After Insurgency

AFTER INSURGENCY

Revolution and Electoral Politics

in El Salvador

RALPH SPRENKELS

University of Notre Dame Press
Notre Dame, Indiana

University of Notre Dame Press
Notre Dame, Indiana 46556
undpress.nd.edu

Library of Congress Cataloging-in-Publication Data

Names: Sprenkels, Ralph, author.
Title: After insurgency : revolution and electoral politics in El Salvador /
Ralph Sprenkels.
Other titles: Revolution and electoral politics in El Salvador
Description: Notre Dame, Indiana : University of Notre Dame Press, [2018] |
Includes bibliographical references and index. |
Identifiers: LCCN 2017055854 (print) | LCCN 2018012975 (ebook) |
ISBN 9780268103279 (pdf) | ISBN 9780268103286 (epub) | ISBN 9780268103255
(hardcover : alk. paper) | ISBN 0268103259 (hardcover : alk. paper)
Subjects: LCSH: Postwar reconstruction—Social aspects—El Salvador. |
El Salvador—Politics and government—1992- | Civil war—Political aspects—
El Salvador—History. | Civil war—Social aspects—El Salvador—History. |
Insurgency—El Salvador—History. | Frente Farabundo Martâi para la Liberaciâon
Nacional—History. | Political culture—El Salvador—History. | Salvadorans—
Interviews. | El Salvador—Social conditions—21st century.
Classification: LCC F1488.5 (ebook) | LCC F1488.5.S67   2018 (print) |
DDC 972.8405/4—dc23
LC record available at https://lccn.loc.gov/2017055854

∞ *This paper meets the requirements of ANSI/NISO Z39.48-1992*
(Permanence of Paper)

For Michelle

entregamos lo poco que teníamos, lo mucho que teníamos,
que era nuestra juventud,
a una causa que creímos la más generosa de las causas del mundo
y que en cierta forma lo era, pero que en la realidad no lo era.
De más está decir que luchamos a brazo partido, pero tuvimos jefes corruptos,
líderes cobardes, un aparato de propaganda que era peor que una leprosería,
luchamos por partidos que de haber vencido nos habrían enviado
de inmediato a un campo de trabajos forzados,
luchamos y pusimos toda nuestra generosidad en un ideal
que hacía más de cincuenta años que estaba muerto,
y algunos lo sabíamos, y cómo no lo íbamos a saber
si habíamos leído a Trotski o éramos trotskistas,
pero igual lo hicimos, porque fuimos estúpidos y generosos,
como son los jóvenes, que todo lo entregan y no piden nada a cambio.

—Roberto Bolaño

Each man
has a way to betray
the revolution.
—Leonard Cohen

Contents

CHAPTER SEVEN
FMLN Veterans' Politics   251

———

CHAPTER EIGHT
Salvadoran Politics and the Enduring Legacies of Insurgency   299

Acknowledgments

This book draws on fifteen years spent in El Salvador. I am deeply indebted to the people I worked with during this period. Through them and with them, I learned about the internal politics of the revolutionary movement and about everyday Salvadoran politics in general. Several of my compañeros or colleagues from those years are still dear friends today. It is impossible to mention all, but Juan Serrano, Ester Alvarenga, Eduardo García, Jesús Avalos, Joanne Knutson, Celia Medrano, Sandra Lovo, Ana María Leddy, Jorge Ceja, Miriam Cárdenas, Juan Barrera, Iván Castro, Julio Alfredo Molina, Vidal Recinos, Flor Alemán, Gloria Guzmán, Mike Lanchin, Miguel Huezo Mixco, María Ofelia Navarrete, Alonso Mejía, Ana María Minero, Julio Monge, Irma Orellana, Michael Levy, Dina Alas, Azucena Mejía, Bettina Köpcke, Leonardo (Alberto) Bertulazzi, Eduardo Linares, Roberto Reyes, Dinora Aguiñada, Raúl Leiva, Alberto Barrera, and Concepción Aparicio hold a special place among them, as does the late—and profoundly missed—Jon Cortina.

I am grateful to the Dutch Interchurch Organization for Development Cooperation (ICCO) and to the International Cooperation Academy of the Dutch Ministry of Foreign Affairs for supporting the first two years of this research project. Utrecht University's Centre for Conflict Studies and its Department of Cultural Anthropology and the Juriaanse Stichting supported parts of my research in subsequent years. Dirk Kruijt, Saskia van Drunen, Carlos Morales, and Nikkie Wiegink read some or all of the manuscript and provided valuable feedback. Chris van der Borgh accompanied many steps in the process of writing this book. I benefited enormously not only from his academic rigor but also from his own considerable experience in El Salvador, which runs partly parallel to mine. Erik Ching provided invaluable feedback and advice. Lotti Silber, a dear friend and intellectual guide for many years, contributed to this study in numerous ways. It was her way of doing anthropology that inspired me to place ethnographic methods at the center of this book. I often made use of the generous sounding board provided by my dear friends, and fellow El Salvador veterans, Darcy Alexandra and Chris Damon, who also contributed with advice on language and translation. The two anonymous reviewers commissioned by the University of Notre Dame Press provided many useful insights that helped improve the final text. I also want to thank the staff at the University of Notre Dame Press for their support, especially Eli Bortz, my editor. I am also particularly grateful to Bob Banning for his outstanding copyediting.

In El Salvador, several institutions and many individuals supported my research efforts. The Salvadoran branch of the Facultad Latinoamericana de Ciencias Sociales (FLACSO) and the Universidad de El Salvador (UES) provided academic embedding in El Salvador. At FLACSO, I am indebted to Carlos Ramos and the late Carlos Briones. At the UES, Carlos Benjamín Lara's work with a new generation of Salvadoran anthropologists gained my admiration. I thank him for trusting me with his students. I thank Jorge Juárez, Ana Silvia Ortíz, Olivier Prud'homme, Alberto Martín Alvarez, and Eduardo Rey—my cofounders at the UIGCS (Unidad de Investigación sobre la Guerra Civil Salvadoreña), the research unit on El Salvador's civil war at the UES—for providing ample opportunities to present and discuss my work in El Salvador, and for sharing their many insights on recent Salvadoran history with me. The UIGCS's ongoing endeavors have made important new inroads for academic scholarship on El Salvador's civil war, involving young and talented Salvadoran students in these efforts. I furthermore thank Mauricio Menjívar and Patricia Alvarenga at the University of Costa Rica for sharing their work with me.

Fieldwork in El Salvador was a treat. I thank the FMLN leadership, in particular the party's general secretary, Medardo González, for giving me permission to work with the Veterans' Sector of this party. Thanks also to the FMLN veterans' collectives FUNDABRIL, ASALVEG, and MV-END, which welcomed me in their midst. The Ellacuría community directive was kind enough to allow me to do fieldwork in their community. I am grateful to the people of Ellacuría for sharing their perspectives on postinsurgent politics with great frankness. I particularly thank Ellacuría residents Anabel Recinos, Francisco Mejía, Dennis Membreño, and Estela Guardado, who helped facilitate fieldwork efforts in various ways. I furthermore thank the many ex-combatants that agreed to interviews and/or helped me with the reconstruction of the life trajectories of their former comrades. Some went to great lengths to do so. I owe them deep gratitude. Five archives holding historical documents related to the Salvadoran insurgency opened their doors for me. I particularly thank Jorge Juárez at the Instituto de Estudios Históricos, Antropológicos y Arqueológicos (IEHAA) at the UES; Verónica Guerrero, at the Centro de Información, Documentación y Apoyo a la Investigación (CIDAI), part of the library of the Universidad Centroamericana "José Simeón Cañas" (UCA); Carlos Henríquez Consalvi at the Museo de la Palabra y la Imagen (MUPI); Ana María Leddy, at the Instituto Schafik Handal; and Angela Zamora and Victoria Ramírez at FUNDABRIL.

Clara Guardado and Yuri Escamilla were wonderful research assistants. I loved working with them and with their fellow anthropology students Alex Leiva, Sofia Castillo, and Ricardo Cook on the Ellacuría case study (chapter 5). Liliana Trejo assisted with the fieldwork on the veteran groups, as did Clara and Yuri. Sonia Barrios at the UCA—El Salvador's Jesuit University—arranged to have graduate students transcribe many hours of recorded interviews. Under the supervision of Sonia and myself, these students, thirty-seven in number, did an impressive job.

Conversations with Wim Savenije, in El Salvador and in the Netherlands, have been valuable for this project. Though we only spoke a few times, Brandt Peterson and Benjamin Moallic helped open new avenues for inquiry and understanding. Marcel Vargas's intellectual irreverence has kept me sharp or, at least, made me sharper. Oscar Miranda and Gerardo Cotto have been two of my closest friends for over two decades. Among many other things, they have served as permanent dialogists on postwar El Salvador.

My family has been incredibly supportive along the way. Thanks to my parents, Gerard and Anny, and to my brother, Henry, for their love and support, no matter what. My aunt Toos and my uncle Frank in Ann Arbor (Michigan) have provided much valuable guidance throughout the years. My Salvadoran family, very much part of the stories relayed in this study, is immensely dear to me. I don't know what I would have done without Diana, the sweetest suegra I could have wished for. When I started this book, Diana was already ill. She passed away in 2015.

My children, Tamara and Simon, have been there every step of the way. The few times I regretted taking on this project were those that forced me to spend time away from them. Both my deepest debt and my deepest gratitude belong to Michelle Melara. She inspired, supported, and suffered this project in ways that merit far greater gratitude than I can express here. I dedicate the book to her.

Figures and Tables

Acronyms

_____

ACISAM	Asociación de Capacitación e Investigación para la Salud Mental
ACJ	Asociación Cristiana de Jóvenes
ACRES	Asociación de Colectivos de Refugiados Salvadoreños
ACUS	Acción Católica Universitaria Salvadoreña
ADC	Alianza Democrática Campesina
ADESCO	Asociación de Desarrollo Comunal
ADG	Asociación de Discapacitados de Guerra
ADIC	Asociación para el Desarrollo Integral Comunitario
AEAS	Asociación de Empresarios de Autobuses Salvadoreños
AES	Asociación Estudiantil de Secundaria
AGEUS	Asociación General de Estudiantes Universitarios Salvadoreños
AIP	Agencia Independiente de Prensa
ALGES	Asociación de Lisiados de Guerra de El Salvador "Héroes de Noviembre del 89"
AMES	Asociación de Mujeres de El Salvador
AMS	Asociación de Mujeres Salvadoreñas
ANDA	Administración Nacional de Acueductos y Alcantarillados
ANDES	Asociación Nacional de Educadores Salvadoreños "21 de Junio"
ANTA	Asociación Nacional de Trabajadores Agrícolas
APDECA	Asociación para la Salud Dental en Centro América
APROCSAL	Asociación de Promotores Comunales Salvadoreños

ARDES	Asociación Revolucionaria de Estudiantes de Secundaria
ARENA	Alianza Republicana Nacionalista
ASALDIG	Asociación Salvadoreña de Lisiados y Discapacitados de Guerra
ASALVEG	Asociación Salvadoreña de Veteranos y Veteranas de Guerra del FMLN "Farabundo Martí"
ASDI	Asociación Salvadoreña para el Desarrollo Integral
ASIPES	Asociación Salvadoreña de Investigación y Promoción Económica y Social
ASOTRAMES	Asociación de Trabajadores de los Mercados
ASOVET 12 DE ABRIL	Asociación de Veteranos y Veteranas del FMLN Histórico 12 de Abril
ASPS	Asociación Salvadoreña Promotora de Salud
ASTAC	Asociación Salvadoreña de Trabajadores del Arte Comunitario
ASVERS	Asociación de Veteranos Revolucionarios Salvadoreños
ATACES	Asociación de Trabajadores Agrícolas y Campesinos de El Salvador
AVDIES	Asociación de Veteranos para el Desarrollo Integral
AVEELSALCOMAR	Asociación de Veteranos de Guerra Comandante Marcial
AVEGUEFOFA	Asociación de Veteranos de Guerra Frente Occidental Feliciano Ama
AVERCH	Asociación de Veteranos de Chalatenango
AVERD	Asociación de Veteranos Roque Dalton
AVERSAL	Asociación de Veteranos Revolucionarios Salvadoreños
AVRAZ	Asociación de Veteranos Rafael Arce Zablah
BFA	Banco de Fomento Agropecuario
BPR	Bloque Popular Revolucionario
BRES	Brigada Revolucionaria de Estudiantes de Secundaria
BTC	Brigada de Trabajadores de Campo

CAM	Cuerpo de Agentes Municipales
CBO	Comité de Base Obrera
CCR	Coordinadora de Comunidades Repobladas de Chalatenango
CCS	Central Coordinadora de Sindicatos
CD	Convergencia Democrática; Cambio Democrático
CDH-ES	Comisión de Derechos Humanos de El Salvador
CDR	Coordinadora para el Desarrollo Rural (San Vicente)
CDU	Centro Democrático Unido
CEBES	Comunidades Eclesiales de Base de El Salvador
CEMUJER	Instituto de Estudios de la Mujer "Norma Virginia Guirola de Herrera"
CIA	Central Intelligence Agency
CIAZO	Comité Interagencial para la Alfabetización en la Zona Oriental
CIDAI	Centro de Información, Documentación y Apoyo a la Investigación (at the UCA)
CIDEP	Cooperación Intersectorial para el Desarrollo y el Progreso
CINAS	Centro de Investigación y Acción Social
CISPES	Committee in Solidarity with the People of El Salvador
CNR	Coordinadora Nacional de Repoblaciones
COACES	Confederación de Asociaciones de Cooperativas de El Salvador
CODECOSTA	Coordinadora para el Desarrollo de la Costa
CODEFAM	Comité de Familiares Pro-Libertad de Presos y Desaparecidos Políticos de El Salvador
CODESMA	Coordinadora de Desplazados y Marginados de La Libertad
COMADRES	Comité de Madres y Familiares de Presos, Desaparecidos y Asesinados Políticos de El Salvador
COMAFAC	Comité de Madres y Familiares Cristianos de Presos, Desaparecidos y Asesinados
COMIN	Comando Internacional de Información
COMUS	Comunidades Unidas de Usulután

CONADES	Comisión Nacional para los Desplazados
CONAMUS	Coordinadora Nacional de la Mujer Salvadoreña
CONARA	Comisión Nacional para la Restauración de Areas
CONAVERS	Coordinadora Nacional de Asociaciones de Veteranos y Veteranas Revolucionarios Salvadoreños del FMLN
CONFRAS	Confederación de Federaciones de la Reforma Agraria Salvadoreña
CONIP	Comité Nacional de la Iglesia Popular
COPAZ	Comisión Nacional para la Consolidación de la Paz
COPPES	Comité de Presos Políticos de El Salvador
CORDES	Fundación para la Cooperación y Desarrollo Comunal de El Salvador
CPDH	Centro para la Promoción de los Derechos Humanos "Madeleine Lagadec"
CPDN	Comité Permanente para el Debate Nacional
CRC	Comité para la Reconstrucción de Cuscatlán y Cabañas
CRD	Coordinadora para la Reconstrucción y el Desarrollo
CREFAC	Centro de Reorientación Familiar y Comunitaria
CRIPDES	Comité Cristiano Pro-Desplazados de El Salvador
CRM	Coordinadora Revolucionaria de Masas
CRS	Corriente Revolucionaria Socialista
CSM	Ciudad Segundo Montes
CUTS	Confederación Unificada de Trabajadores Salvadoreños
DDR	Disarmament, Demobilization and Reintegration
DM-1	Destacamento Militar No. 1
ELAM	Escuela Latinoamericana de Medicina
END	Ejército Nacional para la Democracia
ERP	Ejército Revolucionario del Pueblo
F-16	Fundación 16 de Enero
FAL	Fuerzas Armadas de Liberación
FAPU	Frente de Acción Popular Unificada
FARC	Fuerzas Armadas Revolucionarias de Colombia
FARN	Fuerzas Armadas de la Resistencia Nacional

MU	Movimiento de Unidad
MUPI	Museo de la Palabra y la Imagen
MV-END	Movimiento de Veteranos de Guerra del Ejército Nacional para la Democracia
NGO	Nongovernmental organization
NOTISAL	Agencia de Información y Análisis de El Salvador
NRP	National Reconstruction Plan
OIE	Organismo de Inteligencia del Estado
OIG	Organized interest group
OMR	Organización de Maestros Revolucionarios
ONUSAL	United Nations Observer Mission in El Salvador
ORDEN	Organización Democrática Nacionalista
ORMUSA	Organización de Mujeres Salvadoreñas para la Paz
PADECOES	Patronato para el Desarrollo Comunal de El Salvador
PADECOMSM	Patronato para el Desarrollo de las Comunidades de Morazán y San Miguel
PAR	Partido de Acción Renovadora
PARLACEN	Parlamento Centroamericano
PCN	Partido de Conciliación Nacional
PCS	Partido Comunista de El Salvador
PD	Partido Demócrata
PDC	Partido Demócrata Cristiano
PDDH	Procuraduría para la Defensa de los Derechos Humanos
PMO	political-military organization
PNC	Policía Nacional Civil
PPI	División de Protección a Personalidades Importantes
PPL	Poder Popular Local
PROCOMES	Asociación de Proyectos Comunales en El Salvador
PROESA	Fundación Promotora de Productores y Empresarios Salvadoreños
PROGRESO	Asociación Promo Gestora de Repoblaciones Sociales
PRO-VIDA	Asociación Salvadoreña de Ayuda Humanitaria

PRS	Partido de la Revolución Salvadoreña
PRTC	Partido Revolucionario de los Trabajadores Centroamericanos
PSD	Partido Social Demócrata
PTT	Programa de Transferencia de Tierras
REDES	Fundación Salvadoreña para la Reconstrucción y el Desarrollo
RFM	Radio Farabundo Martí
RN	Resistencia Nacional
RV	Radio Venceremos
SALPRESS	Agencia Salvadoreña de Prensa
SHARE	Salvadoran Humanitarian Aid, Research and Education Foundation
STISS	Sindicato de Trabajadores del Instituto Salvadoreño del Seguro Social
STIUSA	Sindicato Textil de Industrias Unidas, S. A.
STP	Secretaría Técnica de la Presidencia
SV-FMLN	Sector de Veteranos del FMLN
TD	Tendencia Democrática
TR	Tendencia Revolucionaria
TSE	Tribunal Supremo Electoral
UCA	Universidad Centroamericana "José Simeón Cañas"
UCRES	Unión de Comunidades Repobladas de San Salvador y La Libertad
UCS	Unión Comunal Salvadoreña
UDN	Unión Democrática Nacionalista
UES	Universidad de El Salvador
UIGCS	Unidad de Investigación sobre la Guerra Civil Salvadoreña (at the UES)
UMS	Unión de Mujeres Salvadoreñas Pro-Liberación "Mélida Anaya Montes"
UN	United Nations
UNES	Unidad Ecológica Salvadoreña
UNHCR	Office of the United Nations High Commissioner for Refugees
UNTS	Unión Nacional de Trabajadores Salvadoreños
UPT	Unión de Pobladores de Tugurios

UR-19	Universitarios Revolucionarios 19 de Julio
URNG	Unidad Revolucionaria Nacional Guatemalteca
US	United States of America
USAID	Agencia Estadounidense para el Desarrollo Internacional
UTC	Unión de Trabajadores del Campo
UV	Unidades de Vanguardia

List of Protagonists

"Alex." Became involved in the revolutionary movement through church activism. A lay worker and resident in one of the FPL repopulations since the late 1980s.

"Ana." Grew up in a middle-class family heavily involved in the PCS. Participated in the PCS-FAL in different capacities during the war, mostly in exile. After the war, she has developed a career in NGO work.

"Anastasio." A war-seasoned PCS-FAL cadre, he studied law after the war and found employment in a state institution.

"Angel." A former FPL combatant and postwar community leader in one of the Chalatenango repopulations.

"Angela." Fought for the PCS-FAL during the last years of the war, then went back to the university, held several jobs in NGOs and government, and raised a family.

"Antonio." An FPL midlevel cadre, he spent the war clandestinely in San Salvador, mostly in political tasks. After the war, he developed a career in NGO work, without active participation in the FMLN.

"Armando." Participated a few years as a combatant with the FPL in the early 1980s. Became an educator in the Mesa Grande refugee camp and later one of the leaders of repopulation efforts.

"Arturo." Originally from Chalatenango, he fought as a squad leader both for the FPL and for the FAL. After the war he became one of the community leaders in the repopulation of Ellacuría.

"Balbina." From Chalatenango. Developed into an FPL cadre during the war. Settled in a repopulated community after the war and started a farm and a family.

"Beatriz." Having grown up working for the RN in exile, she became a professional artist after the war.

"Bernabé." An internationalist organized with the FPL, after the war he worked for NGOs on behalf of the repopulated communities of San Vicente.

"Cándido." From a family of landowners, he was recruited into the FPL during the 1970s. Lost his wealth during and after the war. One of the animators of FMLN veteran organizing since 2000.

"Carlos." From a peasant family in Chalatenango, he fought for the FPL during the last years of the war. After the war, he settled in a repopulation and did some subsistence farming. After 2000 he became part of the San Salvador municipal police force.

"Carmen." One of the leaders of the repopulation movement, she worked throughout the war in different organizational tasks for the FPL in Chalatenango. After the war she became involved in NGO work. Active within the FMLN's CRS.

"Chabelo." An FPL midlevel military cadre, he was wounded at the end of the war. Initially, played a prominent role in the organization of FMLN war-wounded, but soon broke with the party and settled in his home town.

"Danilo." An experienced ERP cadre, he obtained a government position shortly after the war.

"David." Born in San Salvador, he spent most the war in Chalatenango, where he became a midlevel officer in the FPL guerrillas. After the war, he worked mostly in construction.

"Demetrio." Involved in the ERP's urban structures in the 1970s and 1980s. Different postwar occupations. Was offered a government job late 2009.

"Dionisio Alemán." A senior military cadre with the RN. Involved in FMLN politics and the veteran movement after the war.

"Dolores." Supported the FPL from her family exile and fought in El Salvador during the last years of the war. Worked in several NGOs and, since 2009, with the government.

"Dora." A former FPL member, after the war she worked in public service as well as with NGOs.

"Dorotea." Participated with the FPL masas in Chalatenango and, later, in Mesa Grande. Settled in Ellacuría.

"Edgardo Cornejo." An FPL comandante, he became involved in the FPL radio network after the war.

"Elizabeth." An FPL midlevel cadre charged with political and military tasks during the last years of the war, she returned to her hometown to raise a family and run a farm with her husband, also a former combatant.

"Elsa." Participated with the FPL during the war in different capacities, mainly in the refugee camps. After the war, she ran the family household, which included a tiny convenience store, in one of Chalatenango repopulations. Her husband, a former FPL combatant and political prisoner, migrated to the USA.

"Emanuel." Economist connected to the PCS-FAL, mostly involved in political tasks. Active in different NGOs and a participant in the CRS current after the war.

"Ernesto." An FPL supporter trained in repairing light weaponry.

"Evaristo." Former child soldier and former member of the FPL Special Forces. After the war, he became a police officer and a law student.

"Fabio." An RN cadre mostly involved in political tasks in the capital city. He had a falling-out with the leadership close to the end of the war. Survived on odd jobs.

"Federico." A war-wounded former FPL combatant, he received a scholarship to study medicine in Cuba after the war.

"Felipe." Involved in political work in San Salvador as an FPL midlevel cadre. After the war, he held jobs in municipalities and an NGO.

"Félix." An FPL midlevel military cadre, he found employment in NGOs, as a municipal employee, and, since 2009, as a government employee. Linked to FMLN reformists.

"Fidel." An urban FPL midlevel cadre, wounded several times. Spent a large part of the war recovering in Cuba. Found postwar employment at the UES.

"Fidelina." Daughter of a peasant family from Guazapa, she served in different capacities in safe houses as well as on the rural front. After the war, she settled in a repopulation in Chalatenango, studied to become a nurse, and found employment in a rural health clinic.

"Gabino." A high-ranking FPL military cadre, he became active in postwar politics.

"Gabriel." A PRTC member, he mostly worked in exile during the war. Very active in postwar FMLN politics.

"Geraldine." A political activist from Canada who worked with the FPL in Mexico and in Chalatenango.

"Gerardo." Participated with the FPL in different capacities. As part of the repopulation movement, he stayed in Ellacuría after the war.

"Gilberto." An FPL leader who abandoned this group after the death of Comandante Marcial in 1983.

"Henry." NGO leader and one of those responsible for the ERP's civil-political front in San Salvador. Continued to be involved in NGO work after the war.

"Hernán." An FPL midlevel cadre, he held military as well as political responsibilities during the war. Close to the reformist tendency, he held several municipal jobs over the years.

"Herminia." A leader from the peasant movement in the 1970s, she lived for most of the war in the Mesa Grande refugee camp and settled in a repopulated community at the end of the war.

"Hugo." Integrant of the FPL's Farabundo Martí Radio. Mostly involved in NGO work after the war, he became a government employee under President Mauricio Funes.

"Ignacio." A Catholic priest who participated with the ERP during the war.

"Ismael." An FPL activist with Mexican origins.

"Iván." A fighter for the PCS-FAL, he was killed in the 1989 offensive.

"Jerónimo." An FPL midlevel military cadre, he became a local postwar FMLN leader until a conflict with the party ended in his expulsion.

"Jorge." An urban ERP member, involved mostly in the NGO support structure of the organization. Witnessed the ERP's postwar dismemberment from up close and retired from party politics.

"José." A former FPL cadre, mainly worked on logistics during the war. With reformist sympathies, became marginalized within the FMLN after 2000. Active in veteran politics.

"Josefina." Affiliated with the PCS-FAL during the war, mainly involved in political work. Fought during the 1989 offensive. After the war she distanced herself from the PCS and obtained a job at a state institution.

"Juan." Born in Chalatenango, he became an FPL combatant during the last years of the war. For the last two decades, he has combined season farming in Chalatenango with working first as a municipal police officer in the city, and later as a protection agent for FMLN leadership.

"Justo." Of urban descent, he worked for most of the war in logistics in Chalatenango, for the FPL. He became a municipal employee after the war; subsequently lost his job because of infighting.

"Lilian." An experienced FPL political cadre, she held several positions as a consultant for municipal governments and NGOs before becoming a government official in 2009.

"Luis." Joined FPL combat forces in San Vicente at age ten and came out of the war missing a limb. Since 2000, he has worked as a municipal employee in the capital.

"Magdalena." An ERP political cadre, she broke with the leadership after the war and integrated into the FMLN after the split of 1994.

"Manuel." Part of the RN military leadership toward the end of the war, he became an official in the new police force.

"Marcelo." A former FPL urban commando member, he held postwar jobs in the police force and later in the private sector.

"María." Participated with the FPL masas. Settled in Ellacuría.

"María Ester." A PCS-FAL cadre, she helped organize the reinsertion process for combatants of her organization.

"Mariana." Originally from Chalatenango. Unaffiliated with the revolutionary movement. Repopulated the community of El Roble after the war.

"Mariano." An FPL midlevel cadre during the war, he has worked as a community leader since the war. He also spent several years working in the United States.

"Maritza." An FPL activist from Chalatenango, she settled in a repopulated community after the war.

"Marta." Organized first with the FPL and later with the PCS-FAL. One of the leaders of the repopulation of Ellacuría, she continued to be a community leader after the war.

"Martín." An important cadre for the FPL during the war, he distanced himself from the party in the years after the peace accords.

"Mauricio." From a middle-class family in San Salvador, he participated with the PCS since the 1960s. Served a few years at the front for the PCS-FAL in the early 1980s. Afterwards worked for the party outside the country. Formally renounced party membership after the peace accords and attempted to set up a business.

"Máximo." A South American exile, he was recruited in Europe through the FPL support networks in 1983. Mainly operating from Chalatenango, he survived the war to marry a Salvadoran woman, also a former FPL militant, and make a living working for an NGO. With Funes as president, he became a government official.

"Medardo." Grew up during the war. His family settled in Ellacuría. Involved in postwar community organizing.

"Memo." Fought with the ERP. One of the leaders of the war-wounded FMLN veterans.

"Miguel." A student, he joined the PCS-FAL for the last years of the war. Currently a university professor, not involved directly with the FMLN.

"Miriam." Participated most of the war in urban FPL structures (safe houses). Worked for NGOs in the postwar period.

"Moisés." An RN political cadre during the war. Continued to work with NGOs after the peace accords. Years after the rupture between RN and FMLN, he resumed his FMLN militancy.

"Nadia." A fighter for the PCS-FAL, she was killed in 1988.

"Napoleón." A key PRTC cadre charged with military and political tasks. After the war, he worked for several years for an international organization before returning to El Salvador as an adviser to the FMLN.

"Nicolás." A former PCS-FAL midlevel cadre. Settled in the repopulation of Ellacuría after the war.

"Oscar." Fought most of the war for the FPL. Severely wounded on several occasions. First became involved as a messenger boy. Ended as a midlevel military cadre. Started a family and a farm in a repopulation in Chalatenango after the war.

"Pablo." Native of Cabañas and a midlevel cadre for the FPL during the war. Settled in Ellacuría after the war. Sympathizes with the FMLN's reformist current.

"Pascual." A low-profile RN collaborator during the war, he became involved in the postwar FMLN, first locally, and later nationally.

"Patricia." A former PCS-FAL militant, she has worked as an FMLN political party staff member in the postwar period.

"Pedro." A former FPL military cadre and war-wounded, he worked for years as a security agent at an FMLN office. In 2009, he obtained a security job in one of the ministries.

"Rafael." A midlevel cadre of the PCS in the 1970s and first half of the 1980s, mostly involved in trade union work. Accused of working with the enemy. Though eventually cleared, did not recover his standing inside the party. Became active in the FMLN as a CRS supporter after the war.

"Renato." A Guancora native without affiliation to the revolutionary movement. Fled his home and settled elsewhere in the country at the start of the war.

"René Henríquez." An FPL military comandante. Became a leading figure in the FMLN veteran-organizing efforts after 2000.

"Reyes." A high-ranking FPL cadre. Became one of the leading members of the FMLN renovadores faction after the war and was expelled from the party after 2000.

"Rigoberto." Participated with the FPL in different capacities. Helped organize the repatriation to Chalatenango. Settled in Ellacuría.

"Roberto." An ex-combatant for the FPL. Settled in a Chalatenango repopulation. Worked as a teacher and became involved in local FMLN politics.

"Rogelio." An FPL midlevel military cadre and war-wounded. Worked a range of different postwar jobs. Participated in different FMLN efforts on and off.

"Ronaldo." One of the leaders of the PCS-FAL during the war. Participated with the TR faction after the war. Critical of the official party line of the FMLN.

"Rubén." Fought for the RN during the war, in different capacities. Became a police officer after the war.

"Ruth." Worked for the PCS-FAL leadership in exile during the war. Limited party activism since.

"Rutilio." An FPL midlevel military cadre, he found employment in a municipal administration governed by the FMLN.

"Sandro." A fighter in the PCS-FAL Special Forces, he became active in FMLN party politics after the war.

"Santos." Participated with the FPL in different capacities during the war. A resident of Ellacuría.

"Saúl." A midlevel military cadre with the FAL during the war. Involved in FMLN politics after the war. Left the FMLN in 1998 to integrate into the TR.

"Sebastián." Of urban descent, he participated with the PCS-FAL during the war. Worked afterwards with several NGOs and municipal governments. Unemployed at the time of fieldwork.

"Segundo." Participated the entire war with the ERP in Morazán. Became involved in educational activities and NGO work after the war.

"Sergio." An internationalist with the FPL during the last years of the war. Presently involved in NGO work.

"Severina." Participated with the FPL masas in Cabañas and, later, in Mesa Grande. Settled in Ellacuría.

"Silvio." Mostly worked for the FPL in exile. Developed a postwar career in journalism and communications, with no direct involvement in the party.

"Tino." A former ERP midlevel cadre with vast military experience. Worked for some years for FMLN municipal governments. Unemployed at the time of fieldwork.

"Umberto." The PCS-FAL sent him to San Salvador for political work in the second half of the 1980s. Broke with the PCS in 1992. Now a professor.

"Victoria." Participated with the FPL masas and settled in a repopulated community in Chalatenango. In the 1990s and after 2000, most of her family migrated to the United States.

"Wilber." A PCS-FAL Special Forces member, he worked for different NGOs after the war.

"Yancy." Born in Mesa Grande during the war. Repopulated Ellacuría as a child, together with her family, of which the older members participated with the FPL in different capacities.

"Yolanda." An RN midlevel cadre involved in logistics and human resources during the war. Worked with several FMLN municipalities after the war. Involved in organizing FMLN veterans.

"Zacarías." Supported the RN during the war. Active as an FMLN war veteran.

"Zaira." Grew up on the front in Chalatenango and performed a range of organizational tasks for the FPL. Became involved in social movement activism after the war.

CHAPTER ONE

Echoes of Revolution

But so far the most definite self comes from the Struggle.
Whatever that means now.
—Nadine Gordimer, *No Time like the Present*

The cease-fire of February 1, 1992, ended a hard-fought civil war in El Salvador that had lasted twelve years. The peace accords signed two weeks earlier by the insurgents of the Frente Farabundo Martí para la Liberación Nacional (FMLN)[1] and government representatives received strong international acclaim as "a new beginning for El Salvador" (Wade 2016, 2). "This is the closest that any process has ever come to a negotiated revolution," the United Nations' principal mediator, Alvaro de Soto, declared in the New York Times.[2] De Soto's appraisal became iconic. Many international observers viewed El Salvador's peace process as a role model for ending armed conflict through negotiation of political reforms under the tutelage of the international community. Scores of articles and books extracted lessons learned from El Salvador to be applied in other post-conflict transition processes.[3] Government officials as well as former *comandantes* traveled around the world, sometimes together, to share their experiences as a source of inspiration for other countries crippled by conflict.[4]

The success of El Salvador's 1992 peace accords hinged primarily on the fact that the elites from the former warring parties, though still politically divided, embraced electoral democracy (Wood 2000). In retrospect, Salvador Samayoa, FMLN negotiator and a leading Salvadoran intellectual, referred to the final round of peace negotiations and its aftermath as "the explosion of consensus" (2002, 585).[5] Indeed, the accords constituted the blueprint for an extensive institutional reform process, which included, besides relatively free and fair elections, a new civilian police force, a significant reduction of the armed forces, and an overhaul of the judicial apparatus. The insurgents laid down their arms, demobilized their troops, and entered the electoral arena as a political party. Although scholars also endeavored, to a greater or lesser extent, to point out shortcomings, El Salvador's peace process emerged as a textbook case of democratic transition, at the time that democratic transition was "the hottest theme of the moment" (Domínguez and Lindenberg 1997, 217), certainly in the study of Latin American politics, but arguably also in the study of international politics at large.

Paradoxically, as I myself witnessed up-close, for most former Salvadoran insurgents the transition was a very difficult and often painful process. What democratic transition theory generally tends to interpret as highly positive steps in the process—the demobilization of the guerrilla troops, for example—raised for many of those directly involved complex and uncomfortable questions about the future of their movement. The insurgents' desire for peace mixed with their growing anxieties about the value and worth of previous collective efforts and with concerns about their personal future (B. Peterson 2006). Many wondered whether the outcome had been worth the sacrifice.

This sentiment was particularly strong amongst the rank-and-file and midlevel cadres. In contrast, those holding important political positions within the FMLN generally defended the process. Some comandantes labeled the transition as the "democratic revolution" they had fought for all along, while others framed it as the highest attainable result at the time given the national and international political circumstances.

In 2009 a new outburst of international enthusiasm over Salvadoran politics occurred. Seventeen years after the demobilization of its fighters, the FMLN became the first former Latin American guerrilla front that, having failed to take power through armed struggle, was nevertheless able to win power through the ballot. It was also the first time the Left had won the presidency in El Salvador's history. The pacific transfer of power to the

FMLN, seen as the litmus test of El Salvador's postwar democracy,[6] occurred in a context of left-wing parties rising to power across Latin America, catapulted in part by neoliberalism's waning popularity.[7] For international observers, FMLN president Mauricio Funes became the latest milestone in Latin America's "pink tide."[8] For the FMLN and its supporters, the historical symbolism was compelling, as the party obtained by popular vote the mandate they had been unable to garner through military means (Luis González 2011). Some scholars interpreted the FMLN's triumph as the proof that El Salvador's transition process had finalized; others, as a new, crucial step in "the maturation of El Salvador's democracy" (Greene and Keogh 2009, 668). The first scholarly reviews of FMLN performance in government confirmed the idea of a democratic breakthrough, with the FMLN able to "increase inclusion" (Cannon and Hume 2012, 1050) and "making significant improvements in the daily lives of citizens" (Perla and Cruz-Feliciano 2013, 101).

Thus, after first developing into what Russell Crandall (2016, 69) qualifies as "Latin America's largest and most formidable Marxist insurgency," the FMLN subsequently also transformed into a highly effective peacetime political party. For many of those previously dedicated to revolutionary armed struggle, the Funes election smacked of redemption. In subsequent months, the FMLN party offices throughout the country were flooded by guerrilla veterans and other former FMLN collaborators looking for work and offering their services. As the "Funes transition" unfolded, however, a good part of the former rank-and-file and midlevel insurgents did not see their initial expectations fulfilled, and increasingly expressed criticism, doubts, and anxieties about the FMLN's performance in office. They did so not only as individuals but also through organizations such as associations of FMLN veterans, nongovernmental organizations (NGOs), and a range of social movement organizations.[9]

This book is about how those that participated in the insurgency experienced and helped shape El Salvador's democratic transition. In it, I examine how their historical collective project, what participants refer to as "the Revolution," became remolded in the context of neoliberal peace.[10] I focus particularly on the internal relations of El Salvador's revolutionary movement, and on the postwar accommodations they underwent. The multifaceted transformation of the movement's internal relations played a large part in what I call "the lived experience of postinsurgency." I also document and analyze how the postwar remaking of the movement's internal relations interlinks with the FMLN's contemporary political performance. By this approach, I demonstrate that the reconversion of the FMLN from insurgent movement to an election-oriented party unfolded as a tense and contentious process, which led to the proliferation of internal conflicts. Its relative success notwithstanding, widespread disillusionment surfaced among participants.

The main argument of this book is that the revolutionary movement advanced its engagement in electoral politics mainly by building on insurgent networks, identities, and imaginaries. I contend that the FMLN's electoral success hinged to a large extent on this organization's ability to reconvert a substantial part of its insurgent networks into predominantly clientelist factions. At the same time, factors like the intense political competition between the FMLN and the dominant right-wing party Alianza Republicana Nacionalista (ARENA), pervasive sectarian struggles in the realm of the FMLN, and the scarcity of state resources available for distribution all rendered these postwar clientelist relations relatively unstable and precarious. Considering these political developments in the mirror of the aspirations and sacrifices of revolutionary armed struggle, many former Salvadoran insurgents lamented what they saw as the postwar scramble for public resources, but few could afford not to participate in it. Hence, the experience of postinsurgent politics developed as a peculiar mix of political ascendency and disenchantment.

The present study is based on a total of sixteen months of fieldwork in El Salvador between 2008 and 2015 with (former) participants in the FMLN. In total, I interviewed eighty-nine former insurgents for this project, twenty-six women and sixty-three men.[11] I furthermore relied extensively on ethnographic case studies, for which I performed fieldwork inside the FMLN's political party apparatus, FMLN veteran groups, and former insurgent communities. I also performed research on the revolutionary movement's scattered archives. Underpinning this research lay my own previous experiences with El Salvador's revolutionary movement. Since I lived in El Salvador for a total of fifteen years, my professional and personal life has been permeated by this country's insurgent history. I became involved with El Salvador's revolutionary movement in 1990, while studying in Mexico. I started on a small Fuerzas Populares de Liberación (FPL)[12] collective in the city of Guadalajara. The FPL was the largest of the five political-military organizations that composed the FMLN's united guerrilla front. Early 1992, shortly after the signing of the peace accords, I was transferred from Mexico to El Salvador and assigned to the FPL structures in Chalatenango, a mountainous guerrilla stronghold area during the war. In all, I worked for the FPL for four years, performing tasks that included fund-raising, propaganda, education, and research into the human-rights violations perpetrated by the military and the death squads during the war.[13]

With the peace process advancing and the FMLN functioning as a political party, I gradually started taking a different path, seeking to visualize the largely unaddressed legacy of the atrocities that had taken place during the war, a topic the FPL leadership considered of minor interest. In 1994, I helped found an organization called Pro-Búsqueda, dedicated to the search for the hundreds of young children that had disappeared during the civil war, mostly as a result of kidnappings by the army. Most of the people I worked with in Pro-Búsqueda had actively participated in the insurgency, as was—and often still is—the case for the bulk of the personnel of the many left-wing NGOs in the country. To date, the different contacts and friendships I gained from my time with the FPL have continued to play an important role in my life. I also met my partner and the mother of our two children in San Salvador. Her family participated in the war with another FMLN-affiliated organization: the Fuerzas Armadas de Liberación (FAL),[14] the armed branch of the Partido Comunista de El Salvador (PCS).[15] Our marriage brought me into close contact with many former members of this organization.

Thus, even if I did not actively participate in FMLN party politics after 1994, I continued to be surrounded by former insurgents in the different political and social environments in which I was immersed. Some were involved in FMLN party politics; others were not. However, they all shared common ties and a common history, and lived lives that intersected to a large extent. The evolving story of the revolutionary movement continued to be an inevitable part of conversation. It included the FMLN's internal politics—its schisms, conflicts, and sectarian plotting—often even more than the electoral successes and setbacks. But the story also involved the well-being of the refugee communities, cooperatives, NGOs, church groups, and social movement groups that used to be an integral part of the insurgency.

A BIG CRASH

"If you take into account how great our revolution was, I consider that after the war *nos pegamos una gran estrellada*," "Justo"[16] told me one afternoon in August 2009. "We made a big crash." Justo made this comment while he and I were trying to make a preliminary inventory of the contents of a stack of old cardboard boxes. They were filled with papers and videocassettes, severely damaged by moths and mold: the leftovers of what used to be the archive of the FPL. I had met Justo, a former FPL mid-level cadre who spent most of the war in Chalatenango, through mutual friends in 1992, but we had lost touch over the years, until a joint interest in the protection and preservation of the FPL's historical archive brought us back together in 2009. In spite of Justo's disappointment with El Salvador's former insurgents' postwar performance, the FMLN had just celebrated what arguably was its greatest success in history: Mauricio Funes's triumph in the March 2009 presidential elections. The FMLN had now become the party in power, and a considerable number of former FPL cadres Justo and I knew were moving into important government positions.

That afternoon, Justo and I talked about how within our social circles of former insurgents, opinions on the significance of the election results varied. A few old militant friends talked about it as if it were the realization of the dream they had long fought for. Some warned against early celebration and saw the electoral win as just one step in the long and ongoing struggle to rid the country of the right-wing oligarchy that has held it in its grip for so long. Others argued that the electoral outcome actually constituted one more proof that the FMLN had negotiated under the table with the right-wing establishment. In this reading, El Salvador's traditional powers and their historical ally, the United States, would only have allowed a left-wing victory to take place if the FMLN had become a relatively innocuous part of the system. Justo himself was skeptical of all these different readings. He said he had lost his appetite for political polemics.[17]

Justo's description of the postwar revolutionary movement as a "big crash" acquires depth of meaning when understood within a multilayered and longitudinal context, one that incorporates elements of Justo's own life and personal history within the broader context of the history of the political movement in which he participated. Different episodes of Justo's life are relevant for understanding how and why he frames the experience of the revolution as he does. For example, in the 1970s, being a self-searching urban teenager interested in rock music, he found that the revolutionary movement provided him and several of his closest friends with a community and a purpose. He performed well in these close-knit clandestine networks, where he experienced friendship, solidarity, and comradeship. Taking on large responsibilities early on in life, Justo learned to live by a different name and to hide his revolutionary identity from public sight. He also participated in and bore testimony to violence, and was forced to withstand the horrors of the mounting military and death-squad persecution. In 1981, while passing a military roadblock as a passenger on a public bus, Justo came face-to-face with an elder comrade from his cell who had been captured by the army. The comrade did not betray him, thus risking his life to protect Justo and the revolutionary organization. Over the years, he lost his closest friend, and other loved ones, in combats against the Salvadoran military. In Chalatenango, the FPL's most extensive front, he functioned for several years as a well-respected, midlevel leader, mainly involved in logistical and political tasks, often working directly with the troops.

After the 1989 offensive, while the insurgents were already beginning to negotiate the end of the war, Justo became aware that he suffered from physical and mental exhaustion. He felt he was unable to continue at the front, but he hesitated to present his personal situation to the leadership, because at the time there had been several executions of alleged infiltrators. Justo himself had been ordered to monitor and report on suspected enemy networks amongst the troops and military cadres. He had been instructed that some of the indications of enemy allegiance were "low morale," "inconformity," "complaints of exhaustion," and particularly, "asking for permission to leave the front." But in time, Justo realized he simply could no longer stick it out. He talked to the FPL's political leader of the Chalatenango front at the time, someone he knew well from when they were both still young activists in the 1970s. This comandante proved responsive to his plight. Justo asked for and was granted permission to go to the capital to rest and recover.

His personal experiences in the postwar period provide relevant context to qualify Justo's disenchantment with the transition process. When the peace accords were signed, Justo had been on leave from the FPL for over a year, working in a café in the capital city. He settled with "Felicia," his longtime girlfriend, and their young children, in a small house in the suburbs. Felicia, like him, had spent most of the war in the guerrilla. The FPL did not take him or Felicia into account for the demobilization package, and, though upset with what he saw as their marginalization, he did not insist on being included. Subsequently, Justo did not participate in the FPL final meetings and formal dissolution. Nonetheless, a few years later, with some of his former comrades in public office, he was offered an administrative job in one of the FMLN municipalities. It started relatively well, but after a few years he witnessed his former comrades engaging in personal bickering and become ever more divided. After almost a decade of service, he lost his municipal job as a result of this infighting. It was given out as a prize to one of the participants in a rival faction.

As we were meeting regularly to work on the inventory of the FPL archive, I noticed that Justo had a hard time making ends meet each month. Even though his work on the FPL archives was voluntary, he was hoping that his former FPL comrades would prove sensitive to his economic plight and reward him for his work.

One day Justo told me he had recently searched for the family of "Adelino," the man who had saved his life in 1981. At the time, Adelino and his family had been providing the cover for a major FPL operation in the western part of the country. With FPL funds, they had bought a small coffee farm. Under the house, the FPL built a clandestine workshop, almost a small factory, to make Vietnamese-style mines and other explosives in preparation of the upcoming 1981 guerrilla offensive, the first nationwide armed uprising. Justo had just been in Cuba for extensive training, and he led the team of twelve people working inside the workshop. At night they would sleep on the floor inside the farmhouse, wake early, take turns bathing, have breakfast, and then pack into the underground workshop before dawn, where they would work the rest of the day and only come out again after nightfall. Adelino's wife did the cooking, and the children had to make it all appear as if they were a regular family trying to make a living off the plantation. Adelino used a Volkswagen van with built-in secret compartments to distribute the explosives around the country.

The workshop functioned at full capacity for several months. However, shortly after the offensive, Justo's superior was captured by the military and revealed the location of the workshop. When the raid began, Adelino alerted his comrades through a switch in the house that activated

Leigh Binford emphasizes that the frustration many feel comes from the limited results of the peace accords and the government's obstruction of peace benefits (2002, 205–6). Alternatively, Julia Dickson-Gómez highlights the devastating impact of wartime violence on supporters of the guerrilla and its lasting negative consequences on interpersonal trust and well-being (2002, 2004). Philippe Bourgois points particularly at the insurgents' use of internal violence and concludes that "the revolutionary movement in El Salvador was traumatized and distorted by the very violence it was organizing against" (2001, 19). In his retrospective study *Guerrillas* Dirk Kruijt argues that "the revolutionary ideals of the [Central American] guerrilla generation dwindled away" not just because of the utopian project's failure but also because of important changes in the international political context, including the international demise of the radical left (2008, 171).

The tension between revolutionary aspirations and "on-the-ground" realities constitutes the central element of postinsurgent disillusionment. Such frictions were certainly not absent during the war either. As we see in Justo's case, his wartime experiences—with their kaleidoscope of sentiments—became a heavy load to carry. Postwar developments further deepened the breach between revolutionary aspirations and lived realities, as the utopian horizon receded and participants started weighing what was lost against what was gained, both in collective and in personal terms.

Beyond disillusionment, another element stands out in Justo's story. In spite of manifest disappointment, Justo still expressed a continued sense of belonging. He said: "*We* made a big crash," not *they* made. Justo still saw himself as part of the revolutionary movement, even though he considered it to be in dire straits, and he doubted whether he could still take any responsibility for it. Revolutionary participation has been a defining experience in Justo's life, the experience that, to a large extent, made him the man he was. For Justo, what came after insurgency was to be considered in the light of the achievements of before: "how great our revolution was." Subsequently, in spite of broken dreams, the friendships and other relationships that Justo forged during his time with the FPL continued to play crucial roles in his life after the war ended, not only in affective terms but also in the political and economic facets of his life. Though damaged, and according to some, unrecognizable as a revolutionary movement, some form of insurgent collectivity continued to exist after the war ended.

My thesis is that in order to grasp the lived experience of El Salvador's former insurgent movement, it is necessary to look closely at the paradox that emerges from Justo's story. The networks and the political imaginaries that the insurgents built before and during the war continued to be of great importance to postwar personal and collective destinies, in spite of strong postinsurgent disillusionment. The end of the war implied drastic changes for El Salvador's insurgent movement, but it did not mean a fresh start. The former insurgents took with them into this new phase the collective project they had built up until then. As Justo's account illustrates, revolutionary armed struggle created strong expectations among participants, and what remained of the revolutionary movement in the postwar period had a hard time coming to grips with these expectations.

THE RISE OF ELECTORAL CLIENTELISM

The development of the FMLN from insurgent movement to electoral party changed the way in which FMLN participants made their claims. During the war the priority lay on claim-making upon the Salvadoran government through armed struggle. In the postwar period rank-and-file participants stepped up explicit and vocal claims upon FMLN leadership as power holders. Former insurgents competed with each other in an attempt to position themselves advantageously in postwar political and societal affairs, and patterns of contention thus started to include claim-making within partisan networks. Such claims received an additional boost with the FMLN's 2009 electoral triumph, which opened up new possibilities for access to government resources.

As becomes particularly clear from the ethnographic case studies included in this book (chapters 5, 6, and 7), electoral clientelism started playing a larger role in the FMLN's political performance toward the end of the 1990s, partially substituting the ethos of revolutionary militancy that had helped sustain participation before and during the war. Clientelism helped provide a new framework for continued engagement between FMLN leadership and former rank-and-file and midlevel participants. Wartime sacrifices provided a strong moral justification to be able to benefit in one way or the other from the access to state resources that the FMLN had acquired through electoral means. From a leadership perspective, clientelism functioned as a tool to build a reliable electoral machine. From a nonleadership perspective, clientelism helped translate sacrifices and loyalties, past and present, into assistance with practical solutions for pressing economic challenges. As Javier Auyero (2001, 2007) emphasizes, the operation of electoral clientelism requires extensive mediation and brokerage to take place between levels and groups. This task particularly suited former midlevel guerrilla cadres. Thus, the combined outcome of insurgent accumulation and postinsurgent accommodation was that together they produced the interpersonal networks that allowed the FMLN to successfully compete in postwar electoral politics.

These internal FMLN developments link to broader observations on the continued "presence" of the civil war in postwar electoral politics (Ainhoa Montoya 2013; Wade 2016). The country's dominant political parties are both "sons of war" (de Zeeuw 2010), with ARENA holding a position on the Right comparable to the one the FMLN holds on the Left of the political spectrum. ARENA was founded in 1981, early in the war, unifying factions of far-right anticommunists that saw both the Marxist guerrillas and the US-backed Christian Democrat reformists as their enemies (Baloyra 1982; Melara Minero 2012). ARENA built its wartime partisan networks on traditionally wealthy families, cattle rangers, military officers, urban-based entrepreneurs, and other traditionally conservative sectors (Stanley 1996). Leading figures within ARENA, including founder Roberto d'Aubuisson, an ex-mayor of the Salvadoran army, were also actively involved in eliminating alleged insurgents and other political opponents through death squads and paramilitary groups operating across the country.[20] Such precedents did not prevent ARENA from developing into a successful electoral party. ARENA became the largest legislative force in 1988 and took the presidency in 1989. It was an ARENA-led government that signed peace in 1992.

After the accords, the FMLN soon developed into the largest opposition party. ARENA's and FMLN's combined stronghold on postwar Salvadoran politics also provides an indication as to the continued practical and symbolic weight of the war. Contemporary political campaigning in El Salvador has been characterized as the periodic recycling of "Cold War polarities" (Ainhoa Montoya 2013), by means of a symbolic restaging of the war. For example, in postwar election campaigns, speakers at rallies frequently referred to the war, and particularly to the rivals' alleged abuses, to help strengthen bipartisan divides.[21] Another part of this dynamics played out as a sort of campaigning competition, with "brigades" of activists marking entire neighborhoods in the colors of either FMLN or ARENA, handing out propaganda, waving flags, and plastering every available wall with posters. Sometimes it resulted in (renewed) tensions between activists from the two parties, including small-scale violent incidents (Sprenkels 2014a).[22] And besides "regular" propaganda, anonymous slander campaigns also frequently made their appearance during election time, with false accusations spread through anonymous leaflets or through social media and "troll" activity on the internet.[23] The common thread of all these efforts was that they sought to reframe wartime fears and divides into postwar electoral strategy. The prolonged electoral dominance of ARENA and FMLN suggests this strategy continued to yield abundant dividends.

Hence, it is important to acknowledge that the FMLN's postwar adjustment processes unfolded in counterposition to, or in competition with, ARENA's political grip on the country. Though ARENA's postwar development is beyond the scope of this study, I consider that postwar accommodation processes, albeit with different accents and particularities, also occurred within ARENA-affiliated networks and organizations, where clientelism seems to have played a significant role already during the war (McElhinny 2006).[24] At any rate, as becomes clear from the ethnographic case studies included in this book, the prolonged and intense electoral competition with ARENA left strong marks on the development of the FMLN.

POSTINSURGENCY AS A HISTORICALLY CONSTRUCTED SOCIAL FIELD

How to study the aftermath of an insurgent movement? The most common approach focuses on the "reintegration" of combatants. However, as I argue elsewhere, the notion of postwar reintegration suffers from weak theoretical and empirical foundations which strongly limit its research value (Sprenkels 2014c). Studies on postwar reintegration of fighters have been developed principally under the auspices of international organizations active in postconflict reconstruction efforts, and tend to be highly prescriptive, proposing different policy recipes for demobilization and reintegration programs (Humphreys and Weinstein 2007; Jennings 2008; McMullin 2013). As Norma Kriger points out, most of this research "ignore[s] politics, power and history" (2003, 20), while Anders Nilsson takes critique a step further when proclaiming that reintegration research is in fact "a theoryless field" (2005, 35). Nikkie Wiegink forwards the idea that ex-combatants, rather than "reintegrating" into "mainstream" society, are likely to make extensive use of the relations established during insurgency as a framework for postwar social navigation (2014, 2015). In a similar vein, scholars have recently called attention to the durable political and socioeconomic relevance of postwar combatant networks (Sindre 2016; Söderström 2016).

Another scholarly approach to the aftermath of insurgency focuses on insurgent participation as a form of empowerment or emancipation. Most research embracing this approach has emphasized the impact of female insurgent participation in Latin America on subsequent gender roles and emancipatory agendas. Karen Kampwirth, for example, highlights that though Latin American revolutionary movements of the second half of the last century had an egalitarian agenda, gender equality was not a specific part of it. However, as women became mobilized and played important roles in the revolutionary process, gender concerns eventually also rose to prominence, contributing to "vibrant autonomous feminist movements that emerged after the wars" (2004, 165). Ilja Luciak, similarly, argues that women's "active participation as combatants during the civil wars that ravaged the [Central American] region has now been translated into significant representation in political parties and social movements" (2001, xiii–xiv).

Both Luciak and Kampwirth include the experience of El Salvador in their comparative account. Several additional studies underline how women's wartime participation in the FMLN may have contributed, after reinsertion, to postwar improvement of the political position of women in the FMLN as a political party (Garibay 2006; Luciak 1999; Moreno 1997). Another line of inquiry emphasizes the importance of former female insurgents in forging El Salvador's feminist movement (Blumberg 2001; Cagan and Juliá 1998; Falquet 2001, 2002; Navas 2007; Shayne 2004). Jocelyn Viterna, however, warns us not to equate female guerrilla participation with postwar empowerment too easily: "Those who were empowered during their time in the guerrillas by and large . . . filled high-prestige positions" (2003, 206–7). In her insightful and well-documented book *Women in War*, she further evidences that the guerrilla's internal stratification played an important part in determining what, if any, public political roles female participants were able to take on in the postwar period (2013, 173).

The analytical limitations of the two concepts, reintegration and empowerment, lie in that they both oversimplify a complex and variegated historical process while adding a teleological bias toward a kind of desired end-stage of "reintegration" or "empowerment." Thus, in my view, the questions of whether former FMLN insurgents reintegrated into Salvadoran society or became empowered through previous experiences, and if so, to what extent, present significant drawbacks and complications. Therefore, for this book I approach the matter in terms of identifying the movement's postwar changes and adjustments, and their multifaceted implications, both on a collective and individual level. I focus on the actually unfolding sociopolitical dynamics of postinsurgency and include the complete insurgent demography rather than zooming in exclusively on one particular subgroup. This approach entails thinking about what happens to insurgents after the war as a relational process embedded in a particular historical and political context. It leads me to propose a conceptualization of postinsurgency as a social field, defining this field as a historically constructed space of relations between multiple social agents that were previously connected through participation in insurgency.

Relying on the work of sociologists Pierre Bourdieu (e.g., 1984, 1985, 1990) and Charles Tilly (e.g., 2002, 2003, 2005a, 2008b), theory on social fields has taken flight in recent years.[25] Neil Fligstein and Doug McAdam define what they call "strategic actions fields . . . [as] constructed mesolevel social order[s] in which actors (who can be individual or collective) are attuned to and interact with one another on the basis of shared (which is not to say consensual) understandings about the purposes of the field, relationship to others in the field (including who has power and why), and the rules governing legitimate action in the field" (2012, 9). Society, then, is made up of numerous and variegated fields of this sort, with a great deal of overlap—but also competition—among them. Embedded social actors seek to fashion order in a given field, for example by establishing prestige and hierarchy (Bourdieu 1984). People maneuver in fields—also sometimes referred to as "arenas"—relying on their cognitive capacities to interpret the world around them, to plan for action, and to cooperate with others (Jasper 2006).[26] A range of particular features endow each of these fields with their historical shape and political relevance.

The Salvadoran revolution created a particularly dense and powerful social field for those involved, forming what—both of them employing relational perspectives—Charles Tilly refers to as an insurgent polity (1997, 123) and Kristina Pirker calls the militant habitus (2008, 248). Though a very complex and variegated phenomenon, El Salvador's revolutionary movement was recognizable as a more or less consistent project involving a range of collectives and of individuals with common aspirations, characterized by a culture of militant sacrifice and clandestinity. With the arrival of peace, so I contend, the revolutionary movement's social field entered into flux, as internal relations were subjected to renegotiation and resignification.

THE VARIED PATHS OF POSTINSURGENT RECONVERSION

The FMLN is not the only insurgent movement to have turned into a successful political party. In fact, such political conversion, often in combination with democratic reform, has become a common route of postwar transition (Manning and Smith 2016).[27] Some former insurgent movements turned into dominant political parties, while others shared electoral favor with strong contenders. The phenomenon has been researched predominantly from the perspective of comparative politics, analyzing the strengths and limitations of the conversion process in terms of the new party's political performance.[28] Studies from this perspective point to issues such as party bureaucratization (including negative as well as positive effects), limited leadership renewal, and the constraints of post–Cold War international relations. The lack of trust between leaders, correlated to the experience of war, has been known to affect the willingness of parties to cooperate and to build coalitions, often contributing to the continued polarization of the political system (de Zeeuw 2010; Dudouet 2009; Manning 2007, 2008: Wittig 2016). Nonetheless, many insurgent leaders also display a knack for accommodation. One major overview study on the matter concludes that

> while revolutionaries may speak the language of democracy, their practices do not always mirror this. Many have become as corrupt as the old orders they have overthrown . . . and others have been reluctant or unable to adjust hierarchical battlefield strategies of leadership

to governance in the political arena. The majority, however, have been forced or pushed into adopting variations of the free market development strategies, an approach fundamentally antithetical to the liberationist goals for which they struggled. (Deonandan 2007, 244)

Thus, former insurgent leaderships often embrace a pragmatic stance, both in service of stability and in order to salvage their careers. Entering the arena of electoral democracy also implies the acceptance of political tenets formerly rejected. Leaders tend to water down the political agendas previously envisioned. In this process, it may be difficult to distinguish the leaders' political goals from their personal interests. Indeed, this is a classical theme in political sociology, as far back as Max Weber, who detected "a tendency that appears in every [political] party that lasts, namely that the party becomes an end in itself for its members."[29] Robert Michels extended the argument into what he called the "iron law of oligarchy."[30] Building on his own experiences in the early-twentieth-century German revolutionary left, Michels theorized that party organizations inevitably lean on increased internal inequality, with leadership's detachment from the masses growing over time, until "new accusers arise to denounce the traitors; after an era of glorious combats and of inglorious power, they end by fusing with the old dominant class" (1962, 408).[31]

The right of the political spectrum embraced elite theory most fervently, since many right-wing thinkers conceived of inequality as a necessary feature of the human condition and viewed elite theory as an antidote to left-wing anti-elitist claims. But some Marxists were also influenced by it. Leon Trotsky, for example, analyzed the development of the Communist Party under Stalin in analogous terms. He argued that the party cadres had displaced the masses to assume the control of the state bureaucracy and thus betrayed the revolution (1972, 238). And while for Trotsky elite tendencies had to be exorcized by deepening the revolution and making it "permanent,"[32] Italian Marxist Antonio Gramsci accepted elite tendencies as a given, and argued that revolutionary intelligentsia should profit from it by tutoring for leadership the best and smartest of the subaltern classes (Finocchiaro 1999).[33]

Through thinkers like José Carlos Mariátegui and Paolo Freire,[34] Gramscian elitism was very influential among Latin American revolutionaries who built organizations that professed a highly egalitarian ideology, while at the same time developing a "vanguard," a revolutionary elite with the qualities of a "guiding angel" and the devotion of "a true priest," to recur to Che Guevara.[35] Indeed, Marxist insurgent groups in Latin America were stratified organizations, much inclined to revere their leaders, the comandantes of the revolution.[36] Salvadoran revolutionaries also embraced this transcendent vision on leadership, with figures like Salvador Cayetano Carpio, sometimes referred to as the "Ho Chi Min" of Latin America, and Joaquín Villalobos, proclaimed by his followers as the guerrilla's most brilliant strategist.[37] Did such revolutionary hierarchies also find their way into postinsurgent politics? And if so, how and with what consequences?

The leadership's role and behavior constitutes only part of a postwar transition's story. For a deeper understanding of the process, it is also necessary to look at the insurgency's broader constituencies. Social movement literature suggests that demobilization frequently pairs up with increased "competition among . . . the main actors and their supporters" (Tilly and Tarrow 2008, 97).[38] The high expectations previously generated often fuel internal strife (Owens 2009, 248).[39] Social movement theory also holds that, in spite of such conflicts, "movements do not simply fade away," but instead "leave lasting networks of activists behind them [that] can regroup when . . . new opportunities appear" or that can take on new roles (Tarrow 1998, 164; Kriesi 1996).[40] While some participants respond to new challenges by radicalizing their demands and methods, others instead favor moderation or disengagement.

Indeed, Justo's account of postwar accommodations taking place in El Salvador's revolutionary movement suggests that insurgent participants recurred to different strategies to redefine their engagement with what remained of the movement. While some militants became loyal members of the political party FMLN, others abandoned the movement or sought to voice discontent with the movement's postwar trajectory.

Participation in social movements and participation in insurgencies both rely on a strong investment of affect and on the far-reaching mix of the personal and the political, both aspects able to mark participants' lives well beyond the life span of the movement.[41] However, though social movements and insurgencies have a lot in common, differences in scope and impact also deserve consideration, particularly to the extent that they influence how the two types of movement might accommodate to change.

Revolutionary insurgency is a massive endeavor, as participants seek to generate not just a rebel army, but indeed a separate polity, a force able to effectively topple the regime they challenge.[42] Such a colossal task requires enormous human, financial, and technical resources, and implies developing extensive alliances and relations with groups and individuals that might contribute to its realization (Kalyvas 2006; Tilly 2008a, 16). Violent persecution and sustained clandestinity, furthermore, hold strong implications for those involved (Broderick 2000; Churchill 2014). Revolutionary violence may produce complicity, but is also likely to leave uncomfortable legacies (Degregori 2012; C. McClintock 1998). Thus, war "reconfigure[s] social networks in a variety of ways, creating new networks, dissolving some, and changing the structure of others" (Wood 2008, 540). Jesuit social psychologist Ignacio Martín-Baró made a similar point, just months before his death at the hands of the Salvadoran military, arguing that "when war drags on . . . its power to shape social reality becomes predominant, both in structuring social orders and in people's mindsets" (1989, 3). As is evident throughout this book, El Salvador's long insurgency led to profound entanglements of participants' personal life stories with the movement.

When applying social movement theory to the aftermath of armed struggle, one should state one final caveat. Aside from the debate on the extent to which an insurgent movement and a social movement might qualify as similar, there is also the question of whether a postwar transition should qualify as a situation of the decline or demobilization of a movement, or rather as a new stage in its development. As we shall see in this study, in El Salvador the views on this matter may differ greatly, as some former insurgents claim that the struggle continues, while others complain that the FMLN has betrayed the cause to become absorbed by the system.

SCOPE, OBJECTIVES, AND OUTLINE OF THE BOOK

The political, social, and economic heritage of the Salvadoran insurgency cannot be restricted solely to the FMLN as a political party. This book, therefore, moves beyond providing an account of the evolution of the FMLN from an armed revolutionary movement to a political party. In El Salvador today, hundreds of communities and organizations trace their origins back to the insurgency. Dozens of FMLN war veteran associations exist, and FMLN veterans play prominent roles in a range of political initiatives, NGOs, and government institutions. In other words, the political party FMLN is not synonymous with the social field of postinsurgency. The party is, however, a crucial and central element of that field. Hence, the account I offer of the internal development of the FMLN as a political party comes as a by-product of this study's primary focus: the longitudinal examination of insurgent relations in the transition from war to peace. I research how the insurgents' personal and political networks developed after the war, and how this dynamics played out for different subgroups. The central research question for this study is, In postwar El Salvador, what accommodations took place in the relations that previously sustained the insurgent movement? Other questions addressed extensively are as follows: How do the former insurgents themselves discuss and analyze the postwar accommodations in their movement? And what can these accommodations and their multiple interpretations tell us about the enduring legacies of insurgency in El Salvador?

The academic relevance of this study for scholarship on El Salvador lies in that it provides the most comprehensive examination of the postwar FMLN, of postinsurgent politics, and of the legacies of insurgency in the country produced thus far. Besides its in-depth longitudinal inquiry into insurgent relations and these relations' subsequent postwar vicissitudes, this book offers insight into El Salvador's postwar transition at large, providing new perspectives in addition to recent hallmark contributions on postwar Salvadoran politics by Erik Ching (2016), Irina Carlota Silber (2011), and Christine Wade (2016). It joins less than a handful of ethnographies of postwar party politics in El Salvador.[43] By its insistence on diverse perspectives involving multiple levels and sectors of the insurgents' demography, this study sets itself apart from the many studies on El Salvador's transition primarily based on interviews and expertise offered by major power brokers in the peace process.[44] It also takes an approach very distinct from that of the growing number of former comandantes who have published their memoirs.[45] Though some of these (auto)biographical books hold interesting opinions and anecdotes, they predictably also tend to provide self-congratulatory accounts of the events of the war and its aftermath.[46] I do draw on all of these available sources whenever possible, but I build primarily on the firsthand perspectives of former midlevel cadres and the rank and file.

This study produces a fresh look at the revolutionary movement's social history. Following the lead of life course scholarship, I documented multiple life stories to use these as "small mirrors of . . . social patterns, societal dynamics and change," in order "to grasp these patterns and their dynamics of reproduction and historical transformation" (Bertaux and Delcroix 2000, 70). My personal familiarity with El Salvador's postinsurgency assisted me in the task of generating historicized understandings of networks and institutions, and of the individuals circulating in them (Scheper-Hughes 1992, 29). By this approach, I was able to zoom in on the social genealogies relevant to postinsurgency (Bertaux 1995; Bertaux and Thompson 2007). My study takes further inspiration from a discipline known as a prosopography, a subfield of sociohistorical research dedicated to drawing out and thinking through similarities and differences between individuals in a given group or population (Verboven, Carlier, and Dumolyn 2007, 40).

The academic relevance of this study beyond the case of El Salvador is twofold. First, it provides a novel way of looking at postinsurgency and postinsurgent transitions, by documenting and analyzing the particular dynamics by which an insurgent movement's accumulated historical relations become a factor in shaping subsequent postwar adjustment processes. Both in peacebuilding literature and in transition literature, peace settlements tend to be seen as a new beginning, rather than as a step in the larger process by which contenders attempt to construe political power in specific territories and among specific constituencies. My findings suggest the latter approach might be much more fruitful. In the case of El Salvador's insurgency, the many organizational ties constructed on the ground translated into thick webs of allegiances and loyalties, in which (former) participants played pivotal roles. When peace arrived, the movement's historically constructed political relations, identities, and imaginaries did not simply "dissolve." Instead, they continued to be highly relevant for the transition process.

This is not to suggest that the shape of postinsurgency is bound to be identical in other postwar countries. Comparative politics have taught us the valuable, though still often ignored, lesson that political concepts do not always translate well from one context to the next, given that political communities are specific historical and cultural constructs.[47] What I propose is to ground research on insurgent aftermaths in a thorough understanding of a movement's particular social history. My study proposes to look at what Charles Tilly calls "relational work" (2005a, 77) and how this plays out in insurgent networks as they engage with the transition process. It identifies wartime identities and relations as constitutive elements of postwar politics, rather than looking at these as fading leftovers of defunct ideologies or animosities.

The second broad academic contribution of this study lies in that it encourages rethinking the legacy of revolutionary armed struggle in left-wing politics in Latin America. Most substantially, it suggests reflecting about the renewed saliency of clientelism in left-wing Latin American politics not only as a contemporary rehashing of this continent's long-standing patrimonial tradition, but also—at least in part—as the outflow of the formerly pervasive political culture of revolutionary militancy adapting to the framework of electoral competition. As the democratic election of several former guerrilla participants as presidents illustrates, remnant networks of revolutionary militants have played important political roles in contemporary left-wing parties and movements in Latin America.[48] And with clientelism demonstrating its continued contemporary relevance as a model for political aggregation and electoral competition in Latin America, pink tide governments have proven far from immune (Chodor 2014; Goodale and Postero 2013). In the case of El Salvador, contemporary clientelist networks have, to a large extent, built on wartime affiliations to create vehicles for electoral competition on both sides of the political spectrum. While showing how clientelism developed into a functional contemporary element of left-wing political mobilization in El Salvador, making use of people's socioeconomic needs, in-group expectations, and electoral access to public resources, my study also identifies how inherited militant practices and imaginaries, including sectarianism and conspiracy thinking, actually contributed to shaping clientelist networks. This calls attention to how key elements of armed struggle's political repertoire may have hybridized into contemporary left-wing politics beyond the case of El Salvador.

I have structured this book in two clearly distinct parts. Part 1, consisting of chapters 2, 3, and 4, provides a comprehensive drawing-out of insurgent relations and of the institutional dimensions of the reconversion process that unfolded after the peace accords. As a whole, part 1 focuses much more on organizational and institutional trajectories than on personal life stories, though chapter 3 does provide a personal retrospect of my early years in El Salvador. Chapters 2 and 4 are based on literature review and archival research, only occasionally complemented with interview material. The objective of part 1 of the book is to provide an integral overview of El Salvador's revolutionary movement and of its subsequent multifaceted postwar reconversion process. Its chapters provide insight into the historical development of the movement and, with it, into the "shared baggage" that El Salvador's former insurgents carried along in their contemporary engagement with the movement.

Within part 1, chapter 2 provides an overview of the insurgent movement, from its origin until the time of the peace accords (early 1970s to 1992). In this chapter I examine how aspects like the Marxist-Leninist organizational model, revolutionary militancy, and clandestinity adopted by the Salvadoran revolutionaries impacted on the movement's internal relations. Pervasive sectarianism in the 1970s ended up generating five different guerrilla organizations that united to form the FMLN in 1980. Though now under a shared banner, the five insurgent groups continued to largely rely on separate organizations, consisting of a cadre structure and partially concealed and widely branched networks. Evolving political and military aspects of the war strongly influenced the shape and the functioning of the five separate groups. Chapter 2 elucidates the organizational trajectories of the insurgent groups composing the FMLN and clarifies what accumulated insurgent networks and imaginaries existed at the end of the war.

Chapter 3 serves as an interlude in which I present a retrospect on my own experience with postwar insurgent networks in Chalatenango. Besides helping the reader to qualify the relevance of my own involvement with the FPL in relation to the key topics of this book, it also presents a more intimate, personalized view on the "lived experience" of the immediate aftermath of insurgency. Chapter 4 subsequently deals with the development of the FMLN networks in the first postwar transition years, until the late 1990s. Taking into account the movement's military, political and socioeconomic facets, I document and analyze the insurgency's interconnected peacetime reconversion processes. As in chapter 2, I still focus mostly on institutional genealogies. The shifting priorities of the leadership and the multiple unfolding adjustments caused quite a bit of disarray in different segments of the movement, even though part of the FMLN soon got the knack of electoral politics. Factionalist struggles inside and around the FMLN also strongly resurfaced during the period, fed by electoral competition, ideological divergence, and historical mistrust among sectarian groups. The multifaceted postinsurgent reconversion documented in chapter 4 constitutes a baseline for the FMLN's posterior electoral consolidation and its contemporary political performance.

Part 2 holds this book's main empirical contribution: the ethnographic exploration of the experience of postinsurgency in El Salvador.[49] This effort is subdivided into three case studies, each presented in chapter format. Part 2 grants personal stories and individual experiences of former Salvadoran insurgents a particularly prominent role, while further connecting these stories to insights on the institutional genealogies of postinsurgency.

Chapter 5 revisits the insurgent communities in Chalatenango where I lived during the early postwar years. I present a detailed ethnographic reconstruction of the history of one such community, Ellacuría, in an attempt to straighten out several previously nonclarified issues regarding the specific relations between the insurgency and repopulations like Ellacuría. I then set out to explore the different consequences of these (hidden) wartime connections for postwar community development. Bringing in insurgent history allows for a qualified reassessment of the repopulation's trajectory from its foundation to the present, and helps clarify the principal local legacies of insurgency.

Chapter 6 explores what happened to a group of guerrilla fighters—a particular subset of insurgent participants—after the war ended. It is based on the collaborative effort to trace the identity and the destiny of the individuals represented in eleven historical photographs of guerrilla units. Through an ethnographic technique called photo elicitation, the chapter spins out a dialogue between former guerrilla fighters' postwar life stories and their reflections on the heritage of the struggles that they have been part of. At the same time, the historical photos used in the chapter constitute a detailed sample of postinsurgent life trajectories, putting the former insurgents' postwar destinies and survival strategies on display.

The last case study, presented in chapter 7, homes in on the FMLN war veteran movement, a booming phenomenon in recent years. FMLN veterans' politics constitutes a key facet of postinsurgency. Focusing on the veteran organizing efforts in the first years of the Funes presidency, I provide an intimate account of the political practices among the veteran groups active in and around the FMLN. This last case study unveils the lived experience of postinsurgent politics and examines in detail how the insurgent past is mobilized in postwar Salvadoran politics.

As he did in this introductory chapter, Justo will help guide us through chapter 8, a concluding reflection on contemporary Salvadoran politics and the legacies of insurgency. Several years down the line from when Justo and I worked together on the FPL archives, Salvador Sánchez Cerén, the FPL's former "comandante general," replaced Funes as president of El Salvador, with the FMLN holding on to power for a second five-year stretch from 2014 onward. Justo remained dedicated to recovering the stories about forgotten comrades that, in his mind, nobody in the party hierarchy cared about anymore. He believed they were too concerned with their new status and wealth and that the "old stories" about the movement had become for them but uncomfortable reminders of other values and objectives.

While Justo was sitting on the couch one Saturday afternoon complaining to me, his new partner looked at him disdainfully from the other side of the room. Some years after Felicia, the mother of his children, fell seriously ill and passed away, Justo got together with "Daniela," a woman he also knew from his days at the front in Chalatenango, where she had served as a nurse for the guerrilla troops. Daniela now worked for the government and considered that speaking badly about the FMLN only served to strengthen right-wing forces. "How are things ever going to change if our own veterans emanate such negativity?" she wondered. Justo lifted his shoulders and smiled, before saying, "You are right, my love," and asking me if we should drink coffee or something stronger.

PART 1

_____

DRAWING OUT INSURGENT RELATIONS

CHAPTER 2

El Salvador's Insurgency

A Relational Account

Era la izquierda. Una época que fue también épica.
—Sergio Ramírez, *Adiós Muchachos*

Even though Che Guevara himself had previously qualified the country's tiny and densely populated territory as inappropriate for guerrilla warfare (Harnecker 1983, 77), El Salvador developed one of the strongest insurgent movements in Latin American history. Who was involved in this endeavor? How was this possible? No doubt, a complex range of local and international circumstances fed into the expansion of the revolutionary movement and insurgent warfare in the country. Taking into account the broader Latin American context, the emergence of armed struggle in El Salvador in itself was not exceptional. In fact, its absence would have been much more remarkable. The 1959 Cuban revolution inaugurated a period of revolutionary effervescence across the continent (Castañeda 1993, 55). "During the 1960s, twenty-five pro-violence revolutionary groups emerged in Latin America. . . . By the 1980s, armed groups existed in seventeen of the nineteen countries in Latin America" (Churchill 2014, 23). In El Salvador and other countries, the actions of the military regimes often spurred the growth of such groups, as increased repression convinced many left-wing activists that armed struggle was the only viable option.

Throughout Latin America, Cold War geopolitics and mind-sets interacted with diverse local circumstances, including existing conflicts and tensions with multicausal historical roots.[1] The continent witnessed the multiplication of US-backed anticommunist dictatorships (Brands

2010; Gill 2004; Grandin 2004; Rabe 2011). Relying on strong US support, particularly from the CIA, Latin America's anticommunist forces started developing alliances and forms of coordination that transcended national borders. Also countries like Israel and Taiwan actively backed Latin American anticommunists. In a similar fashion, revolutionary forces constructed networks and alliances that transcended national and continental borders. The Cuban government, particularly its Departamento de las Americas,[2] played a crucial role in such efforts (Castañeda 1993; Kruijt 2017; Suárez Salazar and Kruijt 2015).

The fact that El Salvador was heavily enmeshed in these international dynamics no doubt strongly impacted how the revolutionary movement and the armed conflict evolved. It also helps to explain why, during the 1980s, anything like an evenhanded account of the Salvadoran war and the revolutionary movement was very hard to come by, since scholarly assessments folded into geopolitical divides (Danner 1994; Sprenkels and van der Borgh 2011). Most scholars framed the Salvadoran conflict as the struggle of a legitimate national liberation movement against a bloody military regime sustained by the United States and by an exploitive oligarchy. Such authors particularly pointed at El Salvador's highly unequal land distribution, widespread poverty, and horrific human rights record, and tended to view revolution as something necessary or inevitable.[3] In counterpoint, a second, much smaller group of authors portrayed the insurgents as conniving terrorists and totalitarians, partially composed of foreign infiltrators, and emphasized the potential threat they represented to freedom and security in the Western Hemisphere. This analysis was prevalent in US foreign policy circles (Kirkpatrick 1987, 1988; Manwaring and Prisk 1988). Finally, there were a few attempts toward a "middle road" perspective—a reading of the Salvadoran conflict that was critical of the methods and motives of both the military and the guerrilla, and favored reformist rather than military solutions to the conflict (Baloyra 1982; Zaid 1981).

Academic writing on the Salvadoran insurgency is abundant. Most of the available work, however, attempts to examine the conflict and its background as a whole, and only includes a broad-stroke description of the revolutionary movement. Fewer than a handful of studies actually offer empirical insight into the movement itself. The two most in-depth accounts of El Salvador's revolutionary movement are Jenny Pearce's *Promised Land: Peasant Rebellion in Chalatenango, El Salvador* (1986) and

Yvon Grenier's *The Emergence of Insurgency in El Salvador: Ideology and Political Will* (1999). Interestingly, their findings are radically different.

Pearce offers that the Salvadoran conflict is best understood as a revolution unleashed by "the political awakening of the peasantry," in part because peasants became more aware of their situation through an encounter with liberation theology (1986, 108). "No longer passive and manipulated," the peasants then built their own revolutionary organization to become the key force sustaining the movement. Grenier instead emphasizes the movement's urban character and claims that in the early 1980s "the insurgency moved from the cities to the countryside" (1999, 84) and that "only a tiny minority of rural dwellers joined the insurgency, mostly young men and teenagers, and this as a result of a multiple set of incentives [resulting] from war itself" (135). According to Grenier, insurgency emerged as a result of the explicit political will of a dissenting faction of urban middle-to-upper strata to defy the regime by means of armed struggle (33).

In my view, by emphasizing either bottom-up or top-down aspects, both studies produce incomplete accounts of El Salvador's insurgent movement. A more balanced view requires an understanding of the range of actors and subgroups involved, the different roles they played, and how these roles transformed over time. This is the central endeavor of the present chapter.

An important complication involved in this effort is that the revolutionary movement relied heavily on clandestine relations as a necessary protection from the enemy (Joes 2006). Che Guevara hinted at this when he wrote that "the history of revolutions has a large subterranean component" (1970, 654). In-depth research demonstrates that insurgencies tend to covertly tie together multiple groups and individuals with an amalgam of roles, interweaving political, social, military, and economic aspects (Christia 2014; Staniland 2014).[4] Clandestine relations are inscrutable by design and sometimes difficult to disentangle, even years later. Often, the guerrilla army itself only makes up a small part of the movement (Hammes 2005, 6). In the account of the Salvadoran revolutionary movement I offer in this chapter, I aim to reconstruct the trajectories and itineraries of different, partially overlapping revolutionary networks, zooming in on aspects like clandestinity, revolutionary militancy, and constituency relations. In construing such a relational account, I take guidance from an overall chronology of insurgent development based on FMLN documents.[5]

Before I proceed to the meat of this chapter, a final caveat is in order. Since El Salvador's insurgency was structured in five separate "political-military organizations," I use this term very frequently in this chapter and in the rest of the book. I therefore rely on the acronym PMO. This adds to an array of acronyms referring to different insurgent organizations and networks. Indeed, Salvadoran revolutionaries are renowned for their proclivity to acronyms, and those unfamiliar with Salvadoran politics may struggle with the apparent hodgepodge. Unfortunately, I found no sensible alternative but to also use acronyms, since these pertain directly to the networks and relations I aim to examine. I use the organization's full name plus its acronym at first mention. Subsequently I use the acronym only. When the specific context renders the use of the full name redundant, I only use the acronym and refer to an endnote for further explanation. Should my shorthand get the better of you, please refer to "Acronyms" at the front of the book for a complete list.

"ACTIVE CLANDESTINITY" (PRE-1980): EMERGENCE AND EXPANSION OF POLITICAL-MILITARY ORGANIZATIONS (PMOS)

In El Salvador's left-wing circles of the 1960s, the debate on armed struggle was heavily influenced by an earlier failed attempt at insurgency in 1932, which had ended with the massacre of thousands of indigenous villagers in the western coffee belt of the country, and with the arrest and execution of almost the entire Communist Party leadership, including Farabundo Martí, at the time the country's principal revolutionary. The overall poor organization, coordination, and timing made it easy for the National Guard to violently wipe out the rebellion, ushering in a long period of right-wing military control of the country.[6] Over the next decades, the outlawed PCS led a relatively marginal existence, while gradually rearticulating some of its networks.[7]

In the early 1960s, when armed struggle came in vogue across the continent, the PCS was still small and incapable of garnering widespread support (Lindo-Fuentes and Ching 2012, 66). It was, furthermore, divided on the suitability of armed struggle for the Salvadoran context. In 1961, after much internal debate, it nonetheless set up a group called Frente Unido de Acción Revolucionaria (FUAR),[8] under the leadership of a young Schafik Handal. FUAR was composed mostly of university stu-

"monolithic" unity), and discipline (Lalich 2004, 116; Martín Alvarez 2004).[15] The organization's core was its cadres, following Mao Tse-tung's dictum that the "cadres are a decisive factor, once the political line is determined. Therefore, it is our fighting task to train large numbers of new cadres in a planned way" (1971, 147). Mao also warned that "while boldly enlarging our membership, we must not relax our vigilance against enemy agents and careerists who will avail themselves of this opportunity to sneak in. . . . The only correct policy is: 'Expand the Party boldly but do not let a single undesirable in'" (144). Beyond self-restraint, cadre discipline was to be organized as follows: "(1) the individual is subordinate to the organization; (2) the minority is subordinate to the majority; (3) the lower level is subordinate to the higher level; and (4) the entire membership is subordinate to the Central Committee" (149).

One of the problems the aspiring Salvadoran insurgents faced was the cultural resistance of many of the potential recruits to the use of lethal violence, also connected to the Catholic background of many who were sympathetic to revolutionary ideas. "Breaking the taboo of death"[16] was an important part of the training process for new recruits. Latin America's most eloquent defender of revolutionary violence, Ernesto Che Guevara, proved to be of much help in this.[17] Guevara saw "armed struggle as the only solution for the peoples who fight to free themselves" (cited in J. Anderson 1997, 633). He not only advertised these beliefs; he also tried to put them into practice, most famously in his ill-fated Bolivia expedition (J. Anderson 1997; Castañeda 1997).[18] Two months before his capture and execution in the Bolivian jungle, while facing extremely difficult political and military circumstances and suffering severe physical hardship, Guevara praised the moral benefits of armed struggle in his famous diary. In his view, "this type of struggle provides us with the opportunity to become revolutionaries, the highest level of the human species. At the same time, it enables us to emerge fully as men" (Guevara 1994, 250). Shortly after Che's death, Jean-Paul Sartre qualified him as "the most complete human being of our age" (cited in McLaren 2000, 3). Che Guevara became the single most important source of inspiration and guidance for Latin American (aspiring) insurgents (Castañeda 1993; Debray 1967; Gott 1970; Piñeiro 2006).

Drawing on revolutionary heroes like Lenin, Mao, and Guevara, the Salvadoran PMOs emerged as cadre organizations at the vanguard of the revolution. The cadres had to demonstrate exemplary revolutionary behavior, often referred to as *mística revolucionaria*.[19] This mystique was an important ingredient of the revolutionary militancy, the brand of political activism on which the PMOs were built.[20] Through a spirit of revolutionary sacrifice, the cadres would be able to build relationships with the people and to establish the bonds needed to enlist them in their efforts. Salvadoran revolutionaries, furthermore, embraced clandestine organizing methods explicitly tuned for surviving and growing under the strain of counterinsurgent violence, like the methods proposed in Carlos Marighella's *Minimanual of the Urban Guerrilla* (1969 [2008]) or in Guevara's *Guerrilla Warfare* (1961b), adapting these to some of the specificities of the Salvadoran context.[21] They followed the thesis—vigorously defended by Guevara—that armed struggle would contribute to generating a crisis of the capitalist regime and thus pave the way for a popular revolution.

Both the ERP and the FPL cautiously expanded their clandestine networks in the first half of the 1970s, when both were still small in numbers and had limited operational capacity. In this initial period, both groups experimented with military activities, but generally also, somewhat paradoxically, tried to avoid drawing too much attention (Medrano and Raudales 1994). The PMOs recruited men and women they considered trustworthy, and then trained them to develop an indelible faith in the revolution as well as deep loyalty to the revolutionary party. Responding to different tiers and levels, the PMO networks maintained increasing degrees of secretiveness and protection toward the organizations' core.

The Dynamics of Early Organizational Expansion

The FPL's initial nucleus set up an armed commando a few months after starting the group, and ordered each member of the commando to recruit fifteen collaborators to provide a support structure for the commando. Initially, the FPL mainly recruited from among students and labor union activists. The collaborators provided a pool of potential new FPL cadres. At the same time, this process helped the FPL to penetrate and take over a substantial part of El Salvador's organized labor movement, mainly by infiltrating its leadership (Harnecker 1983, 86, 121).

The PMOs built two parallel and semioverlapping structures: popular organizations and a military structure partially inserted within the former and partially separate. Both were embedded within the overarching internal command structure of the PMO itself, the "Party," the ultimate authority controlling both the political and the military arm of the organization.

Conscious that to embed structures dedicated to armed struggle within popular organizations made these structures susceptible to counterinsurgent persecution, the party adopted an organizational framework that would allow it to survive and grow in these circumstances. To this end, the FPL adopted the following basic principles: "rigorous clandestinity," "strict parallelism and compartmentalization," use of "cell structure for combatants and for the direction of masses," "military centralism," "constant technical revolutionary sophistication," and "strict disciplinary norms" (FPL 1974, 14). Revolutionary mystique helped to generate a mind-set devised to overcome the turbulence and personal sacrifice involved in this kind of organizing.

> The revolutionary organization must abide by a code of high revolutionary morale . . . [and] rely on militants with high revolutionary quality. These must be promoted to the status of militant according to strict selection criteria, which guarantee high revolutionary qualities, [like] unlimited dedication to revolutionary struggle; willingness to make the maximum personal and family sacrifice, to offer their life to the cause of the revolution; deep love of the people; elevated revolutionary internationalism; honesty in their private life; and a discipline of iron. (FPL 1974, 15)

The different categories of participation in the FPL were simultaneously designed to avoid enemy infiltration and allow for expansion, through the testing of potential militants. This model translated into the organization being hierarchical and inscrutable, with a highly dedicated in-group working on expansion as the result of a sort of "covert snowballing." Militants were divided into three different levels: active collaborator, aspiring member, and member. An additional category was that of the regular collaborator who, while not having the status of militants, provided different important services to the clandestine networks, including logistical support, information gathering, and material support for the militants. Obtaining membership was a lengthy and highly selective process, in which only those who "had passed the tests of fire, who had adopted an unbreakable commitment to the revolution, and who were willing to carry out any given task" might eventually qualify (Harnecker 1993, 121).

Militants on different levels were responsible for the recruitment of reliable new adepts, and for this purpose militants mostly recurred to their own social and political networks. New recruits, in turn, could only gain access to higher levels within the organization by demonstrating dedicated and loyal service, which usually included recruitment of others. Starting with the organization's leader (called "first responsible"), all of those involved had someone who was responsible for them. Participants would receive both orders and orientation from whoever was responsible for them, and would usually work in a collective or a cell, a small group of people with specific capabilities the leader could rely upon to perform required tasks. From different organizational components of the PMO, the leadership would handpick (or the participating cadres would name) representatives to the central committee of the organization, formally the highest decision-making body. In practice, given the circumstances, the central committee met in full only on rare occasions, and conduct of the revolutionary process was in the hands of a select leadership group structured around the first responsible.[22]

In early documents, the FPL explicitly proposed a blend of political and military activities that would interlink one with the other in building a constituency for a revolutionary army.

> The armed struggle has demonstrated that, linked to the political organization of the masses, it accelerates the creation and development of the organization, [of the] revolutionary consciousness of large sectors of the people, much more effectively than the sole political struggle of the masses through exclusively pacific means. . . . The revolutionary armed struggle does not scorn other forms of political-economic-social struggle of the masses and its organization for these objectives, but rather believes they should be stimulated and combined in the function of the armed struggle. These means gradually become subject to the fundamental means of struggle that becomes Armed Struggle. Therefore, the one and the other form inseparable parts of the same strategy, the political-military strategy for the development of the prolonged armed struggle of the people.[23] (FPL 1974, 6–7; see also FPL 1973)

One of the main strategies the FPL used to expand their support base was to infiltrate and attempt to take over political organizations previously controlled by the PCS.[24] Apart from labor unions and student organizations, the FPL had considerable success in penetrating and gaining support within Asociación Nacional de Educadores Salvadoreños "21 de Junio" (ANDES),[25] the country's teachers' union and previously a PCS bastion (Sánchez Cerén 2008, 78–80, 86). For example, Mélida Anaya Montes, ANDES's principal leader, simultaneously functioned as the number two in the FPL's secret chain of command for most of the 1970s and early 1980s, identified as Comandante "Ana María." The organized teachers had a strong territorial presence throughout the country, as well as relatively high social standing in different towns and villages, making them a valuable asset for organizational expansion. Other sectors the FPL successfully targeted for expansion were slum dwellers and, particularly, high school students (Harnecker 1993, 139). But the FPL's most remarkable and substantial expansion occurred among El Salvador's peasantry.

This success implied an important break with the dominant Latin American trend at the time. Booming as they were, PMOs across the continent had largely been unable to generate support from the peasant population. The "old" networks of the communist parties and other left-leaning organizations were mostly urban, and rarely connected to significant peasant constituencies. As exemplified in Che Guevara's failed attempt at creating an insurgent movement in Bolivia, the lack of rural support precipitated the defeat of many Latin American guerrillas (Castañeda 1997; Guevara 1994).[26]

Involving the Peasants in the Revolution

How did the Salvadoran revolutionaries cultivate a substantial peasant movement? The Catholic Church, and particularly the ascendance of liberation theology among part of El Salvador's clergy, is commonly acknowledged as the key factor (Berryman 2004; Chávez 2014; C. McClintock 1998).[27] Liberation theologians advocated revolutionary transformation of society for the benefit of the poor, while at the same time promoting progressive social and political transformation of community life, by means of community organizing (A. Peterson 1997). The role of this "popular church" is crucial for understanding the success of the different Salvadoran PMOs, and especially the FPL and the ERP, in mobilizing a peasant constituency in support of their cause.

In the only substantial contemporary account of preinsurgent organizing in rural El Salvador, Carlos Rafael Cabarrús explains how a group of young Jesuit priests, keen to bring new progressive ideas into practice, used the parish contacts in the rural communities to set up a "popular church" in Aguilares, an hour north of the capital city.[28] The pastoral team, made up of priests and seminarians, started the new project in 1972 by living among the peasants in small rural communities for several months in a row (1983, 144–48). Toward the end of this period, a group of "lay priests" was appointed among the community's "natural leaders" to continue the development of the local Christian base community[29] and to serve as a liaison with responsible clergy (145–46). Cabarrús shows that the clergy provided concrete incentives to promote the organizing efforts (training and educational tools, trips to and exchange sessions with other communities, access to funding for small-scale projects) as well as symbolic incentives (attaching positive values to the cultural expressions of peasant communities: folk music, community festivals, and the like).[30] As intended, "the pastoral work almost naturally overflowed into political work" (142).

These efforts facilitated the emergence of local peasant leaders who shared a similar political outlook and worked closely together with the progressive priests and seminarians. The latter also brought in students interested in promoting a revolutionary peasant movement to work with the local groups. While building this popular organization, the clergy moved to keep political parties and other potential political competitors out (1983, 146). In 1973, these new Jesuit-trained peasant organizers, including men as well as women, moved to take over leadership positions within the Federación Cristiana de Campesinos Salvadoreños (FECCAS),[31] a peasant union set up under the influence of the church and the PDC in the 1960s, seen by Cabarrús and others as docile and ineffective until it was taken over by the revolutionary movement (Dunkerley 1985, 99–100; Martín Alvarez 2004, 77).

Throughout his book, Cabarrús emphasizes the need to draw the peasants away from the influence of the traditional powers: state authorities and the landlord's patronage networks. He also stresses the competition that developed between the revolutionary movement and other organizations trying to maintain or gain a foothold among the peasantry (1983, 182). The most important of these organizations was the Organización Democrática Nacionalista (ORDEN),[32] an anticommunist paramilitary organization set up in the 1960s by the military to promote rural organization under the banner of progress and against "communist insidiousness." ORDEN initially functioned mostly as a support structure for the governing political party and as a channel for US and government-sponsored rural development projects.[33] It also organized patrols and coordinated other auxiliary tasks with the military. The expansion of ORDEN in the villages continued until deep into the 1970s, during which time it also increasingly became involved in espionage, coercion, and violent persecution of local activists (Mazzei 2009, 148).[34]

Other initiatives seen as (potential) competitors of the revolutionary peasant movement were not militaristic in nature. The Unión Comunal Salvadoreña (UCS),[35] for example, created in 1966 and funded largely by the United States, promoted the creation of both peasant cooperatives and a peasant syndical movement (Sariego and González 1977). UCS worked together closely with the Catholic Church (via the Catholic NGO Caritas, a partner in the project). Local chapters of the UCS maintained extensive relationships with the governing Partido de Conciliación Nacional (PCN)[36] as well as with the PDC opposition, and both parties worked with the UCS as a vehicle to maintain or extend their rural clientele (5–6). In sum, starting in the mid-1960s, the reactionary Right, the moderate reformists, and revolutionaries were all building support among peasants in sometimes overlapping areas of the Salvadoran countryside.

Cabarrús's empirical data offer interesting insights into the revolutionaries' organizational pragmatism. He describes how those responsible for expansion carefully studied the community and tried to capitalize as much as possible on existing local networks and kinship bonds, as well as on local disputes, adjusting specific organizational strategies used in each community to "win over the people" (1983, 209). Existing traditional ties, such as *compadrazgo* relations, were used to gain local embedding.[37] Different leadership figures or local institutions, including, on occasion, a local chapter of ORDEN, might either be recruited or taken over (if feasible), or might, alternatively, be an opposition target for community organizing efforts (201–2).[38]

Other in-depth field studies were not conducted at the time. However, available data indicate that the preinsurgent organizational expansion elsewhere in the countryside followed a similar path, albeit with particular local adaptations. El Salvador's rural areas, rather than being political landscapes that were "virgin because of abandonment" (Samayoa and Galván, cited in Pearce 1986, 174; see also Todd 2010), were in fact sites of rapid social change in the decades prior to insurgency. Local traditional powers were increasingly intersecting with different external actors, which included political parties, churches, paramilitary networks, emerging peasants unions, and development projects.[39] This development, which accelerated decisively in the 1960s, led to the widespread involvement of different types of support groups and outside allies with rural communities. Thus, in the 1970s, different "activists and their organizations offered alternative sources of economic assistance and protection to peasants directly and through their links with urban and international groups" (Brockett 2005, 164).

In the case of Chalatenango, Juan Fernando Ascoli emphasizes the preinsurgency relevance of local peasant cooperatives promoted by the Catholic Church from the 1960s onward (2001, 21).[40] The training programs associated with the cooperative movement helped peasant leaders from Chalatenango to "develop analytical skills to fully engage social and political activism" and to "create lasting political networks" (Chávez 2010, 139). Chávez, furthermore, points to the success of the Catholic Radio School project, also in the 1960s and early 1970s, and the dynamic social role of the local educators in the church's grassroots activity in Chalatenango (143–49). Initially, the empowerment of these Catholic networks led to increased political influence for the PDC, which in some cases contributed to PDC mayors being elected in Chalatenango municipalities.[41] However, with the intensification of the links between liberation theology's organizational networks and militants of the PMOs, the PDC eventually lost its grip on these areas.

In the early 1970s, some of the most influential clergy had sought connections to the PMOs and the other way around. A few priests and seminarians actually became members of PMOs and started to lead a clandestine double life (Alas 2003, 238; Gibb 2000, 75–85; Kruijt 2008, 53). In some other cases, guerrilla organizers were allowed access to the organizational network the clergy had built up, as was the case in Aguilares.[42] In Chalatenango, one of the first persons to embrace the cause of the FPL was Benito Tovar, a Catholic priest (Chávez 2010, 171). Through him, FPL organizers accessed the local Christian base communities, educational projects, and cooperatives. These FPL organizers provided political education workshops and recruited local leaders to their cause.[43] In 1974, together with some outstanding local recruits, they founded the Unión de Trabajadores del Campo (UTC),[44] trying to emulate FECCAS in Aguilares (Ascoli 2001, 40). UTC was founded simultaneously in the two areas where, apart from Aguilares, the FPL organizing had advanced the most: Chalatenango and San Vicente (Chávez 2010, 158–59).

When channeled in through the clergy, the revolutionary militants encountered an organizational infrastructure they could build upon, with people generally receptive to the revolutionary ideas that had also been promoted by the progressive priests and Catholic lay workers. In line with the model of clandestine expansion, guerrilla organizers actively recruited local leaders as new PMO members, while often keeping them in place in their local leadership roles (Cabarrús 1983, 291). Secret recruitment and insertion within the popular organizations made it possible for the PMOs to operate within a broader movement with a public political presence and to control that movement. Increasingly, the peasant movement started to confront both local powers and the national regime by means of strikes and land invasions (243, 252, 304). In the mid-1970s, organizations like FECCAS and UTC were able to mobilize contingents of between two thousand and three thousand peasants in different antigovernment protests (Cabarrús 1983, 240; Pearce 1986, 163–64).

While the geographic emphasis of the FPL's work was with the popular church networks in the northern and central part of El Salvador, the ERP focused mainly (but not exclusively) on the eastern part of the country. For example, the ERP managed to find an inroad into northern Morazán through the progressive Catholic networks organized by father Miguel Ventura in the parish of Torola. According to anthropologist Leigh Binford, this arrangement made it possible for the ERP to work quietly and clandestinely for many years among the peasants of the area to extend its support base (1997, 33; 2004; see also Medrano and Raudales 1994). While the FPL engaged peasant supporters in confrontational activities with the regime as early as 1974, the ERP gave more attention to clandestine military preparation and only started to engage in protest movement tactics in 1977 (Binford 1997, 32). Also in the central part of the country, the ERP had managed to organize support structures in various progressive parishes (urban and rural). However, a significant segment of that network would split off when the RN was born.

The different PMOs also competed for the loyalty of rural supporters between them. For example, reviewing the events of the 1970s in his Suchitoto parish, directly east of the Aguilares parish and across the Cerrón Grande Reservoir from Chalatenango, former priest and popular church organizer José Inocencio Alas comments that, after 1975, the area "becomes politically flooded. Activists of the five tendencies[45] present themselves in the city and the majority of the cantons (villages). The objective: bring together the largest number of followers and obtain hegemonic power in the region. They are all particularly interested in the Guazapa mountain, which stands majestically a few kilometers from San Salvador. Its northern slopes give exit to Chalatenango, where intensive work is carried out with the peasants" (2003, 237).[46]

Alas's comment is eloquent on the PMOs' active pursuit of peasant constituencies. However, the PMOs simultaneously provided a vehicle for empowerment and social ascendancy for the peasants. Though urban cadres dominated leadership, the PMOs facilitated meaningful internal participation for the peasants, and a significant number of peasant leaders also obtained cadre status during the 1970s. The revolutionary peasant leaders also demanded this space (Chávez 2010, 173). In this sense, it is important to acknowledge that the PMOs and the popular movement they controlled allowed the peasants to participate in a project in which their personal and collective status was framed positively. In the revolutionary parlance of the FPL, the "workers-peasant alliance" was to be the backbone of the revolution and of the new El Salvador that was to emerge afterwards (Carpio 1999, 91). The popular church frequently referred to the organized peasant families as the "chosen people," increasingly so when the struggle became more difficult (Berryman 2004; Wright 1994). Because of their participation in the movement, the peasants were able to engage in and negotiate relationships with other groups and individuals— like political organizers, university students, or priests—on relatively horizontal terms, terms in which, to a significant degree, the peasants' personal and collective aspirations found echo and acceptance.

Simultaneously, the positive framing of the concept of *popular*, meaning grassroots or mass based, also contributed to the emergence of a vibrant cultural production among the organized peasants, which in turn helped sustain the revolutionary movement. For example, with the help of clergy and the rural unions, peasant communities organized local festivals and other cultural activities, mixing traditional religious and peasant motifs with revolutionary themes (Sprenkels 2009, 19–20). The popular church songbook promoted active participation of the population in singing and making music (A. Peterson 1997). Revolutionary songs in vogue in Latin America at the time were often incorporated into the folk repertoire. Rallies, meetings, and festivals featured artistic presentations from urban as well as rural groups (Almeida and Urbizagástegui 1999).[47] The expansion of the revolutionary movement was thus accompanied by new and transformative cultural experiences, helping to create an "oppositional political culture" and to consolidate symbolic and emotional attachments among the movement's followers (Foran 1997, 2005; Jasper 2011).

In the second half of the 1970s, rural activists would frequently play different roles and switch back and forth between these roles when circumstances so required: from lay priest, to peasant leader, to guerrilla organizer (Sprenkels 2001, 209–13). In popular church parishes, clergy, peasant leaders, and militants of PMOs increasingly operated in overlapping networks and roles to actively and consciously build a revolutionary constituency. Being inserted within multiple networks allowed activists to assume roles and responsibilities in political as well as in military work. The use of different roles and identities was a tool for organizational accumulation as well as a defense mechanism. When necessary, members of the guerrilla could pass for union organizers, school teachers, or lay priests.

Mass Organizations and PMO Expansion

Parallel to rural expansion, the PMOs also continued to make headway in the cities, where a number of political events in the first half of the 1970s had fueled revolutionary radicalization within the opposition forces. The fraudulent election of 1972 led to much outrage, with the military imposing its candidate even though opposition candidate and PDC leader Napoleón Duarte had clearly won. Stuffed ballot boxes were followed by a violent crackdown on the opposition. Blatant electoral fraud accompanied elections throughout the 1970s and contributed to the weakening of the position of reformist parties reluctant to engage in armed struggle.

Meanwhile, the PMOs gradually increased covert influence over a significant part of the labor unions, student associations, and urban Christian base communities, both by placing cadres in these structures and by recruiting from them.[48] Insurgent activity took place much to the discomfort of the established political forces. The PCS, for example, after Cayetano Carpio's exit, had rejected armed struggle as adventurist, and instead moved to establish a legal political party with electoral aims, the Unión Democrática Nacionalista (UDN).[49] The PMOs qualified the PCS as "bourgeois" and "collaborationist," and, in turn, the PCS accused them of extremism.[50] Throughout the 1970s, this resulted in bitter and sometimes violent tension between the PMOs and the PCS, which gradually saw its influence shrinking.[51] According to the Christian Democratic leader Napoleón Duarte, the PDC was also affected by the organizational success of the PMOs: "The mass organizations grew as our party [the PDC] withered" (1986, 94). At the same time, the PDC also endured pressure and persecution from right-wing groups like ORDEN. "By the end of the 1970s, [these two extremes] had decimated the Christian Democrats" (92).

Though the intense disputes between the PMOs that occurred throughout the 1970s were often framed in terms of ideological differences,[52] sectarianism might just as well be explained in terms of a competition for constituencies, cadres, and other political resources. Revolutionary rivalry divided the two earliest PMOs (FPL and ERP) from each other, and both opposed the PCS.[53] Revolutionary zeal, repression, and clandestinity fueled distrust and internal power struggles, among and within the PMOs. These disputes would sometimes end in tragedy, as was the case within the ERP in May 1975. In an episode whose exact details and responsibilities are still in dispute today, the ERP leadership executed Roque Dalton, El Salvador's foremost poet and intellectual. Dalton had returned clandestinely to El Salvador from Havana a year earlier to participate in the ERP's urban structures (García Dueñas and Espinoza 2010). His death strengthened the internal divisions within the ERP, giving rise to a new PMO, the RN, initially with very strong animosities toward the ERP. The ERP remained in control of its structures in the eastern part of El Salvador, but lost a significant part of its bases in the central part of the country to the RN (Martín Alvarez and Cortina Orero 2014).

In the second half of the 1970s, the revolutionary expansion provided the impetus for the establishment of overarching popular movements known as "mass organizations." In 1975, the FPL clustered the different popular organizations it controlled into the Bloque Popular Revolucionario (BPR)[54] (Harnecker 1993, 136). The BPR was launched as the FPL's reply to the 1975 massacre of university students on a protest march by the

Salvadoran military, leaving dozens dead or disappeared (Flores Macal 1980, 20). After leaving the ERP in 1975, the RN consolidated control over the Frente de Acción Popular Unificada (FAPU),[55] a mass organization founded in 1974, whose direction they had initially disputed with the FPL, the PCS, and the PDC (Dunkerley 1985, 99). Following the internal rupture, the ERP initially focused more on preparing the military infrastructure that would allow for a popular insurrection. However, the ERP also founded its own "mass organization" in 1977, called Ligas Populares 28 de Febrero (LP-28),[56] after the massacre of several ERP supporters who had gathered in a central square in San Salvador to protest against electoral fraud in the presidential elections.

These mass organizations combined proactive and dedicated organizational expansion with antigovernment rallies, strikes, marches, and occupations of buildings (in the city) and estates (in the countryside) (Brockett 2005, 186–88). At the time, the mass organizations defined themselves publicly as revolutionary movements, but denied having organic ties to the guerrillas (Duarte 1986, 94; Dunkerley 1985, 100). They provided the PMOs with a belligerent protest movement as well as a recruitment pool and a training ground for revolutionary activists. And because of gradually increasing repression by military and paramilitary forces in the late 1970s, the mass organizations themselves also increasingly had to develop defense mechanisms that anticipated the military tasks that were to come for many militants. Cayetano Carpio's slogan "our mountains are the masses" heralded the expansion of the popular movement and connected it directly to the FPL strategy of revolutionary warfare. The underlying message was that Che Guevara had been wrong to discard El Salvador for guerrilla warfare because of its lack of mountains. Instead, the guerrillas might overcome such geographical limitations by seeking cover among the population.

Military or paramilitary violence directed at the PMOs and their alleged supporters occurred with increasing frequency in the second half of the 1970s. It also started to target priests active in the popular church (Sánchez 2015). Rutilio Grande, the Jesuit responsible for the Aguilares parish, was murdered in 1977 together with two of his parishioners (Cardenal 1986). Apart from the military, also paramilitary forces like ORDEN were involved in acts of intimidation and violent repression of revolutionary forces as well as other opposition groups. Meanwhile, the PMOs needed money and weapons in order to consolidate themselves and develop military actions. They carried out bank robberies and kidnappings (a few ended in assassination) of wealthy Salvadorans or other prestigious figures. These actions translated into the accumulation of a significant "war chest," especially by the RN and the ERP (Binford 1997, 33; Rico Mira 2003, 129).[57] The actions also established a type of military presence of the guerrilla forces in the country, and were simultaneously used to push for other demands, such as the release of captured militants. Armed propaganda was another early strategy: masked guerrillas showing off their weapons and distributing pamphlets during brief and unexpected public appearances. Though the revolutionaries suffered from a significant scarcity of weaponry, which they obtained mostly from the black market and by "requisition" of firearms during attacks on the police or the military, they did gradually step up military presence, in part to demonstrate their growing capacity vis-à-vis the enemy, in part to avoid lagging behind the other PMOs.

As indicated earlier, the 1970s buildup of El Salvador's revolutionary movement, though clandestine and highly secretive, did not occur in isolation, but in a context of Latin American revolutionary effervescence. All the different PMOs sustained relationships with revolutionary groups outside El Salvador, and especially with the Cubans, who provided cautious but crucial support for the emerging Salvadoran guerrilla organizations and in turn tried to exert influence on these groups (Castañeda 1993). Of immense symbolic and later also practical importance for the Salvadoran revolutionaries was the insurrectional triumph of the Nicaraguan Sandinistas (July 19, 1979), providing a key rallying cry for the subsequent years: "If Nicaragua won, El Salvador will win" (Perla 2008).

As in the countryside, the revolutionary struggle had also found its way into urban culture. Revolutionaries thought of art as a powerful tool for political awareness raising. Roque Dalton had paved the way, with revolutionary poetry like *El turno del ofendido* (1962) and *Poemas clandestinos* (1975), the essay *Las historias prohibidas del Pulgarcito* (1974), and the novel *Pobrecito poeta que era yo . . .* (1975). He was also the first Salvadoran writer to take on the genre of testimonio, with his milestone rendering of the memoirs of PCS founder Miguel Mármol, a survivor of the 1932 massacre (1972).[58] Manlio Argueta (1977, 1980), Claribel Alegría (1983), and José Roberto Cea (1981, 1984, 1989) would expand on this genre, describing revolutionary sacrifices in the face of military repression. ERP leader Ana Guadalupe Martínez's testimony about her nine months in captivity became a clandestine best seller (1978).[59] Musicians like Tamba Aragón and his Banda del Sol put the Salvadoran struggle to rock (Roque Baldovinos 2016). The different PMOs furthermore produced an impressive array of clandestine publications with different purposes and target audiences (Cortina Orero 2015).[60] While the levels of repression allowed for it, popular artists frequently accompanied rallies and other activities with music, theater, and poetry. Later on, when increased persecution made such activities impossible, artists would sometimes perform inside the war fronts, or tour to gain international support for the cause.[61]

"ACTIVE RESISTANCE" (1980–82): VIOLENCE, TERROR, AND ESCALATION

The March 24, 1980, death-squad assassination of Archbishop Romero is often seen as the "point of no return" in the escalation of the Salvadoran civil war (United Nations 1993; Montgomery 1995a). Romero was the country's foremost advocate for human rights and structural reform, and his death eliminated the one figure who could plausibly have facilitated a negotiated solution to the crisis, convincing many Salvadorans of the inevitability of war (Eisenbrandt 2017). However, it was the October 15, 1979, coup d'état that prompted the dramatic escalation of violence. It ousted the regime of a hardliner general, imposed through fraudulent elections in 1977, which had dramatically failed to contain the political crisis. The coup brought a civil-military junta to power, which included moderate left-wingers, with a program resting on broad reform and the cessation of political persecution, including the immediate dissolution of ORDEN (Majano 2009; Menjívar Ochoa 2006, 267). Archbishop Romero and a substantial part of the Jesuit community in El Salvador threw their support behind the coup (Bataillon 2008, 241–45). It backfired because both anticommunist hardliners and the PMOs viewed the coup as a threat to their position (Galeas 2004, 6; Harnecker 1993, 170).

Major Roberto d'Aubuisson, a high-ranking counterinsurgency official at the time of the coup, abandoned his post and immediately started organizing an underground paramilitary terror campaign. In subsequent months, D'Aubuisson and others were able to galvanize a significant anticommunist (para)military network, which functioned with the support of part of the country's economic elite, part of the military, and most of the formally dissolved structures of ORDEN (Galeas 2004, 12). The "death squads" became the best-known expression of this right-wing shadow force, operating partially inserted within Salvadoran Armed Forces, partially outside it (Stanley 1996). The hardliners increased their share of control of coercive resources through massive engagement in semiclandestine, semigovernmental repression, generating an intractable mix of official and unofficial violence, what Joan Didion described as the "proliferation of . . . shadowy and overlapping forces" (1983, 13). At the same time, the anticommunists publicly mobilized vocal pressure groups, like Frente de Agricultores de la Región Oriental (FARO) and Frente Feminino.[62] D'Aubuisson created a militant anticommunist Right that, in part mirroring the methods used by the PMOs, integrated and combined political and (para)military means.[63]

On the other hand, the insurgents also aimed to sabotage the reformist junta because they were afraid successful reform would undermine their position on the left of the political spectrum. A military victory for the insurgency, like what had occurred in Nicaragua in July that same year, would place them in a much better position (Zaid 1981, 11, 27). The PMOs were pushing hard to consolidate their popular bases and strategic military positions. In the process they increasingly imposed "revolutionary justice" on those they considered their enemies or otherwise a liability to their own safety. In the words of ERP comandante Ana Guadalupe Martínez, "At this time [the end of 1979 and beginning of 1980] all the armed organizations of the Left were committed to an intense campaign of annihilation of the paramilitaries" (cited in Galeas 2004, 19).

Thus, paradoxically, a rise to power of moderates actually led to a dramatic increase of both urban and rural political violence. A horrifying wave of assassinations began in late October 1979, and the formally dissolved ORDEN groups were at the forefront of the massacre (Americas Watch 1991; Menjívar Ochoa 2006). The campaign instigated dozens of massacres of peasant families identified as collaborators of the guerrillas, often perpetrated in joint operations involving paramilitaries and local security forces. In the cities, the campaign included the selective elimination, often through forced disappearances, of suspected left-wing militants as well as the execution of prominent reform-minded opposition figures. Archbishop Romero's assassination took place within this context (United Nations 1993).

vaded the campus of the UES, the most important hotbed of revolutionary organizing, and closed it down on June 26, 1980 (Quezada and Martínez 1995, 67). The killings and disappearances made internal communications in the urban networks falter, often leaving survivors out on a limb (Sprenkels 2014b).[69]

The system of cells and collaborators that had been developed according to the PMOs' secretive and personalized organizational model was vulnerable to being weakened by captured (and usually tortured) militants. It was common at this time for participants in the urban guerrilla networks to lose their nexus to the PMOs because of the impact of repression. The PMOs focused their efforts on the people and means they considered crucial and left many others to fend for themselves. Mostly, the PMOs urged their militants and collaborators to stay put and hang in there until the proposed "final" offensive. The pressure the urban insurgents were under was tremendous, especially if they did not have a good cover (which required money and connections). It was easy to lose track of what was going on even inside one's own organization. Many wanted out: if there were no conditions that warranted going to the mountains (yet), then maybe exile could be an alternative?[70] A hard choice, because it might also mean losing out on what was to come, and many revolutionaries thought victory was near at hand.

In spite of the hardships of repression, in 1980 the PMOs believed political momentum was on their side. "In 1980, we all thought we were going to win," "Gilberto," a former FPL cadre, told me in 1992.[71] The reformist coup failed to sustain the broad coalition which initially supported it. More left-leaning elements left the junta, and only conservative sectors of the PDC and the army remained loyal. In turn, several moderate left-wing organizations allied with the insurgent groups to create the Frente Democrático Revolucionario (FDR),[72] augmenting the amount of urban middle-class support for the insurgents and strengthening their international legitimacy (Montgomery 1995a, 111). Even the PCS had decided to join the insurgency and set up an armed wing called FAL in 1979. The regime seemed to be crumbling, with strong internal divides and the evident inability to control the violence. All these developments further fueled revolutionary zeal.

The proliferation of guerrilla groups (now numbering five in total), different mass organizations, and other political forces gravitating toward the insurgent movement as the crisis prolonged led to an impressive array of acronyms, reflecting both the insurgents' accumulation of strength and their disunity and division. It proved difficult for the different PMOs to create a political unity, a process which passed through several stages to eventually culminate with the founding of the FMLN in October 1980. The FMLN provided the insurgents with an overarching coordinating body, without the five PMOs (FPL, ERP, RN, PRTC, and PCS) having to surrender their organic integrity (Dunkerley 1985, 166).

In this context of growing revolutionary unity, right-wing elements inside the Salvadoran military resorted to another high-profile assassination. On November 27, 1980, security forces kidnapped and assassinated six members of the FDR leadership gathered in the capital for a meeting (United Nations 1993). It was a final blow to the revolutionary movement's aspirations to maintain some type of public presence in the capital city. Except for some segments of the church and the Jesuit university community, all popular groups linked to the insurgency had stopped operating in the cities by late 1980, because of the continued repression (Montgomery 1995a, 102). Thus, as FPL leader Cayetano Carpio wrote in 1982, "When the most difficult moments arrived, we were rendered without the capacity to be able to direct the masses in all situations" (Carpio 2011, 157).

The 1981 Offensive

The long-anticipated "final" insurgent offensive came on January 10, 1981. The FMLN timed it before Ronald Reagan's presidential inauguration (January 20, 1981), in view of his announcement that he would step up military aid to El Salvador. The guerrilla offensive started with forty-three simultaneous attacks throughout the country, including assaults on several major cities and military positions (Bosch 1999, 83). Most spectacularly, in Santa Ana two army officials declared their allegiance with the insurgents, destroyed the barracks, and left to join the insurgency with a small part of the troops (Mena Sandoval 1990). In spite of fierce fighting in several parts of the country, the offensive was far less successful than the insurgents had anticipated. An announced general strike did not materialize. Spontaneous rebellion in the cities did not occur. The US government reacted by rushing military equipment to El Salvador in support

Figure 2.1.   Insurgent relations toward the end of 1980

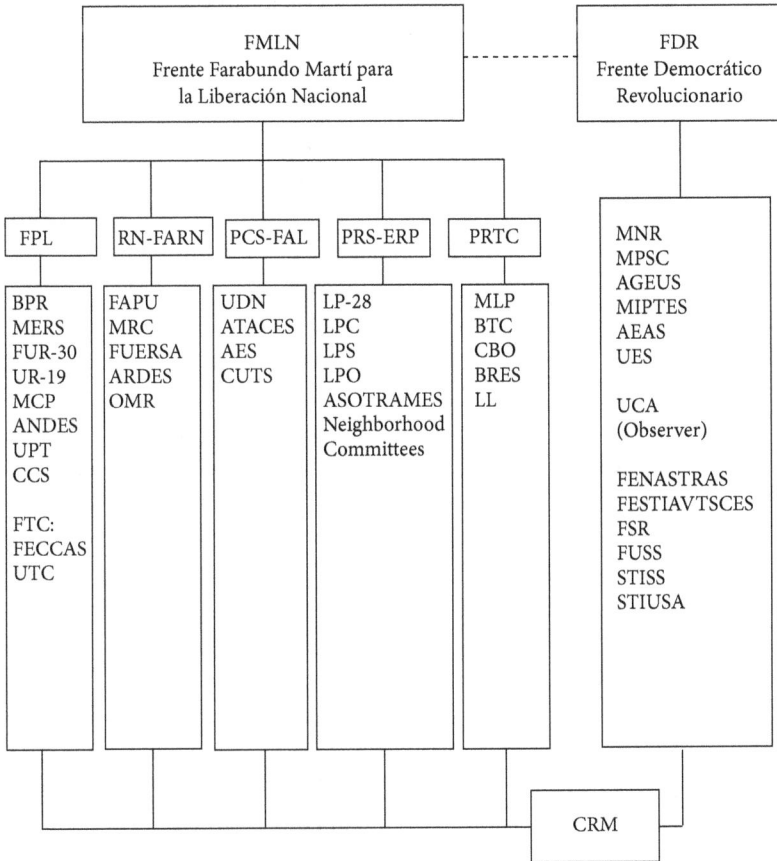

FMLN Frente Farabundo Martí para la Liberación Nacional	FDR Frente Democrático Revolucionario

FPL	RN-FARN	PCS-FAL	PRS-ERP	PRTC	MNR MPSC AGEUS MIPTES AEAS UES
BPR MERS FUR-30 UR-19 MCP ANDES UPT CCS FTC: FECCAS UTC	FAPU MRC FUERSA ARDES OMR	UDN ATACES AES CUTS	LP-28 LPC LPS LPO ASOTRAMES Neighborhood Committees	MLP BTC CBO BRES LL	UCA (Observer) FENASTRAS FESTIAVTSCES FSR FUSS STISS STIUSA

CRM

Sources: Adapted from Armstrong and Rubin (1983, 220–21), Cabarrús (1983, 320), Dunkerley (1985, 303–4), and Montgomery (1995a, 102). For the complete names of the organizations mentioned, see the list of acronyms.

of the army. On January 17, a first shipment consisting of two helicopters and large quantities of weapons and ammunition arrived (Bosch 1999, 100). On January 18, the FMLN announced a temporary retreat and re-named "the final offensive" as "the general offensive." Increased US support and the army's ability to resist the FMLN offensive with relative ease renewed the army's confidence. In the months after the offensive, the insurgents' rearguard areas were further weakened by the large counter-offensive operations mounted by the government (Byrne 1996, 81).

Several things became clear with the offensive. First, it evidenced the insurgents' organizational and logistical weaknesses, which included limited popular backing and a significant lack of firepower.[73] Second, the results of the offensive helped consolidate areas both for the guerrillas (northern and eastern parts of the country) and for the military (the cities and the western part of the country) (Benítez Manaut 1989, 259). Third, in spite of disappointing military results, the FPL and the ERP confirmed their status as the strongest and most effective insurgent military forces. The bulk of the approximately four thousand guerrilla fighters who participated in different tasks during the offensive came from these two groups.[74] The failure of the offensive also revived some of the earlier tensions among the different insurgent groups, especially between the FPL and the ERP. Among other differences, the two groups held completely different analyses as to the reasons for the failure of the 1981 offensive. The FPL argued that the offensive had been precipitous and that more popular organizing was required before a final assault on power could take place, while the ERP insisted that the time had been ripe for insurrection during the first half of 1980 and that, subsequently, momentum had been lost (Menjívar Larín 2006, 272).

The failure of the 1981 offensive had different impacts on the insurgency's rural and urban constituencies. When it became clear that victory was still far away, the PMOs saw their already wearied urban constituency shrink further. A physician for the FPL guerrillas explains: "During the first months of '81 a good quantity of physicians and paramedics arrived [at the front]. . . . [They] thought at the time that the war would end in two months. Most of us got involved in it [the war] with the idea of being back at home and at work in 15 days. After the second month, many abandoned. The front . . . was left behind almost without professionals" (cited in Metzi 1988, 96).

Increasingly, surviving urban insurgents gathered and organized in exile. After the failed offensive, Managua became the de facto headquarters for the Salvadoran PMOs. Nicaragua's capital city provided a safe rearguard from which the leadership organized the war in El Salvador and in which a range of specialized and operational tasks could be performed.[75] Another significant group of (urban) FMLN militants settled in Mexico City (Pirker and Nuñéz 2011). The PMOs started to build support organizations in other countries, through (former) members who had gone into exile as well as by dedicating cadres to this line of work across Europe, North America, and several Latin American countries. The main tasks of these structures were to raise funds and political sympathy for the revolutionary cause. Another specialized task organized (partially) in exile was that of setting up an extensive communication structure, which included press agencies covering the Salvadoran conflict from the perspective of the insurgency and several attempts at launching insurgent radio stations (Leonhard 1999; Cortina Orero 2015).[76] The ERP launched Venceremos Radio in 1981 (Darling 2007, 2008; J. López Vigil 1991), and the FPL followed suit with Farabundo Martí Radio in 1982 (Escalona 2003). Though struggling continuously with attempts by the military to blur the signal, the insurgent radio stations provided the guerrilla movement with a voice beyond the confines of the controlled areas. They also quickly became an important educational and social tool for those living within the different fronts (Darling 2007, 77–79; Henríquez Consalvi 2010).

The repression of 1980 and the failure of the 1981 offensive thus drove many urban PMO supporters into exile while, on the other hand, spurring rural PMO supporters deeper into the war fronts. These moves contributed to the development of a range of specialized operations within the insurgent movement, and to a more structured division of labor, which partially took place outside the war zones and in which urban/rural differences were accentuated. By the time of the offensive, the majority of peasant families that were part of the revolutionary movement had already been displaced from their homes by the repression and had already organized their daily lives around the guerrilla's command structures in the countryside. The PMOs called their supporters *masas*,[77] and each set up specific cadre structures to tend to their own. Generally, the insurgent leadership told their supporters to stay in the area and rely on guerrilla protection for safety, in spite of the military invasions and harsh conditions. Many of these supporters, in fact, wanted to stay and contribute to the fight. On the other hand, if they left on their own account, they risked persecution by the military as well as, sometimes, retaliation by the insurgents for desertion (Sprenkels 2001).

Thus, with the failure of the offensive, the rural base of the insurgents had become even more indispensable in sustaining the war. If kept within the realm of influence of the guerrilla, the peasant families could provide a pool of potential new recruits. Furthermore, the peasants' knowledge of the terrain and their physical resilience, combined with proper training, turned them, generally speaking, into more effective guerrilla fighters than their urban counterparts. The PMOs continued to offer specialized military and political courses to outstanding peasant cadres, sometimes including training in Cuba as well as Vietnam (Castañeda 1993; Kruijt 2008). To a large extent, the ability of the insurgents to overcome the poor results of the offensive hinged on the fact that the remaining rural supporters provided the basis upon which to gradually establish stronger military and political control over the guerrilla's rural areas of activity. Meanwhile, a significant number of urban revolutionaries regrouped in exile and from there were able to diversify and consolidate the insurgent movement's international infrastructure.

"MILITARY INITIATIVE" (MID-1982 TO 1983): CONSOLIDATING THE FRONTS

After overcoming the disarray left by the failed offensive, the PMOs focused on enhancing security and expanding control in the areas they saw as their military rearguard. In part they did so by systematically attacking and eliminating the smaller military outposts in these areas or close to them. This campaign was also a form of retaliation against the paramilitary forces and the military outposts that had participated in the massacres of 1979–80. Those families who were aligned with the paramilitary forces that were originally from the surrounding hamlets had left their houses and brought their families into town, to seek military protection from guerrilla retaliation. The families concentrated literally around the military outposts, in the houses in the center of town, in shacks or tents, and under trees. For example, in Chalatenango, many towns had a small military post in 1980, an inheritance from the earlier preemptive counterinsurgency strategy. The army was reluctant to abandon these posts, and the guerrilla was able to take them one by one, causing significant casualties as well as the exodus of the survivors (Byrne 1996, 82–83). In this period, the FMLN's controlled areas became larger and included abandoned towns. The masas who were organized in support of a specific PMO were mostly living scattered in improvised camps in the area, held few weapons, and mostly moved around to avoid the military operations and the bombing raids. The formal guerrilla forces, consisting mostly of selected youth from the masas camps, were concentrated in nearby but separate camps that functioned under a military regime.[78]

The Salvadoran Armed Forces, with extensive US assistance, resorted to "scorched earth" tactics in order to make the presence of civilian supporters in the liberated zones increasingly difficult and unsustainable. These operations, which had started in 1981, followed a military strategy called "draining the sea" and targeted not only the organized supporters but sometimes also villages on the fringes of the guerrilla areas suspected of offering support (Danner 1994; Sprenkels 2001, 2015). The masas did not wait for the military to arrive and instead ran for their lives, sometimes for weeks on end, in long flights called *guindas*. The guerrilla proved unable to effectively protect the masas from the military, and as a result, hundreds of peasants, mostly women, elderly, and children, were killed by government troops or by famine or disease, and dozens of children were kidnapped, often during the guindas.[79]

Though the PMOs initially urged (and sometimes coerced, depending on the rigidness of the local leadership) the masas to stay within their zone, the disastrous consequences of the large-scale military operations convinced PMO leadership that they were exposing their followers to massacre (Sprenkels 2001, 82). Also, the efforts to protect the masas kept the combatants occupied, diminishing their capacity to strike and cause enemy casualties.[80] The operations provoked the arrival of additional batches of refugees to the camps around San Salvador and at the Honduran border and prompted the organization of a refugee camp further into Honduras, under the auspices of the United Nations (Compher and Morgan 1991; Todd 2010). Mesa Grande, the largest Salvadoran refugee camp in Honduras, harbored close to twelve thousand refugees, most from Chalatenango and Cabañas (Compher and Morgan 1991; Edwards and Tovar Siebentritt 1991). In spite of ongoing harassment by the Honduran army, the camp was safer for the peasant families than the liberated zones inside El Salvador (Compher and Morgan 1991, 31). Insurgent organizers worked to "convert the refuge into a trench for the FMLN" (Ascoli 2001, 98). The different PMOs continued to organize the population in the camps to keep up the contribution to the revolutionary struggle in different ways: setting up workshops to produce resources for the guerrilla army, receiving international delegations, and raising awareness of the crimes committed by the Salvadoran military.[81] And, as described by FPL organizer "Carmen," the refugees were a key source of new recruits.

> They [the FPL] sent me to work in Mesa Grande with a team [in early 1983]. . . . Our task was to send approximately two hundred young people a month [to the front]. . . . We also did some work with the population, to raise consciousness that they shouldn't forget the people that stayed at the front. We said: It's OK for the elderly and the children to go there [to Mesa Grande], but what are all those young people doing there? All these young people growing up: for what really? What will become of them? Where is the contribution of these people?
>
> The problem was that the people already knew what the war was. In the beginning the people didn't know. "Do you want war?!" . . . Everybody said: "Yes!! Yes!! We want war!!!" Without knowing what war really was. But now the people that had been inside [the war] knew what they could expect. The work was first to go [talk] to the parents. . . . We did house visits, from hut to hut, and also in assemblies. . . . There were some families that . . . felt it was hard to accept that their son or daughter would have to continue in the ravages of war, as they had lived it. But the interesting part was when the youngsters themselves said: "No, but the *compañera* is right. . . . We can go fight, you [the parents] can't." . . . A lot of them also remembered what they had lived through, how they had been evicted from their home, the memory of how their mother or their grandmother was murdered. . . . This memory also motivated them to make the decision and say: "*Caramba*, what am I doing over here, when I should go and avenge my family's blood."[82]

For subsequent years, the refugee families in Mesa Grande and their adolescent children became the most important recruiting ground sustaining the guerrillas in the central part of El Salvador (David Spencer 1996; Sprenkels 2001).[83] Not only would the FPL and the RN recruit, but these organizations were also the ruling political powers in the camp. Later on, the PCS-FAL was also allowed to do political work in Mesa Grande and to recruit combatants there.[84] Similarly, with regard to the ERP's work

Security and Internal Strife

As the war consolidated, the PMOs increasingly suffered internal problems related to enemy infiltration as well as to the effects of war and post-traumatic stress on some of their members. César Macías Mayora, a Guatemalan revolutionary recruited into the RN through one of the Salvadoran solidarity committees during his exile in Mexico, arrived at the Guazapa front in 1982 as an RN intelligence chief. In his book, he describes discovering that one of the military commanders was in fact an infiltrator. However, the RN top leadership ignored his reports, until much later, after the infiltrator had been responsible for many deaths. Eventually, the culprit deserted (Macías Mayora 1997, 279–81).[90]

Even with the infiltrator out of the picture, Macías Mayora found that "hate, jealousy, resentments or, in the best of cases, simple distrust was floating in the air" at the front (1997, 281). He discovered then that the local RN military commanders had secretly killed and buried one of their own combatants, a favorite of the rank and file at the front. They subsequently misinformed the people at the front that he had been transferred to another location. When it became known he had been executed, the commanders informed the troops that he had been an enemy infiltrator. A large part of the RN midlevel cadres and rank and file were infuriated by what they saw as a cover-up for murder. In reply, they plotted to eliminate the entire RN military command in Guazapa. The crisis was eventually contained through the intervention of external RN cadres and the restructuring of the military command. Even so, several midlevel military leaders and combatants left the RN to join the FPL or the FAL to avoid later retaliation (1997, 281–88). In Macías Mayora's analysis,

> the reasons for discontent included a complex range of aspects of the revolutionary morale: disrespect for the organization's statutes, . . . different groups being assimilated by the organization without ever achieving a common political-ideological identity, incoherency between political discourse and social practice, unequal distribution of resources (great hardship on the battlefronts and abundance in some of the structures in the exterior, which denoted opportunism), but above all, . . . internal struggles for control of the organization, . . . which had accumulated a substantial war fund. (1997, 284–85)[91]

A different example of the heavy burdens accumulated by the insurgents under the pressures of the war was the events of April 1983 in Managua. A major crisis ensued within the FPL, involving its two top leaders: Secretary General Cayetano Carpio and number two, Comandante "Ana María" (Mélida Anaya Montes). During an FPL Central Committee meeting in Managua, early in 1983, it became clear that while Ana María and her supporters favored further acceleration of the FMLN's unification process as well as the start of peace negotiations, Carpio and his group considered further FMLN unification to be a threat to the FPL, and rejected negotiations as betrayal, at least if such negotiations were to become substantial (Allison and Martín Alvarez 2012, 96). Most sources maintain that subsequently Carpio devotees conspired to assassinate Ana María. Part of the remaining FPL leadership (backed by the Sandinista government) then accused Carpio of masterminding the plot. He subsequently committed suicide (Castellanos Moya 1989; Morales Carbonell 1999; Sánchez Cerén 2008, 191).

The crisis led to a split in the FPL. According to one estimate, up to 30 percent of the remaining urban militants left the organization, some of them seeking to build their own PMO.[92] The split-off included several party intellectuals, some urban guerrilla units, and an important part of the international support network.[93] However, Chalatenango and the other rural fronts remained loyal to the FPL, with the exception of a small group operating near the capital.[94] Under its new general secretary, Salvador Sánchez Cerén—Comandante "Leonel González"—the FPL sported "a leadership with more capacity for coordination and rapprochement with the rest of the revolutionary movement, and more willingness to reach political compromises" (Martín Alvarez 2011, 224). In particular, the FPL started to develop closer ties with the Jesuits and with the PCS-FAL.

"HEIGHTENED GUERRILLA CONTROL" (1984–92)

In spite of the internal troubles described above, in military terms 1983 was a good year for the Salvadoran guerrillas and a bad one for the Salvadoran armed forces (Byrne 1996, 85). Bold guerrilla operations inflicted unprecedented losses on the army (Ibarra Chávez 2009; Salazar 2016). The United States responded to the guerrilla's success by further stepping up its efforts to back the Salvadoran army. In addition to extensive training and significant increases in troop numbers, the US government provided a large amount of modern aerial equipment, which allowed the Salvadoran army to perform quick, large-scale disembarkation operations in enemy territory. Already halfway into 1984, this new modality of warfare forced the guerrillas to break up troops into smaller subunits to diminish vulnerability on their side (Binford 1997, 10–12; David Spencer 1996). While the guerrillas devised a new strategy to wear down the enemy with scattered attacks and sabotage, the United States and the Salvadoran government implemented "low intensity warfare," seeking to isolate the guerrilla forces and combining military means with increased government presence in the countryside, for example through rural development programs (Byrne 1996, 125; Seligson and McElhinny 1996, 213).

Most insurgents, and especially the combatants, perceived the forced return, in 1984, to "guerrilla"-type warfare as a significant military setback. It caused demoralization and led to unprecedented high levels of desertion among the troops.[95] Between 1983 and 1986, the number of combatants was cut almost in half, although this did not necessarily mean that the FMLN's military power was similarly reduced, because the remaining fighters were increasingly well trained and specialized (Montgomery 1995a, 198).[96] In the case of the ERP, the shortage of combatants resulted in a move that previously had been used by the Salvadoran insurgents only very sporadically: the forced recruitment of young people. This soon backfired, because not only did forced recruitment undermine the underground political work of the ERP in the affected communities; it also provoked significant national and international outrage (Byrne 1996, 146; Montgomery 1995a, 173). Furthermore, as the government sought to regain some kind of political presence in disputed territories, the insurgents responded with persecution of the newly established local authorities in these areas. In particular, the ERP executed a number of mayors assigned to towns in ERP territory (United Nations 1993, 288). Under the guise of low-intensity warfare, the armed confrontation continued, but it took a back seat with regard to the political aspects of warfare, in which both public propaganda and underground organizing were highly important.

It was in this context that anthropologist Jenny Pearce clandestinely traveled to Chalatenango to do her research in El Salvador's liberated zones. At the time, she thought of the place as a laboratory for an investigation of a larger scope: the role of peasants in revolutionary processes of national liberation. She was particularly interested in the relationship between urban allies and the rebelling peasants, posing the following question: "Do the peasants become a tool of these 'outside' agents or is a genuine alliance forged, with the peasants producing their own leadership?" (1986, 108). She focused on the local government structures the Chalatenango peasants developed in the liberated zones, called Poder Popular Local (PPL).[97] She called this "a means by which the civilian population could guarantee their needs and organize their society independently of the military command of the FPL" (242). Pearce's account of life at the Chalatenango Front underscores the revolutionary commitment of the guerrillas and civilian population alike. She admiringly relates how, in spite of the war's harsh circumstances, Chalatenango's peasants managed to organize health care, popular education, food production, and women's empowerment largely on their own, while the FPL guerrilla provided a sort of enabling environment for these processes. However, according to Pearce, "When it comes to decisions, it is the PPL which makes them" (252).

Over two decades later, when I shared Pearce's midwar conclusions on the PPL's relative autonomy with "Hernán," a former FPL midlevel cadre active in Chalatenango during the war, he smiled. "You understand. There was a war, and it was necessary to have control," he said.[98] His comment bore no disdain for the PPL. It just seemed obvious to him that the needs of war required strict, vertical control of the affairs at the front. The FPL charged both rural and urban cadres with responsibilities over all aspects of life at the front. Not only were combatants assigned to a specific unit, but also each family had a designated place in the organizational structure of the masas, a structure that regulated essential services and duties. The families involved might distribute specific tasks among themselves, but the overall supervision and coordination was the responsibility of PMO cadres. Thus, all of those present at the front, including the masas, were integrated into the insurgent government, which was hierarchical and militarized, but not overly rigid, since significant cohesion and group empathy existed, and the organization had to constantly adapt to the development of the war (J. Anderson 1993; Metzi 1988; Shaull 1990).[99]

Alas, the way the peasants organized and the tasks they engaged in varied throughout the revolutionary process; however, the FPL's revolutionary jurisdiction remained constant. The PPL was integrated within the insurgents' governance model (Metzi 1988, 219). Its functions included organization of the refugee camps within the area of insurgent control, food production, and the coordination of security for the masses. Simultaneously, the PPL was used to showcase civilian presence in the guerrilla-controlled areas, to denounce indiscriminate military operations against the population, and to raise funds from international cooperation for small-scale refugee projects.[100] Apart from ideological embellishment, these latter functions were also the main reasons to publicly emphasize the autonomous character of the PPL. Hernán emphasized that in the liberated zones of Chalatenango everyone was weaved into the PMO and that, for both military and political reasons, it could not have been any other way.

Two-Faced Power

The less-repressive political climate from 1984 onward made it possible for the insurgents to intensify organizational efforts outside the liberated zones. Two crucial elements that contributed to a notable decrease in political terror were (1) the election of PDC's Napoleón Duarte as president (March 1984), defeating runner-up D'Aubuisson and his ARENA party, and (2) a growing international pressure on the Salvadoran government and military to improve their human rights record.[101] In fact, inside the US Congress, human rights performance became a crucial element in debates concerning financial support for the Salvadoran armed forces. These elements translated into a significant reduction in human rights violations and civilian casualties (Binford 1996, 1999; Sprenkels 2005; Sprenkels and van der Borgh 2011). This allowed for Salvadoran public life, which had largely come to a halt because of the war, to gradually recover. For example, in a gesture of practical and symbolic value, the military abandoned the UES campus occupied in 1980, and the university resumed normal operations.

The key insurgent strategy for the new period was called "poder de doble cara,"[102] which consisted of the construction a civil-political front inside the country, made up of student groups, unions, NGOs, cooperatives, human rights groups, and so on (Binford 1999; Byrne 1996; Sprenkels 2005). "Under the new strategy, the new organizations would present a legal face to the government, insisting on their rights as civilians, while simultaneously collaborating with the FMLN" (Wood 2003, 167). While the military, the government, and their US advisers spoke of "front-groups," supporters of the new insurgent strategy emphasized the legitimacy of what could plausibly be seen as civil society organizations (Sprenkels 2005, 55).

The new strategy capitalized on the remarkable efforts of the different PMOs in building support networks for their cause in Europe, the United States and Canada, and, to a lesser extent, in other Latin American countries like Mexico. The five different PMOs all carried out what they called "international work," consisting of lobbying, fund-raising, and recruitment. The FPL, PCS, and ERP were particularly successful at it.[103] For this work, the PMOs networked with a range of sympathetic left-wing groups, including liberation-theology-influenced churches, as well as with the Salvadoran (refugee) community (Perla 2008; Waller 1991). International work helped generate the political pressure that persuaded the US Congress to condition military aid to El Salvador on improvements in human rights performance (Nepstad 2001, 2004; Sprenkels and van der Borgh 2011). The efforts also led to many contacts in international cooperation, mainly in northern Europe, which made it possible to access financing to set up NGOs inside and outside El Salvador.[104] Thus, not only improved security but also access to external funding made it possible for the PMOs to dedicate cadres to setting up the civil-political front inside the country, with the result that this front expanded rapidly and successfully in subsequent years (Binford 1999; Grenier 1999).

This organizational infrastructure had several functions: to exert internal and international political pressure as a civil movement; to provide cover and resources; and to facilitate recruitment of new collaborators and militants. It provided an opportunity for (exiled) PMO cadres, especially those with university education, to reinsert themselves in urban El Salvador—for example as a university professor or an NGO worker—and thus gain a cover and an income. A few PMO cadres with labor union experience were also able to return and try to revive revolutionary syndicalism. The civil-political front mirrored the experience of the mass organizations in the 1970s, albeit with smaller constituencies, and with more emphasis on NGO work. Regular visits by international delegations helped to provide safety and support for insurgent constituencies within the country (Moodie 2013a).

In the countryside, the doble cara strategy led to the reactivation of peasant organizing. Starting in 1986, the most important political focus of the FPL for the rural areas became the repopulation of war-razed villages. These repopulations were to provide permanent settlements for the FPL peasant constituencies that had been living in the refugee camps around the capital city and for the small groups of masas that were still moving around in the war zones. The repopulation of San José Las Flores in Chalatenango, in June 1986, was the first. In 1987 the first large-scale return from Mesa Grande was organized, with the participation of supporters of the FPL as well as the RN. Additional organized returns took place in subsequent years, leaving Mesa Grande empty by 1992. A similar process took place at the (smaller) San Antonio camp, which housed FPL and PRTC supporters.[105] The ERP organized the repatriation from the Colomoncagua camp, setting up a large settlement called Ciudad Segundo Montes in northern Morazán in 1990.[106]

Apart from attending to the needs of the peasant constituencies they had inherited from prewar organizing, the PMOs also tried to use the new context to protect or increase their support base in the countryside. The ERP was especially active in these efforts in Morazán and Usulután. In an excellent study, Elisabeth Wood (2003) describes how the ERP was able to build a broader peasant support base in Usulután during the last years of the war, by embedding ERP cadres in NGOs and peasant organizations, where the cadres organized small cooperatives. These cooperatives were, in turn, stimulated to claim and occupy stretches of land, occupations which in turn provided the ERP with leverage in the land negotiations that were to come as part of the peace accords (160–92). The FPL organized similar land invasions in neighboring San Vicente, with families from its historical support bases occupying some large haciendas that had been abandoned because of the war (McElhinny 2006). In 1990, small groups of Salvadoran refugees proceeding from Nicaragua, Costa Rica, and Panama also started repatriation to insurgent areas (Morel 1991; Quizar 1998; Nueva Esperanza Support Group 1999).

The 1989 Offensive

In military terms, the period between 1984 and 1992 started out with the fragmentation of forces and the return to guerrilla tactics and small-scale operations. As the guerrilla forces learned to handle the new aerial strength and mobility of the government troops, the war settled into a new stalemate, with the insurgents divided among smaller and more mobile fronts, and establishing effective communication networks between their troops in different locations.

From 1986 onward, the insurgent efforts were characterized by the long and careful buildup to the 1989 general offensive. Crucially for what was to come, the guerrilla forces expanded and consolidated operations on and around the San Salvador volcano, right next to the capital city. In order to boost the number of troops, the PMOs intensified recruitment in all spheres of influence of the insurgents: the refugee camps, the resettled communities, the expansion zones around the fronts, the civil-political front in the cities (which found new recruits mainly among the students), the exile communities linked to the PMOs in Managua and elsewhere, and even, by means of the international work, internationalists willing to be incorporated. The PMOs set up fresh logistical pipelines for weapons and support material from Nicaragua. As far as possible, FMLN war-wounded recovering in Cuba or Nicaragua were patched up. Cuba contributed a significant number of arms as well as financial support (Oñate 2011, 144).[107]

Meanwhile, several attempts at peace talks took place (Martínez Peñate 1995). However, the prospect of a negotiated solution dimmed when, in March 1989, ARENA's candidate, Alfredo Cristiani, triumphed in the presidential elections, renewing mutual hostilities. The second great insurgent offensive started on November 11, 1989, and lasted two weeks. Insurgents were able to take a large part of the capital and, for several days, corner the military. The rural troops connected with urban cadres to organize logistics and orientation within the city. During the offensive, two events made international headlines. On November 15, El Salvador's military command ordered the assassination of Ignacio Ellacuría, a leading left-wing Jesuit (Gould 2015). He was massacred together with five other Jesuits, their housekeeper, and her daughter at the campus of El Salvador's Jesuit university, causing outrage comparable to that caused by the murder of Archbishop Romero a decade earlier (Doggett 1993; Whitfield 1995). The second event was the guerrilla's assault on the luxurious Sheraton Hotel in a wealthy neighborhood of the capital, where FPL and ERP guerrilla forces held several prominent diplomats as well as a group of US Green Berets hostage (Azucena et al. 2005).

The 1989 offensive affected the insurgent groups in several ways. Though military losses had been significant, the guerrilla had little trouble reconsolidating rural positions, in spite of the army's counteroffensive.[108] The army's impact was stronger on the urban front, where previous PMO structures had partially dissolved to mount the offensive. Urban PMO cadres who had blown their covers had to go underground. The government temporarily stepped up the repression and forced some organizations to shut down. By mid-1990, however, most of the insurgency's civil-political organizations were functioning again, now mostly rallying around the peace negotiations.[109]

AN X-RAY IMAGE OF THE FMLN'S CIVIL-POLITICAL FRONT TOWARD THE END OF THE WAR

The success of the two-faced strategy implemented since 1984 resulted, toward the end of the war, in a "dense insurgent network of civil society organizations" (Wood 2003, 178), consisting of organized interest groups (OIGs) as well as of NGOs. With the exception of a few "organismos unitarios," each of the five PMOs built its own specific cluster. Because of this, the civil-political front was characterized by what the revolutionaries referred to as "cinquismo," or "fiveness." For every type of organization (labor union, peasant cooperatives, human rights office, women's group, student association, etc.) one might find five different (but similar) left-wing proinsurgent versions, each affiliated with a particular PMO (Sprenkels 2005, 67–69; Grenier 1999, 68–69). Similarly, each PMO had its "own" repopulated communities, where part of its historical support base had been settled. In correspondence to the size of the cadre structures and the extension of its international support networks, the FPL was the most successful in building this organizational infrastructure, with ERP and RN following suit, while PCS and PRTC made do with a smaller set of communities, associations, and NGOs. The mapping of the civil-political front presented in tables 2.1 and 2.2 helps to give an impression of the extension of the insurgents' nonmilitary networks in 1991.[110]

The role of the FDR requires some clarification. When it was founded in 1980, some senior FDR members were PMO cadres, while others were prominent social democrats who attempted to retain some level of independence from the PMOs. In the alliance with the FMLN, FDR leaders

Table 2.1. Affiliation of the civil-political front according to type of organization (1991)

Organization	OIG	NGO	Mixed	Other	Total
FPL	11	14	6	2	33
ERP	4	7	4	1	16
RN	2	3	2	2	9
PCS	2	6	1	1	10
PRTC	-	2	-	-	2
FDR/CD	-	2	-	-	2
Unitarian	4	3	2	-	9
Total	23	37	15	6	81

Source: See table 2.2.

Table 2.2. Civil-political organizations according to sectors and affiliation (1991)

FPL	ERP	RN	PCS	PRTC	FDR	Unitarian
		Peasants & cooperatives				
COACES	CONFRAS		ATACES			
ANTA/ADC	FENACOA		FUNSALPRODESE			
MCS	COMUS					
FEDECOPADES	FASTRAS					
FEDECASES	PADECOMSM					
FUNPROCOOP	PADECOES					
		Labor				
FEASIES		FENASTRAS	FUSS			UNTS
		FESTIAVTSCES				
		Human Rights				
CODEFAM	COMAFAC	COMADRES				CDH-ES
		IEJES				FECMAFAM
						COPPES
		Women				
AMES	AMS	Las Dignas	IMU	MSM	ORMUSA	UMS
CONAMUS	MCM		CEMUJER			

Table 2.2. (*continued*)

FPL	ERP	RN	PCS	PRTC	FDR	Unitarian
Refugees & repopulations						
CRIPDES	FSM	REDES				CNR
CCR	FASTRAS	CRC				
UCRES						
ACRES						
CDR						
CODESMA						
Health care						
PRO-VIDA	ASPS					
ACISAM						
APDECA						
APROCSAL						
Community development						
CORDES	ASIPES		UNES	ASDI	FUMA	
CREFAC	ADIC		Fundación			
PROCOMES			Cuscatlán			
Education & arts						
Equipo Maíz	CIAZO		ACJ			ANDES
CIDEP						
ASTAC						
Churches						
CONIP	CEBES	Emmanuel	Lutheran			
		Baptist Church	Church			

Source: Based on information from (a) publications including Almeida (2008); Biekart (1999); Binford (1997, 1999); Carter and Loeb (1989); de Herrera (1983); Foley (1996); Gómez (2001); Hammond (1998); Harnecker (1983, 1993); Herrera et al. (2008); Kowalchuk (2003a, 2003b); Manzano Merino (1994); Martín Alvarez (2004); Mata and Martínez (2009); Morel (1991); Orrellana, Foroni, and Nochez (1998); Sollis (1992); Stewart and Jiménez (1993); Sprenkels (2005); van der Borgh (2003); and Wood (2000, 2003); (b) internal documentation from the PMOs, such as PRS-ERP (1992) and FPL (1994); (c) interviews with former insurgents who participated in the civil-political front: "Ana" (November 9, 2007), "Antonio" (July 29, 2009), "Bernabé" (March 17, 2010), "Carmen" (December 11, 2008), "Fabio" (August 28, 2009), "Felipe" (January 30, 2010; February 25, 2012), "Henry" (March 3, 2013), "Chabelo" (January 15, 2010), "Jorge" (January 19, 2010), "Lilian" (January 23, 2010), "Moisés" (August 27, 2009), "Rafael" (December 1, 8, 11, and 16, 2009; January 6 and 14, 2010), "Santos" (August 28, 2007), "Silvio" (May 6, 2009), "Umberto" (May 15 and 20, 2009); (d) a workshop with FMLN veterans (June 2, 2011); and, finally, (e) verification of institutional documents or websites of those organizations still active today.

were mostly dedicated to international political-diplomatic work. Though never formally dissolved, the FMLN-FDR alliance lost protagonism when, in 1987 and 1988, several prominent FDR leaders, like Rubén Zamora and Guillermo Ungo, returned to El Salvador to reestablish small social-democratic political parties in the country with the aim of participating in elections.[111] In fall 1987, these parties formed a coalition they called Convergencia Democrática (CD).[112] This presented a left-wing alternative on the ballot for the 1989 presidential elections and in the 1991 parliamentary elections, when the FMLN itself was still barred from participating.

The unitarian organizations, the most prominent of which was the Unión Nacional de Trabajadores Salvadoreños (UNTS),[113] integrated within their governance structure representations of different groups controlled by the PMOs (Pirker 2008, 229). Alternatively, as was the case with the Comisión de Derechos Humanos de El Salvador (CDH-ES),[114] the different PMOs would reach an agreement to appoint cadres in specific roles within the unitarian organization, mandating cooperation with cadres from the other PMOs in pursuit of joint objectives. In practice, the internal politics of such unitarian organizations were complex. Outwardly, senior organization members represented the same institutional interests. However, these same members had to respond primarily to their superior inside the PMO, leading to tensions in cases of disagreement or conflict (Sprenkels 2005).

At the end of the war the insurgents were also firmly embedded within several other important institutions in the country. As indicated previously, a key stronghold for the insurgents was the UES, with cadres from all the PMOs operating on different levels within the institution, and with the PMOs being heavily involved in UES decision making, such as the appointment of university authorities.[115] Student organizations, like the Asociación General de Estudiantes Universitarios Salvadoreños (AGEUS),[116] as well as a range of smaller, more informal groups, were important for orchestrating public protest, for recruitment of new members, and to ensure internal political leverage for each PMO within the university.[117]

PMO cadres were also active within important sectors of the Salvadoran churches, for example within the San Salvador archbishop's office. The relationship between Catholic institutions and PMOs was complex and ambiguous, because church authorities were autonomous and influence went both ways. For example, the FPL held influence within the

Jesuit community in El Salvador, but the Jesuits also clearly influenced the FPL throughout its history.[118] While in the case of the FPL and the ERP, key ties existed with the Catholic Church, in the case of the PCS-FAL, there was a strong affiliation with the small but active Lutheran Church, and in the case of the RN, with one of the local Baptist churches, as well as with several Christian base communities.

The PMOs also maintained extensive international networks, which included solidarity networks and committees in many countries and cities, most densely developed in Western Europe. In the United States, FPL cadres were heavily involved with three important nationwide groups: Committee in Solidarity with the People of El Salvador (CISPES), Salvadoran Humanitarian Aid, Research and Education Foundation (SHARE), and Sister Cities, founded, respectively, in 1980, 1981, and 1986 (Waller 1991). Senior PMO cadres were charged with coordinating solidarity work in different parts of the world. Among other tasks, they helped international organizations connect to specific PMO constituencies inside El Salvador, supporting projects, for example, to benefit a repopulation or a trade union.[119]

THE NEGOTIATED SOLUTION TO THE WAR

The 1989 offensive coincided with the fall of the Berlin Wall (November 9, 1989). In Nicaragua, the Sandinistas lost the 1990 elections, and the Salvadoran PMOs had to dismantle their Managua headquarters and move part of their infrastructure to Mexico.[120] In Cuba, the USSR's crumbling led to a deep economic crisis. The post–Cold War international context thoroughly complicated the FMLN's long-term military prospects.

The offensive itself and the events that took place during its development had both national and international echoes. The already problematic reputation of the Salvadoran military had received an enormous blow with its involvement in the assassination of the Jesuits, which resulted in El Salvador's first domestic trial against military officers for war crimes (Popkin 2000; Whitfield 1995). Most analysts interpreted the results of the offensive as a military stalemate, and public opinion in El Salvador increasingly shifted toward the option of a negotiated settlement as the best or the only way forward. The perceived need to end the war in order to facilitate economic recovery, furthermore, also helped to throw a large part of the country's economic elite behind the negotiation process (Wood 2000). Meanwhile, Washington also shifted preference from military means to political solution for El Salvador.

Official negotiations between the government and the insurgency resumed in April 1990. The United Nations took on a proactive mediation role, and the peace agenda was divided into sections. The first partial agreement was signed in July 1990 and included the establishment of a UN human rights verification mission in El Salvador. The lengthy negotiation process eventually also translated into significant rapprochement among the negotiators from the different blocs. A growing sense of irreversibility of the peace process disembogued in what FMLN negotiator Salvador Samayoa later called "the explosion of consensus" (2002, 585). Both parties were confident that the UN would provide extensive and reasonably objective verification. Furthermore, the implicit understanding that the international community would pick up most of the (substantial) price tag attached to the accords proved very helpful (de Soto and del Castillo 1994).[121] The peace accords were signed on January 16, 1992, in Mexico City, and led to massive celebrations in San Salvador.[122] Government party ARENA hailed their leader Cristiani as "the president of peace" (Krämer 1998, 184). On the other side, the FMLN victoriously declared that it had "established the basis for a new republic" (FMLN 1992a, 185). "To die fighting for the Peace Accords was worth it, and for this reason, it is worth it to continue the struggle!" Thus proclaimed Salvador Sánchez Cerén—Comandante "Leonel González"—at the FPL's twenty-second anniversary, the first to be celebrated after the cease-fire (Leonel González 1992, iv).

THE LIVED EXPERIENCE OF INSURGENCY IN EL SALVADOR

Given that so many lives came together in the revolutionary movement for so many years, what it meant for those involved varies substantially from person to person. The specific experience of insurgent participation might vary considerably between different specialized units of the PMOs. To form a part of the guerrilla army on the rural battlefront entailed social-political experiences far different from that of operating a clandestine urban safe house in enemy territory.[123] To work somewhere in the chain of logistics was quite different from doing political organizing or participating in special operations. To be a rank-and-file fighter implied different militancy experience from that of a senior cadre. Many insurgents participated in several tasks over the years, but even so, the specific positions held within the organizational networks of the PMO also imprinted significant differences on the lived experience of insurgency.

Nonetheless, it is possible to identify common elements. To be a part of the Salvadoran revolutionary movement meant belonging to what has been called the "habitus" of revolutionary militancy (Pirker 2008). The magnitude of the revolutionary endeavor, the bonding and the enormous investment of resourcefulness and human energy, the dreams that were shared—and often left unfulfilled—the losses of lives of comrades and friends, the strains of war and clandestinity, the internal power struggles and betrayals, all made significant contributions to this communal experience of insurgency.[124] PMO members had to subjugate practically all aspects of their lives to the revolutionary cause. For "Beatriz," for example, the PMO she belonged to represented

> your life, your family, it was everything . . . that gave meaning to your life. The representative of the organization was the one who decided, even your private life in many ways. . . . Well yes, because the main thing was the struggle . . . and not so much personal emotional ties, right? . . . There was a whole process . . . for those who entered [the organization]: to study, to discuss and debate. . . . So you also identified with what you were doing, what you were analyzing, it wasn't something mechanical. . . . I never felt a ferocious, military, arbitrary kind of discipline. . . . The leaders, well . . . I really admired them a lot. . . . And you also knew that your comrade could give his life for you, and I for him, at any given moment. . . . All of this gave you a strong sense of belonging.[125]

"For me joining the FPL was practically like joining a church," "Máximo" told me when I asked him what his experience of participating in the FPL in the 1980s had been like.

Not really as with a "normal" church, but more like Christian communities at the time of the Roman Empire or the first Reform Church communities . . . ; for them the church . . . was their way of life, their community. . . . [In the case of the FPL] behind all that discourse about "popular war," the image that was used . . . was that of the chosen people crossing the desert. We are the chosen ones. We suffer because we are chosen. We are crossing the desert, but sooner or later we, or our children, will reach the promised land.[126]

Each PMO constituted an exclusive and strongly connected political community, a phenomenon Charles Tilly refers to as a "trust network" (2005b, 41). The revolutionary ethos helped integrate hierarchical and compartmentalized—but also extremely tightly knit—PMO communities, frequently referred to as "family" or "bloodlines" by the PMO's members. For the members of the PMOs, the idea of the revolution was what Janja Lalich conceptualizes as a transcendent belief system, feeding into a firm commitment that provided all members with meaning and purpose (2004).[127] Yet such commitment was also frequently characterized by dogmatism and rigidity. The participants' personal identities became strongly dependent on the group context. The combination of ideological zeal and clandestinity converted the Salvadoran PMOs into sect-like organizations, reminiscent of Goffman's "total institution" (1961). However, instead of being closed-off entities with limited interactions with external social agents, the PMOs continuously dedicated a significant number of their cadres to work on organizing and maintaining support networks outside the organizations' core.

Within the habitus of the Salvadoran revolutionaries, to be a member of the cadre was a sacred fulfillment; to become a comandante of the revolution, the highest possible personal achievement. Members were encouraged to think of the revolution as their mother and of the party (the PMO) as their father.[128] Many cadres thought of themselves as the chosen, as "the precursor of the New Man. . . . the most prestigious and superior people of all" (R. Cañas 2002, cited in Kruijt 2008, 54). The PMO cadre system allowed for the organizations' members to spread out on different tasks and to insert themselves in different social circles, while at the same time maintaining a devotion to the PMO and its leadership. Though the different PMOs presented many commonalities, the most important and immediate shared history among the militants was that pertaining to their own specific PMO. The development of their own organization was the common project they shared and worked on throughout the years.

Without extensive clandestine organizing, the insurgency in El Salvador would not have been possible. The influence of this organizing extended beyond the confines of insurgency, as paramilitary death-squad violence, too, operated in clandestine forms, even if these were partially inserted in state structures. As Escobar Galindo, one of the top negotiators from the Salvadoran government, pointed out, "The war has been, in good measure, clandestine" (Montgomery 1995a, 213). Even if all major political actors used conspiracy, in the case of the PMOs it lay at the heart of their efforts.

> The rebels themselves turned conspiracy into a way a life. Most members of the FMLN had to lie about everything in order to survive. They gave themselves new names, made up cover stories, they misled their families, indeed they re-invented almost everything about themselves. This, they all accepted, was perfectly normal in the situation, and naturally they expected everyone else to be doing the same. Worst of all, everyone was always looking for enemy spies and infiltrators. This was especially true of the leadership, . . . [since] lack of vigilance would cost them dear. Thinking in conspiracies was not the slightly crazy attitude it is often regarded in most of the world. In El Salvador in the 1980s everyone was conspiring. (Gibb 2000, 223)

Clandestinity simultaneously allowed for isolation and for integration. Through clandestine organizing, apparently unconnected social sites were actually highly coordinated and complementary components of the insurgent movement. This complementarity was mostly confined, however, to the realm of each PMO. In spite of its symbolic importance for the revolutionary movement, the FMLN had very limited institutional existence. In political, social, and military terms, the PMOs were the true ordering principle of the revolutionary movement.[129]

Notwithstanding differences in size and development, each PMO attempted to create its own "integral" revolutionary apparatus. Different civil-political organizations pertaining to the same PMO were interlinked with each other, on local, national, and international levels, creating both public and covert mutually strengthening networks. Only a handful of people knew the details of PMO involvement in the different organizations. Through the cadre system, the PMOs nonetheless effectively ensured political control within their respective spheres of influence.

PMO sectarianism was another defining aspect of insurgency. The different PMOs continually struggled for primacy within the revolutionary movement, with a particularly strong rivalry between the two largest forces, the FPL and the ERP. The hegemonic pretentions of leadership of different PMOs were commonly seen as the main reason that the insurgent groups waited until late 1980 to establish a common front (Montgomery 1995a, 107). When the FMLN was finally established, with its joint insurgent command made up of the top comandantes of all the PMOs, hegemonic pretentions had to be tempered, but were far from eliminated. The FPL, for example, launched the following rallying cry: "There is only one Comandante, Marcial [pseudonym of Cayetano Carpio] Comandante." In 1981, "at least three times a day, in every village behind the lines, guerrillas, militiamen, and supporters lined up in neat rows to dutifully recite [this] slogan" (Krauss 1991, cited in Kruijt 2008, 61). Throughout the war, the revolutionary movement developed in a constant tension between revolutionary cooperation and sectarian disputes. Numerous sources speak of extensive distrust between insurgent groups in different stages of the struggle.[130]

The lived experience of insurgency has a side generally viewed as positive by its participants, which includes aspects such as discipline, solidarity, and sacrifice, but it also has a negative side, commonly associated with phenomena such as personal losses, (sectarian) intolerance, and internal conflicts.[131] For many, the worst and most painful aspect of the war was the internal purging. Thus far, only high-profile cases like the 1975 assassination of Roque Dalton and the events of April 1983 in Managua are public knowledge. Serious problems with infiltration, defection, and related security issues arose throughout the development of the insurgent movement. Such phenomena, furthermore, sometimes intersected with internal conflicts and disputes.[132] On the rural fronts, security problems varied according to the development of the war, with the period of growing governmental military power in 1984 and the intensification of the war before, during, and after the 1989 offensive standing out as particularly delicate periods. In 1984, the army's increased mobility and airpower improved the effectiveness of planted infiltrators among the insurgents and caused significant security problems on the fronts.[133] Starting in 1988, the preparations for the upcoming offensive led to the influx of new, inexperienced troops and to intensified mobility and

ment persecution, this strategy was sustainable for the insurgents during all of the 1970s and after 1984. In the period from 1980 through 1983, however, repression was so strong and indiscriminate that almost all public organizations tied to the revolutionary movement were dissolved or forced underground.

One of the effects of clandestine organizing was that throughout the revolutionary process a lot of things were not what they seemed from the outside. Clandestinity led to the extensive manipulation of political representation practices and personal identities within the revolutionary movement. The critical importance of security contributed to an internal social climate, in which revolutionary morale cohabited with factionalism, distrust, and overall "wear and tear."

The internal relations of the five PMOs constituted the primary ordering principle of the Salvadoran insurgency. A historicized understanding of insurgency's organizational dynamics helps to size up what various participants accumulated. In particular, the PMOs' recruitment strategies and their ability to constantly adapt to the emerging circumstances of the war supply crucial clues as to who incorporated into the revolutionary movement and why, how, and where they did so. In the process, different actors with different stakes, skills, and resources converged. Through active, intricate, and clandestine weaving of interpersonal relationships, each PMO was able to mobilize people with a wide breadth and diversity of capabilities. These qualities shaped the guerrilla army and the larger community that sustained it.

CHAPTER 3

Interlude

With the FPL in Chalatenango, 1992–95

La sangre cae esta vez, se hará semilla después.
—Guillermo Cuéllar, *Aguilares*

On March 2, 1992, one month after the cease-fire, I made my first trip to a "liberated zone" in El Salvador, traveling together with "Geraldine," my then girlfriend and a fellow activist from Canada. We met our FPL contact in the San Salvador office of an NGO working with refugees and repopulated communities. We then proceeded to board a pickup truck with a dozen other people headed towards Chalatenango. Geraldine was courteously allowed to ride in the cabin while I sat in the back along with half a dozen others, biting through clouds of dust for a large part of the trip. The main road from San Salvador to the northern part of the country was undergoing significant renovation. I had to cling on to the metal frame as we passed one pothole after another. I remember feeling excited and tense at the same time. Not because of the danger—the peace process was going strong—but because of what the trip meant for me. After two years of dedicated work with a Salvadoran solidarity group in the Mexican city of Guadalajara, I would finally be able to witness the revolution from up close.

The year before, "Ismael," a Mexican activist and FPL liaison, had taken me and Geraldine aside and formally announced that the FPL had decided to accept us in its ranks. Ismael had been talking to us about this possibility for some time, as we had grown closer to the organization as we worked on different solidarity projects, which included a day-care center for refugee infants; a weekend *pupusería;*[1] a rural extension project for refugees; and organizing solidarity meetings, talks, and "cultural evenings" with various audiences in the city of Guadalajara. In order to focus on political activism, I had given up my studies at the University of Guadalajara. On behalf of the FPL, Geraldine and I had also been collaborating by hosting party members who came to Guadalajara to recover from illness, receive treatments for war wounds, give birth, or simply rest from the strains of war. Their stories and friendships made life in the large but somewhat stuffy city of Guadalajara seem unreal at times, our ears and minds tuned to the progress of the revolution in El Salvador. Apart from joining the organization, we had also applied to be sent to El Salvador, to work for the FPL there. The party leadership had decided, however, that this had to wait, as the weight of the organization's efforts at the time lay in the peace negotiations taking place in Mexico City.

So we ended up waiting in Guadalajara until the peace accords were signed on January 16, 1992. The party then set up our trip to San Salvador via Mexico City with a family member of one of the FPL comandantes, who was returning, albeit still clandestinely, to El Salvador for the first time after years of exile. We traveled from Mexico City to San Salvador by bus and stayed in a safe house in the capital city for some days while the party figured out what to do with us. Then we learned we had been assigned to a comandante I shall identify as "Cruz Galán," in charge of the FPL's northern front and reputedly a war hero. We were to report to him at the mountain village of San José Las Flores, a repopulated community in the heartland of liberated El Salvador, the area sometimes smilingly called "the People's Republic of Chalatenango." The trip to Chalatenango and the meeting with Cruz Galán was something I had long been anticipating, an impressive moment at my twenty-two years of age.

On the way, there were several military checkpoints, but we weren't stopped. The soldiers just watched traffic go by from a shadowy patch by the roadside. We entered the zone under rebel control and drove for an hour or so on a barely passable dirt road, up and down mountainsides and across riverbeds, before driving into a bombed-out village with an old cobblestone square surrounded by worn adobe corridors and some remnants of sloped tile roofing. From there, our contact walked with us a block and a half to reach the FPL command post installed in one of the few houses still relatively intact, on the edge of the village. The subsequent meeting with Comandante Galán was not exactly what I had imagined it would be. Sitting in deliberation with his high command, rifles leaning upon a muddy fence, he showed markedly more interest in Geraldine than in me. We had not yet been informed of that part of his reputation. The incident, however, did little to dampen the thrill we felt to be there.

The next months we stayed at different guerrilla camps in Chalatenango that had been set up for troop concentration according to the schedule the rebels had agreed upon with the government and the United Nations (UN). In the beginning, camp life was tranquil. We learned to sleep on the floor and to eat beans and tortillas for days on end. Save an occasional hour or two when the generator was run after sunset, there would be no electricity, and nothing to do but chat, play cards, and go to bed early. Days started at dawn, and the *compas*[2] would benignly make fun of us if we weren't up by five. By eight o'clock in the evening almost everybody would be sleeping in their hammocks or on pieces of plastic on the floor. Initially, most combatants would just hang around and play cards to pass the time, while the comandantes and their closest aides would have one meeting after the other. The women would be busy cleaning, washing, and cooking. Occasionally, the troops would parade on the village square. Only once did I witness something other than ceremonious military activity, when in late March 1992 government soldiers moved in close to the FPL positions, in violation of the cease-fire stipulations. Cruz Galán and his second in command immediately mobilized troops to the threatened positions, as UN officials came and went. The crisis was solved by the end of the day with the Salvadoran Army's retreat.

We learned that, apart from the guerrilla army itself, the FPL was everywhere in Chalatenango. Within the liberated zone, all the communities participated in party organizing, practically down to the last family. Each community had its party liaisons for different political and military responsibilities. The leaders of the repopulated communities and the most important NGOs working in the region were directly affiliated with the party. People in the area contributed to the revolutionary movement in different ways, each according to their possibilities. The FPL was involved in community organization, health care, education, and productive initiatives. In the parts of Chalatenango that were outside of FPL military control, insurgent organization was much less encompassing. But the FPL still had some kind of party liaisons in most communities, sometimes in the form of cadres operating clandestinely, sometimes through the help of residents as collaborators. For example, the Catholic Church and the

ANDES teachers union had departmental organizational networks in Chalatenango within which the FPL maintained strong contacts. Apart from size and scope, the main difference between the FPL structures inside and outside the liberated zone was that inside, the FPL often operated in plain sight, while outside, its presence was hidden. With the cease-fire very recent, there was still fear of repression for those living in areas dominated by the Salvadoran military.

In spite of FPL's strong organizational foundations, I gathered that our Chalatenango leadership was somewhat overwhelmed by the multiple commitments that came with the peace accords. Apart from organizing the preparations for disarmament and demobilization of the military structures, several projects had to be set in motion to prepare for the insertion of combatants into civilian life. Simultaneously, leadership faced a race against the clock in order to be ready to successfully compete in the general elections, set for March 1994. This meant opening offices, setting up local directives, selecting candidates, and preparing for campaigning in each town and city. The peace process, furthermore, required the FPL's active involvement in the land reform program, in the creation of a new civilian police force, and in the elimination of thousands of land mines scattered all over the warzones.

Cruz Galán first assigned me to the FPL's departmental propaganda unit. I worked together with a comrade fresh from the capital. Our task was twofold. We had to collect the different materials (paper, ink, typewriters, stencil machines, and the like) left over from the wartime propaganda units active in Chalatenango and bring these to the new office of the FMLN to be opened in the city of Chalatenango. At the same time, we were charged with designing a new propaganda strategy for the FPL in Chalatenango, around the FMLN's new image as a soon-to-be-legal political party that had "conquered peace."[3]

It turned out that retrieving materials stored at the front was a significant challenge. Supplies were stowed away in tatús. These were in out-of-the-way, hard-to-reach places in the mountains, and only a few combatants or cadres knew the exact location. Some of them had already been assigned to new tasks and had relocated to the capital city or other zones. The materials we were able to retrieve (with the help of a few hard-working volunteers from the camps and, on one occasion, with an old mule) carried the marks of their underground sojourn. The rainy season had started and everything turned humid and moldy. Initially, we had to work with stained paper and rusted stencil machines. We coordinated with the national structure of the FPL to get supplies sent in from the capital. I soon learned to practice patience, as even a simple step would require waiting for permission, people, or resources, sometimes for days on end. Then, on June 1, 1992, the FPL in Chalatenango was shaken by Galán's sudden death. We were told he had died of natural causes, although alternative stories soon started to circulate.

AFTER GALÁN'S PASSING, I increasingly spent time at the FMLN head office in Chalatenango city, helping out with whatever I could. In July 1992 the FPL decided to set up a local committee to facilitate the United Nations Truth Commission's investigations of wartime human rights violations. Jon Cortina, a Jesuit priest from the Universidad Centroamericana "José Simeón Cañas" (UCA),[4] El Salvador's Jesuit university, led the committee. He was something of a legend within the FPL, an embodiment of the intimate relationship between the revolutionary movement and progressive sectors of the Catholic Church. In the 1970s he had worked closely with FECCAS and UTC,[5] the two FPL-affiliated peasant organizations that would become hotbeds of insurgency. He remained a firm supporter of the FPL throughout the war, visiting his former flock, now mostly found at the battlefronts or in the refugee camps, whenever he could. When the repopulation movement allowed for the organized refugees to settle in the villages that had been abandoned during the early years of the war, he was accepted as parish priest for the Chalatenango town of San Francisco Lempa, from where he was able to attend to the repopulated communities of San José Las Flores, San Antonio Los Ranchos, and Guarjila.[6] For the insurgents, the repopulation movement meant that the areas they had referred to as "liberated zones" and that had become virtually abandoned as a result of scorched-earth military operations now increasingly also became the place of residence of their historical peasant constituencies.

Our human rights committee functioned with technical assistance provided by the UCA. The FPL provided the personnel, who, apart from myself, consisted of Geraldine and "Maritza," a young woman from one of Chalatenango's leading revolutionary peasant families. Making use of the infrastructure of FPL contacts and collaborators in communities, churches, and NGOs, we set out to document Chalatenango's many wartime atrocities, in order to present this material to the Truth Commission. In this effort, we visited dozens of villages, looking for victims' families willing to share their story. We organized trips bringing victims' relatives to the Truth Commission's office in the capital city. The Truth Commission coordinated field visits with us to document and verify cases in person. During the next six months we worked without pause. Our committee presented over three thousand individual cases of assassinations, forced disappearances, and rape, the vast majority committed by the US-backed Salvadoran army, security forces, and paramilitary units. We furthermore produced detailed reports on dozens of massacres that had taken place in Chalatenango between 1979 and 1992.

The intense labor of reconstructing the history of violence was especially excruciating for those on our team who had suffered persecution, but it also had a devastating impact on the two of us who had not. As it turned out, almost all the Chalatenango families we visited, especially those from the insurgent communities, had endured extreme, brutal violence. In these months, the mountains of Chalatenango revealed for me a very specific geography of terror. Each hamlet had its own horrific tales and many unburied remains laid scattered on the hillsides. I imagined the Chalatenango mountain roads to be engraved with the memory of "one dead body after another, a path of corpses, a line of crosses, all the way up to Honduras," as I wrote in my diary at the time. I experienced frequent nightmares filled with images of terror, such as paramilitaries wielding blood-dripping machetes and shooting helicopters flying overhead. We vigorously hoped the Truth Commission would bring redress to the families we worked with. In our mind, the commission would need to lay the groundwork for criminal prosecution of the perpetrators, for the clarification of the whereabouts of the disappeared, and for different forms of compensation for the victims' families.[7]

These expectations suffered a strong blow when, on March 20, 1993, five days after the publication of the Truth Commission report, the Salvadoran parliament approved a blanket amnesty law, practically burying aspirations for justice and other forms of redress (Popkin 2000; Sieder 2002; Sprenkels 2005, 2012). Our small Chalatenango human rights committee decided to focus on the dissemination of the Truth Commission report throughout Chalatenango, including those areas that had been controlled by the Salvadoran army and paramilitary groups during the war. Additionally, we started a research project on a profoundly troubling issue we had come across in our documentation efforts: the military's deliberate kidnapping of children from peasant families during counter-insurgency operations. The children's families had not given up hope their children might be alive, and had been searching for them for years in the difficult circumstances of the war. Our investigations confirmed that many of the kidnapped children might plausibly still be alive and living with altered identities within El Salvador and abroad. In January 1994 we facilitated a historic first reencounter of a group of kidnapped children with their families in the repopulation of Guarjila, Chalatenango. This work eventually led to the founding of the Asociación Pro-Búsqueda de Niñas y Niños Desaparecidos[8] in August 1994, a group that united the efforts of dozens of families from Chalatenango and elsewhere in search of their children who had disappeared in the war. Pro-Búsqueda started an office in San Salvador, a move that would make me give up my home in Chalatenango in early 1995.[9]

During my close-to-three years of residency in Chalatenango, I witnessed people in the FPL's former "liberated zone" trying to adjust to the many changes that the end of the war had brought. I experienced first-hand some of the excitement brought about by the promises of peace, such as the animated groups of university students who flooded the guerrilla camps during the last months of encampment to give expedited courses to the combatants in an attempt to compensate for the school years missed, or the scores of villagers and (unarmed) combatants who cheerfully loaded themselves in the back of trucks to make the journey to the capital for the May Day march in 1992. I recall the enthusiasm caused by a high-spirited guerrilla unit marching among us on the streets, uniformed and in formation, but unarmed.

I also witnessed the confusion and disarray the transition brought about for many of the guerrilla fighters, especially those who had grown to adulthood in the war. What would they do with their lives if they had never learned anything else but to be a soldier? How were they going to survive if the FPL would no longer clothe and feed them? Combatants who had received sufficient education were encouraged to join the new civilian police force. But what about the majority who had hardly ever been to school? To many of them, the prospects of eking out a living in the poor mountainous soils seemed bleak. Particularly desolate was the prospect for the hundreds of war-wounded facing severe physical limitations as agricultural laborers. My friend Juan Serrano, an FPL fighter from Chalatenango, would describe his situation following the peace accords in these words a few years later: "The life of the guerrilla fighter plunges into terrible uncertainty."[10]

Several demobilized combatants used the reinsertion allowance to buy a boom-box radio or a television set or to go on a drinking binge. The demobilized combatants also received a sort of starter package for "civilian" life, which included a small gas stove, a table and chairs, two plastic water jugs, and cheap kitchenware. Almost everybody complained, and a few were so offended by its content that they refused to receive the package. Other villagers, not in the camps at the time of the demobilization, bemoaned having received nothing, while having fought and sacrificed much more for the revolution than some who had received the package. There were lists for everything, administering eligibilities ranging from plots of land to credit and scholarships, health-care packages for war-wounded, and all kinds of community projects. A person not on the list would get nothing. It didn't matter how much he or she had suffered during the war, how many years of guerrilla duty had been performed or how well the benefit might suit his or her needs.

I befriended one family in Guarjila whose seven sons had all fought for the FPL. Once officially demobilized, six of the seven went directly from the camp to the care of the *pollero*[11] hired to ensure their passage to a new but very different type of clandestine life, that of an illegal worker in the United States. At the time, it was hard for me to comprehend their decision. Was this what they had fought for all these years? One midlevel cadre I knew, a man much appreciated by the combatants because of his wartime valor and his quick wit, traded in his job of working on reintegration projects and became a pollero himself, arranging many former combatants' passage to the North, bribing their way through Mexico.

As postwar reconstruction unfolded in Chalatenango's repopulated communities, I sometimes watched apprehension change into frustration, with the benefits from the reintegration programs failing to meet expectations, while the FPL leadership increasingly left its constituency to its own devices; or at least, so it was perceived. Frustration mostly translated into apathy, with some people deserting communal activities and collective projects, withdrawing increasingly into the sphere of family and personal relations. A few ex-combatants became downright angry with the comandantes, whom they accused of rushing off to the capital and seeking benefits for themselves rather than for the ex-combatants who needed them the most. A particularly telling case was that of the constant rumors regarding the pickup truck that Cruz Galán had acquired shortly after the peace accords. Some claimed that Galán had bought the brand-new Toyota pickup truck with the money that the organization had sent him to set up the guerrilla encampments and pay for the troops' supplies, and that he had done so without consulting the party. The immediate issue was whether this constituted a legitimate form of appropriation of party resources (seen by most as collective property) or not.[12]

In another widely commented-on incident, a recently demobilized FPL official was shot in an attempted robbery of a wealthy rancher just outside the former zone of FPL control. Shortly afterwards, another mid-level cadre I had worked with when transporting propaganda equipment was killed when attempting a holdup elsewhere in Chalatenango. A few armed bandits started mugging passersby on the roads connecting the different repopulated communities, and rumors about the involvement of former *guerrilleros*[13] were persistent. I remember one peasant comment: "Before, the organization would have taken care of it, but now, who is going to do anything about it?"

At the same time, remarkable infrastructural changes were taking place in Chalatenango's former liberated zone. Financed by multiple housing projects, provisional homes in the remains of bombed-out adobe houses and shacks made of plastic and mud were replaced by small cinder-block houses. Home faucets replaced the communal water spigots, and connections to the national electrical network replaced the occasional generator. Schools, clinics, and bridges were built, roads improved. NGOs flooded the communities with scores of productive projects, all of which were supposed to be "sustainable." But only a small handful actually survived beyond the duration of the external financial investment. While they lasted, and from one project to the next, they did provide some kind of income for people that, for the most part, desperately needed it. Nevertheless, for most "beneficiaries," these projects were but a meager consolation and did little to assuage concerns about their future. The many losses of the war, ranging from kin and prewar properties to productive years and physical handicaps, translated into multiple disadvantages that did not begin to be compensated by what some called the "crumbs" of reconstruction projects.

Although I initially felt it was my task to censor apathy or to fend off what I considered excessive criticism with regard to the transition process and the FPL's internal affairs, as my personal relationships with rank-and-file combatants and their families grew closer, I gradually found myself becoming more sympathetic to peasant claims of not always having gotten a fair deal and of feeling "abandoned." I suffered my own, less significant, disappointments with the proclamation of the amnesty law and subsequently with what I perceived at the time as the meager results of the 1994 elections, which right-wing ARENA won comfortably, leaving the FMLN the role of leading opposition party. But above all, I was dissatisfied with the FMLN's reluctance to fight for significant redress for victims of human rights abuses and their families,[14] as well as with its initially very shabby support for our efforts at Pro-Búsqueda. Jon Cortina and I were both disheartened by the FPL leadership's suggestion that our work to find disappeared children might raise false expectations amongst the people in the communities. We felt that the management of expectations hadn't exactly been our leadership's strongest quality in this transition period. From where we stood, we believed the FPL should assign higher priority to its wartime rural constituency.

At the same time, it would be simplistic to state that the FPL leadership started to ignore their rank-and-file as a result of their incursion into electoral politics. In fact, as I witnessed in Chalatenango, the FPL successfully negotiated reinsertion and reconstruction programs to benefit members and constituents, and assigned several senior cadres to overview implementation. However, the revolutionary war had generated, among its participants, deep expectations of societal transformation that stood in stark contrast to the limited immediate benefits of the peace process. As one Chalatenango friend formulated it at the time: "No more overthrowing the rich. We'd better get used to the idea that we will remain poor."

CHAPTER 4

Postinsurgent Reconversion

A revolution is a mighty devourer of human energy, both individual
and collective. The nerves give way. Consciousness is shaken and
characters are worn out.

—Leon Trotsky, *The Revolution Betrayed*

This chapter focuses on the adjustments that took place in the FMLN insurgents' social field, spanning from the peace agreements until the early years of this century. The agreements contemplated three main tracks (demilitarization, institutional modernization, and socioeconomic reform), thus setting in motion what has been called El Salvador's "triple transition" (van der Borgh 2004). For the PMOs, similarly, the transition process translated into complex and variegated adaptations. At the time, the PMO leadership envisioned the need to reorganize insurgent networks to take on postwar challenges.

Internal PMO documentation reveals that, much broader than simply hoping for the best in the elections, the former insurgents' fundamental postwar aim was what they themselves called the "advantageous reconversion which would allow us to turn our accumulated political-military power into a social, political, and productive force" (PRS-ERP 1992; See also FPL 1992). Bourdieu (1984, 157) theorizes "reconversion strategies" as "actions and reactions whereby each group strives to maintain or change its position in the social structure . . . , to change so as to conserve." In sum, what is at stake here is harnessing the social field for the future.

Reconversion strategies therefore unfold in a tension between change and continuity.

PMO leadership indeed envisioned wartime accumulation as a platform on which to build a successful postwar trajectory (FPL 1992, 1994; PRS-ERP 1992). To this end, they developed three core reconversion strategies:

(a) Military reconversion, consisting of two main components: demobilization and reinsertion programs and recruitment of former guerrilla fighters for the new civilian police force.
(b) Political reconversion, for the PMOs to transform into an electoral force.
(c) Broader socioeconomic reconversion of the PMO constituencies, to access peacetime benefits and develop a support base for the new political project.

This chapter delves into how these three reconversion strategies unfolded and to what effect. Existing scholarship only acknowledges the reconversion strategies implicitly, and furthermore deals with them separately and unevenly. While the FMLN's metamorphosis "from guerrilla movement to political party" has drawn a constant stream of attention, mainly in comparative politics, academic reviews of guerrilla forces' broader civil reinsertion, in contrast, are almost nonexistent,[1] with the partial exception of gender aspects.[2] Lastly, as documented later in this chapter and in chapter 5, socioeconomic reconstruction processes in El Salvador's former conflict zones have been researched most extensively. However, available studies mostly do not address the specific role of former PMO networks herein. Furthermore, since postinsurgent reconversion strategies have been studied mostly in isolation from one another, very little is known as to how members or sectors of the movement adjusted to the new situation in relation to each other. This becomes particularly relevant if we bear in mind the convoluted anatomy of the Salvadoran insurgent movement explained in chapter 2. What, then, was the impact of the postwar transition process on the movements' cohesion? How did varied peacetime adjustments redefine internal relations?

The chapter documents how factors like unmet historical expectations and postwar social differentiation among former insurgents helped nurture disillusionment, further fueled by the ongoing, sometimes unsettling, events of the transition period. However, the chapter also highlights that, despite division and deception, the former insurgents still garnered political ascendency, particularly those participants that stayed active inside the FMLN as a political party. The intricate PMO relations inherited from the war played an important role in structuring access to the varied benefits of the three reconversion strategies.

INSURGENT DEMOBILIZATION AND REINSERTION

The Demobilization Process

The peace accords contemplated the complete demobilization of the guerrilla forces. The negotiators did not establish exact locations for the concentration of the insurgent troops, but rather fifteen designated areas, located in the zones of FMLN control. Spread out in these concentration areas, the five PMOs set up a total of sixty-eight individual guerrilla camps (Verhey 2001, 17).[3] Officials from the United Nations Observer Mission in El Salvador (ONUSAL) set up supervision units in the camps and started to register the troops and weapons.

Figure 4.1. Insurgent concentration areas and distribution of PMOs

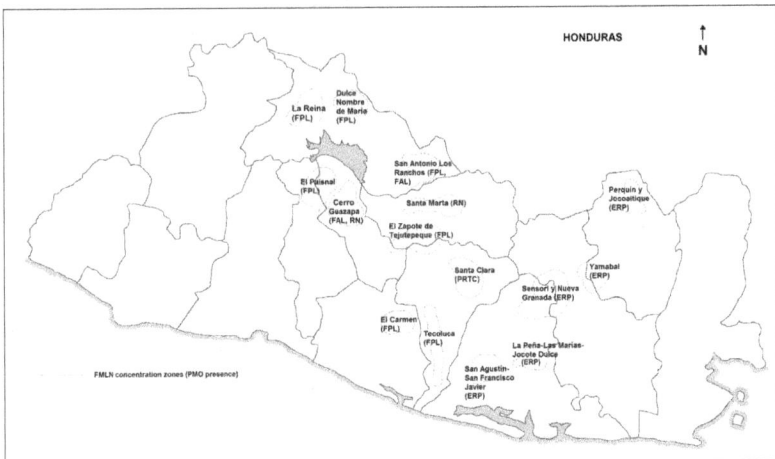

Source: United Nations (1995, 217), Villalobos (1999, 38–41), and an interview with a former FMLN representative on the cease-fire commission (February 23, 2011).

Table 4.1.   Categories of demobilized FMLN members per PMO

PMO	END	Political	Injured	Total	%
FPL	2,583	1,439	1,060	5,082	34
ERP	2,653	463	814	3,930	26
RN	1,554	656	289	2,499	17
PCS-FAL	1,110	996	144	2,250	15
PRTC	652	429	167	1,248	8
Total	8,552	3,983	2,474	15,009	100%

Source: "Proceso de desmovilización del personal del FMLN," cited in Luciak (2001, 49–55).

ONUSAL and the FMLN established the following demobilization categories: military structures, political structures, and war-wounded. After minor delays, military demobilization concluded on December 15, 1992. Political personnel and war-wounded formally demobilized afterwards, wrapping up in March 1993 and November 1993, respectively. The official demobilization figures per PMO read as shown in table 4.1.

Available data confirm the social diversity of the Salvadoran insurgents discussed in the previous chapter. Eighty percent of the demobilized combatants had received no or very limited formal education, while 7 percent had attended university.[4] An estimated 80 percent of the demobilized initially settled in rural communities.[5] Close to 30 percent of those demobilized were women (Pampell Conaway and Martínez 2004, 3).

Reinsertion Programs

The FMLN reinsertion programs were to be included in the National Reconstruction Plan (NRP). Scholarships, pensions, and jobs were listed among possible benefits, but no specific time frames or funding requirements were established (FMLN 1992a, 93–94). Instead, the government, the FMLN, the UN, and several international donor agencies negotiated such provisions in the course of the implementation of the peace accords. The five PMOs, furthermore, set up a combined institution dedicated to reinsertion called Fundación 16 de Enero (F-16).

Salvadoran government officials and some international donors frowned upon granting extensive benefits specifically to FMLN personnel. The United States Agency for International Development (USAID), NRP's largest contributor, was concerned that such assistance might generate "predictable resentment . . . on the part of the general population" (1994a, 16). Thus, initially reinsertion consisted of a very sober package. Most of the funds were instead to be used for reconstruction efforts benefiting communities in former war zones (Bendaña 1999, 55; USAID 1994a, 8). The FMLN, however, repeatedly and successfully argued that, for the stability for the peace process, additional benefits for ex-combatants were crucial.[6] To USAID's dislike, the guerrilla leadership insisted on channeling funds assigned to NRP toward reinsertion programs, which led eventually to an "over tenfold increase in the ex-combatant assistance component" (USAID 1994a, 13). USAID, furthermore, complained that, "as the FMLN developed confidence . . . , it would begin to develop lists and amended lists, each of which would increase the numbers of the FMLN determined and UN sanctioned 'eligible beneficiaries'" (17).

USAID had initially intended for most of the reconstruction funds to expand on the development programs they had administered in wartime, when USAID programs had been an integrated part of US counterinsurgency efforts (USAID 1994a, 8). However, whereas government institutions frequently failed to make use of the NRP, the FMLN jumped on the opportunity (17). The FMLN also mobilized its civil-political front and international work to this end. "The FMLN proved especially successful at lobbying in the US and USAID was pressed to deal directly and often separately with the FMLN" (16). One aspect of this pressure was to execute parts of the program via "FMLN related NGOs," of which USAID identified as many as forty-three (17).

Insurgent reinsertion was thus forged in the dynamics of ongoing negotiations with a host of different institutions and donors. As a result, it consisted of a patchwork of different projects, sometimes working with different logics and time frames. For example, three weeks before finalizing the demobilization process, the FMLN proposed an additional economic reinsertion program for FMLN "officers," entitled From Guerrilla Comandantes to Entrepreneurs (FMLN 1992b, 1992c).[7] Known as "Plan 600," it intended to benefit PMO leadership as well as senior and midlevel cadres with an additional US$7.2 million grant for training, housing, and business ventures. It was accepted and implemented after heavy FMLN pressure.[8] Plan 600 was controversial among former insurgents, as it stepped away from the revolution's egalitarian discourse. Nonetheless, all PMOs eventually selected senior cadres to participate (Luciak 2001, 130–32).

Another 1993 special benefit program for 850 former FMLN child soldiers only met a fraction of its targets (Verhey 2001, 27–28). The failure of "Plan 850" was the exception to the rule. In fact, most of the FMLN re-integration programs not only were implemented but also significantly overspent allocated budgets. In 1994, the NRP framework tallied twelve reinsertion programs, subdivided into four "tracks": a (rural) agricultural track; an (urban) microenterprise track; an academic scholarship track; and the "officers program" (Plan 600).[9] Apart from credit packages, en-tering the rural or urban track would translate into at least six months of vocational training, including a subsistence allowance of US$100 per month. The reinsertion process additionally contemplated rehabilitation assistance for war-wounded veterans and housing programs for ex-combatants in the rural areas.[10] The final beneficiary figures show that 78 percent of the FMLN demobilized chose the agricultural track, 14 percent opted for microenterprises, and 8 percent for academic scholarships.[11]

The cornerstone of the rural reinsertion was the Land Transfer Pro-gram (PTT), which catered to former combatants and FMLN constituents in the former conflict zones (Baumgärtner 1998; del Castillo 1997; McReynolds 2002). The PTT was technically complex because it required solving a host of land-measurement and legal-ownership issues. Further-more, rural property prices skyrocketed because of the PTT, eliciting drawn-out additional negotiations with international funders. By far the lengthiest component of the reinsertion process, the PTT was concluded only in 1999, registering a total of 27,418 FMLN beneficiaries. It resulted in the transfer of 9.5 percent of the total of El Salvador's arable land to the former insurgents (Alvarez and Chávez 2001, 38, 45).

A large part of the reinsertion benefits were extended in the form of loans that had to be repaid. However, payback rates were extremely low. Eventually, after the FMLN and affiliated groups exerted significant po-litical pressure, debts were restructured and subsequently pardoned at the end of the 1990s (De Bremond 2007; Foley 1997; Kowalchuk 2003a, 2005).

Besides the many NRP-related activities, the FMLN actively engaged in additional fund-raising with donors large and small. The largest pro-gram was a European Union program in Usulután, which served three thousand former insurgents for a total investment of $18 million (Verhey 2001, 25). The FMLN also managed to find several external funding sources to provide over three hundred extra academic scholarships to ex-combatants, in addition to the close to seven hundred provided by the

NRP (USAID 1994a, 16). With international support, some small groups of ex-combatants were able to set up cooperative projects which aimed to provide durable employment and income, like Cooperativa Nueva Vida, a printshop run by ERP war-wounded in San Salvador.

Another reinsertion possibility was provided by the new police force established through the peace accords, the National Civilian Police (PNC). The FMLN had negotiated a 20 percent quota for its ex-combatants in the first contingents of this new force, adding up to one thousand available posts (Villalobos 2001, 72). FMLN leadership deemed its quota of strategic importance in order to guarantee the force's neutrality in future political disputes. Nonetheless, the FMLN struggled to find enough candidates in its ranks who fitted the educational profile required to enter the police academy, and thus initially had a hard time making the PNC quota (Bendaña 1999, 25). F-16 registered the incorporation of a total of 408 ex-combatants on the FMLN quota, including several high-ranking guerrilla officers who assumed PNC leadership positions (Sención Villalona 1995, 87). The FMLN managed to remedy the deficit by allowing noncombatant sympathizers of the FMLN to fill in part of the quota, and by negotiating for ex-combatants to be admitted as regular cadets at a later stage, thus giving them more time to fulfill the educational requirement (Costa 1999, 127; Villalobos 2001, 72).

A final major component of the reinsertion provisions was a care and pension arrangement called the Fund for the Protection of War-Wounded and Disabled as a Consequence of the Armed Conflict.[12] Although the fund was established in 1992, political negotiations and struggles over benefits and lists of beneficiaries dragged on for years. Pressure from the associations of war-wounded FMLN veterans—in alliance with beneficiaries from the side of the Salvadoran military—eventually led to significant reforms of the fund in 2001. The war-wounded eventually did receive incapacity pensions and health benefits, but most considered these insufficient. Complaints regarding political manipulation, low benefits, and poor implementation continued for years.[13]

Reinsertion Retrospect

The USAID-commissioned evaluations of the reinsertion process alternated between lamenting the partial FMLN "take-over" and praising the programs' contribution to reintegration and to the peace process (USAID

1994a, 1994b; CREA 1996).[14] Evaluators identified as missed opportunities the lack of attention to women ex-combatants and war-wounded veterans (30 percent and 16 percent of the total force, respectively) (USAID 1994a, 20, 29). In contrast, F-16's evaluation criticized the government's limiting of reinsertion benefits and marginalizing of FMLN ex-combatants, and concluded that "the future of the insertion remains uncertain" (Sención Villalona 1995, 48). "There are no secure jobs, profitability is almost null, the economic activities' future is uncertain. . . . The economic situation of the country . . . is not favorable for the insertion of ex-combatants and [insurgent] landholders. The stagnation of agriculture, commercial liberalization, and the strengthening of the large-scale importation sector . . . threaten to force many small and medium-sized businesses out of the market" (Sención Villalona 1995, 102–3).

In spite of such limitations, PMO leadership did actively frame reinsertion programs as a conquest, and it positioned itself as a champion for insurgent benefits. "The partial success of the reinsertion programs for the ex-guerrilla was due to pressure and efforts by the guerrilla itself" (Villalobos 2001, 41). Leadership not only attempted to maximize the benefits for cadres and supporters (and minimize those accessed by the adversary). It also exerted control over benefit dispensation, acting as a gatekeeper. Proactively, the PMOs were able to draw in a very substantial part of the $356 million invested through the NRP (Verhey 2001, 25). They also procured sizable land assets and a range of other reintegration support programs. The underlying problem lay in the extent to which reinsertion benefits might sustainably satisfy the needs and expectations of those demobilized.

POLITICAL ACCOMMODATIONS: FROM FIVE PMOS TO THREE POLITICAL PARTIES

With the peace accords freshly signed, leadership discussions on new political strategies coincided with the ideological crisis following the demise of the Soviet Union (Bonasso and Gómez Leyba 1992; Montobbio 1999). Simultaneously, within as well as among the PMOs, discussions emerged as to who were to be credited most for insurgent successes, and whether this should be reflected in a larger say for the new period. This exacerbated conflicts between PMO leaders and subgroups. Perceived "historical" differences between the PMOs were reframed in the light of emerging political controversies, reviving factionalism. The FMLN's transition from guerrilla movement to political party generated stark adjustments within and among the PMOs.

The UDN Split-Off

The first public conflict took place around the UDN, the PCS electoral vehicle founded in 1970. Like the other PMOs, the PCS had been involved in establishing civil-political efforts inside the country since the mid-1980s. Part of this strategy had been the UDN's relaunching, initiated with the 1988 repatriation of several prominent exiles, including PCS's Mario Aguiñada Carranza, the top UDN leader. The repatriates also set up an NGO called Fundación Cuscatlán. In the 1991 elections, Aguiñada Carranza won a seat in parliament. With the accords freshly signed, top PCS leaders argued that the role of the UDN had been exhausted and proposed to absorb this party and its patrimony into the PCS structures. Aguiñada Carranza and several other cadres who had been working inside El Salvador argued, on the other hand, that disbanding their project was premature. They believed that significant political relationships and influence would be in peril should the UDN disappear. Furthermore, as a member of Comisión Nacional para la Consolidación de la Paz (COPAZ), the official peace commission, the UDN held a separate vote in the implementation of the peace accords.[15]

Formally, the conflict was settled by means of an "amicable and democratic separation agreement," after which the PCS and the UDN went their separate ways.[16] In practice, the UDN broke into two. A group of PCS militants abandoned the UDN, and another group left the PCS together with Aguiñada Carranza. The Fundación Cuscatlán stayed in the hands of this latter group. According to those involved, defamation, harassment, and intimidation by PCS members severely hampered the functioning of the UDN and its NGO. After the split, UDN members claimed their political efforts were sabotaged by the PCS.[17]

The Crisis around the Truth Commission Report

The 1993 Truth Commission report triggered the first major postwar inter-PMO conflict. Entitled *From Madness to Hope: The 12-Year War in*

El Salvador, the report confirmed that the army and paramilitary groups had committed widespread and systematic abuse. The commission held the FMLN responsible for a much smaller, but still significant number of war crimes. It recommended that perpetrators identified in the report be "disqualified from the exercise of any public function for a minimum of ten years" (United Nations 1993, 166). This restriction affected dozens of army officers, but also the five top commanders of the FMLN and a handful of other former insurgents.

The Truth Commission findings caused quite a stir. Soon after their publication, the minister of defense called a press conference and disqualified the report as "unjust, incomplete, illegal, unethical, partial and insolent" (Rico 1997, 57). The country's leading right-wing newspaper characterized it as "tales, slander, half-truths, and rumors."[18] Five days later, the parliament adopted a "sweeping" amnesty law providing legal protection to those implicated and voiding legal proceedings on abuses committed during the conflict (Popkin 2000, 6).

Joaquín Villalobos, the top leader of the ERP, had previously declared that, under certain guarantees, he would be willing to go to jail together with military officers and oligarchs holding responsibilities for human rights violations.[19] However, the ERP leadership was infuriated when the report came out, claiming that their faction had been disproportionately scrutinized in comparison to the other PMOs.[20] The commission identified six top-ranking ERP members as responsible for the assassination of at least ten different mayors in towns in the eastern part of the country between 1985 and 1988.[21] The report furthermore emphasized the particular responsibility of Villalobos in these cases (United Nations 1993, 139). In contrast, leadership of the other PMOs was not taken on in the report, with the exception of the FMLN "general command," consisting of the five secretary generals. "We are surprised that only one organization was focused on, and precisely almost its entire leadership," Villalobos declared.[22]

The FMLN's communication secretary, ERP's Juan Ramón Medrano, suggested that the report had the "intention to hit only one of the organizations of the FMLN in order to . . . break the unity of the FMLN."[23] ERP leadership claimed that the five PMOs had agreed to be transparent towards the Truth Commission, but that only the ERP acted faithfully, and that the other groups apparently had not provided full disclosure. It also emphasized that the elimination of government-appointed mayors in the conflict zones constituted FMLN-sanctioned policy, even if only the ERP had effectively implemented it.[24] The ERP leadership speculated that the Truth Commission had allowed itself to be manipulated by other FMLN factions to discredit the ERP (Villalobos 1999, 31; Galeas 2004, 47). Internally, ERP leadership spoke of betrayal.[25] In all, the affair caused serious rifts in the relationship between the ERP and other PMOs, especially the FPL and the PCS.[26]

Nonetheless, the FMLN initially did announce it would comply with the Truth Commission's recommendation of temporary disqualification from holding public office. However, the leadership retracted on this issue in the process of negotiating candidacies for the 1994 elections, and the majority of insurgent leaders implicated in the report, including several belonging to the ERP, ended up on the ballot (Sprenkels 2005, 84).

A Fissure within the ERP

Simultaneously, internal tensions had also been building up inside the ERP itself. The leadership, headed by Joaquín Villalobos, rallied in favor of a new postwar ideological profile (Medrano 1992).[27] By 1993, the ERP leadership had explicitly renounced their previous Marxist-Leninist propositions and instead embraced political pluralism, a capitalist market economy and a social-democratic political platform.[28] In September 1993, the ERP changed its name from Ejército Revolucionario del Pueblo to Expresión Renovadora del Pueblo (Martín Alvarez 2006, 128).[29]

A minority among ERP cadres disputed the new course. The strongest resistance came from the ERP's former front in Usulután. The conflict spiraled into crisis when the ERP leadership vetoed the dissidents' candidate for the 1994 parliamentary ballot in Usulután and imposed someone else. The crisis resulted in the expulsion of one dissident and the removal from leadership positions of four others at an 1993 ERP general assembly. The same assembly, furthermore, authorized the leadership to "separate from the Party those that insist in such conspiratorial activities" (PRS-ERP 1993c).[30] The ERP dissidents then, unsuccessfully, tried to enlist the other factions of the FMLN to support their cause.[31] Meanwhile, similar conflicts were simmering within the RN, FPL, and PRTC, but these would not surface until later on in the process.[32]

The 1994 Elections

The run-up to elections was marked not only by rising tensions among the PMOs, but primarily by what appeared as a surge in violence against FMLN leaders and cadres. On October 25, 1993, for example, PRTC leader Francisco Velis was assassinated while dropping off his infant daughter at a day-care center in San Salvador. His murder fit a pattern of death-squad-style killings targeting close to a dozen cadres belonging to different PMOs in previous months. In response, FPL cadres organized a hunger strike in a church in Chalatenango, and the FMLN successfully pressured for the establishment of a special commission called Grupo Conjunto to investigate and eliminate death-squad remnants (Ladutke 2004, 169). Nonetheless, the violence did spark uncertainty or fear of what might happen next and discouraged potential FMLN collaborators from participating in the elections (Morales, Pohl, and Racicot 1995).

El Salvador's first peacetime elections not only included the presence of the full political spectrum on the ballot, but also represented a confluence of the country's two different electoral cycles (three-year terms for representatives of municipalities and parliament, and five-year terms for the presidency) in one event. Several observers championed this crucial step in the peace process as the "elections of the century" (Montgomery 1995a, 248). The FMLN was able to field candidates in 225 (out of 262) municipalities and in all 14 departments of the country (FLACSO 1995, 190). FDR leader Rubén Zamora functioned as the presidential candidate for a coalition including the FMLN. Although many minor irregularities were registered, the elections took place without major incidents, and all parties accepted the results.

The FMLN became the largest opposition party, albeit manifestly behind ARENA, the winner on all fronts. The FMLN won fifteen municipal governments (TSE 1994). With the exception of Nejapa, these municipalities were located in the insurgency's "liberated zones" of the country and consisted of rural constituencies largely made up of resettled refugees.[33] The FMLN also took twenty-one seats in parliament (out of eighty-four). Zamora forced a second round in the presidential elections, which ARENA's Armando Calderón Sol won comfortably (FLACSO 1995; Lazo 1995).

The ERP and RN Abandon the FMLN

Shortly after the elections it became clear that the leadership of the ERP and the RN faction had waited for the distribution of public office in order to force a political showdown with the other organizations of the FMLN.[34] On their first day in parliament, five deputies belonging to the ERP and two belonging to the RN struck a deal with ARENA and effectively sidelined the rest of the FMLN legislators.[35] While many in the FPL, PRTC, and PCS spoke of "treason," the ERP and the RN initially refused to complete a break with the FMLN, but instead proposed to "seek a new internal agreement with which to define the terms of the alliance between the two tendencies" within the FMLN.[36] According to Joaquín Villalobos, the ERP and the RN "[did] not want to be against the system but rather to play by the rules," a commitment that, in his opinion, the other organizations were not ready to assume.[37]

In reaction to this, a new clandestine group called the Frente Revolucionario Salvadoreño (FRS)[38] appeared with a communiqué announcing "death sentences" for Joaquín Villalobos and other dissident leadership.[39] Anti-ERP leaflets circulated among the FMLN militancy showing the ERP deputies embracing their ARENA colleagues accompanied by cries of "traitors" and "sell-outs."[40] President Cristiani, seeking to capitalize on the unfolding dispute, publically threatened to intervene should violence break out within the FMLN.[41] On May 9, the FMLN National Council decided to suspend Joaquín Villalobos and the seven dissident deputies from their official functions within the FMLN, but not to expel them.[42] Shortly after, the leaders who had been expelled from the ERP in November 1993 applied to be reincorporated into the FMLN as a new faction called Tendencia Democrática (TD).[43]

Whatever their position in the dispute, the crisis profoundly affected the militants of the different organizations of the FMLN. The FMLN's September 1994 national convention failed to produce an inclusive solution. The ERP and RN then attempted to force the dissolution of the FMLN. When this strategy proved unviable, the ERP and the RN formally decided to abandon the FMLN in November (ERP) and December (RN) 1994. A few weeks later, the ERP published a sort of epitaph.

It is paradoxical that the RN and ERP, who have long promoted unity, defending that unity at all costs, should be separated from the FMLN. The FPL, who have done so much to destroy the FMLN through the use of blackmail, hegemonic domination, destabilization, etc., today declare themselves its most fervent defenders. They have their motives and it is easy to identify them. Today the bells toll in mourning. They may end up with the money, the flag, and the name (in this order, according to their hierarchy of priorities), but it will no longer be the FMLN with which our people have so long fought. And our commitment is with this people, not with the self-proclaimed archangels of dogma.[44]

The FMLN as a Party of Tendencies

In turn, the remaining organizations (FPL, PCS, and PRTC) resolved not only to stay inside the FMLN, but also to formally dissolve the remaining PMO structures to allow for their full absorption into the FMLN. This new step was presented as a necessity in order to limit the organization's vulnerability to factional conflict. It also clearly bore the mark of strengthening the FMLN vis-à-vis the new ERP-RN project. In the case of the FPL, the decision to dismantle was furthermore prompted, at least in part, by a latent internal conflict between self-proclaimed reformers and revolutionaries. According to Felipe, a cadre close to the FPL political commission at the time,

> Why did we, the FPL, dissolve ourselves as a political organization? Because, within the organization there were different emphases as to the political direction the transition was taking, and the easiest manner of resolving this was by saying: "We would be better off dissolving the organization and all joining the FMLN" . . . because to continue working with these different scripts within the FPL would have brought us to crisis . . . furthermore, we faced and we still [face], I believe . . . some consequences from the party's own events . . . for example, what happened in '83 is a burden that we as the FPL carry up to the present. . . . What happened in '83 happened precisely due to these different approaches within the leadership.[45] And then in '95 there was a situation [a division] that was not going to be resolved the

way it was in '83, but which could have led to some type of split. . . . Therefore, as I see it, what was done was to attempt to avoid a scandalous public split which would have affected the image of the FMLN.[46]

In December 1994, with the ERP and RN out, the FMLN celebrated its second national convention. The delegates, now also including members of the TD, rejected the previous conception of the FMLN as a "party of parties" and replaced it with the FMLN as a "party of tendencies." They were preoccupied with the "unification of the FMLN as a democratic, revolutionary, and pluralist party."[47] The three remaining PMOs announced publicly their decision to dissolve. As of January 1995, the FPL, PCS, and PRTC began to formally integrate substantial parts of previously separate efforts into the structures of the FMLN. By the end of 1995, the three organizations had officially ceased to exist, with their political structures absorbed into the FMLN.[48]

During that same year, a new group called the Tendencia Revolucionaria (TR)[49] emerged, formed by former PCS cadres and led by Dagoberto Gutiérrez. The group claimed to be dedicated to fueling ideological debate within the party. PCS insiders also pointed to personal rivalry between Gutiérrez and Schafik Handal, number one in the PCS hierarchy. In 1998 Gutiérrez and a small group of his followers left the FMLN to establish the TR as a nonpartisan political initiative.[50]

The Partido Demócrata

The ERP and RN formalized their new political project in March 1995 under the name of Partido Demócrata (PD),[51] with the motto "complete commitment to peace." Though programmatically social democrat, the PD in practice prioritized marking political distance from FMLN "extremists." In Joaquín Villalobos's words: "The enemies of the system are our enemies, and those who conspire against it, conspire against us" (PD 1995). In May 1995 the PD signed a political agreement with ARENA called the San Andrés Pact. It outlined reforms such as fiscal modernization, public investment, the privatization of public companies, and a drastic increase of the police force. Shortly afterwards, PD votes helped pass a controversial government bill for sales tax increases (Hernández

Pico 1995). Then, in the summer of 1995, Joaquín Villalobos announced that he had been offered a scholarship to study at Oxford University.[52]

The events of 1994–95 left the ERP and RN militancy in disarray. With few exceptions, the RN and ERP cadres who had been elected to public office on the FMLN ballot in 1994 flowed into the PD. However, support for "the Villalobos line" was much less consolidated among mid-level and lower-ranking militants. Logically, the PD attempted to build on the existing ERP and RN networks as a starting point for their party. However, in the field, political affinities had become divided between the PD and the FMLN. ERP and RN dissidents who had remained inside the FMLN, like those belonging to the TD for example, tried to pull their former ERP comrades towards the FMLN.

Among ERP and RN militants, some questioned the separation from the FMLN on ideological grounds. Others had little confidence that their historical leadership would be able to successfully articulate an alternative political project. Villalobos's decision to move to England, thus effectively depriving the PD of its most visible leader and partially abandoning the project he himself had propelled, stunned friend and foe.[53]

The Emergence of the Conflict between Ortodoxos and Renovadores

As a result of the 1995 unification, former FPL cadres now represented a majority in the FMLN, and Sánchez Cerén took over as party leader in lieu of Schafik Handal. Soon after, new internal differences came to light, pitting two tendencies against each other: a reform-oriented group that would become known as *renovadores* and a group later identified as revolutionary socialists or *ortodoxos*. The FPL played an important role in the new internal conflict that mirrored the debates within the FPL during the last few years of its existence. According to a document produced by a group of anonymous FMLN militants in October 1995,

> while what is spoken about in FMLN meetings is the formation of tendencies corresponding to the parties which constitute it, in reality two tendencies have emerged and are present throughout the FMLN: . . . the conservative tendency, which, without explicitly opposing renovation, seeks to maintain intact the same objectives, methods, structures, conceptions, and leaders from the past; and the renewal tendency, which aspires to develop within the FMLN the

fundamental components of the party project proposed initially by the FPL. . . . Of these two implicit tendencies, that which is imposing itself is the conservative one, given that . . . it has a more organic constitution, based principally upon the structure, ideology, and leadership of the PC [PCS]. . . . The majority of FPL leaders and activists are in favor . . . of renovation.[54]

The document, written from the perspective of FPL *renovadores*, downplayed the FPL's own level of division and insinuated a contradiction within the FMLN between the PCS and the FPL. This strategy was an attempt to ground the political conflict in the FPL's historical identity, drawing on FPL apprehensions toward the PCS as inherited from the 1970s and 1980s. In reality, the former FPL cadres had become increasingly divided between those supporting a "revolutionary socialist" profile, similar to Schafik Handal's position, and those supporting social-democratic "renovation."

The 1997 Elections

The PD's campaigning efforts for the 1997 election were marred by growing internal divisions within the former ERP and RN networks. Many former supporters had become so disillusioned with internal affairs and the postwar political turmoil that they had little appetite for campaigning on behalf of the PD.[55] As a result, the electoral performance of the PD was very poor, gaining only 1 percent of the vote. The PD delivered a sole deputy to the new legislative assembly, which it was able to obtain through its alliance with the PDC in San Miguel (TSE 1997).

By contrast, the FMLN captured 33 percent of the vote, almost doubling its total number of deputies in the legislative assembly and winning forty municipalities, including the capital city of San Salvador. In the run-up to the 1997 elections, the FMLN actively constructed electoral alliances with small center-left forces like the CD and Movimiento de Unidad (MU), an evangelical party (Artiga-González 2006, 2015). Such coalitions helped the FMLN defeat ARENA in major cities like Santa Ana and San Salvador. The FMLN was also able to prolong its electoral mandate in those municipalities already won in 1994, with the exception of three of the five municipal governments previously won in Morazán (Loya Marín 2008, 76).

The FMLN leadership attributed the electoral success particularly to the sustained efforts, since early 1995, to strengthen the organizational base of the unified party. At the end of 1995, the FMLN registered a total of twenty-eight thousand affiliated members, the result of stimulating the participation of former PMO militants in electoral politics as well as promoting the incorporation of new sectors into party activity, especially at a local level.[56]

The Escalation of the Internal Conflict

The simmering contradictions between renovadores and ortodoxos led to increased confrontation after the 1997 elections. In late 1997, the renovadores successfully moved to displace revolutionary-socialist Sánchez Cerén as secretary general and install Facundo Guardado, the 1997 campaign leader and main spokesperson for the renovadores, as the new FMLN leader. A prominent FPL leader before and during the war, Facundo Guardado had started his political career as a key figure in the prewar revolutionary peasant movement in Chalatenango. Guardado's detractors accused the renovadores of manipulating the internal election process. They organized their efforts into the Corriente Revolucionaria Socialista (CRS)[57] as a tendency within the FMLN, while their opponents and the press continued to refer to this group as ortodoxos.[58]

The escalation of the conflict led to both sides engaging in extensive organizational efforts in order to solidify internal support. The growing dispute helped create an environment of mutual distrust and conspiracy, in which the CRS and the renovadores increasingly started to function as two parallel and competing organizations under the umbrella of the FMLN (Dada Hirezi 2002; Ramos 1998, 1999; Zamora 1998).[59]

Considering the favorable results of the 1997 elections and the popularity of figures like Héctor Silva, San Salvador's new mayor, many observers considered that the FMLN had a real chance of winning the 1999 presidential elections. ARENA fielded Francisco Flores, a relatively unknown and unpopular figure, increasing the hopes of the opposition. However, the FMLN's conflict escalated further in 1998, during the selection process for the presidential candidate. As a result, the FMLN's campaign became subordinated to the internal dispute. According to a CRS sympathizer I interviewed for this study, the FMLN's electoral possibilities were sacrificed as follows. "How did Schafik wrest control of the party from Facundo? Their plan was to make [Facundo] presidential candidate so that he would lose the elections and sink himself, while they went about incorporating . . . new affiliates in order to have a majority. . . . Schafik said, 'We are going to lose, but we will lose with Facundo.'"[60]

The CRS refused to support the FMLN's campaign efforts, arguing that, if he won, Guardado would end up selling out the FMLN to the country's right-wing forces. The renovadores, in turn, were furious at what they called "sabotage" of Guardado's campaign. ARENA took the 1999 presidential elections in the first round.

Meanwhile, both sides had been preparing for the FMLN's internal elections by organizing and affiliating many new members in support of their factional position. Soon after the FMLN's electoral debacle, over sixty thousand affiliated militants participated in an extensive process of internal elections defining party leadership at different levels.[61] As a result of this process, the CRS regained control over the FMLN, albeit with a relatively small margin. Guardado lost his position as party leader.[62]

The CRS further improved its internal position within the FMLN through its candidates on the ballot for the legislative and municipal elections in 2000. In these elections, the FMLN performed much better than the year before. For the first time after the war, ARENA ceased to be the largest faction in parliament, with the FMLN leading, thirty-one to twenty-nine. To ensure a legislative majority, ARENA would depend increasingly on support from small right-wing parties. Furthermore, the FMLN won seventy-eight municipal governments, including most major cities, overtaking ARENA in percentage of population governed at the municipal level (TSE 2000).

The CRS Takes Control of the Party

The disputes within the FMLN continued into the decade after 2000, now with the CRS generally holding the upper hand and the reformists internally divided in smaller subgroups. In May 2001, Sánchez Cerén managed to regain the post of party leader, and the CRS appointed its supporters to lead a so-called Honorary Tribunal. In October of that year, this tribunal expelled Facundo Guardado from the FMLN. CRS member and FMLN deputy Humberto Centeno stated in the press that Facundo Guardado was an "infiltrator financed by the right to destroy the party" and that "this is the year of cleansing within the FMLN."[63]

Renovador leader Francisco Jovel and five other deputies abandoned the FMLN's legislative faction in support of Guardado. However, when Guardado launched a new party called Movimiento Renovador (MR)[64] in April 2002, its legislative faction consisted of only four deputies. Jovel, a former member of the PRTC, preferred to ally with former PD activists to establish a new party called Partido Social Demócrata (PSD) (Cañas 2002).[65] Another deputy decided to return to the FMLN in an attempt to avoid expulsion.[66] San Salvador's mayor Héctor Silva also left the party, in his case to join the Centro Democrático Unido (CDU),[67] a new party that continued with the project of the extinguished CD.

Tension remained, and later that year, a group of FMLN activists attacked and partially destroyed the parliamentary office of the MR faction.[68] Similar to what had happened to Joaquín Villalobos's PD years before, the participation of the MR and PSD as political parties in the 2003 elections was not a success. The two parties failed to win a single deputy and were subsequently canceled by El Salvador's Electoral Tribunal (TSE) for failing to meet minimal vote requirements. The FMLN, on the other hand, booked results similar to those of the previous elections, with ARENA continuing to lose ground, but still able to control the parliament through alliances with other right-wing parties (TSE 2003).

A Preliminary Balance of the Insurgents' Political Reconversion

The first decade after the peace accords witnessed the emergence and consolidation of the FMLN as the country's main opposition party. In this sense, the FMLN's political reconversion, "though marred by internal party conflict, has been one of the most successful examples of a guerrilla movement turned political party" (Wade 2008, 145). Surveys indicate that, since 1997, the FMLN performed particularly well among better-educated middle-class segments (Santacruz Giralt 2003). Artiga-González speaks of "the urbanization of the FMLN" (2006, 62). Like its main rival, ARENA, the FMLN gradually developed the ability to field thousands of trained activists before, during, and after election day to participate in campaigning and in the "defense of the vote" (Almeida 2010, 320; Quintanilla Gómez 2010, 37–38). By virtue of the different resources at its disposal, the FMLN was able to "outcampaign" its competitors, with the exception of ARENA.

During the postwar years, each of the five PMOs suffered internal conflicts between groups who can be seen as moderates and radicals, though these conflicts might also be interpreted in terms of a dispute between different aspiring leadership groups. The ERP expelled a group of militants identified as the TD, which later integrated back into the FMLN when the ERP left. The PCS suffered two split-offs, both relatively small (UDN and TR). When the ERP and the RN abandoned the FMLN in 1994, a small RN faction remained inside the FMLN. The FPL remained stable at first, but eventually internal contradictions became a major factor in the conflict between the renovadores and the CRS, a conflict that eventually culminated in the expulsion of Facundo Guardado and the exit of other renovadores, most of them with links to the FPL. The PRTC also became entangled in this conflict.

In general terms, those who split off from the FMLN or were expelled from it were largely unable to articulate viable political alternatives in the electoral arena. The failure of such initiatives contributed to further disintegration of PMO networks involved. In turn, as the revolutionary socialists augmented their control, the FMLN continued to be electorally strong. Postwar political accommodations resulted in former FPL and PCS cadres becoming the FMLN's backbone. The PRTC only represented a small portion of postwar FMLN membership, limiting its political role. On the other hand, for the ERP and RN, the abandonment of the FMLN and the subsequent failure of the PD weakened their political networks considerably.

SOCIAL-ECONOMIC RECONVERSION

The NGO Boom

As we saw at the beginning of this chapter, the socioeconomic development strategy laid out in the internal documents of the FPL essentially consisted of reconverting the civil-political front into a channel for development projects to benefit historical PMO constituents. The international community made available substantial funds for reconstruction efforts in El Salvador and channeled a large chunk of these funds through NGOs

(Boyce 1999; Wood 1999). PMO-connected NGOs generally multiplied their project portfolios, budgets, and staff members. These NGOs mostly attended to demobilized former insurgents, and at the same time they also became an important source of employment, in particular for cadres with a university education.

In the case of the FPL, Asociación para la Cooperación y Desarrollo Comunal de El Salvador (CORDES), an NGO charged with projects for the benefit of the FPL repopulations, is the best example. In the late 1980s CORDES had started out with a single staff member and a few small projects in a borrowed office space at the Jesuit university, UCA.[69] It worked closely with the Comité Cristiano Pro-Desplazados de El Salvador (CRIPDES),[70] the organization which coordinated the support for all FPL-affiliated resettlement efforts. As a result of reconstruction funding, by the late 1990s, CORDES worked with an annual budget of over $2 million and a professional staff of 124 people dedicated to the economic development of resettled communities in the FPL's former war zones (McElhinny 2006, 535). A large part of the insurgent health system providing medical care to FPL troops during the war was absorbed into PRO-VIDA, the FPL's health-care NGO. In 1992, FPL cadres also promptly gave birth to new organizations such as FUNDE, a think tank for alternative economic development; MAM, a women's NGO; and ISD, dedicated to election monitoring.[71]

The ERP's socioeconomic reconversion was initially influenced by its leadership's newfound enchantment with business development and entrepreneurship. In 1992, the ERP set up an NGO called PROESA[72] in San Salvador, dedicated to business development (Manzano Merino 1994, 20). In terms of postwar reconstruction, the ERP prioritized the development of the repopulated Ciudad Segundo Montes in Morazán as a "model" for alternative economic development (Macdonald and Gatehouse 1995). In Usulután, the ERP launched CODECOSTA to coordinate reconstruction and development projects for its settlements (Wood 2003, 181).[73]

On a slightly smaller scale, the remaining PMOs engaged in a similar dynamic of attending to their "own" communities by means of affiliated NGOs.[74] In the case of the RN, the NGO REDES became the most important channel for aid to constituent repopulations, mostly located in Cabañas and in Cuscatlán.[75] The PCS set up an NGO called CRD to obtain projects for the communities that hosted former FAL combatants and their families.[76] The PRTC founded a human rights group named

Centro para la Promoción de los Derechos Humanos "Madeleine Lagadec" (CPDH).[77] The PMOs also set up a couple of new integrated organizations with representatives of the different groups of the FMLN: Fundación 16 de Enero (F-16) for reinsertion projects, and FUNDASPAD, an NGO specializing in electoral training, education, and monitoring.[78]

The previous paragraphs help explain how (former) PMO affiliation continued to be an important ordering principle. As was already the case during the war, the NGOs belonging to the same PMO "family" established horizontal and vertical links, in the form of "networks" or "consortia," in order to facilitate cooperation, bundle projects, and solicit funders (Manzano Merino 1994). NGOs worked primarily with their respective wartime PMO constituencies. "Cinquismo,"[79] with each PMO connected to specific clusters of NGOs, networks, constituencies, and communities, became less rigid after the accords, but certainly did not disappear.

The former "civil-political front NGOs" provided new opportunities for the PMOs during peacetime. According to one observer, "civil-society organizations in El Salvador . . . helped to secure the commitment of higher-level cadres of the FMLN to the peace process by providing employment for them" (Foley 2010, 229). The NGOs relied on the cadres' wartime contacts and organizational experience. They also used discourses around empowerment and social transformation that presented continuities with the insurgents' revolutionary discourse (Silber 2004b). Previous PMO ties equipped NGOs with a crucial asset for development projects: well-organized beneficiaries. As Michael Foley puts it, "The Salvadoran NGOs founded by the FMLN were . . . grounded, thanks to their party ties, in the communities they served" (2010, 171). On the other side of the "development chain," the PMOs' international contacts helped introduce and recommend NGOs with potential donors. Cadres themselves often framed their NGO work in terms of "the professionalization of activism," and thus as a form of continuity of the political commitment acquired during the revolutionary process (Pirker 2007, 17).

The Rural Constituencies of the PMOs

The role of NGOs naturally went much further than providing employment for former PMO cadres. They functioned as a crucial service provider to the rural support bases of the insurgency. This endeavor built on the insurgency's repopulation and land-occupation movement. By 1992, each PMO already had its "own" communities in which its rural support-base had begun to settle, after previously residing in the refugee camps or living a nomadic existence on the war fronts. These communities were also the natural recipients of contingents of ex-combatants, since most had surviving family members in these places. For rural development efforts, the PMOs envisioned the land transfer program (PTT) as the foundation, and the ongoing development work of the NGOs as the catalyst.

The five Salvadoran PMOs all converted their rural base into repopulations.[80] Over a hundred of such insurgent settlements were founded during the last years of war and the first years of peace (Aquiles Montoya 1993, 2001). In accordance with the size of its rural constituency, the FPL gave birth to, by far, the largest number, followed by the ERP and the RN. The PRTC and PCS-FAL were connected to a significantly smaller number of settlements, since their wartime rural constituencies had been much smaller. In the negotiations of the PTT, the PMOs included claims on the properties in the area of existing repopulations and land occupations, but also far beyond. The PMOs not only sought to ensure the transfer of the lands around the communities already settled by their supporters, but also wanted their supporters to be able to take possession of new land with a higher agricultural potential.

By setting up formal community organizations, the PMOs ensured that the repopulations held the necessary political and legal tools to interact with outside entities, including the Salvadoran state (McElhinny 2006, 369). These community organizations negotiated the local implementation of postwar reconstruction projects offered by a range of international organizations and NGOs (van der Borgh 2003). The insurgent NGOs were not the only ones providing support projects, but, contrary to outside groups, they also were important behind-the-scenes political actors (Silber 2011). Postwar reconstruction thus simultaneously provided benefits for insurgents' rural constituencies as well as jobs for some of its (urban) cadres. The interaction maintained and updated historical relations.

Throughout the 1990s, the presence of the Salvadoran state in the repopulations remained limited. Community directives and left-wing NGOs saw government intervention as threatening to community cohesion and alternative development. The ARENA government, in turn, did not prioritize the repopulations in their public investments, because they saw them as opposition bulwarks. The result was that, during most of the 1990s, the repopulations were, politically speaking, still a relatively autonomous society within larger Salvadoran society. In his study on postwar development in the department of San Vicente, McElhinny argues that "a twelve year civil war brought into sharp relief a Salvadoran countryside governed by two parallel states." The political patterns were "so profoundly rooted that they would shape the expectations and behaviors of a generation of Salvadorans" during the postwar transition (2006, 761).

The political spirit of the repopulations as a polity distinct from the dominant Salvadoran state was kept alive. For example, the repopulations did not allow the Salvadoran government to simply roll out its public services, which were seen as of poor quality, unresponsive to specific community needs, and politically manipulative (Binford 1997; Smith-Nonini 2010). Instead, they relied on international cooperation and the NGOs that had sprouted from the insurgency to provide community support and basic services. Subsequently, the repopulations, sometimes backed by FMLN municipalities, would negotiate the terms on which public services were to be gradually reestablished, in arrangements that partially incorporated the human resources and infrastructure provided by the communities and the NGOs.[81]

The success of the PMO repopulations in providing economic prospects for their inhabitants was mixed. The productive projects set up during the 1990s succeeded in providing sustainable livelihoods only for some residents, not for all. Many collective initiatives like cooperatives and community enterprises shut down or ended up in private hands as soon as external funding started to dry up. In spite of the PTT and strong levels of NGO support, the agricultural prospects of the postinsurgent communities were not so rosy. Some repopulations did better than others. In the mountainous areas near the Honduran border, the poor quality of the land hampered agricultural possibilities. A substantial part of the land transferred in southern San Vicente and Usulután suffered from frequent floods. The liberalization of agricultural imports lowered product prices, especially for corn and beans, the staple crops. Due to various circumstances, more than half of the PTT land was still left uncultivated at the end of the 1990s (Alvarez 2003, 16).[82]

At the same time, a good number of insurgent communities were doing better, in relative terms, than nearby villages whose inhabitants had not been part of the insurgency. For example, in the southern part of San Vicente, with extensive support of CORDES and others, the repopulations achieved a level of economic dynamism that differentiated these communities positively from national average (Cummings 2007). There were other relevant achievements. For example, health-care provisions in the repopulated areas in Chalatenango performed well over national average for rural El Salvador (Smith-Nonini 2010). Several repopulations managed to air and sustain community radio stations (Agosta 2007; Ladutke 2004). Part of the earlier international solidarity transformed into partnership agreements in support of local development, as was the case with the Sister Cities network in the USA (Nepstad 2004).[83] Though less frequent than during the war, many repopulations continued to host international delegations and receive collaborations from solidarity groups abroad.[84]

Generally speaking, the repopulations were quite proactive in pursuing reconstruction and development programs (Sprenkels and van der Borgh 2017). Many of the peasants who had been active in the revolutionary movement had the skills to take on leadership roles in the new context (McElhinny 2006). As described in the previous chapter, the insurgent peasants had learned to transit from one political role into the next, and to use different political identities strategically to fit the circumstances: lay worker, cooperativist, union member, guerrilla organizer, refugee, combatant, settler, to name some of the most relevant. The peasant insurgents "saw their participation in each stage as a continuation of their insurgent identity, naturally arising out of earlier choices and experiences" (Wood 2003, 203). Similarly, many of them initially saw postwar reconversion as new step in that historical process. They interpreted or defended the new roles in terms of the continuity of the collective political project built with years of sacrifice (Silber 2004b).

Taking into account the political developments discussed earlier, it may not come as a surprise that socioeconomic reconversion was most controversial and conflictive in the case of the ERP. In 1992, the ERP had formulated the most ambitious economic development targets, with the repopulation of Ciudad Segundo Montes (CSM) as its showcase, under the motto "a hope born in the East for all El Salvador" (Gómez 2001, 136). CSM indeed had a promising start. It was more successful than other repopulations in obtaining technical assistance and international funding.[85] But postwar ambitions suffered dearly from the ERP's internal conflicts and its 1994 split from the FMLN. Community leadership became increasingly divided among supporters and detractors of Villalobos. The ERP's crisis became a vehicle and a catalyst for a range of personal disputes and power struggles. At this juncture, "everyone began to grab what they could,"[86] ruining most community projects. Many CSM inhabitants "pushed collective projects into the background or discarded them altogether in order to focus remaining energies on the household economy" (Binford 2010, 541).[87]

After the 1997 electoral failure of the PD, CSM and other repopulations in northern Morazán "returned to the FMLN fold, albeit under disadvantageous circumstances vis-à-vis the party" (Binford 2010, 547). Disappointment about the shattered dream of a prosperous CSM ran deep. According to several former ERP cadres interviewed for this study, in the late 1990s some CSM inhabitants allegedly wanted to "drink Villalobos's blood" and ERP former top leadership rarely showed its face in the region.[88] The case of CSM is somewhat extreme, but postwar disillusionment was also felt in other insurgent communities with ties to the other PMOs, as poignantly documented in the work of Irina Carlota Silber on Chalatenango (2004b, 2011). Notwithstanding strong community organizing and significant NGO presence, the attention and care received from former PMO leadership and middle cadres was considerably less than during the war. As Rubén Zamora noted, the people in the former insurgent communities started to complain, "They have left us alone; the comandantes drive by in their SUV's and only leave us the dust."[89] For rural constituencies, postwar reconversion by and large meant a return to the political periphery, as well as to a life in socioeconomic conditions that were a far cry from the promises of the revolution (Sprenkels 2004, 38).

In sum, the repopulations—much like the postinsurgent NGOs—managed to adapt to the new context with a combination of continuities and ruptures, of achievements and limitations. In contrast with wartime deprivation, poverty in the repopulations became less extreme. During the war, however, everybody had been equally poor and destitute. In the postwar years, local inequalities gradually became larger, and distribution of benefits and resources became marked by a complex, localized mix of interests, incentives, and remnants of cadre influence.[90] While some settlers were able to obtain cattle and sufficient access to land, others were facing severe poverty. In view of the limited rural livelihood possibilities, many former insurgents started to choose labor migration, mostly to the United States.

The Case of the Labor Unions

Arguably, the FMLN-affiliated labor unions were the least successful in adapting to the postwar circumstances. The 1990s in El Salvador constituted an "era of absolute decline for organized labor" (Almeida 2008, 195), with unions rapidly depleting and deflating. Already during the war, the work of the insurgent unions, though effective as a vehicle for popular mobilization and revolutionary agitation, had been precarious in most other aspects. Particularly, support to the workers they represented tended to be meager and ineffective (Frundt 2002, 31).

In 1992, when the FMLN comandantes were able to take up residency in San Salvador, they displaced leaders of political-civilian front organizations like labor federation UNTS from the spokesperson function they had previously held. The failure of the Socio-Economic Forum,[91] established as a result of the peace accords to promote dialogue between different socioeconomic forces in the country, was another severe setback for the unions. The premature and inglorious ending of the forum not only confirmed private enterprises' continued disdain for the labor unions; it also evidenced the FMLN's apathy toward the unions. According to Tracy Fitzsimmons and Mark Anner, four factors contributed to the unions' demise: political practices inherited from former PMO dominance; postwar abandonment by the FMLN; decline in external funding; and neoliberal reforms, including the privatization of state companies (1999, 115–20).

The case of FENASTRAS illustrates the sliding scale of postinsurgent union organizing.[92] Before, as the largest and most active insurgent labor-union federation, FENASTRAS was the "crown jewel" in the RN's civil-political front: an important source of political agitation, funds, and recruits for years on end. In reaction to the peace accords, FENASTRAS general secretary Juan José Huezo started to maneuver to loosen the union from the RN leadership while at the same time strengthening his personal position (Pirker 2008, 349). The RN leadership had little clarity on whether it wanted to use its influence in FENASTRAS, and if so, how; and they let it be. The scission of the RN from the FMLN further deep-

efforts, but of suppressing the organic character of these links. In practice, the move contributed to the gradual privatization of part of the resources the insurgents had collectively accumulated during the war.

The phenomenon may be best illustrated with the case of the insurgent radio networks: Radio Venceremos (RV) and Radio Farabundo Martí (RFM). In 1992, the staff of both networks had grand plans for their radio stations.[101] The FMLN negotiated their incorporation into the country's legal broadcasting system as part of the peace accords. Both the FPL and the ERP staged public events celebrating the "descent" of the rebel radios from the mountains to new outfits in the capital city, inaugurating a new era of liberty and freedom of speech in the country. Initially, both PMOs continued to envision the radio as an important political tool, and seemed willing to invest in professional reconversion. For example, the FPL agreed to subsidize the RFM operational costs until the end of 1992, with the understanding that afterward the radio would have to be self-sufficient (Leonhard 1999, 30). In this same year, "the rebel stations constituted themselves as commercial enterprises under the names of party members because it was the most agile method for their legalization" (3; see also Escalona 2003, 266).

In support of El Salvador's democratization process, the German foundation Buntstift set up a substantial support project for the radio projects linked to the former insurgency, with its kickoff in January of 1993. Apart from RV and RFM, the other PMOs were also working on launching their own radio projects, and lobbied to have them included in the Buntstift project.[102] However, "those responsible for the 'historical' radios did not want to share the pie and were able to leave them out" (Leonhard 1999, 32). In 1993, RV employed thirty-three people, while RFM had a forty people on its payroll who "considered the radio to be their [personal] reinsertion project" (38). From early 1993, the Buntstift project allowed RV and RFM to obtain high-quality equipment and to cover a substantial part of the operational costs. Both RV and RFM were able to purchase residences for their offices and studios. The networks attempted to complement the income by selling radio advertising and enlisting additional support from international cooperation agencies. In comparison to commercial networks, the staff was large and personnel costs were high.[103]

Radio Venceremos dealt with economic pressures by, on the one hand, trying to raise advertisement revenue and, on the other, reducing personnel. News coverage and other politically oriented items became scarce, and the radio's programming increasingly relied on music. Marketing studies even recommended reorienting radio programming toward contemporary music in English. A large part of the personnel resented the new course, including Carlos Henríquez Consalvi (also known as "Santiago"), the radio's founder and its public icon. Part of the remaining staff rebelled against the press director, seen as the main promoter of the new course, and went on strike. The press director, with the support of the majority of the directorate, pushed through the adjustments. In 1995, the radio dropped the name Radio Venceremos and became "RV stereo." The final traces of political engagement were eliminated from the programming. Early 1996, Santiago was fired and the RV withdrew from the Buntstift project. The network then refounded itself as private corporation. Its ten shareholders included Joaquín Villalobos, as well as the press director and his wife. "The Germans realized that, having trusted in the goodwill of their counterparts, they had financed the consolidation of a commercial radio station" (Leonhard 1999, 43).[104]

Radio Farabundo Martí's postwar journey showed many similarities. The personnel that the radio had inherited from its guerrilla years thought of the radio as ideologically connected to the party, but independent in terms of management. However, when economic pressures aggravated internal frictions, the FPL rapidly intervened and appointed a new director. His proposed "modernization" of the radio alienated the old guard and further escalated the internal conflict. The FPL's political commission then decided to replace him with another cadre, while simultaneously approving the proposed adjustments and firing fourteen staff members, including the most experienced broadcasters. The new director "had been an excellent comandante but knew nothing about radio" (cited in Leonhard 1999, 39). Meanwhile, in the search for audience and advertisement, the radio's political profile was further watered down. In the words of one of the protagonists, "the need to survive was confused with not being critical" (cited in Leonhard 1999, 41). The radio officially changed its name to "Doble FF" in 1995. Like RV Stereo, Doble FF became a commercial network apparently detached from its insurgent past, except for the handful of former FPL cadres functioning as its private shareholders or employees.[105] For those involved, the personal impact was enormous. Years later, FPL veteran and RFM staff member "Hugo" told me that for him the demise of the RFM was "more traumatic than the war."[106]

Some Effects of Changing Logic of PMO Affiliation on NGOs

Many other institutions and organizations with insurgent roots suffered comparable crisis in the postwar years. With a few noteworthy exceptions, most NGOs and grassroots organizations continued to function during the first year of peace with the organic and vertical political orientations that had been used during the war.[107] The majority of PMO cadres who were inserted in these organizations prided themselves on their PMO identity. Consistent with their training, most tended to see their PMO connection as more important and substantial than any other political relationship. Amidst the rapid changes of 1993, leadership of the different PMOs discussed the need to grant more political autonomy to the different organizations under their wings. Coincidentally, some cadres looked at these same organizations in terms of what they might have to offer for personal reinsertion.

The 1994 events concerning the ERP-affiliated human rights group Comité de Madres y Familiares Cristianos de Presos, Desaparecidos y Asesinados (COMAFAC) exemplify the many conflicts that emerged in Salvadoran grassroots organizations as a result of shifting relationships among former PMO cadres.[108] As Salvadoran newspaper *El Diario de Hoy* reported on April 14, 1994, a group of ERP militants had taken over COMAFAC's office and secured the entrance with chains and locks. During an interview years later, when I asked a former COMAFAC activist what had been at the heart of the conflict, she told me,

> The ERP wanted to take over the building [that COMAFAC was using] and put it to use for its own purposes. They told us that after the peace accords, we didn't have to fight anymore. They said we should just go on home, we had done our share. . . . When they saw that we didn't like it, they betrayed us. They even threatened us. This ugly man, . . . he said: all right, old women, you are lucky, because in another era we would have emptied this machine gun on you. They went as far as to threaten us. (Sprenkels 2005, 88)[109]

As ERP's Joaquín Villalobos has argued elsewhere (1999, 2001), he believed that the reforms resulting from the peace accords had largely re-solved the problem and the debt of human rights in El Salvador. Most activists involved in COMAFAC, many of them relatives of people that had been disappeared or assassinated by the military, had a different view. They wanted to know what had happened to their loved ones, and they wanted to fight for justice.[110] When the ERP attempted to take over the directorate and installations of the organization, they resisted. The "old" COMAFAC directorate issued a press release admitting COMAFAC's "organic connection" to the ERP during the war. Now that "the ERP was no longer interested in the defense of human rights," the COMAFAC dissidents wanted independence.[111]

COMAFAC dissidents asked those members of the FMLN leadership not affiliated to the ERP to intervene, but they were told that this was an internal affair of the ERP. They were also told not to make any more public announcements, as these could affect the FMLN negatively in the elections.[112] The alleged ERP plan to take over COMAFAC failed for other reasons. The building that COMAFAC's central office was housed in was not registered under COMAFAC's name, but under that of ANDES 21 de Junio, a union that happened to be mostly controlled by the FPL and the PRTC, not the ERP. This arrangement was set up in the late 1980s in response to formal donor requirements, since COMAFAC was not legally constituted at the time. As a result of the crisis, COMAFAC did lose another residential property (different from the organization's office) previously purchased with donor money that had fewer strings attached. The property in question, which had functioned as a day-care center, ended up in the hands of an individual ERP cadre. During the conflict, COMAFAC's bank accounts were emptied and office equipment was stolen.[113]

On June 5, 1994, COMAFAC held an assembly meeting to determine its future. Those still supporting the ERP were a minority and left the meeting before the election of a new directorate. That same month, two different petitions for the legal registration of COMAFAC were presented at the Ministry of Interior. The faction sympathetic to the ERP abandoned the project soon after.[114] COMAFAC managed to keep possession of its central office and gained independence from the ERP. However, the international donor agencies reacted to the crisis by suspending their support, leaving COMAFAC virtually bankrupt.[115]

Although media-reported conflicts like the case of COMAFAC were sporadic, the NGOs, unions, and social movements that suffered internal trauma after the peace accords were more common than those that did not. Cadres inserted in these groups interpreted talk about independence and autonomy in the light of what was perceived as crumbling cohesion or eroding group solidarity. Formerly, an internal dispute in any insurgency-affiliated organization would have been settled by the cadre appointed by the party or, alternatively, by his or her party superiors. In the new context, this mechanism had faded (it did not disappear completely), and other factors started to play a more prominent role. Some militants interpreted the party's relative hands-off stance as a "green light" to take possession of a particular organization or resources.

The disappearance of formal PMO hierarchies also had potentially positive effects. For example, the RN women's group Mujeres por la Dignidad y la Vida (Women for Dignity and Life; commonly known as "Las Dignas") started to fight for political independence in 1991, sometime before the RN leadership was actually prepared to accept it, and achieved its independence in 1992, which in turn helped it to transform itself into a relatively strong and autonomous women organization (Falquet 1997, 2002; Hipsher 2001, 140). But unlike Las Dignas, most groups had never asked for independence. The staff of most postinsurgent NGOs were uncertain what independence would mean and were divided on what to do with such independence. The fact that CORDES staff "no longer [received] orders," as one CORDES employee phrased it, did not mean that PMO authoritarianism had vanished (van der Borgh 2003, 157). While NGO leadership generally spoke of the need for participation and democracy, their management styles frequently reflected the contrary.

To make things worse, PMO politics would always find its way back into the NGOs' internal sphere. Different conflicts in and around the FMLN were commonly "restaged" in the particular institutional arenas controlled by former insurgents who were directly or indirectly party to these conflicts, as we have seen, for example, in the case of the separation of the UDN from the PCS, or the conflict at COMAFAC. The unitarian organizations suffered the most. The 1994 scission of the ERP and RN from the FMLN had a devastating impact on them. F-16 ceased to exist. NGOs like CDH-ES and FUNDASPAD, or unions like UNTS, survived the crisis but only as a shadow of their former selves, under the particular and personalized control of one of the factions in dispute.[116] Even when the FPL formally no longer existed, the escalating conflict between reno-vadores and ortodoxos brought internal strife to many NGOs, unions, and grassroots organizations formerly affiliated with the FPL. And when the Tendencia Revolucionaria abandoned the FMLN, it caused ripples in a few historical PCS organizations.

Electoral Success and Socioeconomic Conversion

Another area for socioeconomic reconversion emerged with the electoral successes of the FMLN. As is customary in Salvadoran politics, electoral success meant jobs for party militants and supporters. Even if the presidency stayed well out of reach during the 1990s, the FMLN did gradually increase municipal presence, particularly after the 1997 elections, when it won in several large cities, including the capital. While taking the elections in a small town somewhere in Chalatenango or Cabañas would generate only a handful of paid positions, San Salvador and the larger cities provided hundreds of potential jobs. Many of these were distributed among former insurgents.[117]

After the 1994 rupture, which left the FPL and PCS dominating the FMLN, cadres from these two organizations were most likely to access public office. Frequently the FMLN candidate for the mayor's office would also be a former cadre. Beyond positions of public election, former insurgent cadres, especially those with higher education, were generally well-positioned to obtain employment though political and personal contacts.[118] The access of former ERP and RN cadres to such opportunities was considerably more limited, with the exception of those close to the few ERP and RN leadership figures who had stayed inside the FMLN in 1994–95.

A PRELIMINARY BALANCE OF RECONVERSION EFFORTS

However precarious the circumstances of the war had been, for many years the party had provided for the basic needs of the cadres and the rank and file. This proved financially unsustainable during the transition process. Reducing the number of cadres who relied on the party coffers soon became a top priority.[119] For example, several longstanding militants who were engaged in international work were informed that they would no longer receive financial support. Should they decide to return to El Salvador, they were told, they should "first look for work and then look up the party"[120]—a bitter instruction for someone who had dedicated the better part of his or her life to the revolution.

The insurgents' postwar livelihoods were, for the most part, connected to three interrelated possibilities: reinsertion benefits, access to the state (mainly public office and PNC), and socioeconomic reconstruction programs. The first option, reinsertion, was hampered by problems of sustainability. When seen in relation to other reconversion processes, reinsertion programs did have three long-term effects on the postinsurgent social field. Because of the former insurgents' persistent struggle around the PTT and debt cancelation, former rural insurgents were able to take possession of a significant portion of El Salvador's agricultural land. This helped to retain a rural constituency closely tied to the FMLN. Under the prevailing economic circumstances, the land obtained was insufficient, but it nonetheless constituted a durable benefit directly connected to people's former participation in the armed struggle. Reinsertion scholarships prompted the second long-term effect. Hundreds of PMO cadres, primarily of the urban middle class, were able to get degrees that facilitated access to various bureaucratic jobs or political posts.[121] Finally—though the long-term impact of this is less clear—several hundred former insurgents were able to pursue careers within the newly constituted National Civilian Police (Costa 1999).

The constitution of the FMLN as a political party initially provided only limited possibilities for postwar reinsertion, and then mainly for top leadership. Strict hierarchical party control was difficult to sustain without the justification of war and adequate finances. The need to rethink internal governance was complicated by the PMOs' ongoing conflicts over the correct political course for the new period. These conflicts precipitated the formal dissolution of the PMOs, culminating in the 1995 reconversion of the five PMOs into two political parties: the FMLN and the PD. Another small party, the UDN, had split off from the PCS earlier on. The FMLN, a bigger organization from the outset, proved much more successful at the ballots than its dissidents. It was subsequently able to garner a significant number of public-sector office jobs, and filled them largely with people drawn from the former PMO networks. The PD's electoral failure, on the other hand, accentuated the disintegration of the ERP and RN networks, already in disarray because of the split-off from the FMLN.

The FMLN's focus on elections translated into increased bureaucratization and a "low capacity for renewal of party leadership" (Martín Alvarez 2006, 113–15). Internal disputes over candidacies and other electoral calculations clashed with conceptions of revolutionary militancy assimilated in previous years (Martí i Puig and Figueroa Ibarra 2006, 210). The former insurgents were constrained by the logic of the political reconversion they had embraced. "The leaders had to reside in the country's capital; the lifestyle for the leaders began to be different, they had to adopt clothing, housing, and means of physical mobility which clearly differentiated them from the living conditions of their grassroots compañeros. These changes signified a weakening of the internal political relationship and gave rise to a feeling of abandonment within an important grassroots sector of the FMLN" (Zamora 2003, 120–21).

Another review identified a similar downside to electoral politics: "An FMLN deputy . . . complained that his own party had lost what he called the proximity to the people which it had during the war. The system has turned into a political race for power, for partisan interests, and the interests of the country have been forgotten" (Ramos and Briones 1999, 53).

In the interviews I conducted with former insurgents, many argued that the FMLN's "successful" adaptation to electoral politics in the 1990s lay, at least in part, in its capacity to behave much like other "traditional" political parties competing in the Salvadoran political arena. In place of the utopian horizon of the revolutionary era, the party now offered its militancy "bureaucratic incentives": most concretely, access to public office and jobs (Martín Alvarez 2004, 267). Nonetheless, the party's revolutionary past still played a crucial role, not so much as a political agenda, but rather as an identity marker (Martí i Puig and Figueroa Ibarra 2006, 213). For example, the recycling of wartime ideologies was a key component of the struggle between different currents within the FMLN (Ramos 1998, 38). Imputed ideological continuities also allowed for the semantic cohesion of the struggles fought in and sacrifices made over the years. Thus, the revolutionary heritage became an important organizational tool, even more so because "the logic of a leadership based upon charisma and organizational control survived after the revolutionary process was abandoned" (Martí i Puig and Figueroa Ibarra 2006, 208). At the same time, the FMLN demonstrated pragmatism and ideological flexibility in the negotiation of pacts and alliances to strengthen its access to power (Luis González 2003).

The PMOs' wartime accumulation of affiliated NGOs, unions, social movements, repopulated communities, grassroots organizations, and the like jointly provided the framework for a third significant cluster of postinsurgent reconversion strategies. The flow of international resources dedicated to postwar reconstruction and development projects allowed the former insurgent NGOs to grow and multiply. They provided employment to former PMO cadres and captured resources for the repopulations. But not all former insurgent organizations were successful in making the transition to peace. Divergent postwar visions, leadership problems, and echoes of PMO conflict were factors that hampered institutional reconversion (Segovia, Barba, and Suay 2015). As PMO control faded, individual cadres would sometimes take advantage to "privatize" formerly collective enterprises for the benefit of the cadres' own inner circle.

Former insurgents trying to make a career in the NGOs often became involved in debates on tensions between professionalization and activism (Frankland and Rihoux 2008; Pirker 2008; Tarrow 2005). A related postwar discussion unfolded over the extent to which, and the conditions under which, social organizations with revolutionary roots should grant legitimacy to the outcomes of neoliberal democratic transition, a discussion revolving around whether the outcomes of the transition warranted radical and confrontational action, and if so, when. Van Leeuwen referred to this dilemma as "to conform or to confront?" (2010, 91).

In the former conflict zones, the repopulations did not become the utopian "model" communities the revolutionaries envisioned. However, in comparison to other rural communities in El Salvador, they did not do poorly either. Rural participants in insurgency built on their organizational experience and their extensive ties with NGOs to mobilize resources and to constitute local power, in explicit opposition to ARENA, and were only partially integrated within state structures (McElhinny 2006).

The different spheres of the PMO networks remained connected, but more loosely and ambiguously than before. References to historical affiliation coexisted with complaints about lack of attention or even abandonment by the leadership. Though sometimes differently than the insurgents imagined when they laid out their strategy after the peace accords, the three separate dimensions of the reconversion process exterted considerable influence on each other. The political crisis within the ERP, for example, had disastrous effects on the socioeconomic development of the repopulation of Ciudad Segundo Montes (Binford 2010).

Overall, the meager results of reinsertion led to increased demands on the FMLN to procure employment for PMO cadres and rank and file. Those involved in electoral politics, in turn, would visit formerly affiliated NGOs to ask for campaign contributions or to recruit collaborators to staff the voting centers.[122] In spite of limitations, for some PMO sectors the multitrack reconversion process did come near the mutually reinforcing system previously envisioned.

ADJUSTMENT TO PEACE led to many and profound changes in El Salvador's insurgency. During the war, the PMOs constructed complex and sophisticated organizational arrangements, tying together different political, social, military, and economic instruments. With the onset of peace, PMO leadership anticipated a series of postwar reconversions that might jointly strengthen the political collective. In their eyes, successful adjustment required building on the resources accumulated during armed struggle. They devised a range of strategies to turn these into "launch pads" for reconversion (Moallic 2014).

Internal PMO relations played an important role in the postwar reconversion strategies. Most PMO leadership realized that survival as a political force depended, at least in part, on the economic viability of the postwar livelihoods of its cadres and constituents. They were also confronted with neoliberal adjustment policies that sometimes counteracted the negotiated benefits, for example the land transfers. In turn, peace granted the former insurgents the possibility to compete for power in elections.[123]

During the reconversion process, socioeconomic differences among former insurgents soon started to generate tensions. As one study assessing the need for "democratic dialogue" in postwar El Salvador pointed out:

This process [of productive integration into national life] is in many ways simpler with elites than with the rank and file, because with the former it is essentially a process of *reintegration*, whereas with the latter the challenge is really one of *integrating* large numbers of people who had in most cases only a marginal participation to begin with. The FMLN leaders in many cases went to the same schools as their counterparts on the government side in the civil war, and in some cases are even from the same families. But in any event they tend to be well educated, cosmopolitan, middle-aged (thus more experienced) and used to dealing with other elites on terms of respect. On the other hand, the lower ranking participants in the war are largely less educated, provincial and much less experienced (after a 12-year war, many of them have known little else in their adult lives except combat). (Blair et al. 1995; emphasis original)

Postinsurgent reconversion strategies contributed to growing internal differentiation, both between different sectors formerly united in the insurgency and within these particular sectors. In pursuit of livelihoods and careers, former cadres would sometimes even position themselves to the detriment of their former comrades and "privatize" assets previously seen as collective property. A former FPL militant diagnosed the phenomenon as follows: "[In 1992], people begin to think about their life project and this begins to interfere with the collective and partisan projections; . . . it generates a certain type of dynamic where at times it is no longer apparent where the party ends and . . . where the personal begins."[124]

Former insurgents often lamented what they saw as deterioration of in-group solidarity and understood this in terms of the breakdown of revolutionary ideals. The conflicts and ruptures witnessed within and between the PMOs prompted some former insurgents to accuse former comrades of "treason." Increased inequality and the partial privatization of the insurgency's collective conquests contributed to a deep sense of disenchantment. The crudest classification of this phenomenon was that of a former RN militant turned NGO activist who lamented that "the new slogan after the war is 'each man for his own.'"[125] Such sensitivities accompanied and counterbalanced the nonnegligible gains achieved during the first decade of postinsurgency.

Disillusionment notwithstanding, many former insurgents relied on the interpersonal ties developed during the war to survive in peacetime. The manner in which, and the extent to which, they were able to do so differed significantly depending upon their position and standing, and upon which PMO they had belonged to. It also depended on the particular skills they had developed during their revolutionary career, some of which allowed for peacetime reconversion more easily than others. All PMOs formally dissolved as organic entities, but this did not mean that they also disappeared as relevant interpersonal networks.

PART 2

———————

ETHNOGRAPHIES OF POSTINSURGENCY

CHAPTER 5

Inside Chalatenango's Former "People's Republic"

Siguiendo a la organización es que nos vinimos p'acá.
—Severina, inhabitant of Ellacuría

In 2009 I organized a fieldwork seminar for Salvadoran anthropology students in Ellacuría, a repopulation with a little over five hundred inhabitants in northeastern Chalatenango. One of the students' assigned tasks was to perform a survey which interrogated the local inhabitants on family background, wartime participation, and political preferences. Three elements stood out from the survey results. The first was the fact that almost half of Ellacuría consisted of families who had their roots not in Chalatenango but in the neighboring department of Cabañas, and that only one family considered itself as originally from this village. The second was that, apart from a majority of FPL participants, several former PCS-FAL insurgents had also settled in the community. Finally, we stumbled over an interesting paradox: almost two decades after the peace accords, the political support for the FMLN in Ellacuría continued to be very high, while, in contrast, appreciation for community organization and local leadership was slight.

The three issues, though uncontroversial in themselves, did generate interesting questions. For example, why was there only one native family among the local inhabitants, if the repopulation movement's slogan had been "return to our places of origin"? Why did people from Cabañas decide to repopulate Ellacuría and stay there after the war, rather than returning home? Why were there both FPL and PCS-FAL families in the community? How to interpret the limited enthusiasm of Ellacuría's inhabitants for local politics? Why, in contrast, was there still such strong continued public support for the FMLN as a political party? When I set out explore these questions in ethnographic fieldwork, the local inhabitants often recurred to stories about clandestine relationships in the community, stories that previously had been censored or shared only in the realm of the revolutionary movement. As anthropologist Olga González points out, "Secrecy is a component of truth, particularly in a context of war" (2011, 210). Insurgent participation, so I learned, played a larger and more contentious role than is often assumed, and held strong implications for the lived experience of the repopulation movement and its aftermath.

THE STUDY OF EL SALVADOR'S REPOPULATION MOVEMENT

Over the years, the repopulations have spoken to the imagination of many revolutionaries, "fellow travelers," and students of revolution and political change. The peasant families that repopulated abandoned towns, while the war was still raging, testified to the resilience and resolve of the insurgency's grassroots supporters. A significant part of the international sympathy for the Salvadoran revolutionaries was channeled into the repopulations. With it came a steady flow of international visitors eager to catch a glimpse of the guerrillas and to learn from the transformations taking place in these communities. As Brandt Peterson explains, "The importance of the repopulations to the FMLN cannot be overstated. They showed the world the revolutionaries as community organizers and defenders and gave a face to the FMLN supporters, contradicting the US and Salvadoran governments' insistence that the guerrillas had no significant support among the rural poor. They also provided the FMLN combatants with bases in civilian populations, allowing the revolutionaries 'to move among the people as a fish swims in the sea'" (2006, 166–67).

The repopulations became a display window for revolutionary El Salvador, a laboratory for a new and just society (Lindsay-Poland 1989, 34). "The remarkable achievements of the [Salvadoran] refugees . . . are not only a triumph of will and courage but also an inspiration for those who seek some escape from the despair and torment that have settled over Central America and much of the Third World," Noam Chomsky wrote.[1]

In part because of this inspirational role, El Salvador's insurgent re-populations have been studied extensively. Over the last two decades, the bulk of social science scholarship on rural community development in El Salvador has specifically focused on repopulations.[2] Most authors emphasize the substance and depth of the transformations that have taken place in particular features of community life as a result of the participation in the insurgency and its organizational legacies. For example, Molly Todd (2010) offers that the refugees, and later the *repobladores*,[3] in spite of the dire circumstances of war, were able to turn their disadvantageous condition into a method of political empowerment and thus transform themselves, from dispossessed and persecuted into citizens. Elisabeth Wood (2003) documents how rural insurgents were able to redraw the land-property maps in the coastal regions of Usulután. John Hammond (1998) ponders how the alternative popular education system the insurgents set up during the war helped empower both individuals and communities, and equipped them to contribute to a larger collective struggle while at the same time challenging the status quo of social inequality in the country. Sandy Smith-Nonini focuses on the achievements of the popular health system forged during the insurgency and then consolidated in the repopulations, which helped local women with little formal schooling to become popular nurses and health promoters (2010).

A very different reading on the repopulations comes from anthropologist Julia Dickson-Gómez (2002, 2004). In her account, war trauma and unresolved grief draw a heavy burden on community life. She describes the repopulated community as reverberating with distrust, confusion, and resentment. For Dickson-Gómez, talk of cooperation and development constitutes no more than a thin veneer over torment and division (2002, 2004). "The war taught campesinos [peasants] that people, neighbors as well as government forces, are capable of betrayal, extreme violence and duplicity. Similar behavior is therefore expected in the future. Neighbors' potential for violence and betrayal is communicated through accusations of envy and gossip" (2002, 420).

The work of anthropologist Philippe Bourgois on peasant supporters of the FMLN partially concurs with Dickson-Gómez, but is unique in that it connects findings from two very different moments in time. His first stretch of fieldwork was in 1981, when, in the midst of war, he joined the insurgent masas in Cabañas and was forced flee with them from a crushing military operation (Bourgois 1982). After the war, Bourgois reconnects with some of the people he met under these circumstances (2001, 2002). These encounters lead him to rethink some of his earlier conclusions about the relationship between the peasants and the FMLN. Not only the violent government persecution but also the internal guerrilla violence has left deep wounds.

[Earlier,] it was difficult for me to perceive and portray the revolutionary Salvadoran peasants as anything less than innocent victims, at worst, or as noble resisters at best. The urgency of documenting and denouncing state violence and military repression blinded me to the internecine everyday violence embroiling the guerrilla(s) and undermining their internal solidarity. As a result I could not understand the depth of the trauma that political violence imposes on its targets, even those mobilized to resist it. This is not to deny, however, that the peasants also took pride in mobilizing. (2001, 28)

Leigh Binford, a student of the insurgent communities in northern Morazán, takes issue with Bourgois's retrospective reassessment. He considers that, save a few exceptions, the insurgents' government was relatively benign. According to Binford, the ERP acted with "moderation in the application of disciplinary violence," and actually succeeded in diminishing some forms of everyday violence amongst the peasants, like domestic abuse (2002, 204). Binford thinks that the repobladores' negative portrayal of guerrilla experiences may be linked, at least in part, to "the frustration felt by former rebels and their supporters" with regard to postwar marginalization and the continued socioeconomic inequalities in the country (205). In a later piece, Binford extends this argument by ascribing a variety of problems with postwar development in the repopulation of Ciudad Segundo Montes to its postwar integration into national and international capitalist circuits of production and exchange (2010).

Several other scholars, like Kowalchuk (2004, 2005) and Brandt Peterson (2006), have also called attention to the loss of morale among El Salvador's former revolutionary peasants. Especially eloquent is anthropologist Irina Carlota Silber's work on a repopulation she calls "El Rancho" in Chalatenango. Reflecting on the voices of the female repobladoras she befriended, Silber analyzes their growing disillusionment with development projects, community affairs, and revolutionary politics at large

(2004a, 2004b, 2006). Later, she also reflects on how a good part of El Rancho's repobladores became caught up in a new type of displacement, that of living clandestinely as a migrant worker in the US (Silber 2011, 2014).

Scholars like M. Cruz (2004a, 2004b), McElhinny (2006), and Smith-Nonini (2010), on the other hand, reject pessimistic readings and emphasize what they view as enduring positive effects of empowerment, in spite of the hostile neoliberal context these communities have had to survive in. Anna Peterson urges us not to ignore "real material and political gains" (2005, 75).

Scholars disagree both on the nature and on the extent of the transformations that have taken place in the insurgent repopulations. The disparate readings reviewed here might respond, in part, to the many rapid changes that took place in the repopulations over the last decades as well as to possible regional and local differences between communities studied. The use of distinct methodological and interpretive lenses appears to be another factor of weight. An additional issue is that, even though most scholars acknowledge that the repopulations' genesis is connected to the FMLN, the specificities of the relations between the repobladores and the PMOs remain understudied.[4] Especially during the war, the study of PMO ties qualified as a complex and delicate matter.[5] Their existence was exactly the accusation that the Salvadoran government and the military used in their attempts to obstruct or discredit the repopulation movement. Furthermore, the notion of PMOs operating behind the scenes did not harmonize with the portrayal of peasant agency that most scholars aimed for. They thought of the repopulations essentially as a project of moral empowerment, leaving military implications uncharted.

THE REPOPULATION MOVEMENT IN ITS HISTORICAL CONTEXT

By the mid-1980s most peasant PMO supporters who had survived the repression were located in refugee camps, while only small groups had remained sheltered in the insurgent stronghold areas. Dozens of church-managed refugee camps existed, mostly around the capital city of San Salvador.[6] Additionally, there were three major camps in Honduras, not far from the border with El Salvador: Mesa Grande, Colomoncagua, and San Antonio.[7] The guerrilla played an important role in the Honduran camps, with each PMO managing its own network of cadres and attending to their "own" masas. Affiliation was distributed as follows: the FPL and the RN, later joined by the PCS-FAL, in Mesa Grande; the ERP in Colomoncagua; and the PRTC together with a small contingent of FPL in San Antonio.[8] In 1986, these camps harbored approximately twenty-two thousand refugees.[9]

Lengthy and complex political negotiations preceded the establishment of the first repopulations.[10] With the war dragging on, and in the context of the Central American peace process,[11] strong international pressure emerged on behalf of the permanent resettlement of Salvadoran refugees (CIREFCA 1989; Sollis 1992).[12] The Catholic Church, concerned with the unsustainable situation in the camps they were running, became a persistent advocate for repopulations.[13] The Duarte government was partially open to the idea. The Salvadoran army was wary that, unless restricted and controlled, repopulations might improve the insurgency's military and political position.[14]

Early 1986, two large military operations resulted in the detention of small groups of masas in the mountains of Guazapa and Chalatenango (Edwards and Tovar Siebentritt 1991, 50–51). Their lives were respected and they were handed over to the Catholic Church. The FPL leadership, meanwhile, debated whether it made sense to continue with the masas at the front. The remaining families were exhausted. The argument to keep them in hiding to prevent massacre had proven to be no longer valid. It was decided that a group would descend at dawn from the mountains into the town of Dulce Nombre de María in Chalatenango.[15] They locked themselves inside the church. Soon, the military came, forced open the doors, captured the entire group, and transported them to the 4th Brigade barracks. A few days later, they were released and taken to the Calle Real refugee center, where they were reunited with those captured earlier.[16]

This same group then prepared the return to Chalatenango. They selected an abandoned and overgrown village in the middle of the FPL rearguard. On June 20, 1986, a group of some 120 refugees founded the repopulation of San José Las Flores.[17] Progressive sectors of the Catholic Church buttressed the initiative,[18] and the Sisters of the Assumption established a small convent in town. In subsequent months, several families that had still been accompanying the guerrillas also settled in Las Flores. Similar repopulation experiences followed later that year in other parts of El Salvador, like El Barrillo, for masas affiliated with the RN, and Panchimilama, for masas affiliated with the PCS-FAL.[19]

In 1987, repopulation efforts received an additional boost with the re-patriation of thousands of refugees from the Honduras camps to found communities in Chalatenango, Cuscatlán, and Cabañas.[20] Most families that participated in this return were organized with the FPL, except for the group that settled in Santa Marta, Cabañas, which also included RN-affiliated families.[21] Several repatriation rounds followed between 1988 and 1992, establishing dozens of FPL repopulations in Chalatenango, as well as its bordering departments of Cuscatlán, Cabañas, San Salvador, and La Libertad.[22] The RN founded several new repopulations around Suchitoto.[23] The ERP waited until the 1989 offensive to start repatriation from Colomoncagua, and concentrated on one large settlement in northern Morazán. This repopulation would be baptized as Ciudad Segundo Montes, in reference to one of the Jesuits murdered during the offensive.[24] The ERP also engaged in occupations of agricultural estates, mostly on the coastal plains of Usulután. The FPL did the same on coastal plains of San Vicente.[25] The PRTC and PCS-FAL, with much smaller peasant constituencies, sponsored only a handful of repopulations.[26]

The Salvadoran military never stopped venting concerns that "the re-populations could be turned into covers for rebel cadres, logistical help, recruiting, and even intelligence in favor of the guerrilla" (Lindsay-Poland 1989, 34). It targeted the repopulations with "hearts and minds" campaigns as well as with frequent harassment.[27] Repobladores were often detained at roadblocks or arrested for questioning. Though military violence was much more contained than in previous years, killings did occur incidentally.[28] Most repopulations concentrated the people around what had been the village center. It was thought that individual families should not live out of sight.[29] Organization was the repobladores' most important defense. When required, the entire repopulation would mobilize instantaneously, and protest would resound in the capital and abroad.[30] Strong cohesion was also necessary to overcome economic hardship. Attempts to resuscitate agricultural production rendered limited results. Communities relied on external funding (Thompson 1995, 134–35).

Frequent assemblies took place to distribute responsibilities and to elect authorities, including regional representatives. A multitier organizational structure "defended the rights of people in their communities, formed a body to negotiate with the military, and provided a forum of discussion for regional policy, services and economic initiatives" (Thompson 1995, 137). For example, insurgent repopulations linked to the FPL set up the Coordinadora de Comunidades Repobladas de Chalatenango (CCR),[31] which was in turn linked to the CRIPDES[32] as its national umbrella (Keune 1995, 261).[33] Insurgent repopulations elsewhere in the country enjoyed similar backing.[34]

In Jon Cortina's words, the repobladores "lived at the service of the war" (Sprenkels 2009, 27). At the brink of peace, however, the repopulations also served another objective: occupied land strengthened the insurgents' land claims during peace negotiations.[35] PMO cadres told the repobladores: "You have to take over land now, to be able to negotiate it later."[36] By the late 1990s, El Salvador held at least one hundred villages that trace their origin to the insurgent movement (Aquiles Montoya 2001, 154).[37] In northeastern Chalatenango alone, twelve insurgent repopulations had been founded by 1992, among these, Ellacuría.

Figure 5.1. Insurgent repopulations in northeastern Chalatenango (1986–92)

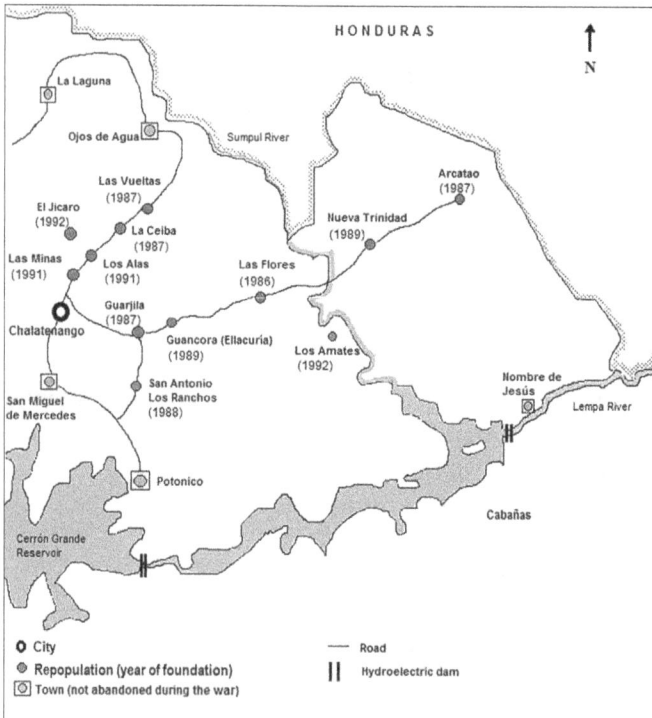

Source: Salazar and Cruz (2012), complemented with the author's knowledge based on his residency in the area between 1992 and 1995.

COMUNIDAD IGNACIO ELLACURÍA: ITS ORIGINS RECONSIDERED

When it was repopulated, on October 28, 1989, the community was not yet called "Ignacio Ellacuría." One could say that this is the community's insurgent name. Before the war, the plateau housed a *caserío*[38] called Guancora, part of the Guarjila *cantón*,[39] all pertaining to the city of Chalatenango. People also used to call the place Corral de Piedra, in reference to its many stone fences, a result of years of piling up the abundant stones found scattered over the plateau to clear the fields, mark off properties, and help regulate the movements of the grazing animals. Before the war, Guancora was a mountain hamlet, home to a dozen extended families, mostly dedicated to subsistence farming and raising pigs to sell. A few families a little better off owned cattle. Guancora's relative isolation was reduced in 1978, when the new road carved between the city of Chalatenango and the village of Arcatao passed straight through it. A few inhabitants had bought pickup trucks to help transport pigs and cattle to and from the market.

When war broke out, life in Guancora quickly became dangerous. Several disturbing events took place. According to one survivor, residents of Guancora were harassed and threatened, and forced to pay extortion money by either the guerrilla, the paramilitaries, or both. One night, a group of masked men appeared in the village and kidnapped and raped several adolescent girls.[40] When a small delegation of the National Guard came from Las Flores to keep watch in Guancora, the guerrilla attacked and killed them. According to Dorotea, an elderly Guancora native, subsequently "everyone left because the war was coming."[41] Guancora was gradually abandoned between mid-1980 and mid-1981. Not only did the violence escalate, but word was that it would become a lot worse in the future. Guancora's families spread out to seek shelter in different locations inside El Salvador.[42] One of the last families left in the rainy season of 1981. They had left their fields planted with beans and corn. When a few men went back to try and harvest, they were murdered.[43] Guancora "became desolate, . . . only the dogs remained, many dogs, howling."[44]

Unlike some nearby villages, Guancora was not a stronghold of revolutionary organizing, and those who abandoned their homes did not seek guerrilla protection. "Dorotea" explained that her husband, Bernardo, was the only one in Guancora that secretly collaborated. In 1980 the National Guard, joined by paramilitaries, beat up Bernardo with a large stick and left him for dead. The family sent word to the FPL. They sent a party to transport him deep into the mountains, to the Laguna Seca camp. Bernardo spent the next three months in the guerrilla field hospital. His family joined him there. From then on, they moved around the mountains of Chalatenango as FPL masas. In 1982, they left for Mesa Grande.[45]

Repopulating Guancora

Several of the organizers of the 1989 repatriation of Guancora still live in the community today. They recounted their experience with a level of frankness that, for several reasons, would not have been possible before. For example, when asked about his particular role in organizing the return, "Gerardo," one of the leaders of the return effort, insisted that he wasn't really a refugee; the FPL had sent him to Mesa Grande to work there as a logistic coordinator in a storage facility. Among other things, his task was "to build a tatú inside the camp in order to be able to provide or store some rifles." His family's participation in the return was connected to the continuation of his involvement in clandestine logistics, but now from inside the front. He explained: "One had to be cautious in those times; today because more than twenty years have passed, it's possible to talk about some of these experiences."[46] These types of stories, previously handled only on a need-to-know basis inside the FPL, took on a prominent place in the repobladores' retrospect.

The story of the resettlement of Guancora starts with the 1989 negotiations around continued repatriations from Mesa Grande to El Salvador. These negotiations were tenser than previous rounds, mainly because of the increased reluctance of the new Salvadoran government, led by ARENA president Cristiani, to allow the repatriations to go forward. With peace talks failing and relations between the government and the FMLN deteriorating further, popular organizations inside El Salvador once more started suffering increased persecution. Marta, another repatriation leader, offered her interpretation:

The first and the second [repatriations] [1987 and 1988] went well. But then, the [government negotiators] no longer wanted to help us or grant us permission. Because they said: if everybody wants to go, we

are screwed, because these people are there in support of the guerrilla. And this was true. Indeed, we were part of this project. . . . [The
repopulations of] Los Ranchos and Guarjila were already functioning . . . and, obviously, they knew precisely that the people in
these communities had come to strengthen the movement. They
said that these were the lakes in which the guerrillas hid; that from
here the people's army was strengthened. All these things, they . . .
were well aware of.[47]

In 1989, the Salvadoran government and the armed forces were also
aware that the FMLN was working on a significant military buildup. On
the other hand, the UNHCR, the Honduran government, and the international community at large still strongly favored the continuation of
the repatriation process. The refugee leaders rejected any new delays for
return and started to organize protests in order to demand immediate
return. Pablo, a FPL organizer in Mesa Grande before returning with the
group repopulating Guancora, explained that the leadership knew what
was coming: "We knew, [although] not everyone, that the offensive was on
the way."[48] The FPL ordered Pablo to coordinate the return and to take his
family with him, but he refused the last part. As a midlevel cadre, he knew
what was coming, and he decided his family would be safer in Mesa
Grande. The bulk of the families he organized for the return did not have
this knowledge. "A few of us disobeyed. For example, in my case they told
me, in an internal meeting: 'You have to go with your sons!' 'No,' I told
them, 'I will go there because it's what I already know. . . . The next day I
will join [the armed struggle], . . . in whatever place I am, but my family
I will leave behind [in Mesa Grande].'"[49]

According to Pablo, half of the families that he enlisted for the repatriation to Chalatenango were from Cabañas, specifically from an isolated
area northwest of Villa Victoria, down toward Lempa River. This was
Pablo's home region. Before the war, Pablo had already been one of the
leaders of the FPL's expansion in his native cantón and surroundings.
When the families were forced out of their homes, he became one of the
leaders of the FPL masas from Cabañas, and he played an important role
in the guindas and in the masas' eventual flight to Honduras. A good
number of the people he organized and prepared for the return were connected to him through these experiences. Some also belonged to his extended family.[50]

Why then did these people from Cabañas head for Chalatenango, rather than returning to their home region? Indeed, the repopulation movement was also present in Cabañas, with the founding of the Santa Marta repopulation in 1987. Pablo's explanation went as follows. Before the war and during its first few years, both the RN and the FPL had been very active in northwestern Cabañas. When Santa Marta was repopulated, "bases" affiliated with the RN as well as with the FPL participated. Also in the 1989 return, one of the repatriation groups leaving from Mesa Grande would go to Santa Marta. But the orientation that Pablo had received from the FPL was to organize families to go to Chalatenango. The main reason for the FPL's decision was that the RN, not the FPL, dominated Santa Marta. In fact, the reports that the FPL had from the FPL families living in Santa Marta were not positive: FPL constituents felt discriminated against by the RN leadership. Previously, in negotiations among the different PMOs, the FPL leadership had decided to "leave" the northwestern part of Cabañas to the RN and to focus instead on Chalatenango and Cinquera (southeastern Cabañas) both in terms of military efforts and in the consolidation of the presence of social bases in these areas. Without this arrangement, so Pablo considered, "Our history would have been different. We would not have hundreds of families from Santa Marta living here in Chalatenango."[51]

An Ellacuría community leader I have called Arturo confirmed: "A lot of people from Cabañas came here. . . . These were the Party's political orientations. 'You will go to Chalatenango.' Right? 'Join these other people [the repobladores who had already settled in Chalatenango].' Many people went, because in that time you had to be obedient."[52]

Timing was a key issue in the return effort. Because of military plans—the final offensive was at hand—the PMOs active in Mesa Grande (FPL, RN, and PCS-FAL) were eager to organize another repatriation before November. The Salvadoran government, on the other hand, was stalling the negotiations. In this context, with time pressing, several hundred Salvadoran refugees abandoned the Mesa Grande camp and marched on the Honduran city of San Marcos, where they occupied a church. The Honduran military then surrounded the premises. The protest became an international news item. In less than a week, the refugees obtained permission for repatriation.[53]

As in previous rounds, representatives of churches, NGOs, and international observers accompanied the repatriation caravan of October 1989.

Approximately twelve hundred refugees participated.[54] The Salvadoran government still proved reluctant to allow the returnees to enter the country. At El Poy, a Honduran-Salvadoran border crossing, the group was stopped and rigorously checked. The Salvadoran authorities took one of the repatriation leaders and one international observer into custody. Intense communications followed between the remaining leaders of the repatriates, UNHCR officials, the Catholic Church, and government officials, communications that resulted, later that day, in the release of the detainees and permission for the repatriates to enter the country.

Inside El Salvador, the caravan split up. According to the negotiated agreement, one group was to travel to the repopulation of Teosinte, established a year earlier as the first repopulation in western Chalatenango. A second group headed for the previously repopulated community of Santa Marta in Cabañas. And a third group was to settle in La Lagunita, just outside of San José Las Flores. This group continued on to northeastern Chalatenango.[55]

The group that Pablo coordinated arrived in Guarjila on the night of October 27 and was met with a large celebration, which included delegations from the other repopulations in the area, organized under the banner of the CCR. The next day, the repatriate caravan continued up the road further into northeastern Chalatenango. However, rather than moving up to La Lagunita, the caravan stopped and unpacked a few kilometers earlier, in Guancora. Pablo explained why.

> This place [was] visited very frequently by the enemy . . . , because it had the requirements to set up ambushes; a lot of stone fences. . . . It was like a transit zone to get to El Alto, to get to El Portillo [preferred locations of guerrilla camps in the area] . . . , and it was here that they [guerrilla fighters] were ambushed. . . . This is why, as I am telling you, it was an orientation directly from the FPL, from the leadership.[56]

Gerardo confirmed this reading and added that the military also regularly set up mortars nearby. Guancora "was a strategic location for the armed forces," but with their presence, the repobladores "had won the place [from the military]."[57] Nonetheless, when the new settlers arrived to Guancora, the Salvadoran military was not there.[58] Because of the heavy guerrilla presence in the area, the Salvadoran armed forces were unable to maintain a permanent base in northeastern Chalatenango. In the second half of the 1980s, they did regularly organize incursions using specialized counterinsurgency units, often with backing provided by the air force and by less-experienced infantry troops. When the military did enter northeastern Chalatenango, Guancora was one of their preferred sites.

The head count the organizers used for the repatriation was ninety-five families, consisting of four hundred people.[59] Arturo confessed that the actual number was somewhat lower. "Well . . . talking in earnest, here the information given was intended to benefit the people. 'How many families are there?' 'Ah, some hundred and eighty families!' That way the material support arrived for one hundred and eighty families. This allowed us to help the compas [guerrillas]. In other words, . . . we said we had more . . . inhabitants then we really had."[60]

The returnees had brought as much as they could from Mesa Grande. Sheets of corrugated steel, wooden planks and beams, and plastic, a lot of plastic, were lowered from the trucks and used to build shacks that served as provisional housing. Hand mills and stones for grinding corn and cooking disks were installed. Food supplies for the first few weeks had been brought from Mesa Grande. The community sent delegates to apply for permits to get supplies past the army roadblocks. While exploring the ruins of the community, an adolescent accidentally stepped on an army mine hidden in one of the abandoned houses, and injured his leg.[61] Thus, the repatriates suffered their first casualty.

In the first few days, as everybody collaborated in making Guancora habitable, a group of eighteen men who had participated in the return from Honduras disappeared from the community. They incorporated into the guerrilla forces, with the preparations for the November 1989 offensive in their final stage.[62] Arturo was one of them. Most of them had been recruited previously, in Mesa Grande, to incorporate immediately after the return.[63] "Ernesto," a repoblador who had acquired experience with weapon repair at the front and in Mesa Grande, set up an improvised workshop just outside of the repopulations to repair guerrilla weaponry whenever circumstances allowed.[64]

According to Jon Cortina, the acting parish priest for the area, when the offensive itself started on November 11 (thirteen days after the arrival at Guancora), the dominant sentiment in the repopulated communities was "fear, because there were few guerrilla fighters, since they were all at the offensive. The people were afraid that the army would take advantage of the lack of defensive capacity in order to make incursions into the com-

Figure 5.2.   Arrival in Guancora

Source: Courtesy of Anabel Recinos.

munities and even to take revenge. As a matter of fact, trenches were built in case there were bombings, in order for us to be able to hide in the trenches" (Sprenkels 2009, 32–33).

Things nonetheless remained calm in northeastern Chalatenango until after the guerrilla offensive lost steam. The retaliatory military incursions began in December. When the Salvadoran army troops appeared in Guancora, they installed themselves on the edge of the new settlement. The repobladores of Guancora were forced into an uncomfortable cohabitation with the armed forces. Going to the river to wash and get water became problematic, because the army was installed there. Several incidents occurred in which repobladores who did venture a little bit outside of the perimeter of the Guancora settlement to fetch water or firewood were shot at.[65] In December 1989 and January 1990, there were ongoing combats between the soldiers and the guerrilla forces in the area. In spite of animosity toward the repobladores, for the soldiers the repopulations, paradoxically, also were a relatively safe place in hostile territory. As Marta explained: "They also used the community to save themselves. In order to avoid combat in the mountains they came to the communities, and they didn't come just to hide, but also to force the families to give them food."[66]

The Guancora Massacre and Its Aftermath

What the community residents had most feared occurred on February 11, 1990. That day,

> five people were assassinated and several more were wounded in a bombing attack executed by the Salvadoran Armed Forces. The attack started at 6:25 in the morning and continued for more than two hours. At 8:30, a helicopter equipped with missiles flew over the village at very low range and opened fire against some of the buildings. Seeking protection from the bombing, some people hid in the community chapel. Others hid in a house that was targeted by the fire of the helicopters and in which five people were killed. The victims were Ana Beatriz López, two years old; Blanca Lidia Guardado, two and a half years old; Isabel López, ten years old, José Dolores Serrano, eleven years old, and José Anibal Guardado, twenty-eight years of age. (CODEHUCA 1992, 40)

The night before, the soldiers had left Guancora. A large contingent of soldiers had spent the night in La Lagunita, a few kilometers north, and in the morning part of these troops set out for Guancora on the main road. At the last curve before completing the ascent to the Guancora plateau, FPL guerrillas ambushed the army. After the attack, the guerrilla retreat faltered.

> On the outskirts of Guancora there was . . . the shoot-out . . . and they [the guerrillas] killed about three soldiers and recovered [a] machine gun. . . . Imagine, the compas retreated. Then, the soldiers said: 'Shoot! There they go, inside the community!' . . . These matters are not told, but yes, the retreat that occurred was not appropriate. In other words, . . . [the guerrilleros] retreated in the midst of the people, and [the soldiers] shot here inside [the community].[67]

Aviation appeared quickly, with guerrilla fighters still running through the community. Two of them hid behind a brick house, one of the few prewar houses still standing. Inside this house, a group of repobladores had sought refuge from the firefights around them. A helicopter targeted the house with two rockets. After the impact, the fighters quickly took off and disappeared. María, the mother of two of the children killed, narrated that she saw them take off from behind the destroyed house and disappear.[68] The attack killed five and left sixteen people injured.[69] The military subsequently occupied Guancora and militarized the perimeter of the house it had targeted. According to a song the repobladores sing in commemoration, "They didn't want the people to see the brutal massacre they had committed."[70] After the massacre, authorities arrived in the community to "verify" the events, under the gaze of military occupation.

Salvadoran newspaper *La Prensa Gráfica* reported four days later that army troops and the guerrilla engaged in "tough combat" in a "refugee camp" in northeastern Chalatenango, resulting in the death of five civilians, six guerrilla fighters and one soldier. The newspaper referred to an official report, which denied any responsibility of the air force in the incident. It attributed the death of civilians to subversive elements that had attacked the community with "terrorist catapults," without clarifying what exactly this term referred to.[71] In spite of the international denunciations of the massacre, the event bore no further consequences for the officials involved or for the Salvadoran army in general. As far as the victims' families were aware, no apologies were made, no compensation offered, and no other measures taken.[72]

On July 22, 1990, five months after the massacre, the repopulation of Guancora adopted the name of "Ignacio Ellacuría" as a tribute and a token of resolve, following the example of Ciudad Segundo Montes in Morazán.[73] Like Montes and others, the Jesuit Ellacuría had been assassinated by the military in November 1989. Marta explains that, taking into account that the repobladores were not Guancora natives, the community sought to adopt a name "that was better suited for the history that we were building."[74] The attending priest in Guancora at the time was Jon Cortina, himself a survivor of the 1989 massacre at the UCA (Sprenkels 2001, 31). The ceremony that rebaptized the community was organized by the CCR and drew dozens of religious workers, human rights activists, and international visitors to Guancora. Repobladores from the surrounding communities flocked in to show their support. For a crowd that one observer estimated at three thousand people, José María Tojeira, head of the Central

American Jesuits, proclaimed: "We will continue to tell the truth and work for peace and justice in El Salvador, like Ignacio Ellacuría did" (Carranza 1990, 318, 325). An excerpt of Tojeira's words that day reads as follows:

> Members of the community of "Ignacio Ellacuría." Live your future with faith. You have not built your communal life on idols, on ill-gotten money, on unjust social differences, on unequal development. On the contrary. The essence of your life has been solidarity, mutual support and consciousness born and raised during the suffering of repression, of exile, of threats. The war continues to be a great affliction for you and yet you continue to believe in love, in peace, and in the communitarian option of living like brothers and sisters. Continue on your feet, community Ignacio Ellacuría, giving us the example of liberty, even though there are roadblocks that want to restrict it, render unto us your testimony of peace in the midst of war, shouting to us your message of love for the land amidst so many that bargain with it.[75]

A week after the rebaptizing ceremony, the community once more suffered nearby mortar fire (Carranza 1990, 320). However, July 1990 was also the month that the FMLN and the government signed the first significant agreement toward peace in San José, Costa Rica. This document paved the way for the installation of a United Nations human rights verification mission in the country. Over the next year and a half, as peace negotiations progressed, military abuses in the repopulated communities indeed became less frequent (Johnstone 1995, 18–21; Katayanagi 2002, 71; Samayoa 2002, 341).

Clandestine Networks within the Repopulation

Local food production got off the ground slowly, and the repopulation depended on donations to purchase food at the market. Gerardo, one of the leaders charged with this task, was relieved of agricultural duties and worked full-time on provisioning the community, bringing in supplies from Chalatenango and other locations. Pablo, the first community president, had left Guancora shortly after the massacre to perform FPL duties elsewhere, which left Gerardo as one of the principal FPL liaisons.[76]

Gerardo helped facilitate the distribution of the goods both to the community and to the guerrilla forces. This was a delicate job for several reasons. For starters, even if the community generally supported the insurgency, not everybody had the same levels of participation, and not everybody was affiliated in the same way. Ellacuría's location indicated that it was bound to be an FPL-affiliated repopulation. Furthermore, as we have seen, the FPL coordinated the repatriation. Ellacuría's participation in the CCR connected the community with the broader organizational realm of the FPL. However, the PCS-FAL had recruited some Ellacurían families back in Mesa Grande, prior to the repatriation. This particularity touches upon a previously undocumented episode of the refugee and repopulation movement. Arturo explained:

> From '85 onwards, the PC [short for PCS-FAL] was present in Mesa Grande. It was then that three blocks were formed: on one side the RN, which consisted of people from Cabañas; the FPL; and then the PC. . . . They started recruiting internally, because I myself changed to the PC. So, I fought for some time with the FPL, and later in '87 I switched to the PC. I had some problems with some FPL leaders and I crossed over to the PC. . . . If you'd had responsibilities, they took better care of you [in the PC]. Since the FPL was large, it didn't have a lot of material and economic resources, but the PC, because they were few, they had everything. Whatever one asked for, it was granted. Out of convenience many people changed to the PC, it is that simple. . . . This is why the PC grew . . . here in Chalate[nango]. . . . This happened to us in the war, we recruited amongst ourselves. Instead of going to recruit where it was necessary.[77] I remember we had this discussion: "Damn, they are taking people away from us." "But well, . . . it is all the same, they are going to fight the enemy." This is how the PC [PCS; also below] grew, because many people . . . were born in the FPL, were leaders in the FPL, but ended up with the PC. . . . [Therefore] the PC became all mixed in with us in this repopulation; we arrived *revueltos* [scrambled].[78]

One of the implications of this mix of PMO affiliation was that both the FPL and PCS recruited inside the community. For example, more than half of the Guancora repatriates who subsequently enrolled in the offensive fought with the PCS-FAL.[79] Not only the FPL had political cadres inside the community, but also the PCS-FAL. Pablo and Gerardo served as FPL liaisons for the repatriation, and Marta had a similar function for the PCS-FAL. Nonetheless, Ellacuría was a CCR community, meaning that the community's broader support structure was affiliated with the FPL. The community's school and the health services were set up and coordinated with the CCR, and linked with the larger efforts in the larger nearby repopulation of Guarjila.[80] Also, as we saw earlier, FPL-affiliated families were the majority in the community.

Even though in Ellacuría the FPL and PCS-FAL worked closely together, they did not always trust each other with everything. As part of the FMLN, the two organizations were striving toward similar goals, but on occasion the different affiliations also generated competition over resources and loyalties within the community. Furthermore, the fact that the inhabitants were all considered "social bases" of the PMOs did not mean that everybody in the community supported the insurgency to the same extent. To make the internal politics of the community even more complex, both the FPL and PCS-FAL suspected that the Salvadoran army might have hidden informers inside the community.[81] As a consequence, Gerardo had to organize part of his work within the community itself in a clandestine manner.

> There was something we called the *colchón*, the surplus. . . . Because one way or another, it had to be done and . . . we didn't want to hurt anybody. . . . You know within the community different sorts of thinking existed. The distribution had to be done as indicated, but a surplus was left over and this we passed on [to the guerrilla]. There was one person [of the guerrilla] charged with supplies. . . . We handed the supplies over to him and this was something we had to do. How? We had to invent how. . . . This was how we participated [in the struggle] . . . and even so, we asked everybody and told them: "We need you to give us a pound of corn. We're not asking for all of it. We're asking for one pound." Together it added up to quite an amount. . . . Separate from the group, some people complained why [give our food to the guerrilla]?[82]

The repobladores were also involved in military support tasks for the guerrilla. For example, Gerardo remembered,

We had to go and leave [food] to those who were on the lookout, [and] others who were on missions and who had to eat. We left tortillas for them. But this was a job . . . quite separate. . . .[83] It wasn't easy, they were fighting [there were combats]. The only thing was that there were stone fences. . . . We went to a fence, they were on the other side, then we had to look on all sides, how . . . and who we could send. There were people that told us: "Yes, man, you already know, whenever you say." These people were already in place. So we would tell them: "Look, go and leave this." It was a well-coordinated job and above all strategic, in order to avoid these things being discovered. In other words, it was a clandestine job, to use that term, among our own people because . . . these were difficult times. Since this is now in the past, it is not a problem to tell [you] this.[84]

Through (lower) cadres, the FPL and the PCS-FAL both had their own clandestine networks in Ellacuría, which organized repobladores into hierarchical support structures. Commonly, the more prominent members of these clandestine networks would also perform public functions, like serving on the community directorate. Thus, the PMOs kept a check on the community's internal political processes. The PMO superiors, often located in the guerrilla camps, sometimes also in NGOs or unions, offered political orientations and distributed tasks to be performed at the community level. Local PMO liaisons regularly reported on their work to their superiors. All this work happened in clandestinity. PMO clandestinity constituted a sort of parallel universe in the community, elusive to outsiders, but very consequential for the repobladores themselves.

Military Harassment and Infiltration

Those involved in clandestine work had to be wary of the military. When stationed in or near Ellacuría, soldiers would always attempt to extract information from the repobladores. The same happened at the roadblocks. Gerardo was forced to interact with the military regularly on account of his logistical responsibilities, which required frequent travel to Chalatenango city. He was often subjected to scrutiny.

At the time it was necessary to request permits at the "DM-1" [military compound, to bring supplies to the village]. . . . Then they would decide that they didn't feel like giving the permit, they sent you to the "4th Brigade." So, . . . since I [did] as many as three trips a week, sometimes they would take my clothes off to see if I had anything. . . . And they would ask me: "And the *cadenas* [elastic marks]?"[85] I knew well what they were referring to. "What are you talking about?" I would tell them. "You are pretending not to know"; they would tell me, "Take off your clothes to see if you have any shrapnel in your body."[86]

In a change of strategy, the military approached Gerardo on one of his market trips.

I had a habit of going to the cathedral [in the city of Chalatenango]. . . . One day I was sitting there when I sensed that behind me was a sergeant, and he says: "Look mister, they want you to go [to the military compound, located next to the cathedral]." "Alright," I told him, since I was already there; "I will be there shortly," I told him. "No, you will go with me." "In that case," I told him, "wait here for me a little bit." I told him, "I am going to get some money that a man is holding for me." This is what I told him, right? So I went to see someone who was a comrade, he collaborated with the guerrilla, and he worked there [in the church]. . . . I told him: "Look [name], . . . something is happening. If I am not back in two hours or three, come and look for me."[87]

With this warning out, Gerardo returned to the soldier waiting for him at the entrance of the cathedral. The soldier accompanied him across Chalatenango's central square into the military garrison, where he brought Gerardo straight into the colonel's office.

[The colonel] told me, "You were called to my office to work with us." "What do you mean?" I asked him. "It is easy . . . ," he told me, "you will go Arcatao, Nueva Trinidad, Las Flores, . . . to Los Ranchos, Guarjila, y Las Vueltas [all repopulations in northeastern Chalatenango]." "To do what?" I asked him. "You will . . . distribute propaganda." . . . "That's tough," I told him. "Understand that I have a lot of children that depend on me." . . . "Those are the ones that you will be providing for." "That's what you say! . . . If I go to any of these places, I can assure you I will have another [problem]." "Why?" he asked. "If the soldiers find me," I told him, "they will treat me as a guerrilla." . . . "Don't be afraid, the thing is that I will tell them and we will give you a piece of paper in order to prevent anything from happening to you." "Paper is worth nothing," I told him. "Think it through," he told me. He went to a locker and took out two stacks of . . . bills. "This stack is yours and a lot more." The situation was quite difficult. [I went in] at eight o'clock and I left the place at noon.[88]

Gerardo's account is eloquent with regard to the interaction between the military and the repobladores at the end of the war. The military frequently and routinely resorted to obstruction, intimidation, and sometimes detentions, but they rarely committed the extreme abuses of the early 1980s. Gerardo hence acquiesced to the order to enter the military compound, but not without making sure he got word out concerning his whereabouts. Should he be detained, different organizations would soon demand his release. His testimony also shows that the military attempted to build a network of collaborators inside the insurgent communities. It is not clear to what extent they actually succeeded in that, but Gerardo did indicate the need to hide certain insurgent activities from the residents of Ellacuría. Even though the population of "Ellacuría" was made up entirely of supporters of the FPL and the PCS-FAL, it could not be ruled out that the army also had its informers there. In fact, PMO leadership was convinced of infiltration taking place.[89]

ELLACURÍA AFTER THE WAR

Reinsertion, Reconstruction, and Development

The first postwar years translated into considerable instability in Ellacuría.[90] For one, the repopulated families had to determine whether it would be more beneficial for them to move back to their hometowns, to claim their original holdings, or to stay in the community. Furthermore, the PMOs also offered the possibility for some families to settle on estates acquired within the framework of the PTT, like those in San Vicente and

Usulután. The repobladores understood that if they wanted to move else-where, it would be easier to do so before land, houses, and other projects were assigned. Much depended on what reconstruction benefits could be expected where. Potential support from extended family or close friends was also an important consideration. On balance, a majority of the Ella-curía residents decided to stay put, while a significant minority sought opportunities elsewhere. Families from other repopulations sometimes served as replacement. For example, several families from Cabañas that had initially repatriated to Santa Marta moved to Ellacuría in 1992, out of discontent with political affairs in Santa Marta.[91]

Just before the end of the war, the PCS-FAL decided to set up its "own" repopulations in Chalatenango and founded Las Minas and Los Alas. They persuaded a few PCS-FAL-affiliated families to leave Ellacuría and resettle in their communities. Other PCS-FAL-affiliated families stayed behind in Ellacuría. The PCS-FAL also persuaded dozens of families from other repopulations in the area to make the move, either because of the ties these families had established with the PCS-FAL in Mesa Grande (which usually meant that the family's youngsters were fighting in the ranks of the PCS-FAL) or because the families were seduced by the promise of better economic prospects.[92] However, a conflict emerged within the Chalatenango leadership of the PCS-FAL in 1992, which contributed to the decision by the second in command in the PCS-FAL hierarchy to abandon Las Minas and settle in Ellacuría. He brought a few PCS-FAL families and some demobilization benefits with him to Ellacuría.[93]

As FMLN troops concentrated for demobilization, some veteran combatants residing in Ellacuría moved to the camps to qualify for demo-bilization benefits. Several demobilized ex-combatants furthermore opted to settle in Ellacuría, mostly because they already had family there. Some thirty Ellacuría individuals formally demobilized, a little over half from the ranks of the FPL and the rest from the PCS-FAL.[94] The remainder of Ellacurían households were classified as *tenedor*.[95] This distinction between demobilized (often also referred to as ex-combatants) and tenedor was relevant because of the eligibility criteria for different projects. Several housing projects, for example, were specifically destined for the demobi-lized. The PTT also distinguished between tenedores and demobilized, and this distinction was relevant for the timing and terms of the transfer (more favorable for ex-combatants) (Alvarez and Chávez 2001).

The most urgent matter for Ellacuría was to legalize property owner-ship. Eviction of the repopulation was not likely, since the FMLN would not allow it, and hence it would jeopardize the peace process. However, the land Ellacuría was established on was all private land, owned by small-holders now living elsewhere in the country, the only exception being the one native Guancora family that had participated in the repopulation process. In the previous two years, the community directorate had ad-ministered the land, assigning housing tracts and plots for farming. The Ellacuría directorate administered the land collectively and without a legal base. This matter became particularly urgent given that major recon-struction programs were being launched in the former conflict zones. For example, programs to build houses demanded that a potential beneficiary owned the land the house would be built upon. Support programs for co-operatives demanded similar clarity regarding the legal status of com-munity resources.

The PTT got off the ground very slowly, but the acquisition of land, and particularly of the settled areas of the community, was too urgent to wait. Furthermore, it was unclear at the time whether the PTT would be able to help solve the property questions inside the constructed areas of the repopulations. Therefore, the repopulations petitioned the solidarity groups that had supported them during the war to donate money to pur-chase land. In the case of Ellacuría, the sister city of Detroit proved a valu-able ally. The Sisters of the Assumption, actively involved in "buying the town" of Las Flores, were also able to channel donations to Ellacuría.[96]

The urgent need for land acquisition was confirmed by an unex-pected appearance, in 1992, of another group of aspiring settlers in caserío El Roble, two kilometers west of Ellacuría. They occupied a stretch of land that the Ellacuría directorate had planned on claiming. Like Guancora, El Roble had been abandoned at the beginning of the war. Like most of Guancora families, the people from El Roble had not joined the guerrilla, but had looked for refuge in the cities. Several of El Roble's families stuck together and settled in a squatter's community at the outskirts of Santa Tecla, near the capital. With the signing of the peace accords, they decided to return to their old home. This return to El Roble was not organized through a PMO, a church, or the government. The participating families simply rented a few trucks in which they placed their belongings and drove to Ellacuría. There, they drove the trucks as far up the mountain as they could, unloaded, and quickly moved everything up to El Roble, including a very old man they had to transport in a hammock.

The directorate of Ellacuría immediately organized a delegation to get them out. They went up to El Roble, told the newcomers they had to leave, and when they refused, picked up the newcomers' belongings, including the old man in the hammock, and brought them down to Ellacuría to place them by the side of the road to await transport. The Ellacuría repobladores then escorted the people from El Roble on the road towards Chalatenango. A few months later, the same group made another attempt to resettle. This time they traveled lightly and avoided passing through Ellacuría, crossing on mountain paths instead. When the Ellacuría directorate learned there were people living in El Roble, they again sent to have them evicted. Soon after, a delegation of the people from El Roble returned once more, this time with property titles to back their claims to the land. They also had contacted ONUSAL. In view of these developments, the Ellacuría directorate and the CCR decided to allow the resettlement of El Roble on August 25, 1992.[97]

Fortunately for Ellacuría residents, the bulk of the original landowners from Guancora and surrounding areas did not consider returning and were willing to sell their properties. Only a handful of the original owners were interested in holding on to their land, either because they saw it as a good investment or because they were thinking of going back to farming in Guancora. Since the documentation of landownership was far from perfect, and the original owners scattered, there were cases in which alleged owners sold more than what actually belonged to them.[98] In the period between 1992 and 1994, the directorate was able to obtain the water sources, tracts for houses (already in existence or to be built), and an additional two hundred acres of farmland close by.[99]

At the same time, Ellacuría became considered for a broad range of internationally funded projects.[100] Some projects were simply directed at making the place more habitable, like installing latrines or infrastructure for drinking water. Other projects favored social aspects, like the construction and operation of a small day-care center and of a *casa de la mujer*.[101] The most ambitious efforts aimed to reactivate the local economy. In 1994, a community cooperative called Planes de Guancora was founded with the idea of promoting collective farming and providing technical support as well as a safety net for individual farmers.[102] Other projects included the establishment of a small shoe factory, a weaving workshop for handmade cloths, and an egg farm.[103] Arturo, a community directorate member during most of the 1990s, explained:

> We have tried to form . . . a cooperative, but to be honest . . . it didn't work, in practice. Because after the peace accords there were many, many projects . . . and they [all] were a complete failure. . . . We were only accustomed to fighting, to killing each other, not to administering [projects], right? The same thing happened . . . in every community. . . . Taking into account . . . that for a variety of reasons it was very difficult to manage community projects, . . . we have focused on contributing on a social level.[104]

In 1994 ARENA won the municipal elections in Chalatenango city, but in 1997 the FMLN took over. One of the community leaders from Ellacuría took a seat on the municipal council, and the community directorate was able to obtain a few projects through the municipality. In the subsequent nine years of FMLN municipal administration, these projects included the cement paving of several of the community's dirt roads, the development of a basketball court and a football field, and the building of a community youth center. When ARENA regained Chalatenango in 2006, municipal funding for projects in Ellacuría dried up.[105]

From previous insurgent affiliation, Ellacuría inherited a durable relationship with the NGO CORDES, which, over the postwar decades, continued to implement small community projects, such as vegetable production for family consumption. Another legacy was the continued support from Detroit, coordinated through an NGO called the SHARE Foundation. The "sister-city" bond maintained a community vehicle (a pickup truck doubling as an "ambulance") and a small scholarship program for community youngsters attending high school or university.[106] Additionally, over the years, an international NGO called Plan International supported projects directed at child education and nutrition.

Ellacuría: Two Decades after the Peace Accords

As I strolled around the community in 2012, the remains of various postwar development efforts were conspicuous. Close to the center of the village, the former Casa de la Mujer, with fading purple paint, and its surrounding piece of land had been fenced off, apparently to serve as a grazing

area. The abandoned structure itself at least still had a roof on it, and a
door with a lock. Only the bare walls remained from an edifice built in
1992 to house the shoe factory. The project was abandoned in 1994. Afterward, the inhabitants of Ellacuría stripped everything else to use for other
purposes. A little further out from the community center lay the remains
of the egg farm. On the other hand, the school that was begun in 1992
with international donations was in very decent shape. The "popular
education" teachers who had provided education in Ellacuría since the
founding of the community were replaced by government-employed
teachers in 1994, after attempts to accredit the community's educators as
formal teachers failed. The community still owned the school building,
but the school administration was in the hands of the national authority
of the Ministry of Education.

Most remarkably, the houses in Ellacuría had become a far cry from
the shacks built after people returned there from Mesa Grande. Virtually
all families obtained brick or cement-block houses through the various
housing projects dating from the reconstruction period. Besides Ellacuría's characteristic rustic stone fences, many now had additional metal
fences around properties with grown fruit trees and often also a few dec-
orative plants. Over the years, most had made substantial housing additions, and several families completely rebuilt their homes. Most houses
now had a separate kitchen area—equipped with both a traditional wood
stove and a modern gas stove—and long corridors, characteristic of El Salvador's traditional rural homes. Some Ellacuría homes also incorporated
"villa"-style architectural elements, a mix of Mexican and US aesthetic
influences which has spread in the Salvadoran countryside particularly
over the last decade. All homes had electricity and running water.

"Purely on remittances," "Yancy," one of Ellacuría's university students, clarified when asked about the community's remarkable level of
home improvement.[107] As happened in other insurgent repopulations,
many inhabitants of Ellacuría migrated to the United States over the last
two decades.[108] On occasion, entire families made the trip and established
themselves in that country. But more often, part of the family, often the
elderly and the children, stayed behind and received remittances. Arturo
elaborated:

> If I take stock, almost all families [from Ellacuría] already have family
> members in the United States. . . . They have grown accustomed . . . to

go and get their . . . remittances each month. . . . I think that at this point in life a lot of people would struggle hard should they stop receiving their remittances, right? Because they have become very . . . accustomed to this. . . . If you look you will see that the youth only wear Nike shoes. . . . Now almost everybody no longer wants a regular television, but rather a flat screen. Not a cheap cellular phone, but one with a camera, with whatever else they put on those things. . . . A lot of families depend one hundred percent on remittances. . . . With electricity available: a refrigerator, a television set, domestic appliances, and all this paid for with only remittances. . . . Beds, but not the ones from before made out of ropes. . . . Remittances, you see. . . . So you see, a lot of compas have improved their lives. Unfortunately the families in Ellacuría, and this the same in every other place, my brother, they have not valued the work of the compas over there [in the United States] and in practice they have squandered [the money]. We have informed . . . this to the [community] assembly. The problem is that one cannot meddle that much . . . in telling them: "Hey there, don't buy so much!"[109]

Although concerned with migration's costs and consequences, Ellacuría's leadership saw no alternatives.

We had a meeting to see how we might stop migration. What are we going to offer to them? Nothing, nothing, nothing, nothing, nothing! Sure, the land, to grow. But agriculture doesn't render! . . . What the people harvest is for them . . . to eat, nothing more. . . . People used to tell me: "Look [Arturo], I am going to leave." "That's fine. Have a good one. Congratulations and do your best then." What else could we do? Because if I told them: "Hey man, don't leave." [He would reply,] "Alright, you give me a job then." And, with what means?[110]

Labor migration started timidly in the aftermath of the demobilization process, as former combatants were developing new survival strategies. It picked up pace toward the end of the 1990s. Of the thirty demobilized FMLN combatants who settled in Ellacuría in 1992, ten were residing in the United States in 2009.[111] Many *tenedores* also decided to make the journey. Initially only men, but soon also several women left, either to join their husbands or to try to make it on their own. Some that left, especially those that left early on, were later able to pay the coyote's fee to transport other family members.

Even though certainly relevant, international labor migration by those who had actively participated in the war was still a minority option. However, a big boost occurred towards the end of the 1990s when the United States became a common option for recent school graduates who had realized that, besides subsistence farming, there were few opportunities for them in Ellacuría. Many families from Ellacuría now possessed extended family networks in the United States, able to receive youngsters eager to migrate. Even so, the ever-growing costs and dangers of the trip, combined with the 2008 economic crisis, moderated the migration drive. Ellacuría also housed several deportees who now tried to get by once more in their hometown.

Doubtless, labor migration to the United States constituted by far the most significant postwar phenomenon in Ellacuría. This is true not only in economic terms, but also in terms of community development in a broader sense. Ellacuría families, fragmented by migration, developed a range of transnational bonds. In spite of the distances, families often maintained extensive communication, by phone, by sending video recordings of family events back-and-forth, and, for the young people, by means of Facebook and other internet tools (Alarcón Medina 2015). Also, visible in the architecture are new cultural elements that Ellacuría families embraced through their exposure to Mexican-dominated Latino culture in the United States, different both from the traditional Salvadoran peasant repertoire and from that of the revolutionary struggle.

Labor migration also helps explain that Ellacuría's population has grown only modestly, even though birth rates have been high. A 2002 community survey registered 557 inhabitants, 44 percent of them under fifteen years of age (Calderón Vandenberg 2002, 31). A 2007 Ministry of Health community survey registered 552 inhabitants, a decrease of 5. Meanwhile, the number of homes increased considerably. In 2002, there were 119 homes in Ellacuría (Calderón Vandenberg 2002, 31). In 2009, my students identified 142 Ellacuría homes, an increase of 23. Those living in the United States not only helped those left behind to improve their homes; they often also sent money for the construction of new homes, to be used upon return. Thus, in 2009, there were over a dozen nicely built, uninhabited homes awaiting family members in the United States.

LOCAL POLITICS IN ELLACURÍA

One element I focused on during fieldwork was understanding how the relations between Ellacuría residents and the FMLN might have changed over the years. "Here all of us continue to support the FMLN," Pablo told me, "but the way people participate is not the same as before."[112] Separately, Arturo concurred and elaborated.

> Before . . . when we used to go to protest marches in San Salvador . . . , everybody was on that truck. Not anymore! If they don't bring in a bus, a large comfortable bus, then they would rather not. Now everybody travels by bus, sitting down, none of that traveling in the back of a truck. If the bus is old, they won't go. Even sometimes with a good bus, the people don't want to participate, it is coming to an end. . . . [The party] has neglected us in close to 100 percent. . . . Even though they might tell you over there that the party is all of us. But then I say: "I can be very much part of the party, very much part of the FMLN, but if my comrade is up there, is eating well, as they say, is making good money and he doesn't remember me, then I'm not going to make a big effort either." . . . More and more, the FMLN is becoming an electoral party, it's that simple.[113]

In spite of these complaints, Arturo also made it very clear that he would always remain loyal to the FMLN.

> I vote for the FMLN and I feel that that's where I will die. I won't change parties, even if only horses remain in the leadership. . . . Because that's where I was born, I have never voted for any other party. . . . I tell them . . . that they only use us for the elections. When the elections are coming, then the comrades come to meet with us and to organize us in the local committee, that we have to help over there and . . . we paint and glue on [propaganda], we set up political activities, there we go. . . . Before, when we were fighting in the guerrilla, we had a different vision, which I sense I have not achieved in practice.[114]

These comments are interesting for several reasons. Arturo offered a substantial critique on the FMLN, but not without emphasizing his loyalty. His main disappointment seemed to be what he perceived as limited reciprocation for his efforts and those of his local comrades. He partially questioned FMLN leadership for not living up to its former vision, while at the same time he also censured what he considered to be growing political apathy in the community population.

Nonetheless, as had appeared in my students' survey, Ellacuría inhabitants tended to esteem the FMLN highly, while showing disaffection with community organization and local leadership. Indeed, practically all of Ellacuría's elderly manifested pride with regard to insurgent affiliation and wartime contributions. They spoke admiringly of recent electoral victories, which many viewed as a type of historical redemption for their cause.[115] But tones and dispositions changed when discussing community affairs. One woman I spoke to extensively explained reluctance to engage the subject as follows: "When someone goes around saying certain things, they start to consider you as a *contrario*."[116] "Saying what?" I queried. "Well, how some within the community have taken advantage." "And what happens then if you say such things?" I asked. "Well, they marginalize you even more," she replied.[117]

It should not be surprising that Ellacuría, like any community, has its disputes and divisions. In fact, an absence of such internal divergences would be a stunning discovery. What is relevant for this study is whether Ellacuría's postwar political rifts bear any significant relationship to the community's insurgent history. I found that it did. For example, I learned that a few individuals with strong PMO ties had increasingly dominated Ellacurían politics. They were some of the most experienced former cadres residing in the community. After the war, they harnessed control over local affairs, using positions within the directorate and within local FMLN structures. Ellacuría's residents were divided with regard to their support for these leaders, with a substantial number expressing discontent.[118]

The Issue of Land

Scraping beneath the surface, I learned that landownership was a central bone of contention. With the failure of collective production, the fields around Ellacuría had become an intricate barbwire patchwork. One night, as we were sitting on plastic chairs in his patio, Pablo recalled how, before and during the war, he and his comrades used to sing "A Desalambrar"

(Take down the wire fences), a protest song that called for collectivization of land to benefit poor peasants. Pablo made a bittersweet joke that people were now obsessed with fencing off their plots.[119] Ironically, these plots were often not the property of those putting up the fences. Close to half of Ellacuría's families still depended on community lands to be able to grow crops.[120] The members of the directorate held significant sway over who got which piece of land to cultivate, since they distributed collective farm-land each year to petitioning families.[121]

There was also another issue at play. At the time of the PTT, the directorate had played a central role in negotiating and assigning properties. According to Pablo, roughly half of the land obtained through the PTT for the Ellacuría families was close-by enough for them to farm; the rest was too far away.[122] Some stretches of land, furthermore, were of much higher quality than others. Hence, even though the nominal value of the PTT land assigned per beneficiary was similar, the real value differed. According to some who ended up with relatively useless land, the directorate had maneuvered to favor their relatives and friends with access to the best properties.[123]

An additional complication was that the community did not formally own part of the communal land. The reason for this was that, when the directorate bought most of the land, Ellacuría's community associations[124] did not exist yet in legal terms.[125] Therefore, in order to be able to buy land, the directorate had to get the transactions registered on personal titles. The directorate recurred to namesakes, selecting acting directorate members or individuals closely associated with them. After the community association was legalized, several namesakes subsequently did not transfer their nominal property.[126] To make things worse, the Ellacuría directorate files from the 1990s no longer exist. Allegedly these were lost when a group of children charged with cleaning out the community office accidentally destroyed part of them. According to other sources, the papers were lost in a deliberate fire.[127]

The ambiguity regarding the ownership of communal lands fueled speculations within the community that some (former) directorate members were retaining their nominal property as a bargaining chip, or that they might be maneuvering in order to safeguard private ownership in the future. For example, one family that had been working the same piece of land since the 1989 repatriation learned that this communal plot was legally registered under the name of a community leader. They repeatedly requested the property to be transferred either to their name or to the name of the community. The owner refused. There was gossip that he sought to will the property to his son. In another example, the namesake owner of the tract of land assigned to a communal women's project decided to fence it off to let his animals graze there.[128]

When asked what could be done, some claimed they would like to see substantial reform, but that they had few hopes for this to happen anytime soon. According to Pablo, the issue of land was beyond repair, because "they all have skeletons in the closet." He thought that too many of Ellacuría's leading families were implicated to make a wholesale solution viable. The only thing that could be done was to defend the right of the most vulnerable families to use community land.[129]

Political Dissent and Discomfort

"Severina" and "Santos," an elderly Cabañas couple with numerous offspring, shared their disillusionment with local politics at length. Because of how their reflections contribute to understanding Ellacuría's postwar community politics, I include a lengthy excerpt from the interview transcript.

> *Severina*: . . . We've already seen that it's the same for us no matter who they put on the directorate . . . , because with [mentions the name of community president] the same thing happened. . . . When he was in charge . . . he handed out the smallest plots . . . , but he himself profited, because he took a plot here and another there. . . . Whoever is in charge, . . . we already know that they will continue with the same old dirty tricks, . . . this is where we lose hope . . . , this is where I tell you that we are screwed. We have this community [which] clearly . . . is all about *compadres, ahijados* [godfathers, godchildren] and the like. . . .
> *Santos*: Compadres . . . or brothers cannot be directorate members [together] in a cooperative; they can be workers there, but not part of the directorate, and this is the problem here. . . .
> *Severina*: The problem today is that we have two brothers from the [name] family in the directorate . . . but the thing is, I told [a historical leader] to his face, whether he is inside or outside the directorate, [he] is manipulating the members, because [he] and [the community

president at the time of the interview] are compadres, you see? . . . Another fine thing they did: the plots they distributed when [mentions a leaders' name] was in the directorate! . . . Look, the dirt we have in this community, one year wouldn't be enough to uncover it all! Here we have things that are unjust, because . . . we all come from a time [of equal poverty] . . . and then everybody started grabbing for himself. . . .

Santos: Always as directorate members . . .

Severina: To regain equality, we would have to go back: those that have a lot have to cede, and those that have small [properties] will get more. But this requires cleansing, an honest job, as we say. As a directorate member, if he wants to work honestly he could, but no, because they already have [dirty hands]. . . . Clearly, the one who has most is [a former president of the directorate]. His family is small. [Another community leader] has plots everywhere and they are just five people. . . . This I can say to their face: they are the ones in charge here! I think of [mentions a community member who favors the directorate] like she is the protégée of these monsters. What she does is to not say anything. She says: "I don't like problems, I don't like to get mixed up in anything."[130]

"The fault lies with individuals, not with the organization," Santos emphasized several times when we continued to speak at length about postwar community politics.[131] He revisited various episodes to contextualize the current animosity between his family and community leadership. The antecedents included disputes over water distribution, over the PTT, over private ownership of community land, and most recently, over the refusal by one of the community leaders to allow an access road to a plot of land Santos farms. On different occasions, local leadership allegedly called Santos as "stubborn as a *guardia*,"[132] accusing him not only of inflexibility, but also of the wrong politics.[133]

I asked Santos and Severina why they hadn't returned to Cabañas instead of settling in Ellacuría. Severina replied, with some anger in her voice, that they ended up in Ellacuría because they followed instructions. Santos interrupted, offered a neutralizing smile, and emphasized their "obedience'" in repopulating Chalatenango, in accordance with party guidelines, rather than seeking to return to Cabañas or look for a home elsewhere. Looking back on the political journey his family embarked on for the last decades, Santos offered only praise for the FPL and the FMLN. The explanation he chose to share with me placed the blame for his family's predicament exclusively on the abuse of local leaders, and kept it far from party politics and the broader political process. I gathered that Santos wanted to avoid being confused with a "contrario." If he were accusable of right-wing sympathies, his criticism could easily be dismissed and, in Ellacuría's particular political context, worsen the sociopolitical position of him and his family.[134]

When I spoke to Ellacuría's leaders about internal affairs, they emphasized that they have done a lot to benefit different members of the community as evenly as possible, while taking into account a range of specific needs and circumstances. They remarked that, logically, there are always people who will disagree with a given decision or who claim a larger share. As a directorate, they have the task and responsibility of looking out for the common good. Their intention was to put community resources to the benefit of all.[135] They pointed out, however, that it was virtually impossible to keep everyone satisfied. Unfortunately, they said, not everybody is aware of what it takes to contribute to an organized community. Nonetheless, even if people think differently, that did not mean the directorate would exclude them from community projects or benefits. On the contrary, they claimed to make specific efforts to avoid marginalizing anyone.[136]

Community Leadership and Sectarianism

Postwar frictions in Ellacuría cannot be understood without reference to the community's insurgent history. A key element of this history entailed that the most important community assets were seen as benefits acquired collectively, by means of a struggle in which all participated and all made great sacrifices. Hence, families like Severina and Santos's considered they were entitled to an equal share. Nonetheless, significant inequalities existed, and, somewhat ironically, status and privilege that were acquired through insurgent participation played a role in them. Key community leaders derived their position in part from having been PMO cadres.

Exceptions also existed. As we have seen earlier, Pablo also held cadre status during the war and was the principal leader of the return effort. Why then hadn't he grown into one of Ellacuría's principal postwar leaders? When discussing his current position in the community, he explained that he left the repopulation between 1990 and 1993, which had disconnected him from ongoing developments at the time.[137] When he came back to settle in Ellacuría, he found others in control. Additionally, PMO sectarianism played a role in Pablo's marginalization. The two principal postwar leaders had wartime links with the PCS-FAL as well as with the FPL. Pablo, on the contrary, only had contacts within the FPL. During the FMLN's internal disputes between the revolutionary socialists and reformers in the mid-1990s, Ellacuría's leaders sided with the revolutionary socialists. According to Pablo, this led to apprehensions toward former FPL militants in the community with no PCS-FAL connections, who were presumed to be on the side of the renovadores.[138] Initially, the FMLN leadership in Chalatenango was more favorable to the renovadores, but when that current faltered at the national level after 1999, most of Chalatenango's renovadores aligned with the new FMLN mainstream. Chalatenango's revolutionary-socialist sector, which included the local former PCS-FAL cadres, subsequently saw its local political position strengthened because of the national outcome.[139]

Pablo said that local leaders in the repopulations frequently take advantage of divisions in the FMLN to the benefit of their own power position. He illustrated his argument with what happened in the case of his home region of Santa Marta, Cabañas. After the FPL left the political control of this area to the RN, tensions arose between the remaining FPL families and local RN leadership. Toward the end of the war the situation escalated, and there were several violent incidents. Tensions continued in the postwar period, and motivated many FPL families to leave Santa Marta and resettle elsewhere, in places like Ellacuría or in the repopulations around Suchitoto and near San Pablo Tacachico (located in the La Libertad department). Pablo considered that these "were surely not mistakes committed at the highest level (of leadership), but rather by mid-level cadres."[140]

It's a shame. Because in Santa Marta, I think that's why so many people lost their political commitment because of this matter, it made them lose their perspective. A lot of people, leaders! For example a woman called Carmen: a leader! And now: a leader of ARENA! Now they use her in their rallies. She was a historical comrade with a true fighting spirit. She felt abandoned. Abandoned by the FPL, I mean! Today she is an enemy, an enemy politically speaking. . . . [Years before, during the war] when they started sending compañeros over there [to Santa Marta] in order to [address this situation], well sometimes the RN captured them. . . . [He names an important FPL leader in Chalatenango during the war] went something like three times, and they even wanted to . . . [he does not finish this sentence]. They [the RN] killed our compañeros. My niece was shot with a machine gun. . . . Yes, because of politics! It is shameful to be telling this.[141]

Broader historical and political cleavages appear to help make sense of postwar community affairs. As we have seen in the case of Santos and Severina, these include the "master" cleavage between FMLN and ARENA, with its strong symbolic roots in the war. As becomes clear from Pablo's account, they also include perceived cleavages within the FMLN, including the sectarian PMO identities inherited from the history of the insurgent movement.

Visiting Ellacuría in 2012, Pablo confided to me that he was not going to vote for the local FMLN candidates in the municipal elections, because what he called "the PCS line" dominated in the candidacies. He considered that if this group won, the result would be further marginalization for himself and other people in the community. He was not alone: some sectors within the FMLN in Chalatenango city were working "under the radar" to have people abstain or vote for a non-FMLN candidate. Also, Pablo now pondered voting for a right-wing party, though not ARENA. He emphasized that this did not mean he no longer considered himself to be part of the FMLN. "We must not allow them [supporters of the PCS line] to take that away from us."[142]

FROM THEN TO NOW: EXPLAINING POSTINSURGENT INEQUALITIES

To reconcile the revolutionary past with the postinsurgent present was a difficult task. In the period between 1992 and 1995, when I lived in Chalatenango myself, idealistic stories about the building of a new kind of society in the repopulations were already dwindling down. Since then, revolutionary disenchantment and political intrigue have been constant in my conversations with repobladores from the area.

Take Juan, a repoblador and ex-combatant from San José Las Flores, and an old friend from my Chalatenango years. When I interviewed him for this study, he told me it was hard to believe how much his town had changed. "Here in the community presumably we were all equal; we were all equally poor when the war ended. If one of us ate, we all did." According to Juan, two decades later, in Las Flores a few families have become rich, while other families are struggling to survive. These "new rich," as Juan calls them, dominate local politics. Most commented upon was one repoblador who had been the local mayor for the FMLN for five consecutive terms and also owned the largest local supply store.[143]

> *Juan*: Today, . . . we live here but it is not with the same spirit, right?, like at the time of the war, when we lived all united. There is so much difference [now]. What happened is that there were people who held leadership positions in the community, they took advantage and took things that belonged to the community and, as a result, they are in a better economic position.
> *Ralph*: So, . . . today, if we compare the poorest family in the community with the wealthiest family, how much difference is there?
> *Juan*: Uuuuuy! Shit!
> *Ralph*: Ten times wealthier?
> *Juan*: Ten times? More . . . !
> *Ralph*: Twenty times?
> *Juan*: Perhaps more! Because in this community we have . . . a lot of very poor people. . . . If we compare them to the wealth that other people here have accumulated, they are poor. . . . For example, the people have received construction materials to build their homes as well as the plot for their house, and that's good, but . . . behind all of that, things are hidden. . . . In order to justify a project, . . . they give the people something, but more of it stays in the hands of other people [of the leadership] than what is given to the people. . . . When I think about everything they used to tell us back then, the idea of the revolution, the idea to change this country, today we can see that it's really not that easy.

In Juan's perspective, the FMLN's form of engaging in local politics had become increasingly similar to what he identified as the historical right-wing practices of patronage politics.

Today the left-wing ideology is maybe to set us apart from the right, but in the end I think it's just about the same. . . . Whoever comes here has to become part of the FMLN, because all of us are part of the FMLN, right, and that's how we work, in support of the party, . . . but is there a big difference between left and right? In truth, I don't see much. . . . What the political parties do is that they contact [someone who is a leader] and they start working with him so that he works the people for them to work for the party. So what this person does is he invests for these people to elect him in a post. . . . Yes! Because I go see a person "x" and I tell him: "Look, I need this much money, because I don't have any." This person gives him the money. Then, the people take this as a commitment to be there for that person when the time comes. . . .

Ralph: Now I have to repay this favor . . .

Juan: Aha! Aha! That's how things work here. For instance, the mayor, he gives handouts to the people so that they will support him and he will remain in office. . . . So how are things done here? He that has wealth dominates! That's the one who ends up being the candidate and that continues to be the mayor. . . . In other words, the project is no longer that of changing things for the benefit of the people, but for the benefit of his own pocket.[144]

Juan thought the Las Flores mayor acted "like the *cacique* from before."[145] Apart from his economic dominance, over the last two decades he has established *compadrazgo* (godparenthood) with many local families. These compadrazgo networks overlap community organization and local party politics in ways that legitimize the accumulation of power by one or several dominant families.[146] For repobladores like Juan, the stark contradictions between the discourse of the revolution and postwar realities practices have not gone unnoticed.

One night in the repopulation of Las Vueltas, west across the mountains from Las Flores, a colleague and I sat down with "Elsa" and "Victoria," two women I have long known, both repobladoras with extensive community-organizing experience. We chatted to catch up on family affairs. At some point, the conversation turned to local politics, and became ridden with retrospective disappointment. Elsa commented on how she had recently asked a well-known Las Vueltas FMLN leader for a lift to San Salvador. He traveled to San Salvador frequently and was one of the few residents with a pickup truck at his disposal. Elsa lived a half-hour walk south of Las Vueltas, on the road to San Salvador. Nonetheless, his reply had been that if she wanted a lift she should first come to his house, because "on the street I won't stop for anyone."

Once she had gotten started on the subject, Elsa had no good words left for local leaders. She claimed that they were all swindlers. After the peace accords, the community received cattle, horses, and goats, all bought with donations. According to Elsa, "The most astute put their brand mark on them and said: this one is mine." The community pickup truck was sold, and, so she claimed, "two of [the directorate] ate up the money. . . ." Elsa offered several other examples of appropriation of community goods by local leaders.

Then Victoria told a story to illustrate that this type of abuse also occurred during the war. Shortly after the repopulation of Las Vueltas, with the war raging, one FPL leader had received a significant sum of money intended to provide for the guerrilla troops and their expenses at the front. The man had taken the money and made a run for Honduras. As a result, the repobladores from Las Vueltas had been ordered to increase their war contribution and to tighten their belts, along with the troops. Victoria's story was about how ordinary repobladores and combatants sometimes served to fatten corrupt guerrilla leaders. Her retrospective lesson was that they should have seen it coming: peace benefits would not be equally distributed.[147]

Several leaders from Guarjila, the region's largest repopulation, received similar harsh criticism in my interviews. According to Guarjila resident and lay worker Alex, community organization had failed in many regards. He considered that former revolutionary leaders had, over time, become a conservative political force and an obstacle for development. Alex illustrated this with how the directorate handled the community bakery, which was equipped, financed, and staffed for several years by means of international donations.[148]

All community projects were like the Soviet Union, and all of them failed. They all failed! . . . Today people want to be the owners. And they do not want to work with the directorate that pays them "shit" and bosses them around as if they were employees. . . . I can talk about . . . the case of Guarjila: money like you wouldn't believe, projects like you wouldn't believe . . . and each project has failed and that's why people think: "Why am I doing this [to participate in community projects]? I don't need this anymore." . . . [For example,] the communal bakery, . . . like in the Soviet Union, the products that came out were "shit." We had a cafeteria, extremely filthy! . . . This was the product of our communism, right. This was our product and it was called "shit." . . . [So] [a Guarjila resident I shall name "Liduvina"] set up her own bakery. . . . [A baker from the city of Chalatenango offered] to train six women [from Guarjila], to make different types of bread. . . . He is very good . . . ! Only [Liduvina] went and she was really criticized [by the directorate], like you wouldn't believe. This is how we slow down our development. . . . "Why is she going with [him]? She is too ambitious! Why is she doing this? Damn, she won't make any money there!" Because that was the deal with the baker [that she wouldn't make money], but she went every day, for six months, and very submissively, but she learned. . . . So [Liduvina], the most criticized, "the whore," because for them [the directorate] that is what she was . . . [now] she has a very good business. Her product, everybody buys it.

Ralph: And the communal bakery?

Alex: It closed.

Very little had been learned from the many truncated development projects in Guarjila, Alex claimed. In 2010, any given project that arrived to the community was still liable to be mismanaged, in particular by some of the older, more experienced leaders. Like Las Flores, Alex claimed, Guarjila also has its new rich, like the family whom I shall refer to as the Sánchez family, well known in Guarjila and surroundings. A large family, with strong wartime revolutionary credentials, the Sánchezes had many supporters as well as detractors in northeastern Chalatenango at the time of fieldwork. For example, when I discussed the matter with "Oscar," a veteran community leader from the area and someone I know very well from my Chalatenango years, he told me, "Look, I know that the [Sánchez family] is really criticized. But I believe they have gotten where they are because they are united, it is a large and united family. They work hard and they've known what to do. What's wrong with that? The thing is that people don't see that, they only see what they have, and that's where envy can come into play."[149]

Alex only partially concurred with Oscar's view. In his perspective, things started to go astray when, just before the peace accords, insurgent leaders like the Sánchez brothers oriented everybody not to buy any land, because this would be acquired collectively. "Land is not bought but conquered" was the slogan at the time (Alvarenga and Baumgärtner 2008, 11). According to Alex, the Sánchez brothers and a few other leaders started to quietly purchase some of the best land in the area privately, before the PTT drove the prices up. The next step up for the Sánchez brothers was that, when the different reconstruction programs got underway, they made sure they were on every possible list.

> *Alex*: [The Sánchez family] applied for . . . all available projects, but as a family. They took advantage as a family and their development was incredible. Don [Andrés, one of the Sánchez brothers,] has incredible parcels, . . . because they knew how to handle money . . . [Andrés] is incredible for business. . . . So, they have acquired their wealth like the people from before. . . . [Andrés] is Guarjila's old power. . . . But [Andrés] . . . always wears mismatched shoes to put on the facade of a poor farmer. . . .
>
> *Ralph*: But the image still persists of these communities as places in a sense . . . extraordinary, revolutionary and with [revolutionary] track record . . . ?
>
> *Alex*: . . . Some people think we are something that we are not, and some [people from the community] want to take advantage of this. . . . Because [of] this revolutionary energy that existed before, right? [The repopulations] drew the attention of the whole world and brought incredible solidarity, right? Each year and in every different stage, right? . . . It's an image, this is sad, but it is true; it's an image that allows you to sell yourself.

The "image" that Alex referred to concerns Guarjila's insurgent status. Its community leaders continued to present Guarjila to outsiders as a revolutionary bulwark. They still frequently recur to the use of revolutionary discourse that presents the community both as a place of historical heroism and a continued popular alternative, engaged in an ongoing struggle with the "system" sustained by the right-wing elements that continue to dominate the country. According to Alex, this discourse contrasts painfully with Guarjila's social reality. In his view, Guarjila's poor have in reality lost faith in each other and in themselves. Violence, crime, vandalism, domestic abuse, and alcoholism have become common fare in the community. Alex offered that the most loyal and genuine followers of the revolution ended up paying the price for believing in the revolution too much and looking out too little for their personal interests. "I would say that the most revolutionary people in the communities are the poorest. People that really committed themselves, who fought and believed. . . . Good militants! They attended the meetings, the protest marches, right? They believed [in the revolution] and [now] really are the ones furthest behind."

Alex's reflections point to a remarkable paradox. While Guarjila's revolutionary heritage might still be used to "sell" the community to outsiders, those with "genuine" faith in the revolution itself might have actually become increasingly marginalized inside the community. In any case, similar to what we encountered in other repopulations, Alex's account of postwar Guarjila suggests that the repobladores there saw revolutionary aspirations diluted with a sobering dose of realpolitik.

ELLACURÍA'S CROSSROADS

Two initiatives that emerged in Ellacuría during the time of fieldwork emblematized the current state of the repopulation project. Ellacuría's community directorate promoted the first one. Its goal was to obtain a legal change of name of the community from Guancora to Comunidad Ignacio Ellacuría. The repobladores' use of the latter had become less frequent over the years, with most using the names Guancora and Ellacuría alternately, or solely referring to Guancora. For strictly legal purposes, the location was still called Guancora, since the Salvadoran government never formally sanctioned a new name. To change it would entail a procedure involving the departmental governor, the Ministry of Interior and the Parliament. Previously, with ARENA in power, Arturo and other directorate members thought that attempts to legalize the community's new name would be futile. After 2009, with Mauricio Funes as president, the directorate set up a meeting with Chalatenango's newly appointed departmental governor, followed by a formal petition initiating the procedure.[150]

The directorate saw this initiative as a way for the inhabitants of the community to remember where they came from, and to educate younger generations about their home village's history.[151] For the directorate, flying the name Ellacuría constituted a political allegory, a rephrasing of one of the FMLN's principal postwar slogans: "The struggle continues." The directorate said the entire community was behind the petition. Indeed, as far as I could tell, the repobladores either supported the initiative or were indifferent to it. I suspected that, in any case, many would continue to use the name Guancora. Nonetheless, the initiative could be interpreted as a form of updating communal commitment to the insurgent heritage. Which might prevail: the community's traditional name or its insurgent name? With Ellacuría's internal politics in mind, this matter gained significant symbolism.

The second initiative generated various questions on the heritage of the insurgent repopulation project in Ellacuría. It concerned the intended repopulation of La Pinte, in Cabañas. Pablo was born and raised there, an hour by foot from Santa Marta and two hours' walking from the town of Villa Victoria.

In several conversations, Pablo had talked to me with enthusiasm about La Pinte, "such a beautiful place" and the place of origin of a dozen of Ellacuría's families. Abandoned at the start of the war, La Pinte had never been repopulated. The problem was that it could only be reached by foot or on horseback. With the FMLN in government, Pablo had taken the initiative to put together a delegation of La Pinte natives to petition for the construction of a dirt road into the La Pinte valley. However, prospects were not good, since technical obstacles made the project very expensive. Nonetheless, Pablo had already enlisted several families originally from La Pinte interested in a possible return, families currently living in Ellacuría and in two other repopulations. One obstacle was that this time it would be very difficult to find resources and projects to help finance the process. Another difficulty was that the elderly tended to be more enthusiastic with this project than the family youngsters who had never lived in La Pinte or did not even know the place. Therefore, some were held back because their children would not join them there. Pablo nonetheless seemed determined to go through with his plan.[152]

What to make of Pablo's yearning for La Pinte? In what ways would this repopulation expedition be different from the one Pablo had organized in 1989? I could not make up my mind whether the idea of several of Ellacuría families eventually returning "home" to La Pinte, over three decades after the exodus of war, symbolized a defeat or a new beginning. For Pablo and his followers, should they undertake this step, the enormous task of making La Pinte inhabitable once more would probably leave little time for reflection on these matters.

IN HIS STUDY on a "revolutionary town after the revolution," Daniel Nugent portrays how the peasant supporters of the Mexican revolution, those that did most of the fighting, profited little from the broader benefits generated by the process, especially when compared to other groups involved. Nugent cites a peasant leader who called his town folks *cartuchos quemados*, "the burnt or spent cartridges of a struggle in which the victory went to other social classes" (1993, 3). For peasants participating in insurgent movements, the shift from revolutionary prominence to post-revolutionary marginalization is a phenomenon that, indeed, has occurred in numerous historical contexts. But the fact that peasants might not cash in on revolutionary participation as effectively other participating groups does not mean that their participation might not generate any rewards, or that their communities might not be transformed through the experience of insurgent participation and its aftermath.

In order to study such transformations, it is important to consider with care the insurgent relations that affected or involved the peasantry. Therefore, I started out this chapter with a review of the role the PMOs played in the repopulation movement. I showed how strategic considerations of the PMO leadership were instrumental in drawing out the settlement patterns of this movement. The repobladores relied on their affiliation with a particular PMO to organize their return. The repopulations allowed the PMOs to reconvert existing peasant support bases into a settlers' movement. The repobladores continued to be connected to the PMOs through political-military networks that were inserted clandestinely within the community itself. This was the manner in which the inhabitants of the repopulations lived "at the service of war."

The repobladores' postwar disillusionment might be interpreted in part as a backlash to insurgent grandiloquence. Its emergence as a predominant sentiment probably says more about the high expectations invested in the revolution than it does about postwar development in itself.

Nonetheless, it must be understood that for a generation of repobladores—as well as for those who have lived with them or have studied them over the years, myself included—it is very difficult not to perceive the repopulations in the mirror of past promises.

These promises were generated in several different spheres of interaction: that of the PMOs with their rural supporters, that of local leaders and their followers, that of international delegations and observers eager to support a new society in the making. After the peace accords, the inherited expectations were subsequently larded with development discourses, and community organization became the panacea for reconstruction and development programs (van der Borgh 2003). The community directorates gained relative independence from the PMOs, right at the time that they started to manage significant amounts of money and make crucial decisions with regard to the distribution of resources. Those who were both well positioned and willing to embrace a "pragmatic" approach thrived. Once socioeconomic differences became more evident, the repobladores started to reconfigure community relations in accordance with emerging differentials, and old-fashioned compadrazgo-based patronage regained prominence.

At the same time, and somewhat paradoxically, ideological discourses inherited from the revolutionary period persisted. Political identities forged during the insurgent participation became a crucial tool in local politics. It resulted in the continued intertwining of insurgent history, party politics, development projects, and community organizing. As a consequence, the FMLN's major political battles and cleavages from the war and the postwar period were restaged and reenacted on the micropolitical level in the repopulations.

Some researchers, struggling to rhyme insurgent promises with the repopulations' present realities, seek to explain postwar development in terms of the encroachment of neoliberalism and its effect upon the communities, as the story of how "the neoliberal model gradually established itself in the former war zone" (Köpcke 1999, 260; see also Binford 2010). Postwar popular organization in the repopulations then became a story of continued resistance in these disadvantageous circumstances. It is true that some factors of crucial importance to the repopulations, like labor migration and prices of agricultural products, are certainly contingent upon neoliberal globalization (Kay 2015). One could also argue that the shape and character of many development projects, as well as the role of local government, suffered significantly from the preponderance of neoliberal policy recipes during the 1990s (Silber 2011). As McElhinny points out, the "rewriting of prewar property relations provoked by insurgent communities" occurred together with "a secular shift toward individual modes of production," partly inspired by neoliberalism (2006, 350).

Nonetheless, a focus on neoliberalism should not obscure the complicity of PMO legacies in generating the present-day inequalities in the repopulations. The repopulations' postwar trajectories cannot be understood without considering the impact of insurgent history. The safeguarding and deepening of privileges gained by some in the course of the revolution has been a very important part of that mix. Community organizations, former revolutionary leadership, and FMLN party politics all contributed to hollowing out the egalitarian promises of the former "People's Republic of Chalatenango."

CHAPTER 6

Postwar Life Trajectories
of Former Guerrilla Fighters

Definitivamente no es lo mismo hablar con alguien que ha estado
siempre en el partido, que hablar con alguien que le tocó rebuscarse.
—Wilber (ex-combatant of the FAL)

While the comandantes' postwar trajectories are well known, much less is
known about what happened after the war to rank-and-file and middle
cadres. Where are these "ordinary" Salvadoran guerrilla fighters now?
What are the main livelihood strategies they used to survive after the
peace accords? How did they experience and make sense of the postwar
transition? The historical photographs of guerrilla units featured in this
chapter were put to work to find out what happened to those portrayed
and, in the process, to reflect on the legacy of insurgency. Findings delin-
eate how, after insurgent demobilization, former guerrilla fighters continued to rely extensively on PMO networks inherited from the war as
part of postwar livelihood strategies. They furthermore illustrate the
impact of the internal dynamics of postinsurgency on the lives and livelihoods of former guerrilla fighters.

SAMPLING POSTINSURGENT LIVES

How to build a faithful sample of the former insurgents' postwar life trajectories? I asked this question as I was already engaged in ethnographic

fieldwork with several FMLN veteran groups. It quickly became clear to me that only a reduced number of guerrilla veterans were politically active as such. Hence, if I limited the mapping of life trajectories only to those currently participating as veterans, this would predetermine my sample. What then about former fighters who no longer participated in politics? Or what about those who were active in other political sectors or groups, rather than collectives of war veterans?

To obtain a broad overview of postinsurgency, I needed a methodology that could accommodate such a variety of postwar alternatives. Building a sample by "snowballing," based on my contacts and informers, would inevitably carry the imprint of my own position and that of my informers.[1] I considered using lists of reinsertion beneficiaries, but here I also encountered several problems. For example, what about those who, like explosives expert Justo in chapter 1, had not participated in the demobilization and reinsertion process? Over the years I have met many former insurgents who participated extensively during the war, but who did not formally demobilize or participate in reinsertion programs. I also met youngsters who had never participated in the guerrilla army, but who, mainly through family connections, were channeled into the camps in 1992 to increase the FMLN's numbers.

At any rate, using reinsertion beneficiaries for sampling life trajectories proved to be impossible, since I was unable to obtain comprehensive lists of FMLN beneficiaries. This was mainly because the Fundación 16 de Enero (F-16), the organization in charge of coordinating the reinsertion and reintegration programs, fell apart in 1994 as a result of internal strife within the FMLN. At the time, Salvadoran NGO Fundación para el Desarrollo (FUNDESA)[2] inherited the existing programs and archives of the F-16. Contracts with donor organization stipulated a ten-year safeguard period of all the documentation concerning the reinsertion programs. When this period expired, the institution evacuated and burned the F-16 archives—so FUNDESA's director declared.[3]

Luckily, a more interesting alternative for sample building appeared to me in the course of fieldwork. During one of my visits to Chalatenango, I looked up "Federico," an old friend and an ex-combatant who had come out of the war with numerous scars and one glass eye. Halfway into the 1990s, Federico was a smart and affable but restless young man, disillusioned with the lack of peacetime opportunities and unsure of what route to take into the future. Then he heard that the FMLN was giving out scholarships to study medicine in Cuba. His application, together with his guerrilla credentials, secured his place among one of the first groups of students to enroll in Cuba's Escuela Latinoamericana de Medicina (ELAM).[4] Already a physician, in 2009 he was close to finishing his specialization. When we talked over the phone in 2009, Federico was particularly eager to talk to me, because he was in the process of writing his memoirs, and he wanted my advice.

Via email, Federico forwarded a well-advanced manuscript the next day. It held vivid descriptions of the battles he had participated in and of the comrades who had died in the process. It also recounted in detail how he himself had been gravely wounded and how he miraculously survived. We agreed to meet a few days later to go through the manuscript. While sitting at his kitchen table in one of the repopulated towns in Chalatenango, we discussed my feedback notes. Then we came to talking about one of the pictures illustrating the document. It depicted a guerrilla combat unit, posing before the camera in a relatively informal formation. "This is me," Federico said, when he pointed at the face of one of the young men at the back of the formation, peeking over the shoulders of his older comrades. When the image was made, Federico, sixteen years old, had recently been recruited together with other adolescents from the repopulated town of San José Las Flores into the guerrilla army. This was when the insurgent forces were gathering strength in preparation for the November 1989 general offensive. One of the FPL's cadres who were involved had taken the picture as a souvenir.[5]

As we discussed the photograph, it turned out Federico knew quite a bit about those who had been there with him that day. A few had been killed in combat during the last years of the war. Several of the survivors had settled in repopulations after the war. Federico had stayed in touch with most of them. The photograph only included a handful he had completely lost track of. The discussion of his former comrades' postwar endeavors proved a rich source of information, as our conversation extended to why people's lives had developed the way they did, and as different stories and anecdotes about those in the picture came on the table. The photograph stimulated what I perceived as a well-grounded analysis of postinsurgent life trajectories.

Federico offered to talk with ex-combatants he knew to reconstruct what had happened to the incogniti in the picture. I also printed a copy of

Source: Photograph by Francisco Ramírez Galán. Used by permission.

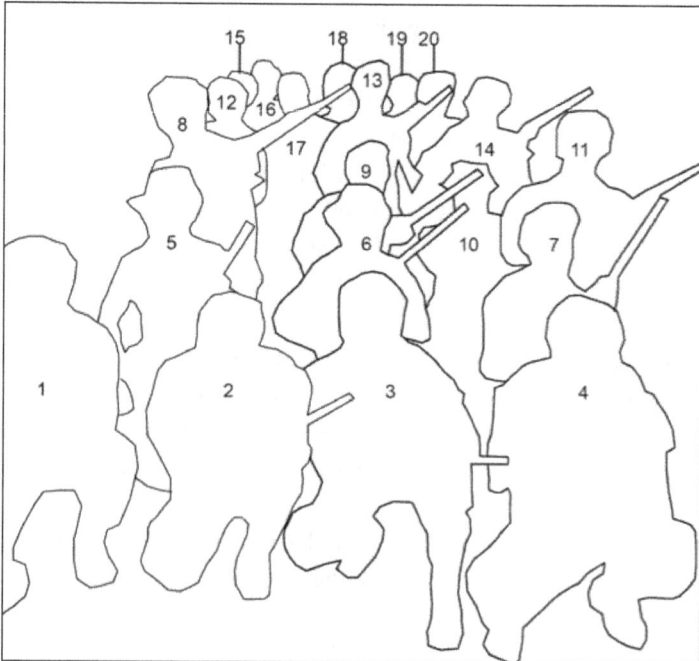

Figure 6.1. FPL, San José Las Flores, Chalatenango (October 1989)

1. Works with the FMLN in San Vicente.
2. War-wounded. Combines agricultural activities with running a transportation service in the FMLN-affiliated settlement he moved to after the war.
3. Migrated to Canada after the war and works in a landscaping company.
4. Migrated to the United States after the war.
5. Entered the PNC after the peace accords as part of the FMLN quota. Still active as a police officer.
6. A farmer in a repopulation in Chalatenango.
7. Combines agricultural activities with working as an NGO-appointed dental technician in a repopulation.
8. Killed in combat in 1990 in Chalatenango.
9. Works odd jobs in San Salvador. His family still lives in San José Las Flores.
10. A farmer in an FMLN-affiliated resettlement.
11. Migrated to the United States after the war.
12. A farmer in an FMLN-affiliated resettlement.
13. Killed in combat in 1990 in Cinquera, Cabañas.
14. Migrated to the United States.
15. Identity unknown.
16. Killed in combat in 1990 in Cinquera, Cabañas.
17. Works for the municipal police corps in an FMLN municipality.
18. Entered the PNC as part of the FMLN quota after the peace accords; later left for the United States.
19. War-wounded. Granted a scholarship to study medicine in Cuba. Finishing his specialization.
20. Identity unknown.

the image, and consulted with several ex-combatant friends and acquaintances in Chalatenango to fill gaps and confirm the information Federico had already provided. Over the next few months, we met a few times in Chalatenango and in San Salvador to compare our findings and to fill in missing information. We were able to identify all the fighters except one, and we mapped out nineteen different trajectories, spanning more than two decades and several countries, all captured in one single photograph.

An experienced guerrilla leader led the group and was assigned a few seasoned fighters as squad leaders (they feature in the first row of photograph 6.1, with the leader on the far left). The rest were inexperienced adolescents, mostly from the repopulation of San José Las Flores. Although this unit participated in the offensive with little previous combat experience, they did not suffer any casualties at first; not until later on, when in the aftermath of the offensive they withdrew from the capital back to the guerrilla rearguard areas and became engaged in heavy combat around the town of Cinquera.

In the period between the offensive and the peace accords, Federico's unit participated in numerous operations in Cabañas and Chalatenango. On April 2, 1991, in an operation meant to take over a well-secured hydroelectric dam between Chalatenango and Cabañas, a landmine blew up close to Federico's face while he was advancing toward a position, crawling on the ground. His comrades retrieved his injured body and transported him by hammock into the mountains. After a few days of indescribable suffering, Federico finally reached a field hospital in the repopulation of Guarjila. There, shrapnel and dirt embedded in his upper torso and face were removed. After several weeks of treatment, he was then sent to a specialized clinic in San Salvador, where he received the treatment that allowed him to save his one remaining eye.

GUERRILLA PHOTOGRAPHS AS RESEARCH TOOL

For Federico, many stories were encapsulated in his unit's photograph. The appeal of our approach consisted of the photographic image combined with the life stories we collected, and the depth both acquired because of each other. No longer was it a photo of an anonymous group of guerrilla fighters, whose intrinsic meaning largely depended on the ideological associations it evoked; instead it had become a compact but comprehensive retrospect into the lives and times of a group of rank-and-file guerrilla fighters.

John Berger suggests that "the thrill found in a photograph comes from the onrush of memory" (1992, 192). Indeed, by providing a stereotypical image of a belligerent group of guerrilla fighters, the picture inevitably evokes a past era. However, at the same time, the knowledge Federico, I, and others had gathered now also allowed us to look at the picture with different eyes, to partially "liberate" the image from its frozen time, and qualify its meaning beyond the aesthetics of revolution or warfare.

Federico himself commented on the picture with a complex mix of sentiments. There was reminiscence over the revolutionary and combative spirit and the sense of brotherhood he felt had accompanied their war efforts at the time. There was nostalgia for his youth, which also represented the time his body was still intact, without the physical injuries he would now carry for the rest of his life. He also recalled how hard his recruitment had been for his mother, a woman who had already suffered great hardship because of the war. Federico also shared many comments on the other fighters in the picture, and we reflected on how their lives had turned out two decades later. There was talk of what was lost and what might have been gained and by whom.[6]

"A photograph is both a pseudo-presence and a token of absence," Susan Sontag writes (1977, 16). The experience with Federico's photograph opened my eyes to what a powerful mnemonic device we had come across. As ethnographer Douglas Harper claims, "that extraordinary sense of seeming to retrieve something that has disappeared belongs alone to the photograph, and it leads to deep and interesting talk" (2002, 23). Federico's photograph helped him to historicize his own life and, in the process, move away from commonplaces that are usually exchanged in conversation on the war and its legacies. Instead Federico now grounded his reflection on these large subjects more explicitly in his personal history and that of his comrades.

I was impressed by our approach's double capacity to map postinsurgent life trajectories and at the same time generate interesting and relevant conversation, as in an ethnographic fieldwork methodology known as "photo elicitation" (Harper 2002, 2003; Pink 2004). With the results of Federico's picture, I became convinced of the broader potential of this method—a form of "group portrait–based life-story reconstruction"—for this study. I set out to build a sample of life trajectories based on photographs of groups of guerrilla fighters. For this purpose, I collected wartime photographs from various sources: the personal collections of former combatants; the archive of the Museo de la Palabra y la Imagen (MUPI),[7] a Salvadoran NGO dedicated to collecting photographs and other materials pertaining to the civil war and other aspects of El Salvador's history; and the archive of wartime photographs collected by the Instituto de Estudios Históricos, Antropológicos y Arqueológicos (IEHAA-UES),[8] a research center at the University of El Salvador. From these sources, I initially selected several dozen group photographs. During the final months of fieldwork, time constraints pushed me to make a final selection of eleven photographs to focus on, which are presented in this chapter.[9]

The life trajectory reconstruction efforts based on the guerrilla photographs were both painstaking and rewarding. For one thing, even though pictures of guerrilla activity in El Salvador are relatively abundant, the number of suitable pictures I was able to lay a hand on was quite limited. This related to the particular circumstances of the war. On the one hand, at different times throughout the conflict, the PMOs allowed or promoted the documentation of their troops for propaganda purposes. As we have seen in chapter 2, the different factions of the FMLN strongly relied on private international support in Europe and the United States. To nurture support for their cause, the PMOs produced significant numbers of propaganda and communication materials, including photographs (Cortina Orero 2015; Darling 2008). Also, journalists were allowed at times to enter the guerrilla fronts and document their activities.[10]

On the other hand, during the war photographs of guerrillas were also a potential security threat, should they fall in the hand of the enemy. For example, they could be used to identify and target individual insurgents and their families. Especially in the early years, photographs would often present the guerrilla fighters covering their faces with scarves. As a result of these two contradictory incentives, I found images of El Salvador's guerrillas to be relatively abundant, but mostly not suited for the kind of mapping and tracing of individual identities that I was now aiming for.

Even though progress on reconstructing the life trajectories of those in the photos was often slow and difficult, the veterans responded with enthusiasm to my endeavor, and insisted I should carry along despite prac-

participated in the PCS youth group and who left Managua to join the FAL in 1987—only three survived the war.

Some years later, we invited Wilber to our house to thank him once more for his cooperation in the search for Nadia. We talked about how he had experienced the process of demobilization and his reinsertion after the peace accords, and I asked him if he had any photographs of his former guerrilla unit. The next time we met, he produced two photographs (6.2 and 6.3) from around the time of the peace accords. With the help of the friends that he had stayed in touch with, Wilber was able to trace what had happened after the war to the different combatants in the photographs.

The Guazapa volcano, where this unit operated most of the time, was a highly disputed area during the war. Since combat was frequent, the survivors developed strong military skills. According to Wilber, the fighters in this group, though youthful in appearance, were actually highly disciplined and experienced. Several of these combatants, like Wilber, had started out as child soldiers, proved their valor in combat, and were eventually selected for this elite unit. Wilber himself had entered the war in 1983 when he was eleven years old. As Jocelyn Courtney has pointed out, in El Salvador's war, the use of child soldiers was common in both the Salvadoran armed forces and the guerrilla forces (2010). Indeed, under-age combatants appear regularly in the photographs.

For Wilber and his comrades, the value of their military dexterity became uncertain as a result of peace. Wilber had known little else besides combat and felt helpless with most other matters. In retrospect he considered that the first years after the war had been the most difficult in his life.

> It was incredible to think [that] the war was over and I was alive! . . . We never believed . . . that we were going to stay alive. . . . The first generations that joined the war died, others joined and died. Compañeros who began the war and who were still alive at the end were very few. . . . We don't know how to do anything, we don't have anyone to take us in, what are we going to do? What are we going to live off of? Most importantly, we don't know if really the enemy is going to respect those peace accords or if once we've turned in the weapons and are trying to conduct normal lives, as civilians, if there is going to be a witch hunt and they will begin to kill us [or] put us in jail. So it was a question of uncertainty in which we did not know whether to be happy or worried.[15]

Source: Photograph by Juan José Figueroa. Used by permission.

Figure 6.2. FAL Special Forces unit, Guazapa (late 1991)

1. Employed as a personal protection agent for FMLN leadership.
2. Active as a personal protection agent for FMLN leadership.
3. Enrolled in the university and pursued a career in FMLN politics.
4. Went back to school and then worked as an employee in a private enterprise.
5. Worked for over a decade as a personal protection agent for FMLN leadership. Killed in a robbery after cashing paycheck.
6. Migrated to the United States.
7. Worked for different FMLN-governed municipalities.
8. Became a police officer on the FMLN quota. Killed years later, in his home, allegedly by delinquents.
9. Obtained a job in the police force of an FMLN municipality. Migrated to the United States in 2000.
10. The head of this unit. Pursued a career in FMLN politics. Also owns a family store.
11. Worked for a while as a fare collector on a bus after the war. Current situation unknown.
12. Employed as a personal protection agent for FMLN leadership.
13. Found employment in two different FMLN-affiliated NGOs.
14. Employed at an FMLN municipality.
15. After the war, got a degree and pursued a career in FMLN politics.
16. Employed as a personal protection agent for FMLN leadership.
17. Became an automobile mechanic in his hometown.

Source: Photograph by Iván Montecinos. Used by permission.

Figure 6.3. FAL, demobilization camp, Guazapa (December 1992)

1. A municipal employee. Went back to school and got a university degree.
2. Went back to school after the war and now works with an NGO and is involved in FMLN party activities.
3. Worked with an (FMLN-affiliated) NGO after the war.
4. A government employee. Also went back to school and got a university degree.
5. Was employed at an FMLN municipality but lost the job in 2009 because of a change in municipal administration (from FMLN to ARENA).
6. Killed after the peace accords in a violent-crime incident.
7. Identity unknown. Reportedly recruited in 1992 from a family with links to the party in order to "fill the quota" for the demobilization of the FAL, but never actually participated in the guerrilla forces as a combatant.
8. Identity unknown. Situation similar to that of number 7.

From my years in Chalatenango, I recall that the fear of being targeted by political violence was a common motif among the demobilizing insurgents.[16] Furthermore, ill prepared for civilian life, including a generally very low educational level, many fighters were very uncertain about their personal prospects. According to an observer present at one of the camps at the time, the demobilization itself constituted "a moment of terror as much as celebration" for the insurgent troops (B. Peterson 2006, 181). Among the demobilizing combatants, the promises of civilian participation in Salvadoran society discorded with concerns about what was to come, as well as with the weight of violence and loss inherited from the war.

"Sandro," one of Wilber's comrades within the FAL Special Forces and a devoted co-worker on the mapping of the photographs, had also entered the war as a child. He declared that for the first two years after the peace accords the only thing he could think of was that he would have been better off dead than forced to return to a "civilian" life that, for him, did not exist. The photographs, more than providing him with an opportunity to reminisce about the war, for Sandro meant a return to his personal plight after demobilization, when it had been very hard for him to find new grounding.

The stroke of luck that helped Wilber along while in the demobilization camp was that he reencountered his family. He had not seen them in almost a decade and thought they were dead. When the demobilization camp was dismantled, his sister gave him a place to live. The vocational training course, awarded as part of his reinsertion package, did not captivate him, but the stipend helped him get by for several months after demobilization. Then he managed to get a poorly paid part-time job as the weekend security guard for one of the PCS NGOs in San Salvador. During the week, he would hang out with former comrades in one of the FMLN offices in the capital.[17] "These were the meeting places for the compañeros who did not have work. We didn't know what to do with ourselves; we didn't have any social circle other than that of compañeros consoling one another."[18]

Sandro eventually emerged from his postdemobilization blues. He attended high school, then university, and got a degree. He worked for different NGOs linked to the PCS. During the decade after 2000 he participated extensively in FMLN party activities, both as a volunteer and in a professional capacity, mostly as a consultant. Initially his activism was motivated by his desire to counteract what he saw as the negative influence of the renovadores movement in the party. He now considered that the FMLN's problems were far beyond the issue of the conflict between renovadores and ortodoxos, and included what he saw as widespread opportunism on all levels.[19] Sandro stated he "would have preferred to die in the war instead of having to see all that now can be seen in the party."[20] To my surprise, in spite of his cynicism and disillusionment, Sandro nonetheless continued to participate actively in FMLN politics.

What was depicted in the photographs was not always what it appeared to be. For example, photograph 6.3 demonstrated that not all of those who demobilized as combatants had actually participated as such in the guerrilla. According to their comrades, numbers 7 and 8 in the photograph participated in the demobilization process to "fill the quota" of combatants agreed upon with the government and the UN. Wilber and Sandro acknowledged that those in the picture were not the only ones who performed such a function in the FAL camp in Guazapa. A similar phenomenon was again documented in photograph 6.4, which depicts a guerrilla unit of the PRTC at the time of demobilization in Nacaspilo, on the border between the departments of San Vicente and Cabañas.

According to the former PRTC combatants who contributed to the reconstruction of the life trajectories in photograph 6.4,[21] more than half of those depicted were not actual combatants, but people from repopulated communities linked to the PRTC who had been asked to join the camps for the demobilization process. Although some of these people might have participated in the war in previous stages, the ex-combatants who provided information on the photograph were only able to provide information on those they had fought with, as they were not familiar enough with the rest of the group. More than what was found in the photographs of the FAL units, the most important trend in this group consisted of postwar insertion into rural livelihoods. Some of the combatants who were demobilized in Nacaspilo were given the opportunity to settle on the coast of Usulután and participate in a shrimp-farming project. Others settled in the PRTC repopulations around Santa Clara and San Esteban Catarina (northern San Vicente) and in Nuevo Gualcho (northern Usulután).

Source: Photograph from the IEHAA-UES archive. Used by permission.

Figure 6.4. PRTC, demobilization camp, Nacaspilo (1992)

1. Became an FMLN municipal employee after the war. Years later joined the PNC.
2. Works in the División de Protección a Personalidades Importantes (PPI) as a security agent for FMLN leadership.
3. Farms in a repopulated community.
4. Migrated to the United States after the war.
5. Returned to home community to farm.
6. Farms in a repopulated community.
7. Farms in a repopulated community.
8. Became an employee at an FMLN municipality after the war.
9. Settled in a repopulated community; runs the household.
10. Migrated to the United States after the war.
11. Farms in a repopulated community.
12. Identity unknown.
13. Farms in a repopulated community.
14. Identity unknown.
15. Farms in a repopulated community.
16. Farms in a repopulated community.
17. Identity unknown.
18. Settled in a repopulated community as a housewife. Left for the United States years later.
19. Runs a household.
20. Initially joined the PNC. Later became a mechanic.
21. Returned to home community to farm.
22. Migrated to the United States after the war.

23–49. Unknown identities. The former combatants who provided the information about this photograph indicated that these individuals proceeded from the PRTC's rural support base and entered the camp to fill the demobilization quota.

REVISITING LAGUNA SECA

A former internationalist fighter for the FPL drew my attention to the existence of a photograph of a large group of combatants reunited at a camp in Chalatenango called Laguna Seca that would become the pièce de résistance of my reconstruction efforts. Initially, I thought it would be extremely difficult to map the photograph because of the large number of fighters and because it had been taken early in the war. My impression changed after I showed the photograph from Laguna Seca to David. At the time, I had been interviewing David, an experienced former FPL guerrilla fighter and midlevel cadre, concerning his military activities during the war. When I handed him the photograph, his emotions got the better of him. He had been there. Short in size, he was hidden from the photographic lens by his comrades lined up in front of him. David vividly recalled the scene.

On December 29, 1981, the FPL troops had gathered in Laguna Seca, a preferred campsite high up in the Chalatenango mountains, to prepare the assault on a military outpost, located a good thirty kilometers of rough mountain terrain to the northwest, directly on the Honduran border. David indicated with his finger where he had been standing with his squad, recalling the exact order of the formation in which he participated that day. One of the reasons that David had become so emotional was that it had been the first time he had seen some of his comrades again after their deaths many years ago. For David, the photograph brought back many people who had not survived the war, but whom he still remembered very well. He feared their lives might soon sink into oblivion because of the lack of tangible evidence of their existence.

After months of research, David and I, with the assistance of numerous other FPL veterans, eventually identified all the individuals in the picture. Of fifty combatants in total, twenty-seven were killed in combat. Being the earliest picture of a guerrilla formation that I used in my research, it made palpable for me and for those I worked with on this photograph the strong personal losses that surviving veteran combatants carried with them into peacetime, something that Wilber referred to earlier in this chapter.

The Laguna Seca photograph also renders testimony to the social composition of the FPL guerrilla during the first years of the war. For example, the group had quite a few combatants of urban descent (at least twelve), a much larger proportion than would be usual in later stages of guerrilla warfare.[22] Of the fifty fighters, seven were women. Interestingly also, the photograph features three internationalist fighters, two from Chile and one from Argentina, all three with officer ranks. Of the six guerrilla leaders conducting the inspection, only one is of rural descent.

A significant number of the rank-and-file guerrilla fighters in the photograph became military leaders later on in the war; that is, if they lived long enough, as was David's case. When the photograph was taken, he still served as a regular combatant, but in subsequent years he became a platoon leader with the rank of lieutenant. David grew up in a working-class neighborhood in San Salvador. In 1980, when he was sixteen, the FPL sent David to Cuba for training, after he had already served some years in urban guerrilla structures. From there on, he spent the remainder of the war in Chalatenango. Over the years, David, though known to have a taste for irreverence, became a disciplined and fiery military cadre whom the FPL leadership trusted with numerous delicate missions.[23]

Part of his appeal and effectiveness lay in the fact that he was close to his troops, often preferring to spend time with them rather than seeking the company of higher-ranking officers and other insurgent cadres. In retrospect, it was not hard to understand for me why David must have been of tremendous value to the FPL. During our mapping of the Laguna Seca photograph, David proved gifted with extraordinary perceptiveness and the memory of an elephant. He joked that he might not have a diploma to show for it, but that he graduated from the university of the war.

Nonetheless, his self-proclaimed rebellious character finally did get him into trouble with the FPL's military command toward the end of the war. According to David, the reason for this conflict was that he was one of the few midlevel cadres who dared to question how the leadership was handling the prospect of peace. His personal conflict with the leadership, which had some earlier wartime precedents, escalated and turned ugly. David was stripped of his military ranks and degraded to rank-and-file combatant during the concentration phase for UN verification of the guerrilla troops. David claims: "They even went so far as to comment that they hadn't killed me because the United Nations had me in their registry."[24]

Source: Photograph from the IEHAA-UES archive. Used by permission.

Figure 6.5.   FPL, Laguna Seca, Chalatenango (December 1981)

1. Killed in combat at Cerro San Fernando, Chalatenango, 1986.
2. Chilean internationalist fighter. Squad leader. Left the front in 1983 because of health problems. Current situation unknown.
3. Member of Chalatenango's military command. Died of natural causes in June 1992.
4. Argentinian internationalist fighter. Detachment leader. Killed in combat while trying to exit the front during the month of April 1983, between Guazapa and Apopa (San Salvador).
5. Killed in combat in Cinquera, 1984.
6. Committed suicide after a personal crisis in 1983, after girlfriend was killed in combat.
7. Killed in an ambush in Dulce Nombre de María, Chalatenango, 1989.
8. Killed in combat at Cerro Miramundo, Chalatenango, 1983.
9. Killed in 1984 or 1985 by government troops in Suchitoto.
10. Killed in combat in Nueva Trinidad, Chalatenango, on January 31, 1982.

11. Radio operator. Killed with Comandante "Susana" (Virginia Peña) and two other combatants, in Las Cuevitas, Chalatenango, on July 12, 1986.
12. War-wounded. Worked after the war in a project at an FMLN municipality and as a night watchman at an NGO; eventually studied law. Makes a living providing legal services.
13. Killed in Potonico, Chalatenango, April 1983.
14. Killed in the second attack on Potonico, in 1983.
15. Worked for some years with an NGO. Currently a mechanic at a municipal workshop in an FMLN municipality.
16. Killed by a landmine in 1984 or 1985.
17. A government soldier captured by the FPL who decided to fight along with the insurgency. Killed in the assault on the Cerrón Grande dam and electricity plant in June 1984.
18. Killed in combat in Chalatenango, 1983.
19. Killed in the attack on Veracruz, Chalatenango, 1986.
20. Severely wounded in the attack on Nueva Trinidad in 1982. Currently works as a farmer in a repopulated community in Chalatenango and receives a pension.
21. Killed in San Salvador during the FMLN offensive of November 1989.
22. Killed in combat during the attack of San Isidro Labrador in 1982.
23. Living in Santa Ana and working for the FMLN in various capacities.
24. Demobilized in Cinquera and moved near the capital. Mother of a member of San Salvador's municipal police.
25. Female combatant. Runs a family store near the capital.
26. Deserted in 1983. Rumored to be an infiltrator in the ranks of the guerrilla. Current situation unknown.
27. Killed in combat in Chalatenango, 1988.
28. Now works for a women's NGO.
29. Currently lives in the repopulation of Santa Marta, Cabañas; works for the municipal police corps in an FMLN municipality.
30. Killed in an exchange of fire with government troops while crossing the Cerrón Grande Reservoir, between Chalatenango and Cuscatlán, in 1983.
31. Killed in a reconaissance mission in Las Vueltas, Chalatenango, 1983.
32. Killed in combat in 1983 or 1984.
33. Killed by bombs or grenade fire in the "Radiola" front in Cabañas, 1985 or 1986.
34. In spite of multiple war wounds, at the demobilization in 1992 he headed a platoon. Currently works at a municipal workshop in an FMLN municipality.
35. Killed in combat at Cerro Miramundo, Chalatenango, 1983.
36. After the war, returned to work as a farmer on family property in a small village in Chalatenango.
37. Fell ill at the front in 1988 and was killed by allergic reaction after having been administered penicillin.
38. Chilean internationalist fighter, left the front in 1986, afterward worked in Cuba as a representative of a Chilean revolutionary organization. Current situation unknown.
39. Suffered significant war-wounds in his legs. Became a driver at an NGO with FMLN roots after the war.
40. Became a farmer and a community leader in a repopulated community in Chalatenango. Suffered war wounds.
41. Left the front to give birth to a child, and the surviving former comrades did not hear from her again.
42. Became a farmer in a repopulated community.
43. Currently lives in Usulután; works for the municipal police corps in an FMLN municipality.
44. Made a career in the FMLN after the war, serving in various leadership positions, including as a deputy in the legislature. Abandoned the FMLN in 2007 after internal dispute; returned to farming. Lives in a repopulated community in Chalatenango.
45. Killed during the takeover of Jutiapa in 1983.
46. Killed in combat during the assault of the 4th Brigade (El Paraíso) in Chalatenango, December 30, 1983.
47. Left the front after the combat death of her partner Medardo, an FPL fighter. She presumably moved back in with family in San Vicente. Current situation unknown.
48. Killed in combat during the assault of the 4th Brigade (El Paraíso) in Chalatenango, December 30, 1983.
49. Deserted and applied for exile in Mexico. He became a taxi driver in New York City.
50. Lives in a repopulated community and works as a farmer.

In David's account, the main issue that pitted him against the guerrilla army's command was the distribution of postwar privilege.

[Leaders] were selecting some people at their own discretion. . . . You began to see some vehicles, . . . some money being moved and things like that, which I really disagreed with . . . , because, they were already taking advantage. . . . There were things that I saw . . . that indicated that we were going to end up screwed over, others maybe partially screwed over . . . and others much better off. . . . [One FPL commander] what did he do? . . . From money that . . . was for the budget for the Front, he bought himself a vehicle . . . , just like that, without asking anyone else's opinion. . . . There were tons of other things, very palpable things that nonetheless were silenced. . . . From the outset they gave some people an opportunity: some as security guards, others began to earn a little money back when we were all concentrated [in the camps], others were inserted into projects; . . . some of them were granted positions that were almost like phantom jobs [receiving a salary without having to work]. . . . The famous 600 Plan for the officials. . . . What did they do? . . . Who were the officials who benefited by those projects? Their [the officials'] women [wives and girlfriends] became the officials! . . . Everyone said: "Wait a minute, what happened here? Why were these women [suddenly] officials?" . . . I'm not saying that they do not deserve their credit, but people always questioned this.[25]

Even though the comandante in charge died—of natural causes—during the demobilization process, David continued to have problems with Chalatenango's FPL leadership, including the head of the demobilization camp where David was sent to hand over his weapons. At first, David had decided he wanted to stay to live at the demobilization camp, a beautiful venue, situated in a pine forest high up in the Chalatenango mountains. However, he reconsidered because he anticipated that socioeconomic conditions would not be very favorable for those who settled there. "There was a housing project [for the demobilized combatants who wanted to stay at the camp], but from then on, I believe, things evolved very differently. [The camp leader] came and diverted [the project]. He distributed the houses among other communities. [The leader who was mentioned went on to live in one of these houses.] . . . Two other projects were approved [for the camp location], but the party kept the money for itself."[26]

Thus, in David's view, while he was being marginalized, others were offered benefits. The fact that he addressed such issues with other comrades gained David the label of *resentido*,[27] a distinction that he shared with several other veteran comrades who had vocalized strong criticism on how the party was handling the reinsertion process. In turn, David decided to maintain his distance from the party. He went back to the capital and reconnected with his mother, whom he had not seen for over a decade. He taught himself to weld metal structures and worked in different construction jobs.

On occasion, he went back to Chalatenango to visit his old friends. He told me, "[One time I discovered that] they had spread rumors about me, in Guarjila, Las Flores, that whole area [northeastern Chalatenango], that I was . . . leading a band of thieves."[28] Even though the accusation was deeply hurtful to him, to avoid further problems David did not pursue any investigation as to who had planted the rumors. Instead, he resolved to visit Chalatenango more frequently, to avoid becoming an outcast. His former comrades from the demobilization camp granted him a piece of land to build a rancho on. David began to divide his time between the capital and his plot in the Chalatenango mountains. David's wife, also a former FPL guerrilla fighter, supported their home and children in San Salvador through a security job with one of the FMLN leaders. David did the same by taking welding jobs wherever he could.

Apart from David, another former guerrilla fighter called Rogelio also greatly helped me along in the identification and reconstruction process of the Laguna Seca photograph. Like David, Rogelio recalled many details of the day the picture was taken. Even though the data that both provided largely coincided, I invited David and Rogelio to my home in San Salvador one day to work on the photograph together and, hopefully, clear out a few of the remaining doubts. It was fascinating to see them work together. Rogelio convinced David of the identity of one of the fighters by carefully reviewing the implements on his belt. David in turn convinced Rogelio that he had made a mistake in one of his identifications, by recalling that the comrade Rogelio had in mind was actually on a mission elsewhere in Chalatenango that day.[29]

For Rogelio himself, the photograph constituted a memory of his revolutionary prime. He had been a guerrilla leader early on in the war.

However, after he had miraculously survived a helicopter attack in 1982, he was sent to Cuba for a lengthy recovery. He only went back to work for the FPL in Nicaragua in the late 1980s, in matters of intelligence and logistics, and never recovered his former status in the FPL. After the peace accords, Rogelio worked for several years as a night watchman at a San Salvador–based NGO with FPL ties, while during the day he did restoration carpentry on a colonial building in an FMLN municipality. He also became involved in local FMLN politics in the city where he settled with his family, a working-class hub near San Salvador. However, the more he learned about the local FMLN administration, the more disappointed he became. Meanwhile, as a member of the neighborhood directorate, he became involved in a protracted political conflict, through which he was directly confronted with corruption and abuses involving FMLN officials. As he attempted to convince some people he knew in the top of the FMLN about the severity of the local abuses he had witnessed, he found that, even though they showed some concern, their efforts to correct the wrongdoings were minimal.

Like David, Rogelio manifested bitter disappointment with the FMLN's postwar record. "They made *moronga*[30] from the blood of the compañeros," he told David and me during our meeting over the La Laguna Seca photograph. As in David's case, Rogelio's main grievance was also the distribution of privilege. To illustrate his point, Rogelio recounted his participation in an FMLN campaign meeting some years after the peace accords. Under the leadership of the former comandantes, a long list of tasks was distributed among the participants. According to Rogelio, toward the end of the meeting, when he remarked that he might need some financial support in order to be able to accommodate the different party responsibilities along with his daily work, the comandante snapped at him: "Where is your political consciousness, [Rogelio]?" Hurt by her remark, he got angry and publicly recalled that she was earning good money as an FMLN deputy in the legislative assembly while he was struggling to make ends meet. He said he shouted back at her: "And your consciousness, compañera, is it worth 17,000 colones!?"[31]

I found two other former guerrilleros who helped me reconstruct the Laguna Seca photograph in the municipal workshop of a city close to San Salvador. "Rutilio" was well known among the former FPL guerrilla fighters, in part of because of his much-commented-on adventures in Cuba. Both Rutilio and his former comrades liked to tell the story of how he, while recovering from war wounds in Cuba, had plundered the liquor cabinet of one of the FPL comandantes there and gone on a monumental drinking binge that ended up with the Cuban police apprehending him in a La Habana nightclub. After the war, Rutilio settled into one of the re-populations in Chalatenango. Though he was originally from elsewhere in El Salvador, he preferred to make his home in Chalatenango, where he had spent most of the war. In 1997, the opportunity arose for Rutilio to work for a municipal police force near the capital. Some years later, he managed to be transferred to the municipal workshop to work as a me-chanic. There he worked with another former comrade also featured in the Laguna Seca photograph. Amidst broken-down municipal garbage trucks and heaps of metal debris, together they helped me to fill in some of the remaining gaps in the reconstruction of the photograph.[32]

Two of the survivors in the photograph pursued political careers in the FMLN after the peace accords. Most successful was a man I shall call "Gabino," who under his legal name served as FMLN deputy in the legis-lative assembly several times. However, when I looked him up in 2010 to seek his help with the Laguna Seca photograph, he had fallen out of grace with the party. After a conflict in 2007, he left the FMLN, arguing political differences and lack of internal democracy. At the time, in what appears to have been an unsavory plot, one of the members of his security staff was accused of involvement in a case of kidnapping for ransom. In March 2010, I found that Gabino had returned to peasant life, farming a stretch of land in his wife's home village in Chalatenango. He was reluctant to talk to me about his truncated political career, but he was very impressed with the photograph and collaborative in completing and contrasting informa-tion. When I told him I was particularly interested in finding out what had happened to the different fighters since the peace accords, he offered a grin and said: "The problem was we could not all live off politics."[33]

"This was my unit in 1985," David said, after handing me back a copy of photograph 6.6. "Where are you then?" I asked. "I do not appear," he answered. I asked why not. "I never liked to be in pictures," he smiled. It was a matter of security, an instinct that, according to David, fighters like him who also had urban guerrilla experience had developed more acutely than those with a peasant background.[34] This image depicted part of what the FPL at the time had called the "vanguard units." In 1985, this unit was operating under David's command around the area of the Montañona in Chalatenango. All its fighters came from a peasant background. With the

Source: Photograph from the IEHAA-UES archive. Used by permission

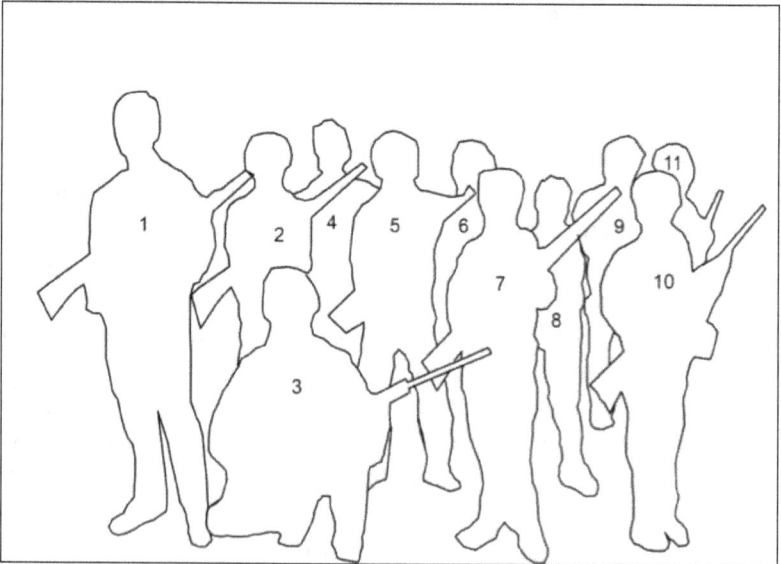

Figure 6.6. FPL, La Montañona, Chalatenango (1985)

1. Killed in combat on Cerro Quequeque on December 31, 1990.
2. Severely injured during the 1989 guerrilla offensive and left behind by comrades. Presumed dead.
3. Currently in the municipal police force of a city governed by the FMLN.
4. Deserted at the end of 1985. Currently a farmer near Ciudad Arce, La Libertad.
5. Deserted near the end of 1985. Ambushed and killed by Honduran army on the way back to the Mesa Grande refugee camp.
6. Female combatant killed in combat in "El Común," Dulce Nombre de María, Chalatenango, February 1987.
7. Killed in an attack on the "El Refugio" military installations near La Palma, Chalatenango, 1988.
8. Female combatant. Worked after the war for many years as a personal bodyguard for member of FMLN leadership. Currently works for a municipal police corps.
9. Deserted in Chalatenango, late 1988. Currently lives in Sweden.
10. Deserted from the guerrilla in Chalatenango in 1985. Current situation unknown.
11. Killed in combat in La Laguna, Chalatenango, in 1985 or 1986.

exception of three individuals, the unit consisted of recent recruits from the Mesa Grande refugee camp in Honduras.[35] David considered that 1985 had been one of the bleakest years of the war. Aviation and counterinsurgency battalions had forced the insurgents to split up into smaller units and to engage in a war of attrition. Insurgent faith in victory had suffered several blows. Morale among the troops was generally low, and so it was in this unit.

Like in any army during wartime, desertion was a capital offense. The guerrilla commanders considered desertion to be not only a problem of discipline but especially also of security. Deserted combatants might defect or otherwise fall into enemy hands. They could voluntarily or involuntarily disclose secret information that could put the guerrilla organization at risk. As David explained, some of those who deserted were actually already infiltrators who left the guerrilla to contact their army liaison. Sometimes combatants deserted with the idea of joining the enemy.[36] However, most were simply young people fed up with guerrilla life and desperate to leave. Though desertion, defection, and infiltration constituted problems for the insurgents throughout the war, they became worse during spells of adversity.

One of the fighters depicted in this photograph agreed with David that two of the unit's combatants deserted because they could not endure the hardship of war, one did because he might have been an informer, and a final one deserted because he had no choice. This last one had actually been one of the finest combatants of the group. At the end of 1988 he had asked permission to visit a nearby repopulation because of a family emergency. When the comandante denied the permit on trivial grounds, he decided to go anyway. When he returned to the camp two days later, it was rumored that the leadership was about to apprehend him for infiltration. He decided to desert before he'd be executed. Through family connections and with the help of a priest, he was smuggled out of the area and applied for political exile at an embassy in San Salvador. As of 2010 he still lived in Sweden.[37]

The ex-combatant in question was very lucky, because it is known, though still scantily documented, that a significant number of guerrilla fighters who were the object of similar accusations did die at the order of the comandantes, at the Chalatenango front as well as elsewhere in the guerrilla (Juárez 2015). According to David, one of the problems that contributed to this soldier's postwar marginalization from the circles of

Figure 6.7. FPL, San José Las Flores, Chalatenango (early 1990)

1. Head of this platoon. Entered the PNC after the peace accords; still active.
2. Left for the United States in 1996.
3. In the PNC for some time, but then decided to migrate to the United States.
4. Farmer after the war in a repopulated settlement in Chalatenango.
5. Stepped on landmine, severe war wounds. Currently lives and works in a repopulated community in Usulután.
6. Identity unknown.
7. Migrated to the United States and worked there for some time, but was caught and deported back to El Salvador. Now works with the FMLN providing security to one of their offices.
8. Farmer after the war in a repopulated settlement in Chalatenango.
9. Now a farmer in a repopulation in Chalatenango.
10. Left for the United States after the war ended.
11. Farmer in home community in Chalatenango.
12. Works at the PNC.
13. Farmer in home community in Chalatenango. Occasionally, works as a bricklayer.
14. Returned to home village to farm. Died from unspecified illness shortly after the war.
15. Held several jobs related to the FMLN. Also worked in the United States for some years. Currently involved in NGO work.

El Zapotal. He was interested himself in the matter as well, since, he explained, he had personally recruited the adolescents from El Zapotal featured in the photograph. Mariano had been working the expansion zone as a political cadre before the offensive. He then returned to the guerrilla army, leading some of his own recruits.[39]

On the way to El Zapotal, we caught up on what we had been up to and commented on political affairs. I told him that initially I had been somewhat surprised when I found out he had left to work in the United States a decade earlier. He explained that he had obtained a travel visa, which made the step to go north much easier than for most. He had worked mostly in landscaping and had done reasonably well there, he said, but the nostalgia for his family and his country had gotten the better of him. Upon return, he had done some farming and resumed his political activism.

Mariano was much milder in his evaluation of the postwar FMLN than David or Rogelio, earlier this chapter. He too spoke from experience. In the 1990s he spent a term as a member of an FMLN municipal council, and currently he had been heavily involved in the local campaign activities for the 2009 elections. He said that many former comrades bore unrealistic expectations and criticized too easily. Mariano considered it logical that political and socioeconomic progress would be slow, and he knew it was contingent both on the level of unity within the Left and on the level of opposition from the Salvadoran Right.

Mariano had recently agreed to work on the directorate of an organization that supported Chalatenango's repopulations, though he said he was now repenting a little bit, and had difficulties fighting off depression, which he believed to be the effect of everything he had been through during the war. One of the FPL comandantes he had worked with during the war had recently been appointed as a government minister, and Mariano was speaking to people close to the minister about the possibility of a job in landscaping, a task he considered better suited for his present state of mind.

In El Zapotal, Mariano still knew many people from before. He also remembered the location of the homes of some of the families we needed to contact for the photograph. Close to noon, many of the men had already returned from their fields. The farmers in El Zapotal also remembered Mariano and greeted him with respect. In a few hours we were able

Figure 6.8. FPL, Chichontepec Volcano, San Vicente (December 1991)

1. Returned to school after the war. Currently working as a physician in San Salvador.
2. Worked in one of the municipalities the FMLN gained in the 1994 elections and later migrated to Italy.
3. Migrated to the United States after the war.
4. Moved to a repopulated community in the area, runs her household, and became an evangelical preacher.
5. After the war, made a career in FMLN politics, serving in various leadership positions and public office; abandoned the FMLN in one of the postwar political splits. Involved in several business activities in his place of residence.
6. Lives and farms in a repopulated community.
7. Lives and farms in a repopulated community.
8. Migrated to the United States after the war; works in cleaning and maintenance.
9. Lives and works in Canada.
10. Employed as a personal protection agent for FMLN leadership.
11. Migrated to the United States after the war; makes his living as a gardener.
12. As a child, during the last years of the war, performed odd jobs around the camp; migrated to the United States after the war.
13. Current situation unknown.
14. Lives and farms in a repopulated community in the San Vicente province.
15. Lives on the streets and struggles with addiction.
16. Identity unknown.
17. Migrated to Canada and has remained there.

unfolding events made the leadership suspicious of advanced levels of enemy infiltration and a considerable number of rank-and-file troops fell victim to the purges, possibly as many as hundreds.

According to Luis, several of the comrades in the photograph had lost family members at the hands of Mayo Sibrián and his accomplices. This picture thus portrays double survivors: San Vicente's FPL combatants who survived the catastrophe of war as well as that of the internal purges. Mayo Sibrián himself was executed on the orders of the FPL top leadership only months before the photograph was made.

Luis considered that, even though Mayo had certainly committed abuses, his execution constituted more of a cover-up than an act of justice. According to Luis, several other former FPL cadres active in San Vicente had been involved in the purges and had contributed to their escalation. He also claimed that those who had collaborated with a recent controversial book on the Mayo Sibrián killings—written by Galeas and Ayalá (2008)—involved people partially responsible for the events. According to Luis, the accusations against Sibrián and former FPL secretary general Salvador Sánchez Cerén[41] featured in the book should be interpreted, in part, as attempts to put the blame solely on them.[42]

After the war, Luis moved to the capital and became involved in initiatives for the FMLN war-wounded. He helped his peers from different parts of the country organize around their particular interests and demands. Through his FPL contacts, he was able to get a job in the San Salvador city government in the late 1990s. In 2009 and early 2010, at the time of our interviews, Luis still held that job, but feared he would soon lose it on account of the new municipal administration, led by ARENA. His work at the San Salvador municipal office had provided him with a decent income as well as sufficient room for activism with the FMLN and the FMLN war veterans. As I witnessed in other veterans, he combined continued activism with considerable disillusionment and deep mistrust of postwar left-wing politics.

> What happened in El Salvador? . . . I've been wracking my brain. What the hell happened? . . . Revolutionary dynamics generally begin with theory and little by little create processes, until consciousness is achieved. . . . I think in our case this process occurred the other way around. We beat the shit out of each other while knowing zero theory. It is due to this ignorance that we are where we are. . . . At this point

in the race, compañeros who . . . fought hard . . . give thanks to God for being alive, and with this all is said! There is little consciousness of what was done. And there is someone who is reaping the fruits of this. . . . There were twelve years of sacrifice . . . who benefited from this? Therefore, my question is: Was this process revolutionary?[43]

For Luis, the answer to his own question was clear. What he had witnessed in the postwar years had little to do with revolution, nor with democracy. According to Luis, FMLN politics had degenerated into power games and individual interests, particularly income generation. Politicians thrived through manipulation and by using former comrades as "ladders" to prop up their personal ambitions. In order to figure out what went wrong and to find alternatives, he longed for theoretical understanding. Luis always carried a stack of old books in his backpack, with titles reminiscent of the sixties' revolutionary candor.

A significant portion of FPL forces stationed near the capital in the last years of the war is featured in photograph 6.9. Soon after it was taken, the troops were concentrated for verification by the UN and the demobilization process began. This is a particularly mixed group in terms of personal background and geographic origins. For example, some of these combatants were recruited and forged in FPL strongholds like Chalatenango, and then sent to the "Frente Sur" (southern front) during the last years of the war. Several others had their roots in the displaced communities around Aguilares. A few had been recruited in the cities during the buildup for the offensive, and afterwards had remained at the front.[44]

The leader of the troops in the photograph went on to become a prominent FMLN leader in the postwar period. In 2000, he was elected mayor of an important city close to San Salvador, and he has been reelected numerous times since. Over the last decade, he has become one of the principal leaders of what is considered the "moderate" proreform sector of the FMLN. Several fighters in the photograph have worked in his municipal administration. A significant number of the demobilized combatants of this group chose to integrate into the PNC. In total, nine former combatants from this group joined the police force, and eight of them still remained there at the time of fieldwork for this study.

One of the remarkable features of the photograph is how strongly it communicates the excitement and joy of the war being almost over. This is the happiest of the photographs of guerrilla units that I came across.

Source: Photograph from the IEHAA-UES archive. Used by permission.

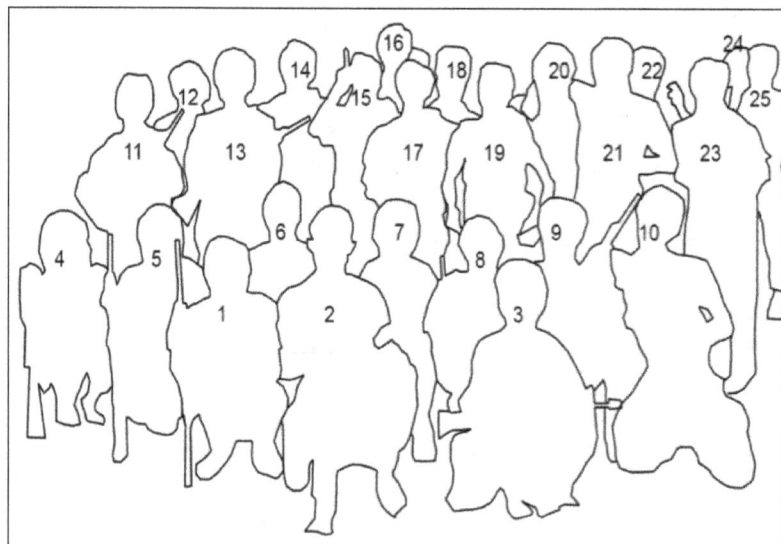

Figure 6.9. FPL, Southern Front, La Libertad (first days of January 1992)

1. Found employment in a municipal job, using her FMLN connections.
2. After the war, migrated to Belize in search of work, then returned to El Salvador and now works as security personnel at an NGO.
3. Identity unknown.
4. Went back to school and managed to get a job in the administrative area of the PNC.
5. Migrated to the United States in search of work after the war and continues to live there.
6. Entered the PNC force after the peace accords as part of the FMLN quota. Still active as a police officer.
7. Allegedly became involved in criminal activity and became a member of a youth gang after the war.
8. Employed first as a security agent for FMLN leadership for several years then migrated to the United States in search of work. Recently returned to El Salvador.
9. Entered the PNC as part of the FMLN quota after the peace accords. Still active as a police officer.
10. Went back to school after the war and got a university degree. Works as an employee in the country's judicial system.
11. Lived and worked for a number of years in a repopulated community after the war, then migrated to the United States in search of work.
12. Pursued a career in FMLN politics after the war, serving in several senior leadership positions.
13. Entered the PNC as part of the FMLN quota. Still active as a police officer.
14. Owns a small mechanic workshop near the capital; migrated to the United States in search of work, but only stayed there for a few years.
15. Had several odd jobs, then migrated to the United States in search of work. After some years was deported; currently lives in San Salvador and works as a security agent for the PPI department of the PNC.
16. Entered the PNC as part of the FMLN quota after the peace accords. Still active as a police officer.
17. Made a career in the FMLN after the war, serving in various leadership positions in the party and in public office.
18. Lived and worked for a number of years after the war in a repopulated community. Then migrated to the United States in search of work.
19. Killed shortly after the war, during an armed robbery at a bus stop in San Salvador.
20. Got a job at a municipal police corps through FMLN connections. Also runs a small family store in hometown.
21. Current situation unknown.
22. Entered the PNC as part of the FMLN quota. Went back to school. Currently a bureaucrat at a government ministry.
23. Through his FMLN connections, now has a senior position at a municipal police corps.
24. Works at the PNC.
25. Works at the PNC and recently obtained a university degree.

Most combatants smile and look relaxed. Note what seems to be a bottle of wine (held by number 21). My friend Dolores, however, who had fought with several of those featuring in this photograph, contemplated the image with a mix of pain and joy. She certainly recalled the feeling of happiness, or rather of relief, that the war was over. For her, the war had been a nightmare, and the advent of peace a form of rebirth. Of urban middle-class descent, she came from a family situation that had put her in the middle of the revolutionary war since she was a child. She grew up predominantly in safe houses and in exile. Rather than romantic appeal, she emphasized the powerlessness and anguish she felt while serving the guerrilla.

> I joined the struggle, the revolutionary process, not in a conscious manner. I'm talking about at first. Because my parents are the ones who joined, and therefore, indirectly, my siblings and I myself [joined]. It wasn't a situation in which I saw the need to join because of my own social consciousness. Along the way I began to develop this consciousness. I saw the party kind of like my father, see? [laughing] . . . That is, I had to do what the party told me to do even if I did not agree. . . . I knew that my destiny . . . was to come to El Salvador. . . . Bottom line, I did it out of obedience.[45]

She traveled from Nicaragua to El Salvador two months before the 1989 offensive and was posted in a safe house, where she had to defend herself from the insistent advances of a leading FPL cadre. When the offensive was about to start, she was instructed to incorporate into a military unit. "In a single week . . . I lost about ten pounds, we didn't eat, it was anguishing, it was terrible. For example, they sent us to get food. . . . There . . . the person who went ahead of me, they killed him. It was traumatic. . . . We were advancing and it was said that we had to go back . . . and the man, trying to save his own life, went ahead of me, if not, well, that bullet was meant for me."[46]

During the offensive, the officer in charge of her squad was also killed, along with several other comrades in her unit. What was most difficult for her to process was how this experience contrasted with what she perceived as the disinterest of ordinary Salvadorans in the struggle and its cause. "Incredible how we were sacrificing ourselves, and people on the street were acting as if nothing was going on, having parties! . . . That which they have told us so many times, so much doctrine. . . . 'Where are the people,' I asked myself, 'who were supposed to take the streets and support us once they saw what was happening?' So I began to be disillusioned and that is why I was very happy that the war ended."[47]

After the peace accords, Dolores initially registered for FMLN affiliation through FPL structures, but when her enrollment had to be formalized by her reaffiliating with the FMLN, she did not go. While her husband, also a former guerrilla fighter, was more involved, she kept her distance, though always supporting the party in campaigns or by volunteering on election day. Dolores went to the university, held several jobs with NGOs, and raised a family. For her, reinsertion had not been difficult, but rather the start of the "normal" life she aspired to. According to Dolores, reinsertion had been much more difficult particularly for people with a peasant background.

> [After the war], when I went out to some communities, I met people who had been with me, sharing life in the safe houses, now back living in the same poverty situation [from before the war], living in poor people's houses. So I said, "jeeze" right, "so much effort and then to come back to the same thing." . . . I think there was a lot of idealism . . . with respect to the transformations [we would achieve], right? I think there was a lot of romanticism . . . in our heads. . . . I was taught that we were all going to be equal, that we would all have opportunities. . . . Really, I believed that was how it was going to be. . . . I saw a peasant and . . . even in terms of sentimental relationships I thought that . . . Well, I never had a peasant boyfriend, but my compañeras, my girlfriends, sometimes had [peasant] boyfriends, and really these relationships eventually ended . . . once peace returned, and life went on. I have some friends whose husbands were peasants, and now they are not together because they have different perspectives, different worlds.[48]

Reinsertion was difficult for Dolores's father as well, a middle cadre who came out of the war tired and empty handed. He held a range of jobs that have allowed him to get by. "It has always been the political contacts that have given him the opportunity to work." Dolores herself also obtained a new position. After Mauricio Funes became president, her party contacts brought her in as staff in one of the ministries.

THE ERP AND THE RN: LESS RECONVERSION,
MORE DISINTEGRATION

Being less familiar with the ERP than with the FPL, I found it much harder to get support for mapping life trajectories based on photographs of ERP units. Both my limited success and the reflections ERP veterans shared suggested that the remaining interpersonal connections between ERP ex-combatants were weaker than what I had come across in the case of the FPL and the FAL. The evocation of wartime interpersonal relationships was invariably clouded by the ERP's internal events of 1992–95, which had left deep marks among the former militancy. For example, Tino, a former student from the capital who had spent the entire war as an ERP military official in the mountains, considered that

> the whole political framework that had been created to take power was lost. . . . The ERP and RN . . . clearly allied themselves against the FMLN. . . . And then the ERP lost itself in the subsequent whirlwind of confusion. . . . "Is this treason?" "No, the compañero is not a traitor." See? We weakened ourselves. . . . We, the compañeros who were there, did not have the capacity to visualize what to do at that moment. . . . The only thing that occurred to us was automatic dismantling, you see? . . . Everyone took off every which way.[49]

On a personal level, the experience of the ERP's postwar disintegration had been much more traumatic for Tino than the war itself, so he said.[50] According to another ERP veteran, the profound disappointment with postwar affairs had made many former ERP militants renounce political activities altogether and withdraw completely into the sphere of family life.[51] Tino told me ERP members were sometimes looked down upon or made fun of by veterans from the other PMOs. In fact, as an aspiring professional, Tino considered that his ERP affiliation had constituted more of an obstacle than a benefit to him in his postwar career. He had suffered several long periods of unemployment, something he attributed in part to the ERP stigma he carried. Finally however, through one of his ERP contacts who had remained inside the FMLN, he did manage to get a well-paid job in municipal government. Unfortunately, he lost this position a few years later because of political conflicts among different FMLN factions within the municipality and again found himself unemployed. Over the last years, Tino had visited and reconnected with many former ERP comrades and had found that many, like him, had difficulties finding steady employment. He said that they provided mutual support and helped each other by sharing contacts for job opportunities.[52]

Though the unit portrayed in photograph 6.10 was small, mapping it turned out to take longer than mapping any of the other photographs in this study, even when I had managed to contact one of the people featured in the picture. Besides Tino and others, "Segundo" contributed substantially to the process. A former ERP combatant of rural descent, he entered the war when he was eleven years old, after part of his family had been massacred in Morazán. Like his fellow child soldier Wilber from the FAL, he never considered he would come out of the war alive.

The ERP had provided Segundo with a sort of family in which he had grown up and matured while submerged in the hardships of war. "We owe our lives to a whole lot of people who are dead and buried," he said. Although he recounted with indignation several stories of abuses that occurred inside the ERP, overall he believed that values like solidarity and sacrifice had held the upper hand in the organization during the war.

After the peace accords, Segundo eventually found employment at an NGO run by a former ERP midlevel cadre he had worked with during the war. Though he held little respect for the former ERP leadership, he also believed that their actions were not fundamentally different from those of the other PMOs. In his opinion, after the war, everyone was seeking "personal advancement." He found that among his former comrades there were many of "those who turn their backs [on others] once they have seen dollars." For Segundo, not only leadership, but also rank and file had lost their moral compass after the peace accords. "In peace time we brought out all the miserable aspects of ourselves that we have within us."[53]

When I showed photograph 6.11 to RN veteran Moisés, it confronted him with painful irony.[54] What he saw was a group of his former comrades offering a salute to the FMLN flag, the political project the fighters had been told by their leaders would guarantee the continuity of their struggle. However, a little over a year later, the ERP and RN leaderships were already enmeshed in a deep conflict with the FMLN, leading to the separation of the ERP and RN from the FMLN. "What would these comrades in the photo have thought if they had known what was coming?" Moisés wondered. "What did our leaders do with so much effort and sacrifice?"[55]

Source: Photograph from the MUPI archive. Used by permission.

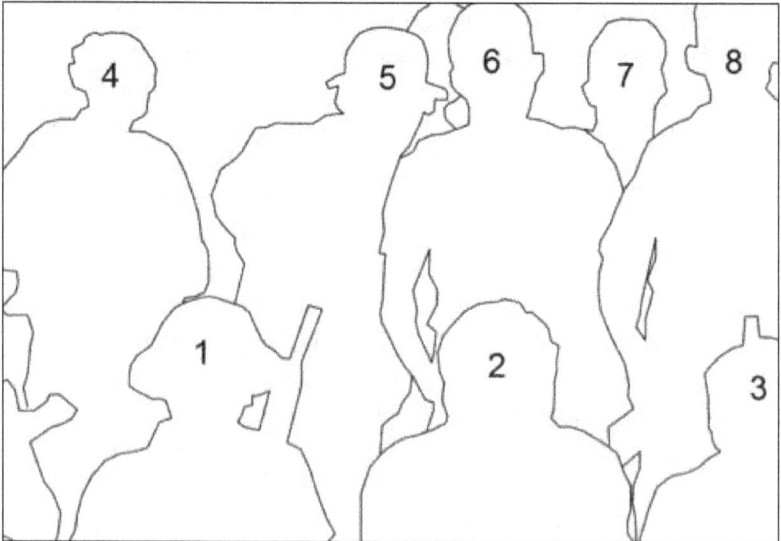

Figure 6.10. ERP, Guazapa (1984)

1. Farms in a repopulated community in Morazán.
2. Migrated to the United States.
3. War-wounded. Farms in a repopulated community in Usulután.
4. Demobilized with the ERP, resumed university career, obtained a government job.
5. Abandoned the ERP when on leave outside the country. Continues to live outside El Salvador.
6. Killed in Cerro Los Lirios (Guazapa) in 1985, when FAL and ERP troops encountered and mistakenly engaged in combat.
7. Farms in a repopulated community.
8. Identity unknown. Presumed to have been killed in combat.

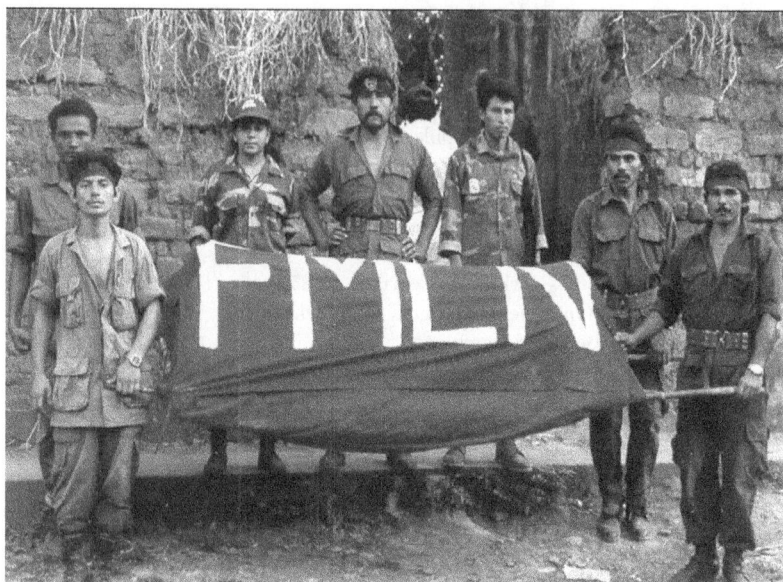

Source: Photograph from the IEHAA-UES archive. Used by permission.

Figure 6.11.   RN, demobilization camp near Suchitoto (1992)

1. War-wounded. Lives off pension combined with agricultural activities.
2. Joined the PNC.
3. Lives in a repopulated community near Suchitoto; works at home and participates in the community radio network.
4. A former soldier. Joined the RN after having been made prisoner by the guerrilla in 1983. Farms in a repopulated community and complements his income by working with the local community radio network.
5. Lives in San Salvador and has a job at an FMLN municipality.
6. War-wounded. Works as a driver for an NGO.
7. Farmer in a repopulated community.

Moisés believed that, similar to what happened with the ERP, his comrades at the RN suffered from a double rupture: the break-off of the RN from the FMLN and the RN's internal decomposition. "We ended up practically in the air," he commented. As a result many former comrades had become bitter and had distanced themselves from politics, so Moisés thought. Moisés himself battled for several years to regain entry and acceptance into the FMLN, which he finally achieved through his involvement in NGO work. "The peace accords," he said, ". . . generated for us a huge ideological vacuum which the Right ably took advantage of, sowing discord to the extent that many who were heroic compañeros during the war were weak, very weak during peace time . . . and hence were easy prey to the happiness of right wing fantasies."[56]

For Beatriz, who spent most of the war working for the RN in Managua, the photograph of the RN's demobilization process provoked mostly sadness, though also a hint of nostalgia for the loss of revolutionary innocence. For her, the idealistic image of the revolutionary struggle had already been dented by her personal experiences in Cuba and Nicaragua during the war. She remembered: "[After the war,] I began . . . to hear some dreadful stories, to see the war-wounded, completely drunk, . . . in sorry shape, abandoned . . . and these others raising their own salaries in the legislative assembly and living a very normal and bourgeois life, and all the deaths from before not bothering them a bit."[57] Thus, the internal development of the revolutionary movement in postwar El Salvador provided further "fuel for [her] disenchantment."

> Where is the utopia? . . . I'm not saying that they did not believe in it, themselves, in a given moment or that they [some old revolutionary leaders] were fighting to make themselves millionaires. I know that . . . back then it wasn't that way, but now it is terrible, because . . . they became corrupted. It is so difficult to find someone who really maintains and defends his ideals. . . . Radical discourse . . . is effective because we live in a radical reality. . . . That is, you can go to any barrio, . . . and you will become radicalized because . . . the social injustice is too much, there is too much shit going down to not say: "Yes, I'll take up arms . . . ," and if you want an enemy, you can easily find one. . . . Too many differences, too much egoism. . . . That is, those who have money are dreadful and those who become rich end up just

the same way, this is the incredible part, they turn out just the same. . . . There is no difference.[58]

While for Moisés it had been manipulation by right-wing forces that had weakened the RN's revolutionary leadership, for Beatriz the contradictions between revolutionary promises and the RN's internal realities were at the heart of the matter. For her, power and privilege were the postwar ordering principles, beyond alleged contradictions between Left and Right. In any case, I found out during fieldwork that it is not easy to find a former RN militant who ponders the postwar trajectory of the organization with anything else than dismay.

THE PHOTOGRAPHS AS A SAMPLE OF POSTWAR LIFE TRAJECTORIES

The same photographs that helped ground reflection on the experience of postinsurgency also rendered a small quantitative data sample on the postwar destinies of FMLN guerrilla veterans.[59] Our mapping efforts identified a total of 191 individuals, 174 males and 17 females. Of these, 188 are Salvadorans and 3 are internationalist fighters. In all, an estimated 75 percent of the sample derived from the photographs consists of individuals with a prewar rural background. Of those depicted, 36 did not survive the war. For 10 fighters, we were unable to establish whether they survived the war. These were mostly individuals whom their comrades lost track of during the war, in most cases because they abandoned the insurgent forces prior to the war's end. The pictures (seven out of eleven) that were taken after the 1989 offensive do not reflect wartime casualties because the fighting was (almost) over. In contrast, the four photographs taken before the 1989 offensive also provide an impression of the risks and losses that accompanied the guerrilla fighters through the war.

According to our informers, a total of 145 identified individuals in the photographs survived the war. Of this group, we established basic elements of their postwar life trajectories in relation to their principal livelihood strategies from the time of the peace accords until the moment of our mapping efforts (2009 and 2010), thus spanning close to two decades. Since part of this group employed several principal strategies over the course of these years, the total of postwar livelihood strategies used amounts to 189. (See table 6.1.)

Table 6.1.   Guerrilla fighters' main postwar livelihood options

Rural livelihoods	37 (20%)	**Private Sector Employment** (*continued*)	
Farmer in a repopulated community	31	Provides legal services	1
		Doctor	1
Farmer in hometown	5	Bus-fare collector	1
Farmer elsewhere	1	Transportation services	1
		Evangelical	1
Civil service employment	40 (21%)	Odd jobs	1
National Civilian Police (PNC)	17	Construction	1
Municipal employee	11		
Municipal police corps	8	**Migration**	35 (18%)
State or government employee	4	Migrated to United States	27
		Migrated to Canada	3
FMLN-employed	24 (13%)	Migrated to Belize	1
FMLN security personnel	12	Scholarship in Cuba	1
Career in FMLN politics	8	Exile in Sweden	1
"Works with FMLN"	4	Migrated to Italy	1
		Outside of El Salvador	1
NGO-employed	13 (7%)		
NGO employee	11	**Other**	18 (9%)
Community radio	2	Current situation unknown	9
		Victim of lethal criminal violence	4
Private Sector Employment	22 (12%)	Died of natural causes	3
Runs the household	7	Lives on the street	1
Runs a family store	3	Gang member/crime	1
Mechanic	3		
Businessman	1	**Total**	189 (100%)
Private sector employee	1		

SCENARIOS FOR POSTWAR LIVELIHOODS

In spite of the predominantly rural background of the fighters, only 20 percent built up rural livelihoods after the peace accords. A group of similar size left the country to try to make a living elsewhere, mainly in the United States (18 percent). Civil service employment provides the largest cluster of postwar livelihoods (21 percent). Additionally, a good number (13 percent) found employment within the FMLN itself, either as political activists or as bodyguards for FMLN leaders. As illustrated earlier in this chapter, a closer look at the stories behind the trajectories calls attention to the prominence of the links and networks forged during the war and their impact upon the livelihood strategies of the former guerrilla fighters after the war.

Although one segment of veterans did find employment and built livelihoods independently from insurgent ties, the aggregate findings from the photographs indicate that a large number of former guerrillas continued to rely on the party and on its networks. Examples of livelihood options that fit this category include those employed by the FMLN, the municipalities, the PNC, and the NGOs. Although party affiliations lay at the root of having gained initial access to these jobs, the control and intervention of the FMLN with regard to these forms of employment varied significantly, as will be explored in the next section. In general terms, levels of party involvement were extremely high in party employment, very high in municipal employment, relevant in NGO employment, and instrumental but formally restricted in PNC employment.

Overall, the data from the photographs indicate that the socioeconomic reconversion process that the PMOs envisioned for their structures during the first years of the transition period (see chap. 4) did take place to a significant extent. This is especially true for the cadre segment. In the case study of Ellacuría we already saw how former PMO cadres were able to position themselves favorably in the local community. Data from the photographs suggest that the highest-ranking surviving members of the different units often went on to build careers in FMLN politics, albeit with mixed success, as illustrated in the case of Gabino from photograph 6.5, whose political career was aborted because of internal conflict.

Civil Service Employment

When the FMLN won its first major urban municipalities in 1997, a significant number of those elected were former PMO cadres (Urbina González 2006; Zamora 2003). Sometimes the FMLN had also recruited popular local figures either as mayoral candidates or as candidates for municipal council, but former cadres invariably functioned as the support team for such "outsiders."[60] Electoral success meant jobs for party militants and supporters. While winning the elections in a small municipality somewhere in Chalatenango or Cabañas would generate only a handful of positions, San Salvador and the cities around it were able to provided hundreds of jobs for FMLN militants, most of which were

distributed among former participants in the PMOs. By grace of their political contacts, former insurgent cadres, especially those with an education, were generally well positioned to obtain senior functions within
the FMLN municipalities.[61]

Typically, the election or the appointment of former PMO cadres
would motivate unemployed former comrades to contact them and leave
their résumé for consideration. Likewise, FMLN officials were looking for
people they trusted both personally and politically to serve on their staff.[62]
Former insurgents who had remained active in the political circles of
postinsurgency could use historical as well as contemporary political relationships in their quest for employment (see, for example, the case of Luis,
described in this chapter). Those who had remained more at the margins
of postinsurgent politics were still able to make use of the strong personal
ties established with individual cadres during the war.

This process benefited former participants of the five PMOs in different proportions. Because of the FPL's strength inside the FMLN, former
members of the FPL were particularly well positioned, as were former
cadres of the PCS who had decided to remain inside the FMLN after the
break-offs of the UDN (1992) and the TR (1998). Because of the 1994 rupture, former ERP and RN members who had remained in the FMLN were
now a small minority, much like the PRTC, whose influence inside the
FMLN was limited because of the small body of cadres and constituency.
In consequence, former ERP, RN, and PRTC cadres and rank and file,
generally speaking, had less access to these new opportunities for employment than cadres from the FPL and the PCS.

In the larger cities, municipal jobs were varied, and required different
levels of experience and schooling. Though insurgent experience could go
a long way in terms of political credentials, the candidates' résumé also
needed to fulfill the minimal requirements of each particular function.
Such a filter meant that the former guerrilla fighters of rural descent
without much formal schooling still had limited possibilities of obtaining
public employment. Municipal security was the one field in which the
peasant guerrilla fighters' experience and schooling were usually deemed
sufficient. For example, when Héctor Silva won the San Salvador mayoral
race in 1997, he appointed a former FPL comandante as the head of the
municipal police force, called Cuerpo de Agentes Municipales (CAM).[63]
The new head of the CAM, in turn, appointed several former FPL military
officers as his aides. In subsequent years, the CAM employed dozens of

at a later stage in the postwar careers of former insurgents. This occurred especially after Funes won the presidential election, and a significant number of former PMO cadres active in Salvadoran NGOs then accessed government functions (Moallic 2010).

With former cadres occupying senior positions in NGOs, opportunities for rank and file to be considered for different lower-ranking jobs within an NGO also multiplied. Rogelio and Wilber were not the only former fighters who worked as night watchmen after the peace accords. Many FMLN-affiliated NGOs would commonly hire former guerrilla fighters as night watchmen as well as for a range of other jobs. Another reason that the former PMO connections remained relevant was that the NGOs commonly located their activities and projects in the repopulations founded by their former PMOs.

Migration

The strong anti-imperialist stance of the insurgent movements appears not to have affected the United States' strong appeal to the former insurgents. The country emerges from the photographs as by far the largest recipient of former insurgents who opted for migration. The finding that 18 percent of the former guerrilla fighters in the photographs migrated outside of El Salvador is remarkable also in view of the sacrifice previously invested in the revolutionary process. As documented in the previous chapter, in the insurgent communities migration rapidly transformed into a key postwar livelihood strategy. This connected to the relative failure of the land transfers and the rural reinsertion programs to provide durable and sustainable family incomes for many of the beneficiaries.

The migration numbers that emerge from the photographs resonate with those from the previous chapter as well as with other sources. A Catholic priest based in northern Morazán with close ties to the former ERP constituency there estimated that among the former ERP combatants from this region, approximately 30 percent had left for the United States in the two decades after the war.[70] "Pedro," a former midlevel cadre who had been in charge of the demobilization process for the FPL in Los Ranchos, told me that close to 70 percent of the troops that demobilized under his command had left to work in the "North."[71] The photographs' findings suggest that this estimate is likely too high. Nonetheless, Pedro's comment reflects the prominence that labor migration acquired in postinsurgent

Chalatenango. Estimates regarding former guerrilla fighters' involvement in transnational migration tend to surpass overall national rates.[72]

The question of how relevant the networks built up by insurgents during the war were for migration is difficult to answer. I recall from my own participation in the 1990s that one of the best-known polleros active in FPL postinsurgent communities was a former midlevel cadre, a young urbanite who had fought side by side with the peasants. When I saw him again in San Salvador in 2009, he confirmed that he had channeled hundreds of comrades to the United States. In recent years he had left the pollero business to dedicate himself to agribusiness projects in El Salvador and Belize.[73] Even if inherited ties from the insurgent period might have played a role in some early migration trajectories, extended family networks are no doubt the most relevant factor in the establishment of migration patterns. Available research shows that, once the first relatives migrate and establish themselves, they become the principal point of reference for those in El Salvador seeking to go north (Bibler Coutin 2007; Silber 2011). In all likelihood, the labor migration of the former FMLN fighters was built more on family ties than on old insurgent networks.

Rural Livelihoods

Though still considerable, the number of guerrilla fighters from our sample who chose agricultural livelihoods (20 percent) is very low compared with the data from the reinsertion programs, where 80 percent chose an agricultural track. Findings suggest that many of those who demobilized into the repopulation communities and accessed land transfers and reinsertion credits did not convert these resources into a principal livelihood option in the long run. Many former fighters eventually preferred other options, such as migration and FMLN-related employment.

I found that very few of those identified in the photographs farmed outside of the area of the repopulations. The vast majority of the fighters who chose agricultural activities after the war settled in the insurgent repopulations rather than returning to their hometown.[74] As we have seen in the previous chapter, PMO ties were certainly relevant for the eventual agricultural livelihoods of the former guerrilla fighters. This was especially true in the early stages, with the decision to settle in an insurgent repopulation and to apply for land in the PTT. This resulted in the absorption of the former guerrilla fighters in rural communities in which insurgent politics continued to play a prominent role in everyday life. However, this does not mean that all former guerrilla fighters-turned-agriculturists have remained heavily involved in FMLN politics. This is predominantly the case for local leaders, often former cadres in the PMOs, or for those who have become involved in the FMLN veterans' movements that I will discuss in the next chapter.

THE TRANSFORMATION OF PMO NETWORKS AFTER THE WAR

As we worked together on the Laguna Seca photograph, I became aware of how David, in spite of his relative marginalization from the party, had been able to keep in touch with many of his former comrades. David said he liked to attend FMLN rallies not for the speeches offered but in order to meet old comrades. In spite of his reputation as *resentido*, David still had many friends among his former comrades. He liked to catch up and share anecdotes of the events they lived through together. The comradery he felt with his peers contrasted with the distance he perceived from his former superiors. He claimed that the comandantes from the FPL leadership with whom he had worked closely during the war now often did not greet him and sometimes did not even recognize him when standing face-to-face. According to David, on such occasions, the comandantes' bodyguards observed him closely, eying whether he might carry a weapon and inquiring what he wanted. "These sons of bitches think they can behave this way just because they live off the party," David said.[75]

In spite of his difficulties with the FPL around the time of demobilization, and the distance he had maintained since, David had declined several opportunities over the years to work as a protection agent for FMLN leadership himself. He preferred the relative freedom he enjoyed as an independent welder, moving from one job to the other and occasionally resting for some weeks if he felt like it. Nevertheless, after Funes's election, he had handed his résumé to a former FPL cadre holding a political post in San Salvador. Welding had taken a high toll on his eyes, and he wanted something different. David hoped for a job that did not involve security work; he said he had done enough of that during the war. David saw little contradiction between his critique of postinsurgent party privileges and his attempt to obtain a job through the intercession of his former comrade. It was not the "party" that would help him, but rather a close friend who happened to still be involved with the party. David furthermore considered that his wartime contributions more than justified his access to a job and benefits.[76]

David's anecdote suggests a process of "personalization" of former PMO relations. Party officials might now be more willing and able to favor their personal networks by means of their position of power than they would have been in earlier periods of the revolutionary process, when party control and discipline were more severe and the revolutionary ethos more restrictive of personal favoritism. What seems to matter the most in the postwar years are personal contacts with former PMO cadres in high places. In El Salvador's political slang, such contacts are called *conectes*.[77] They are characterized by their capacity for resolving different types of problems through personal influence. When conectes link to party politics, they allow for the mobilization of personal as well as political favors.

Thus, being a former guerrilla fighter might not, in and of itself, be of much help when looking for a job. For example, although its limited spread prevents reaching definite conclusions, the sample from the photographs suggests that the networks of former FPL and FAL fighters evolved somewhat differently from those of ERP and RN fighters. Most notably, while former FAL and FPL fighters were very likely to have found employment linked to the party, such as municipal employment, security jobs, or a political career, the sample of former PRTC, RN, and ERP fighters shows lower presence of these types of livelihoods. This finding, pending further corroboration, resonates with what several of the former ERP and RN members expressed during interviews for this study. The ERP and the RN suffered much higher levels of postwar disintegration. This is related to their break-off from the FMLN (1994) and the electoral failure of the PD (1997). As a result, former ERP and RN cadres obtained less access to public office. Subsequently, the former combatants from these organizations had fewer opportunities to opt for public sector jobs.

The use of insurgent ties for present-day problem solving is not just a bottom-up process. These ties are also an asset that (aspiring) leaders may want to exploit for a range of political purposes, from political campaigning to rolling out diverse projects and ventures. David expressed his opinion of his former FPL comrades, now FMLN leaders, as follows:

They use you to take one step after another [up the ladder]; . . . if you accept it, you keep covering [them] up in silence, for convenience, [or] for whatever reason it may be, they keep on using you. "You, come here! Here we can have you doing such-and-such; we can project you this way." But if you . . . don't share the same criteria, they cut you off . . . or they simply don't involve you anymore. . . . They only select people and then when they need help for something, a signature or whatever it may be, they just look you up, you see. . . . If they think you can reach a point at which you could force out so and so . . . Not that! Oh no! "If that is a risk then let's push him out beforehand, let's cut his wings so that he doesn't go any further." . . . This is why many people for convenience . . . don't give their opinion, they bow their head, or they turn a deaf ear. . . . So for convenience, I better stick to this and leave it be.[78]

David's former comrades have asked him, "You [David], why haven't they given you a job somewhere, in some municipality?"[79] They have also told David repeatedly to work on his temper and his pride.

Many people . . . have said to me: "Look you bastard, the best thing [to do] is to act in such and such a way, because . . . your problem is that you have always been very off-the-cuff!" . . . There are things that one has to shut up about, that is the key piece. . . . Why? To keep your little job . . . to maintain your status in the party. . . . All of this is what [everyone] is trying to preserve. . . . Everyone's inclination, of course, is to have a job and to survive. . . . If you don't stick to your party . . . where they know you, . . . you are even more fucked, you see. You don't have a lot of space, because [out there] they don't know you and you end up bouncing around in life you see, any which way, trying to defend yourself and look out for yourself, you alone.[80]

David's empirical understanding of FMLN politics and its intimate connections to postinsurgent livelihoods reflect years of accumulated experience. Indeed, of the dozens of former insurgents that I interviewed or spoke with extensively for this study, I did not meet a single one who had not used his PMO network at some point to help solve life's significant problems. Most commonly, PMO contacts were used to obtain employment, but use of these contacts could also include getting leverage to be used in interpersonal disputes or interaction with different institutions. David furthermore made explicit what I found to be a broadly shared sentiment among former rank-and-file and middle-cadre guerrilla fighters. The dissatisfaction with postinsurgent politics that was stated time and again was not that privileges for former insurgent participants were incorrect or unethical in themselves. On the contrary, the issue for most was that they were insufficient and distributed unevenly. Ex-combatants almost invariably considered that they deserved more than they had obtained: a better position than that of a municipal police officer with a lousy pay, or than having to take orders from people they did not recognize as their superiors. Former guerrilla fighters complained that they were barred from better-paid jobs because they lack the right diplomas. Some of the indictments of such supposed bureaucratic "rules" that I overheard were "They didn't ask for our papers in order to go to war," "When I went to the mountains they didn't ask for a diploma," and "How is one supposed to have a diploma if, instead of going to school, we went to war?"[81] Unfortunately, some believed, the leaders had only taken good care of their closest personal friends and allies. Often, the ex-combatants' main chagrin seemed to be their relative position in comparison to that of those former comrades now holding well-paid jobs.

The bottom-line argument I heard over and over was that the ascendency of these leaders had only been possible as a result of the contributions of "ordinary" guerrilla fighters like them. What was often expressed as the typical rank-and-file sentiment could be summarized as follows: if we made the greatest sacrifices, if we contributed most of the dead and the bulk of the firepower, why don't we get a larger share of the fruits of power that the FMLN has obtained? I found that this sentiment also played a pivotal role in the political organizing of the FMLN veterans' movement, the subject of the next chapter.

CONCLUSIONS: PMO NETWORKS AND POSTWAR
LIVELIHOOD STRATEGIES

Most former combatants were not content with the way in which the internal relations within the revolutionary movement developed during the postwar years. Their retrospective analysis was heavily tinged with a sense of loss and disillusionment. At the same time, their reflections also clarified the extent to which the former insurgent relations continued to play an important role in their lives. In the postwar period the majority of former guerrilla fighters depended to a very significant extent on the socioeconomic opportunities contingent on insurgent affiliation. Most commonly, PMO contacts were used to obtain employment, but prior affiliation could also provide leverage to be used in interpersonal disputes or for access to certain state-run services, like health-care benefits. When a former guerrilla fighter became gravely ill, for example, his or her former comrades might well look to the party to intervene in getting proper medical care in El Salvador or even in Cuba. The former insurgents did not consider such actions to constitute a kind of favoritism, but instead viewed them as morally necessary and correct, as a sort of inherited debt of internal solidarity from the former PMOs.[82]

Generally speaking, postwar "reintegration" of guerrilla fighters depended upon the social networks generated by their former PMOs. Most individual opportunities for former fighters emerged from collective projects inherited from the insurgency: the PNC, the NGOs, the insurgent repopulations, and, especially, employment related to the FMLN's performance as a political party. Preexisting differences among the insurgents in background and education significantly impacted the availability of postwar opportunities. As the PMOs' formal organizational structures and control mechanisms were dismantled, the weight of internal relations shifted from strict party structures and hierarchies to more personalized and less formal connections.

Access to public office and NGOs, though often contingent on inherited PMO relations, also implied a certain bureaucratization of these relationships. Once appointed to a specific post, former cadres also became gatekeepers who had to respect minimal suitability criteria for specific posts. Furthermore, if being channeled into a particular job could be interpreted as a favor at first, once an employee obtained a formal work contract, this also granted employment stability partially independent of *conectes* or of broader party politics. The labor situation nonetheless continued to qualify as relatively precarious, as illustrated by the stories of former insurgents who were forced out of their jobs because of political conflicts or changes in public administration. Even in a bureaucratic setting, interpersonal ties were key.

The different life trajectories recorded and discussed in this chapter illustrate how insurgent identities remained highly relevant for socioeconomic prospects almost two decades later. For example, David's marginalization within the FPL in the final months of the war subsequently impacted on his postwar career. In a broader sense, the FMLN's internal conflicts helped to differentiate socioeconomic opportunities, placing former FAL and FPL members in a more favorable position. Also, within-PMO distinctions were found to be relevant, with former cadres showing high levels of postwar ascendency, and rank and file making much more limited progress. This finding dovetails with Jocelyn Viterna's conclusion on former female FMLN combatants: their levels of postwar empowerment varied significantly according to "within-guerrilla distinctions" (2003, 208; 2013). Nonetheless, in spite of growing inequality among former insurgent participants, the photographs also demonstrate that PMO networks remained highly relevant for postwar rank-and-file livelihoods.

The demobilization of the guerrilla forces and the formal dissolution of the PMOs precipitated drastic changes in the former guerrilla fighters' immediate social context. Especially former ERP and RN combatants, but also members of the other PMOs, often interpreted these adjustments as a form of disintegration of their PMO "community." However, such interpretations should be understood in the light of what the PMOs meant to their constituents before 1992, when these organizations served as an all-encompassing social environment. While the PMO networks suffered many ruptures and adjustments in the postwar period, the stories and trajectories encapsulated in this chapter's photographs evidence the continued importance of the interpersonal ties forged during the insurgency, not only for sociopolitical, but also for economic aspects of life.

CHAPTER 7

FMLN Veterans' Politics

Lo que los hermanaba era el sectarismo con el que se combatían.
—Horacio Castellanos Moya, *El sueño del retorno*

In the late 1990s former FMLN guerrilla fighters started to organize around their identity as war veterans. Though friendship ties and nostalgia played important roles in the emerging movement, the FMLN veterans also engaged in political activities, showing the FMLN leadership they were a force to be reckoned with. FMLN veterans' organizing soon became heavily intertwined with the FMLN's internal conflicts.

The political life of veterans' groups documented in this chapter offers a view into what Veena Das calls "the underlife of political parties" (1990, 12). The chapter examines the intricacies of participation in postwar FMLN politics, and it touches upon key aspects of how the FMLN functions internally. The chapter is based on comparative multisited ethnographic fieldwork (Falzon 2009; Marcus 1995) with three veterans' groups. The first was the official Sector de Veteranos del FMLN (SV-FMLN),[1] a part of the FMLN party apparatus.[2] The second consisted of FPL veterans who gathered around an NGO called FUNDABRIL.[3] This collective included a few people I knew from my previous participation in the FPL.[4] The third group was called Movimiento de Veteranos de Guerra del Ejército Nacional para la Democracia (MV-END),[5] and consisted of small numbers of ERP, RN, and PRTC veterans, proclaimed Marxists-Leninists. This collective presented itself as operating left of the FMLN and regularly published a critical bulletin.[6]

I start this chapter with a review of the rise of the FMLN veterans' movement, which doubles as a window into the development of the FMLN in the decade after 2000. Then I present my fieldwork findings from the three groups, focusing on such aspects as the following: How were the veterans' groups organized? How did they speak of their political engagement? What were their goals? How did the different groups position themselves in relation to the FMLN, the Funes government, and each other? In the course of my fieldwork, the Funes government set up a special benefit program for FMLN veterans, which became an important arena of contention for the veterans' groups I was studying. This process provided me with additional insights on the practical logic of veterans' politics, as veterans' organizations were actively renegotiating their relationships with the government, the state, and the FMLN.

THE EMERGENCE OF THE VETERANS' MOVEMENT

In 1998, hundreds of former guerrilla fighters attended the first national FMLN veterans' meeting in Chalatenango. Most were former FPL, but contingents from the other PMOs also showed up. There were speeches and music. Several head of cattle were sacrificed for meat and soup.[7] Early FMLN veteran organizing took its key from the FMLN war-wounded associations, born after the peace accords and, since then, involved in a lengthy struggle with the government over benefits.[8] The rather complex story of the FMLN war-wounded associations merits a study in itself.[9] In a nutshell, the two most important war-wounded groups were the Asociación Salvadoreña de Lisiados y Discapacitados de Guerra (ASALDIG),[10] the original FMLN war-wounded association founded in 1992, and the Asociación de Lisiados de Guerra de El Salvador "Héroes de Noviembre del 89" (ALGES),[11] a 1997 split-off, which the FMLN leadership eventually recognized as the legitimate representative of the war-wounded. Since these associations had already proven able to obtain benefits, and to show some muscle to the government as well as to the FMLN leadership, they constituted an important source of inspiration for the veterans. Furthermore, several of the veterans' initial leaders were war-wounded veterans who aimed to branch out their work to include all veterans.[12]

The veterans' early political engagement soon became intertwined with efforts to gain strength inside the FMLN. As we saw in chapter 4, in the late 1990s the FMLN's internal politics were dominated by the tensions between reformists and CRS supporters. Internal strife continued in the decade after 2000, even after the expulsion of reformist leader Facundo Guardado in 2001.[13] The drawn-out dispute constituted a motivation for some veterans to engage in FMLN politics, either because they wanted to support a particular faction or because they felt they needed to step up because the leadership was making a mess of things.[14]

In 2002, the FMLN leadership authorized a provisional secretariat to take on the organization of veterans and supported it with a budget. Headed by a former FPL cadre considered to be a CRS supporter, the secretariat planned a nationwide organizational process that was to culminate in a national assembly meeting to formally constitute the FMLN veterans' sector.[15] These efforts ran parallel with another, more transcendental internal party process. In July 2003, the FMLN held an internal election to confirm its candidate for the 2004 presidential election. The reform-oriented within the FMLN profiled Oscar Ortíz as a possible opponent to Schafik Handal, the CRS candidate. Ortíz, a former FPL field comandante who had gained popularity as the mayor of the city of Santa Tecla, had launched an internal current within the FMLN called Fuerza Por El Cambio[16] in support of his aspirations. The internal election resulted in a victory for Schafik, but also demonstrated that the reformists were still a force to be reckoned with inside the FMLN.[17]

Political tensions among veterans had been evident throughout the preparatory activities. Besides CRS supporters, the provisional secretariat also included reformists and other dissidents. When everything was ready for the launch of the veterans' sector, the secretariat's leader suddenly took ill and died. This increased leadership's concerns with the potential impact of the constitution of the FMLN Veterans' Sector on Schafik's campaign. In view of the party's ongoing disunity, it was perceived that organized veterans might become a key factor in the internal power struggles.[18]

What followed was a complex tug-of-war. The FMLN's political commission first authorized preparations for a national assembly in Nejapa, but then withdrew its support after the provisional veterans' secretariat had already fixed a date and sent out the invitations. Most of the secretariat's members then refused to call the meeting off.[19] It was subsequently boycotted by another group of veterans who obeyed the instructions from the CRS leadership to cancel the meeting. In a last-minute move, when it became clear that the Nejapa assembly would go forward, the CRS group then decided to hold a parallel "national assembly" meeting to constitute their "own" veterans' sector, in one of the FMLN offices in San Salvador. Here, former RN field comandante "Dionisio Alemán," one of the CRS sympathizers active in the provisional secretariat, was elected national coordinator. The other national assembly meeting, that same day in Nejapa, drew a much larger attendance (estimated at fifteen hundred).[20] At this meeting, former FPL field comandante "René Henríquez" was elected as national coordinator.

According to newspaper coverage of the Nejapa assembly, the veterans' main grievance was that they had been "abandoned" by the FMLN. The veterans' authorities elected in Nejapa claimed that "the majority [of veterans] are in a difficult situation and know very well that organizing is the only mechanism through which they can resolve their most urgent needs." They intended to "work for the just demands of the veterans' sector" while also "[supporting] the FMLN from a qualitative and quantitative perspective," under the premise that as veterans they were "the heart, mind and soul of the FMLN."[21]

During the following months, a struggle evolved around which of the two veterans' groups would be accepted as the FMLN's "official" veterans' sector. Favoring the Alemán group, the FMLN leadership had publicly rejected Henríquez's aspiration to be recognized as the only legitimate representative of the veterans.[22] However, the FMLN leadership did not reject Henríquez's leadership completely. In an attempt to decrease animosities, they initially allowed him to represent some of the veterans. Both veterans' groups now aimed to expand, mainly by strengthening their territorial organization. The Henríquez group was by far the more successful in this effort, organizing a range of local assemblies and installing departmental and municipal veterans' directorates. Though this group was dominated by the FPL veterans, those that participated in it represented several different currents, with contacts all over the country. Their common agenda was determined by the double objective of strengthening the FMLN veterans movement and of countering CRS influence.

On November 11, 2003, Schafik Handal attended a rally of the Henríquez sector, in which he asked for the veterans' support in the campaign and praised them for being "the moral reserve of the FMLN."[23] Five days later he attended a similar event of the veterans' sector led by Alemán and expressed himself in the same terms.[24] In an attempt to boost their legitimacy, Alemán and his group worked hard to get a significant attendance for their own assembly with Schafik. Also in this meeting, the attending veterans demanded recognition from the FMLN leadership. According to a report in *Diario Co Latino*, one ex-combatant expressed himself as follows: "We are not going to deny our support to Schafik, we are going to struggle to vote and try to win, but we want them to recognize our quota of power within the FMLN."[25]

With this genie out of the bottle, FMLN leadership tried to curb the veterans while at the same time trying to avoid public controversy in the run-up to the elections.[26] The result was that the Dionisio Alemán group lowered its profile considerably and participated in the elections mostly from a position within other party structures. The Henríquez group continued to publicly pressure the FMLN for recognition, while contributing to the presidential campaign as a separate structure under the banner of the FMLN. For example, they formed their "own" campaign committees in different localities and organized a support caravan for Handal.[27]

Behind the scenes, René Henríquez and his aides looked beyond the election. With Handal way behind in the polls, they anticipated that his defeat would allow the reformists to pressure for new leadership.[28] Such a scenario would help the veterans to strengthen their internal position and to negotiate their demands. The group's avid participation in the Handal campaign was motivated in part by the need to be able to divert accusations of disloyalty that could undermine their position later.[29]

Meanwhile, the 2004 electoral campaign unfolded with unprecedented levels of postwar tension and polarization between ARENA and FMLN. Both camps, but especially the Right, developed a dirty campaign filled with wartime rhetoric and personalized attacks.[30] Militants from both parties were involved in violent incidents. The worst of these occurred during an ARENA campaign tour in northeastern Chalatenango on October 27, 2003, and resulted in twenty-three people wounded.[31] In March 2004, ARENA took the presidency once more in the first round and with considerable margin. The FMLN responded with accusations of "massive fraud."[32]

VETERANS' GROUPS AFTER THE 2004 ELECTIONS

The standoff between the Fuerza Por El Cambio and the CRS entered a new phase after the election. Handal interpreted his defeat as yet another indication that ARENA and the oligarchy would ultimately resist the FMLN's democratic ascendency, manipulating the system in their favor (Handal 2004, 11). Additionally, Handal considered that the FMLN had been weakened from within through the growing influence of the Right over parts of the militancy. In response, Handal called for restricting internal elections, reducing the number of affiliates, and making the party less permeable to newcomers (17). He also argued for strengthening the FMLN's ideological profile by drawing on the endurance of the Cuban revolution and on Chávez in Venezuela. In fact, the CRS had for some time already been actively involved in strategic coordination with Cuba and Venezuela.[33]

The participants in the Fuerza Por El Cambio, on the other hand, responded to the defeat by demanding that Handal and other leaders step down. When this did not occur, they started to prepare for the next round of internal elections, scheduled for November 2004. Henríquez's veteran group played an important role in this campaign. Their bulletin *Veteranos en Marcha*[34] railed against the CRS, labeled as the "group controlling the party leadership [with] the opportunistic behavior of the Right."[35] According to *Veteranos en Marcha*, the CRS leadership constituted a "clique controlling the FMLN: what it does is promote political clientelism in order to strengthen the circle of power they have constructed."[36]

According to *Veteranos en Marcha*, a group of FAL cadres headed by José Luis Merino (Comandante "Ramiro Vásquez") constituted a shadow leadership in the FMLN top echelons, with control over strategic decisions and party finances.[37] In October 2004, the Henríquez group publicly supported Ortíz as the new FMLN coordinator.[38] In one of the last bulletins before the internal elections, *Veteranos en Marcha* showed particular concern with the emergence of a third force, which consisted of a group of mostly former FPL cadres that had distanced themselves from both the CRS and the Fuerza Por El Cambio, and had called for party unity. This force identified itself as "terceristas" (a third way). *Veteranos en Marcha* called this new force "the duro-blandito current," in reference to a type of Salvadoran cheese enigmatically called hard-soft, and warned "militants not [to] be surprised by the maneuverings of the Conservative Clique [CRS leadership] and their hard-soft allies . . . against the Fuerza del Cambio [*sic*], whose efforts they will attempt to defeat, accusing it of being 'center-right' and 'social-democratic.'"[39]

The FMLN's internal elections took place on November 8, 2004. The election resulted in CRS's Medardo González, supported by the terceristas, narrowly beating Oscar Ortíz for the position of coordinator. Ortíz initially did not accept the results, but later decided to cease his opposition.[40] Between late 2004 and June 2005, some Fuerza Por El Cambio supporters left the party, or were expelled from it, while others decided to lie low.[41] The FMLN's political commission accused a group of FMLN deputies connected to Fuerza Por El Cambio of being bribed by ARENA.[42] Some of the dissidents tried to set up an alternative political project called Frente Democrático Revolucionario (FDR).[43] Its fate would not be very different from those of previous FMLN split-offs.[44]

Following Ortíz's loss, the Henríquez group fell apart. Medardo González confirmed the Dionisio Alemán group as the only veterans' sector recognized by the party. Henríquez and his followers were expelled from the office they had inside "1316," the FMLN's national seat in San Salvador. Files and equipment were thrown out on the street, and individuals banned from access to FMLN installations. Several former FPL cadres who had been at the forefront abandoned the group. René Henríquez himself had been offered an attractive job as head of security with a large state institution, which led to his resignation from the veterans' leadership.[45]

Following Handal's lead, the FMLN put a stop on primaries and internal elections after 2005, returning to a system based on nominations controlled by the party's top leadership. To justify this, the FMLN leadership dusted off the Leninist principle of "democratic centralism" and presented it as a guarantee for the party's ideological unity and internal discipline (López Bernal 2015, 12). The move also affected the veterans' groups, since it eliminated opportunities to organize veterans' support groups for FMLN primaries. Thus, the public presence of the FMLN veterans' movement became much less pronounced.

Nonetheless, after the withdrawal of FPL "heavyweights," a small group of veterans continued to meet as the "nonofficial" veterans' sector.[46] They attempted to strengthen the ideological profile of the sector by calling themselves Marxist-Leninists, and they critiqued the FMLN leadership for having sold out to the system and for having negotiated with the oligarchy under the table. Consisting mostly of ERP and FPL veterans, this group was loosely organized and operated rather invisibly. René

Henríquez and his aides considered most of these veterans to be radicals.[47] According to some veterans, the FMLN leadership internally accused the group of being infiltrated by veterans on the payroll of the Organismo de Inteligencia del Estado (OIE), the president's intelligence office.[48] The participating veterans considered these accusations to be a scheme designed to discredit and marginalize them.[49]

Within the FMLN another development was taking place at the time. After the failure of Handal's bid for the presidency several FMLN leaders favored a switch to more confrontational opposition strategies, building on closer linkages between the party and "*el pueblo*," in particular left-wing social movements. The idea behind this was that increased social mobilization and protest would weaken and wear out the government of President Antonio Saca.[50] Handal died suddenly of a heart attack in January 2006 and was hence unable to witness the results of this new strategy personally. The massive outpouring of mourning caused by his death confirmed Handal's personal status within the FMLN as well as the continued dominance of the CRS (Bichkova de Handal 2009; L. González 2006). In March 2006, after a campaign again riddled with violent incidents, ARENA defeated the FMLN in the legislative elections by a narrow margin (34 to 32 seats). In the same elections, the FMLN managed to retain the capital city, albeit by a tiny margin, and after a tense postelection standoff around the hotel where the votes were counted.[51]

The rise of a more radical militant atmosphere inside the FMLN had several effects on the remaining veterans' groups. The "nonofficial" veterans' sector initially echoed the strategy, which synchronized well with its ideological profile. The veterans anticipated that an emphasis on social mobilization and protest would help radicalize the popular bases of the FMLN, something that might help strengthen the political influence of experienced Marxist-Leninist activists. Small in numbers, the nonofficial veterans sought to insert themselves into ongoing grassroots struggles in the hope of gaining influence within these efforts.[52]

However, this social mobilization strategy backfired after the student protests of July 5, 2006, in which an FMLN militant identified as Mario Belloso killed two police officers with an M-16 rifle (Moodie 2010, 212; PDDH 2006). Inside the FMLN, the Belloso case triggered extensive talk about enemy infiltration (Sprenkels 2014a). The controversy around Belloso did not benefit veterans' organizing efforts. Those who had remained active in the "nonofficial" veterans' sector were wary that, because of these veterans' radical stance, the FMLN leadership might intend to use them as scapegoats in the Belloso affair and its aftermath. As a result, this group of veterans lowered their profile and partially demobilized after July 2006, with a few members continuing to meet and work underground.[53]

The FMLN's troubled internal political climate improved in 2007 as the combined result of two events. In July 2007, several social movement groups staged an antigovernment protest in the town of Suchitoto, which was met with strong government repression.[54] The Saca administration then attempted to apply the new antiterrorism legislation it had pushed through after the events of July 5, 2006, to obtain lengthy jail sentences for those arrested during the protests. This led to international commotion, with family members setting up a "political prisoners" committee and the FMLN rallying behind the detainees, who were finally released and cleared of charges eight months later.[55] The Suchitoto incidents united different groups of militants in and around the FMLN in favor of the detainees and in rejection of the criminalization of social protest (Ladutke 2008).

Another event that helped calm the waters within the FMLN was the selection of Mauricio Funes as the FMLN's presidential candidate, announced formally on September 27, 2007.[56] With the FMLN leadership opting for a strong, independent, and charismatic candidate, the possibility of winning the election created a new horizon for FMLN constituencies, including the veterans' groups. It was understood that a possible Funes presidency would not only grant the FMLN access to power, but also broaden the possibilities for different left-wing sectors that had lost strength within the FMLN but had historical connections to people in the Funes entourage. The veterans anticipated new power-sharing arrangements within the Salvadoran Left, and new possibilities for historical militants to reengage. In this context, the social mobilization strategy was abandoned, and the upcoming election became the priority matter. Several of those who had played a leading role in the 2003–4 veterans' movement now inserted themselves into the Funes campaign.

I started my fieldwork with FMLN veterans in May 2009, just prior to Funes's inauguration as the new president.[57] Because of this timing, my fieldwork coincided with the start of a new era of intense networking and organizing among veterans.[58] Not only the veterans but also the war-wounded engaged in renewed organizational efforts and activism. They rallied for the payment of a debt that ARENA had accumulated with the beneficiaries of the war-wounded protection fund, a debt that Funes quickly agreed to disburse.[59] When, in late 2009, it became clear that the Funes administration was considering establishing some kind of compensation program for FMLN veterans, organizing intensified further.

SV-FMLN: THE FMLN'S "OFFICIAL" VETERANS

Arranging the Fieldwork

A personal assistant of FMLN general coordinator Medardo González invited me to the 1316 office to discuss my petition to research the FMLN veterans' movement. Having not been inside 1316 for some ten years, I was impressed with the changes. The garage had been transformed into a waiting room. At the office's entrance, there was a receptionist, who registered all visitors. She pushed a button to unlock the door to go inside, into the central hallway. Access to the stairway leading to the second floor was shielded off with metal bars and an electric lock. The assistant led me upstairs into the building's main meeting room, transformed from a bare room into a comfortable space. Its walls were decorated with posters and portraits of Latin American revolutionary heroes, from Farabundo Martí to Hugo Chávez.

As we sat down, the assistant excused Medardo González's absence, due to an unforeseen urgent engagement, and said that the FMLN leadership had discussed and accepted my petition. The FMLN was very interested in my research, he said, since the veterans constituted one of the FMLN's largest sectors, a sector, furthermore, renowned for their revolutionary stamina. The FMLN Veterans' Sector, he claimed, included some six thousand veterans. They had already informed Dionisio Alemán, the coordinator of the Sector de Veteranos del FMLN (SV-FMLN), of my research project, and had instructed him to collaborate with my effort. The assistant suggested I arrange a meeting with Alemán to discuss details.[60]

Alemán worked mostly from "229," FMLN's smaller, downtown San Salvador office.[61] When I explained in our initial meeting that my intention was to participate in different meetings of the veterans' group, Alemán's reaction was bereft of enthusiasm. It was only after considerable insistence on my part that he agreed to let me attend the weekly Monday-night meetings with the veterans from the department of San Salvador.

Furthermore, I would be able to meet with the SV-FMLN national directorate, but not sit in on its meetings, since he claimed these had a more internal character. Also, I would not be allowed to record the meetings I participated in, but instead I was confined to taking notes.[62]

The Monday-night meetings of the FMLN veterans from San Salvador were held in the partially roofed back patio of the "229" office.[63] The venue was spacious, able to hold up to one hundred people, though white plastic chairs were less abundant. One drawback was that, in the rainy season, the noise of the water drops hitting the tin roof would drown out the speaker's voice. The meetings' attendance varied considerably, from some twenty participants on quiet evenings to close to one hundred in the best-attended meetings. All the participants were over forty years old, and at least 80 percent were male. Most attendees were regulars, even though almost all, except for Alemán, would miss or skip meetings. Set to start at six, the meetings normally began half an hour later, because Alemán attended short bilateral consultations while the arriving participants were greeting and chatting, fetching coffee, and buying sweet bread from a veteran who always dropped in with her large round basket of bakery products.

The meetings developed according to a set format. After the initial delay, Alemán walked to the front, welcomed the participants, and proposed an agenda. Other members of the veterans' directorate would take a seat either next to Alemán or in one of the front rows. Alemán's two most prominent aides were "Yolanda" and "Gabriel." Yolanda functioned as the treasurer and was the only woman on the directorate. I learned she also held a post in the FMLN municipality of Mejicanos. Gabriel, an elderly doctor who spent the war in exile, participated in the directorate of the veterans and that of the FMLN's "professionals sector." Rafael, another directorate member, always sat in the back. He doubled as one of the animators of the El Salvador–Cuba Friendship Committee. At the end of every meeting, Rafael would try to enlist the veterans in ongoing activities in support of the Cuban Revolution. Indeed, among SV-FMLN's regular attendees, many simultaneously participated in other FMLN activities, sectors, or committees.

Normally, the agenda Alemán proposed consisted of three elements: reports, activities, and agreements. Since Alemán participated in different internal FMLN meetings on a senior level, his reports mostly consisted of a rather lengthy account of the relevant issues discussed there. This included the "party line" with regard to current events. Then other directorate members would take over, speaking mostly on what was expected of the veterans with regard to upcoming events, while trying to recruit volunteers to take on concrete tasks. At this point, participants would ask questions and ventilate opinions more actively. Finally, to wrap up the meeting, Alemán would confirm the distribution of tasks and stress the importance of participating and being visible as veterans in upcoming party activities.

As the meetings ran to their end, usually around eight o'clock, most participants were in a hurry to leave, because they relied on public transportation to get home.[64] Some stayed behind because they wanted to discuss something with Alemán privately, or because they needed to arrange practical matters with Alemán or other members of the directorate. The members of the directorate would usually stay later because they needed to coordinate their activities for the upcoming week. Having a vehicle at my disposal, I would usually stick around until Alemán was finished with his bilateral meetings, and offer him and others that might need it a ride home.

This Is Solidarity! Distributing the Opportunities of the New Funes Administration

As to what was discussed during the meetings, what stood out was the issue of *gestiones*, which referred to the efforts of Dionisio Alemán and other members of the directorate to procure job opportunities for the veterans. Another recurrent topic was what the veterans saw as the emerging tension between President Mauricio Funes and the party, spurred mainly by the president's nomination of a significant number of cabinet members who did not belong to the FMLN and by his apparent lack of interest in party affairs. A final recurrent item was a project for a monument for the guerrilla fighters killed during the 1989 offensive in the city of Soyapango, close to the capital.

Frequently, Alemán's political analysis and the issue of job opportunities mixed. For example, on August 24, Alemán referred to Funes's orientation to respect the posts of municipal and ministerial employees inherited from previous administrations. Only those occupying *puestos de confianza*[65] were to be replaced. This led to a lively discussion. Yolanda offered that the definition of puestos de confianza required reconsidera-

ring to a situation the FMLN was facing in Mejicanos. "There are forty comrades working as members of the CAM in Mejicanos who don't want to pay their party quota," she said. Yolanda and others had spoken with them and explained: "There are thousands of veteran comrades who don't have work and you don't want to pay the five dollars to the party." Gabriel backed this up: "Schafik used to say that the party quota needs to be institutionalized; anyone who fails to pay their quota for two months in a row should be thrown out of the party." Alemán then intervened to emphasize the importance of his effort with the ministry. "Be assured that we are going to continue placing comrades [in job positions]; we already managed to do so with one contingent, but there will be more!" This statement was met with a spontaneous and thundering applause.

With the applause dying out, someone in the group stood up and said, "Those ten comrades that already have work can offer their solidarity with those who have not been hired."[68] The proposal was that those members of SV-FMLN who had obtained a job donate part of their income in order to provide assistance to those who had not yet found a job. His comment was also met with strong and persistent applause. Gabriel then once more insisted that the objective of procuring jobs for veterans was not only economic, but also political. "The role that we are going to play is an important one," he said, pointing out that the ministries were filled with right-wingers and corrupt employees. Gabriel, who appeared to be particularly inspired this evening, also emphasized the importance of strengthening the solidarity among the veterans. He said, "For those for whom we found work, . . . we want to see you here in the Monday meetings in order to strengthen ourselves ideologically." Such a task was apparently needed, because according to Gabriel, "When one first begins to feel the change in one's pocket then one forgets about others, who may be in rough shape. 'Comrade: do you want to come with us to the march?' 'Well, you know, I can't!' 'Why not?' Because he already resolved his problem and has forgotten the others, this is how we are as Salvadorans."[69]

A veteran from Guazapa spoke to denounce how in his municipality the ministry's agricultural packages were hoarded by local ARENA and PCN leaders so they could hand them out in exchange for registering for party membership or simply sell them. Gabriel had attended a meeting in Santa Marta the week before in which "there were many accusations of corruption" with regard to the matter of agricultural inputs. A veteran from Santa Marta present at the meeting explained that the problem was that those involved in negotiating the packages had "a corrupt trajectory" linked to an NGO active in the region. Alemán, who had also attended the meeting in Santa Marta, interrupted: "They appear to be with the FMLN." The Santa Marta veteran replied: "No, they are businesspeople!"

Gabriel picked up on this exchange by going off against NGOs: "[They] have gotten rich off the international cooperation in recent years, do not work at all with the party and even motivate people to not go to the marches." Alemán backed him up by stating, "We don't have any money, [and meanwhile] the NGOs are running around with shitloads of money, sucking it all down." Many social organizations, Gabriel claimed, were only empty shells that served to fill the leaders' pockets and prop up political aspirations. After Funes's election, social movement activists were reorganizing themselves. According to Gabriel, this was a good thing, but he warned that leaders should coordinate with the FMLN—"so those damned rightists don't catch us with our pants down." He proposed inviting some leaders to participate in SV-FMLN, "but not too many, because if so they could slip in infiltrators." Alemán closed the meeting by emphasizing the need to organize the veterans to be able to jump at the opportunities the Funes government could offer. "If we are not alert, others are going to eat the cake, and then we should not sit around complaining."[70]

A week later, the Monday-night meeting focused on the preparations for the upcoming celebration of the twentieth anniversary of the FMLN's November 1989 offensive. After the meeting, I waited for Alemán, Yolanda, and Gabriel to finish up in order to give them a ride home. As we were getting into the car, a veteran I call "Zacarías" approached me and asked if I could take him along. Alemán, Yolanda, and Gabriel were conversing about which names to put on a list for five new job openings for the veterans in the postal service, a subdivision of the Ministry of Interior. After some time, Zacarías asked why they did not put him on that list. Yolanda replied that he was already on another list for jobs at a government institution called Administración Nacional de Acueductos y Alcantarillados (ANDA).[71] Zacarías explained that he had presented himself at the job interview but had not been called afterward. Yolanda said that out of eleven veterans interviewed, ANDA had accepted seven. However, one of the seven was not going to be able to take the job. Her contact at ANDA had assured her they would call at least one more, and possibly several, of those that had been interviewed. At this point we neared Alemán's house, and I stopped to let him out. Alemán told Yolanda to finalize the list together with Gabriel. The journey continued and Zacarías insisted upon being included in the list for the postal service. Gabriel intervened with a favorable comment. Yolanda recited the list she had been working on to present to their contact at the postal service the next day. Gabriel suggested one name to replace with Zacarías. Yolanda agreed. Zacarías, very content, then said: "Thank you! This is solidarity! It is not about talking but about helping out the comrades."[72]

During my fieldwork, SV-FMLN was able to procure a significant number of job openings for veterans in a range of different state agencies. However, veterans frequently complained that they had not been included in the lists or that the positions offered were not to their liking. In particular, openings for security agents and prison guards were met with reluctance. The Veterans' Sector leadership, meanwhile, lamented that their contacts in different state agencies sometimes failed to deliver on their promises, hiring fewer compañeros than agreed upon previously, for example. They strongly criticized government functionaries who resisted meeting with the veterans or who refused to make concessions. On the other hand, they also censured cases in which veterans had not shown up for the job interviews or had abandoned their new posts, stating that such incidents reflected negatively on the sector as a whole. "Let us not be seen as irresponsible," Yolanda implored.[73]

The Soyapango Monument

Early in 2009, the municipal government of Soyapango, a large urban center bordering San Salvador to the east, had granted the veterans a location for a monument for fallen guerrilla fighters at a traffic intersection in an area where heavy fighting had taken place. The project was cosponsored by a reputable FMLN militant and senior state official, who had enlisted an artist to design the monument. The initial plan was to inaugurate the new monument on November 11, 2009, in celebration of the twentieth anniversary of the 1989 offensive. After a few meetings, however, this time line was declared unrealistic, and the goal was changed to placing the first stone.[74] The veterans had calculated they needed around ten thousand dollars for the monument, but so far they had raised only a fraction of that amount. Alemán said that fund-raising had to be done with ordinary militants and collaborators, but especially with "mayors, legislative assembly members and governors."[75] The veterans were handed numbered paper bonds and lists to register the donations. Money and lists were to be handed over to Alemán at the latest on October 12, 2009.

Simultaneously, the veterans began preparation of the upcoming celebration of the offensive. Two people working with the FMLN's "cultural commission" joined one of the meetings to discuss different ideas with the veterans. One problem was that the municipal administration of San Salvador had passed into ARENA hands earlier that year, and the new mayor was presumed to not allow the offensive to be commemorated on the capital's central square. The veterans responded to this presumption with indignation. A few offered to turn the celebration into "a political offensive," to "take the streets" and stage reenactments of the offensive across the city, "whether mayor Quijano likes it or not."[76]

As the celebration date came closer, plans became ever more modest. The monument project suffered new setbacks, making it impossible to place the first stone in November. Alemán, furthermore, lamented the meager results of the fund-raising campaign, complaining both about some prominent FMLN figures' reluctance to donate and of the passivity of the veterans in their fund-raising efforts.[77]

Then, a few days before the celebration, Hurricane Ida caused flooding and damages across the country. The government declared a national emergency. The FMLN immediately mobilized its militancy toward emergency relief. The FMLN's political commission further scaled down the celebration of the offensive, relocating it to the modest venue of La Bermeja Cemetery in San Salvador, by a monument for the FMLN's "fallen heroes" built some years before. Around 150 militants attended the celebration on the morning of November 11. Not Alemán, but Medardo González gave the keynote address. SV-FMLN participated with a salute to the fallen and placed a floral arrangement.[78]

The Monday-night meeting of November 23, 2009, served to evaluate this celebration as well as the veterans' participation in the FMLN emergency relief efforts. With regard to the first item, I perceived considerable disappointment among the veterans due to the fact that not even the first stone of the Soyapango monument had been laid, the modesty of the celebration, and the small role given to the Veterans' Sector at La Bermeja Cemetery. During the discussion, a regular participant asked Alemán for permission to read something he had written about the difficulties with the monument. He stood up, unfolded a sheet a paper, and started reading out loud.

> It is inconceivable that in a Revolutionary Party . . . in order to honor the memory of the heroes and heroines of November 11, '89, through the erection of the monument to those who gave their lives for the cause, one should have to beg and plead for the support of some legislators and high government functionaries when . . . they have a moral obligation [to support the project] given that they have their positions and seats because of them.
>
> And if this is what is done to [those that have fallen], now we shall see what they do with [the survivors]; . . . the men and women comrades of the FMLN Veterans' Sector are viewed in many municipalities in a disparaging manner, as if they were members of the opposition or of contending parties, when it was we who sacrificed our youth, our social standing, our professions, our work, our intellectual formation, our families, and even our lives to make a more just and dignified society for all a reality, one in which many others today enjoy a number of privileges. And it is precisely to them that these remarks are directed, given that, enjoying as they do these privileges, how is it possible that they do not recognize the reason why they are enjoying their positions?[79]

The veteran finished his comments with a heartfelt cry for the veteran leadership to take "action on the matter" and to "make [the party] comply fully with its statutes, principles, and values." Shaking with emotion, he then handed the piece of paper to Alemán, accompanied by the ovation of the participants. He also handed out a few extra copies.[80] Alemán took advantage of the moment's solemnity to emphasize the importance of raising awareness within the party of the veterans' historical role and to vindicate the veterans as a sector. He also insisted on the need to resume and continue fund-raising activities for the monument.

Then the meeting moved to the evaluation of the emergency relief after Ida. Several veterans had participated in FMLN brigades that helped to clean up the mess from flooding and mudslides and worked to distribute aid to affected communities. They said that ARENA had also mobilized its militancy to provide relief. The veterans accused local ARENA politicians as well as ARENA emergency brigades of hoarding the aid, distributing it to their own constituencies, or storing it to sell later for profit. Pro-Cuban revolution activist Rafael, who had participated extensively in these activities, exhorted that it was not enough for the militants to help clean up. "Along with carrying around a shovel, pick, and wheelbarrow, you need to go talk to people. You need to explain to them the cost that this disaster signifies in the midst of the overall plundering that the Right has carried out [under the previous administrations]."

Alemán explained that "emergency aid activities are highly humanitarian, but they are also propaganda and counterpropaganda activities." One veteran said that the key task was to "avoid letting the aid reach the people involved with the other political group, in other words, ARENA." Rafael agreed that the veterans should not be naïve: "The political enemy also takes advantage of emergencies." Several veterans, furthermore, complained that not all the brigade participants showed exemplary behavior. For example, "There were those who said: 'We're the only ones who came while the legislative assembly members are kicking back.' . . . They were saying inappropriate things to people. One group of compañeros began to change into clothing that had come in the donation bags; they were a bad example. That aid was for the people. Or party activists who say, 'Can I grab a pound of beans?'"[81]

Fund-raising for the monument continued to lag behind,[82] and after several new delays, the placement of the first stone of the monument was finally scheduled for January 10, 2010, the date of the anniversary of the first large insurgent offensive, in 1981. A brigade of volunteers from among the veterans worked to clear the site and prepare it for construction. The first Monday-night meeting of 2010 was dedicated to preparing the upcoming event. Alemán reported that the fund-raising tally was now up to three thousand dollars, an announcement met with applause. This was still short, but a decent step in the right direction. Among the veterans, several had not yet presented their lists. Yolanda exhorted those present to bring in the money from the bonds sold and return those that had not been sold. Holding up a five-dollar note, Alemán announced, "[We have just received] a donation from a compañera for whom we had found a job, . . . because she had just received her first month's pay." Again, there was applause from the group.

The monument's cosponsor had sent a representative to the meeting, who offered advice on fund-raising. Through his comments, we learned that Alemán's group had actually not been responsible for bringing in most of the money, but had only raised three hundred dollars so far. The cosponsor had brought in the remaining twenty-seven hundred dollars. The representative's advice was to canvass much more actively during large events attended by party militants. Last month, he said, together with some helpers, he had sold 160 bonds during the commemoration of the El Mozote massacre and 250 at the National Convention. After this comment, Alemán once more proposed to step up the veterans' efforts to sell bonds. One attendant then offered: "I know who is loaded... the legislators!" This comment was met with laughter from part of the group and with a somewhat sour face from Alemán. He proposed that after the January 10 event plans would be developed to undertake a new fund-raising push. He conceded that the FMLN leadership should also contribute.

For the January 10 event, Alemán's immediate concern was to obtain a strong attendance, in terms of both dignitaries and audience. According to the veterans at the meeting, the latter would not be difficult. "In the offices of different city governments there are people who are there because the veterans recommended them. So, they can go. There are a ton of employees. In Cuscatancingo there are more than three hundred employees; many are there because we recommended them; it is the same in San Marcos."[83]

Another veteran agreed: "The problem is not for us to gather together two hundred militants. They'll be there. The problem is raising the money." With the topic once more on the table, another veteran suggested: "We need to ask the guys in the ties for money" (*los corbatudos*), which again caused some hilarity.[84]

On January 10, the decoration commission had adorned the site with little red flags and a handmade banner in honor of the fallen combatants. The event featured short speeches by Alemán and others, as well as a very lengthy address by Soyapango's FMLN mayor, who emphasized the historical continuity between yesterday's combatants and today's FMLN. The party's general coordinator, Medardo González, participated by symbolically placing the monument's first stone, under the applause of onlookers, who numbered roughly one hundred people, mostly dressed with FMLN T-shirts, hats, and other party identification items. The next day, a picture of Medardo González placing the first stone, with the veterans looking on, featured in a national newspaper.[85]

The event was evaluated in the Monday-night meeting two weeks later. Alemán seemed content. He honored a group of veterans from Soyapango who had worked the entire week before the event to compact the dirt for the plateau upon which to place the first stone. The meeting gave them a strong round of applause. The veterans agreed to set up two commissions: one headed by Yolanda and three other veterans who would visit senior officials and dignitaries to solicit more financial contributions. A second commission was charged with organizing a fund-raising festival. These and other efforts allowed the completed monument to be inaugurated on November 14, 2010.[86]

SV-FMLN's Internal Environment (and My Presence in It)

Early on in my fieldwork, Alemán invited me to present myself to the SV-FMLN national directorate. I was granted half an hour to discuss my research project with the group, which consisted of the leaders of the Monday-night meetings along with a few representatives from other departments. I explained that my research was aimed at understanding the long-term dynamics of postwar reinsertion of former FMLN guerrilla fighters, as well as the political role of the veterans in the postwar period.

Figure 7.1.   Monument to the heroes of 1989, Soyapango (2011)

Source: Photograph by Yuri Escamilla. Used by permission.

This double focus was received well. Although the veterans' stated primary concern was "to return the party to the true line of revolutionary mystique, which it has lost," the directorate underlined that the sectors' marginalization was not only political, but also economic.[87]

Alemán also emphasized the socioeconomic plight of the FMLN veterans. He explained: "Insertion in civilian life is easy. I just take off the uniform and I am a civilian. The tough part is insertion in economic life."[88] Alemán explained that they considered it part of SV-FMLN's work to help the veterans improve their social-economic position, but that with ARENA in power such an effort had been very difficult. With Funes, there was talk about the possibility of opening up programs for FMLN veterans. With the aid of the UES, SV-FMLN was in the process of performing a "census" of veterans, which was to include basic socioeconomic indicators. Alemán asked if I could help, and I agreed to provide technical assistance with regard to the format of the census and data processing, hoping that this contribution would help to make my integration into the group smoother.

As it turned out, for reasons unbeknownst to me, the collaboration with the compañero in charge at the UES did not function properly.[89] In general, my fieldwork with SV-FMLN developed with awkwardness, not least because I felt the sector's leadership, especially Alemán, to be weary with my presence. For example, it took weeks of persistent requests to get Alemán to pass me a copy of the SV-FMLN work plan. When he finally did, he indicated that I would be allowed to read it and take notes, but not to make a photocopy. I was to return the document to him after the meeting. Among other issues, as part of the political context in which the veterans had to operate, the document took on the matter of infiltration and betrayal within the FMLN, which resonated partially with the distrust I perceived in Alemán. As I hand-copied from the document into my notebook,

> These [false] leaders . . . had already tasted the delights of exercising power for personal benefit through holding public offices, and they were still within the party [FMLN], but they no longer had either principles, ethics, nor revolutionary morals, and they furthermore created divisions within the party, . . . organizing groups . . . revolving around their personal interests, . . . trying to move the party to the Right. . . . In order to do this they took advantage of the party's

statutory democracy, which they themselves had drafted, as well as of flawed party conventions where . . . they blackmailed and tricked party members. It is important to point out that many of these leaders, over the years, became traitors who are now working with the Right, . . . but who have left, like it or not, a few remnants within the party, who will only be eliminated over time.[90]

The document indicated, "The Veterans' Sector and FMLN war veterans are the historic-moral reserve of our party, those who can and ought to transmit our experience together with all our party members and the people," by using the sector's "principles, discipline, mysticism, and solid revolutionary objectives," which had been accumulated through years of struggle and sacrifice and thus could function as a counterweight against negative influences within the party.[91] But, I wondered, weren't the dissidents also almost invariably seasoned war veterans, with years of struggle and many personal sacrifices on their slate? How to determine what qualified as "truly" revolutionary, what constituted "treason" and what was simply a disagreement on a political topic? What to think of the announced purging of emerging "traitors" within the party?

During the meetings I attended, the veterans regularly talked about the FMLN being infiltrated, as well as about the idea that their own sector could be prone to infiltration, and about the "next traitors" that had already sold out.[92] Whereas during the war a significant number of lives were lost because of such suspicions, these references now mainly served to explain perceived internal contradictions and to disqualify certain groups or individuals. In the minds of the veterans, infiltration and the breeding of treason were tools that the Right used with the ultimate aim of destroying the FMLN. The SV-FMLN veterans saw the Right as constantly manipulating and conspiring against the FMLN. On occasions, elaborate conspiracy theories would be discussed and validated during the meetings. For example, after the devastating Haiti earthquake (January 12, 2010), various comrades argued that the United States had secretly provoked the disaster in order to establish a stronger military presence in the Caribbean to close in on Venezuela. According to these veterans, the US military used earthquake provocation as a pretext to invade Haiti, repressing and killing people in the process. This theory was unanimously accepted in the group.[93] I did not intervene in the discussion, but skepticism must have been written plainly on my face.

Given that the FMLN, and the Veterans' Sector in particular, was an environment rife with distrust, I imagine it must have been difficult for Alemán and his aides to have an outsider present at their meetings. They must have been aware that I was bound to stumble across some of the weaknesses and contradictions of the veterans' organizing efforts, making it hard to keep up the image of being a collective that was "worthy, unified, numerous, and committed," which is what most social movements strive for (Tilly 2004, 4). Indeed, SV-FMLN's relatively precarious level of organization became ever clearer to me as fieldwork progressed. Territorial structures outside of San Salvador were barely functional. To outsiders like me, Alemán attempted to paint an image of SV-FMLN strength that was difficult to hold up over the course of numerous meetings. For example, in one of my earlier meetings with the SV-FMLN directorate, Alemán maintained that there were as many as sixty thousand or seventy thousand veterans that the directorate could organize into SV-FMLN, if only they managed to carry out the registration properly.[94] In reality, as far as I witnessed, active participants constituted a few hundred veterans at the most.

As it turned out, SV-FMLN did not have a registered membership body. This was the main reason they wanted to have a veterans' "census," hoping that registration would strengthen the organization. Mainly, they wanted to be able to present lists and data that allowed the veterans to apply for benefit programs, with the SV-FMLN leadership functioning as mediators in this process. As Alemán expressed in one meeting: "We need to do a census in order to be able to say to the government: 'We have 4,000 farmers, we need help for them.'"[95] The lack of registration became more pressing with SV-FMLN aiming to participate in government programs that emerged during the last months of 2009. For example, Alemán explained that the Ministry of Agriculture was setting up programs with the European Union and Brazil that might include veterans as beneficiaries. The same ministry was negotiating with Cuba to train selected peasants to become licensed agronomists. And the Ministry of Health had requested data concerning the veterans and their places of residence.[96]

Meanwhile, Alemán became increasingly restless with the fact that the UES was not producing any results. Finally, toward the end of my fieldwork, Alemán and Yolanda invited me to a meeting in 1316 to discuss the matter. Alemán stressed the importance of making headway with the registration of the veterans because of the urgency of seeing how the

SV-FMLN could give their "comrades some benefit . . . with the new government." He complained about the lack of support his organization had had so far, also from within the party, and said that the effort to organize veterans has been almost his alone. Nonetheless, Alemán claimed he so far had gathered some three thousand veteran-affiliation forms. What he needed was for these forms to be processed into a database. He furthermore wanted to organize some new rounds of affiliations in different localities of the country, and he needed people to help fill out new affiliation forms. Alemán indicated that he preferred not to have other sections of the party involved but that he wanted to be directly in control.[97]

Alemán's concerns regarding veteran affiliation made more sense to me in light of what I had learned from different participants in the Veterans' Sector during bilateral interviews. Directorate member Rafael, for example, had pointed out to me that SV-FMLN participants were predominantly former RN militants. Outside of RN circles, Alemán's influence and standing were limited. Most of those who attended meetings and other activities had ties to the RN during the war and knew Alemán from this period.[98] In fact, while I was saying my goodbyes to the group, one of the meeting participants said: "It may appear that we are an RN group, but we represent all FMLN veterans."[99]

FUNDABRIL-ASALVEG

The second group I worked with for the study on the FMLN veterans' movement was organized around an NGO called Fundación 1 de Abril (FUNDABRIL). In June 2009, René Henríquez, the man who had been Alemán's competitor for the leadership of FMLN veterans in 2003–4, now worked as managing director of FUNDABRIL. The NGO's name referred to the founding date of the FPL (April 1, 1970). It was set up in 2004, as the continuation of an initiative called FPL Assets Committee, an entity established at the FPL's 1995 final congress, with the task of administering part of the FPL's accumulated capital for the benefit of its former militancy (Luciak 2001, 232). In 1995, this Assets Committee had taken charge of funds and properties amounting to well over $1 million.[100] It was also mandated to safeguard part of the FPL's historical archive.

The Assets Committee was assembled by a group of seasoned FPL members, mostly midlevel cadres. For the first years, this committee functioned as a small, separate office inside the 1316 FMLN office (one of the FPL properties that passed on to the FMLN in 1995). Based on the liquid assets available, it set up a credit line for former FPL militants. It also provided a legal-support fund for a few FPL militants who continued to be incarcerated in foreign countries for activities connected to the FPL.[101] As it turned out, the FPL properties inherited by the Assets Committee almost invariably presented complex legal-ownership issues. These difficulties made it impossible for the committee to cash in without first investing significant amounts of money, a risk the members were hesitant to take, especially when it came to properties abroad.

From 1995 to 2003, most of the committee's funds were invested in the credit program for militants. This money gradually evaporated because of poor administration and extremely low payback rates on outstanding loans. In the words of one of the committee members: "Every [party militant] asked for loans as if among friends, and it turned into a mess, a real disaster."[102] The Assets Committee money was furthermore used as a solidarity fund for former FPL militants facing an emergency or to support meetings and celebrations, like the FPL's anniversary.

FUNDABRIL was born as an attempt to revamp the Assets Committee and protect it from the FMLN's internal conflicts of 2003 and 2004.[103] At the time, it had been functioning in close coordination with Henríquez's veterans' group, which, as we have seen, was expelled from the FMLN office in November 2004. In fact, as I learned, most of the materials that had been thrown out on the street in front of the FMLN's 1316 office after Ortíz's 2004 defeat in the internal election were now stored in FUNDABRIL's office. Nonetheless, FUNDABRIL's political profile was not one of clear-cut dissidence from the FMLN mainstream. Members held diverse opinions regarding FMLN politics, though most did favor some kind of reform.

After working for a period without an office and with their papers spread out over the homes of several compañeros, the FUNDABRIL directorate rented a small office in 2007. The organization had inherited a significant portfolio of outstanding loans to different FPL militants. The directorate had sent out a letter to the debtors, informing them that interest would be forgiven in the case of prompt repayment. Results were modest. FUNDABRIL collaborator José, a university lecturer, said he was one of the few who had paid back their loans. The directorate also considered hiring a debt recovery agency, but finally voted against it to avoid conflicts. According to José, the fundamental problem was that the former FPL militants thought the money belonged to them.[104]

In view of this situation, the FUNDABRIL directorate considered that obtaining funding for new projects constituted a more promising avenue. They invested some of the remaining Assets Committee funds in the appointment of a managing director. In addition to taking over responsibilities such as the FPL veteran solidarity fund, FUNDABRIL aimed to "contribute to the human development of veterans and war-wounded and their families, through social, economic, cultural, and other kinds of projects and programs."[105] FUNDABRIL had written half a dozen proposals in this direction and was busy trying to get them funded.[106] The group also supported another area called "historical memory." During my fieldwork, the main activity for this area was to organize the FPL's historic archive, stored in moldy boxes at the FUNDABRIL office. This was the activity I volunteered to support.

Veterans' Organizing Efforts

Several members of the FUNDABRIL directorate held experience in international cooperation and fund-raising. To underpin project proposals, they had commissioned a mapping exercise "to get to know the socioeconomic situation of male and female FMLN war veterans with the goal of promoting development projects" (FUNDABRIL 2009, 3). This mapping focused on fourteen preselected repopulations and found that veterans suffered widespread illiteracy, chronic health problems, and generally precarious livelihoods (FUNDABRIL 2009). According to Henríquez, the people in these communities summarized their situation as follows: "Here we are abandoned and in bad straits." A logical predicament, he explained, since "veterans were reinserted within agriculture, which the government made unviable. How were they to ever get ahead?"[107]

Within FUNDABRIL different visions existed on what should be done to improve the veterans' standard of living. FUNDABRIL leaders who held NGO experience tended to favor the possibility of promoting development projects. These would not only bring concrete benefits to the veterans, but also allow FUNDABRIL to stop spending the remaining Assets Committee money, they argued, since project funding could help pay for office and staff. Henríquez and some others instead favored veterans' organizing. If fund-raising resulted in projects for veterans, these were considered a welcome addition, but this group's key interest was to provide the veterans with political leverage vis-à-vis the Funes administration. Like Alemán at SV-FMLN, Henríquez and several other FUNDABRIL members viewed the Funes administration as the opening of a new political playing field in which veterans might finally be able to make a mark.

Thus, Henríquez left fund-raising efforts mainly to the "NGO people" in FUNDABRIL and worked on behalf of the reemergence of a veterans' movement. In order to distinguish this group of veterans from the Alemán group directly aligned with the FMLN, Henríquez's group identified themselves as veterans of the "historic" FMLN. In previous years, Henríquez had focused mainly on maintaining informal relationships among key FPL veterans. Now, he and others were continually organizing meetings in and outside the FUNDABRIL office with their various contacts. As José indicated with an enigmatic smile: "They are engaged in conspiracy."[108]

These activities led to some tensions within the FUNDABRIL directorate. Some members were wary that involvement in veterans' politics might jeopardize the organization's reputation and make it vulnerable to being labeled as an FMLN dissident group. Some FUNDABRIL members active inside the FMLN considered that the organization should not be openly involved in veterans' organizing. Soon after, in July 2009, Henríquez was offered a job in the Funes administration. His task would be to help organize the government's social dialogue with veterans.

FUNDABRIL appointed "Dora" as the new director. She was also a former FPL member, and lost her job in the municipality of San Salvador two years earlier due to a conflict with a rival FMLN faction.[109] She had some NGO experience dating back to the war and was expected to work mainly on fund-raising. Hernán (Henríquez's closest aid), José, and some other FUNDABRIL members now worked to set up an autonomous structure for the veterans' organization. On August 9, 2009, José invited me to attend the first formal assembly of the Asociación Salvadoreña de Veteranos y Veteranas de Guerra del FMLN "Farabundo Martí" (ASALVEG),[110] which was held on the premises of a former FPL-affiliated union. A notary public swore in the freshly elected directorate.[111] As José confirmed to me, one reason to create the association was to see how its members could "make sure [they] were included among those receiving the packets that the government was about to hand out."[112]

FUNDABRIL-ASALVEG: Insights and Perspectives on Postinsurgency

Over the next months, while FUNDABRIL attempted to raise money for projects for veterans, ASALVEG tried to expand its membership and organizational structure in preparation for the upcoming round-table dialogue with the government. The FUNDABRIL office served as a gravitational point for former FPL militants, in particular those that were not positioned as well within the FMLN. This allowed me to (re)connect with former FPL cadres, who were now active in various professional environments. My presence at FUNDABRIL, normally one or two days a week, allowed me to get a feel for different issues at play among former FPL cadres. Both in informal conversations and during interviews, I discussed their personal experiences with postinsurgency and reflected on the postwar trajectory of the FMLN.

One of the first people I interviewed was Cándido, a father figure among the veterans. An FPL loyalist to the bone, he denied that the FPL had ceased to exist in 1995. When he took his revolutionary oath, it was for life, so he considered. A member of a family of wealthy landowners, Cándido sold his properties and invested his money in the revolution. His last remaining property, an extension of mountainous terrain he had bought in Chalatenango during the war as part of the FPL's clandestine logistical support for the front, was lost to him during the 1990s when, in Cándido's version, a former FPL comrade swindled him out of it. Cándido survived on a small monthly stipend from FUNDABRIL.[113]

Cándido had been one of the animators of the FMLN veterans' organizing process in 2003–4. In the ensuing conflict, FMLN leadership accused him and several of his comrades of being OIE agents working for the Right. The FMLN's attitude toward the veterans showed him that "the idea of solidarity [had] disappeared." He considered several of the current FMLN leaders to be "perverse." In his view, the FMLN had become "a commercial venture . . . which [was moving] ever further away . . . from the real interests of [its members'] struggle." Of poor health, Cándido expressed deep sadness and regret for a revolution that never was.[114]

I also interviewed Lilian, who headed the FUNDABRIL directorate. She held a long track record as an adviser to NGOs and FMLN municipal governments. With Funes's rise to power, she had obtained a senior position in a government agency. Throughout the 1990s and the first years of this century, she had been very active in FMLN party politics. She had since distanced herself as a result of overall disillusionment with how the party had evolved.

> I cannot stand to be in the party apparatus of the Frente (FMLN) right now. . . . It is pathetic, the situations that occur there. . . . I was in the municipal [directorate of the FMLN in a large city], but I didn't know how to play the game on that level: . . . the intrigue, the manipulation of the people, the private interests of certain groups. . . . It really is a waste of time! . . . There is no analytic capability. . . . It is just activism, . . . nothing else.[115]

Related to this lack of analytical capability, one of Lilian's frustrations with the FMLN was that "the only central issue was the elections." Another problem was what she saw as a distorted relationship between the public good and the party, as she witnessed when serving on an FMLN municipal directorate:

> It was the period in which the divisionism began and [a local FMLN leader] came [to the meetings] just to criticize people, one after another. So anyway, . . . no one questioned him. . . . People were more interested in supporting him because later, he could give them a job. . . . And then there was the issue of corruption. To give an example, they named someone to collect the money [party dues] . . . and when we asked him for a financial report, it was always delayed. Finally, . . . [the dues collector] said that since he was in charge of collecting the dues, that money was for him, and then along comes [the leader], who says that he was right because that was how he [the dues collector] survived financially because he didn't have a job. . . . Imagine! And everyone accepted this type of thing! . . . The message that [the leader] was giving [the employees] was that "you are all there representing [the party], so you all owe fidelity to the party, not to the municipal government." . . . So what does this generate? They weren't good employees! . . . What did he say to them? "Look, we haven't brought you here to be crabs in the ass. You all shouldn't be criticizing anything . . . , that is why we hired you."
>   Within the mayor's office, the people from the party didn't want to punch the time clock, because they were from the party, right? And what did they say to me? . . . "I gave so many years [to the struggle],

and now I have to come and punch a time clock?" This was the response. . . . Then there was [one] who was a wounded veteran. . . . He didn't want to work. . . . He simply showed up to read the newspaper because he was a party militant and he was a wounded veteran. Imagine! What a deformed situation! . . . He only showed up . . . to cause problems. But these were the people who supported the directorate. At election time they raised their hands for so and so. . . . This was party life . . . in the 1990s and it is still this way today. . . . And what makes me saddest is that people don't say anything! They don't even have the ability to give their opinion! They are completely shut down! Or [they are] afraid to give their opinion, right? Imagine, the type of party we have![116]

Nonetheless, Lilian was much milder in her opposition to the FMLN's top leadership than most other FUNDABRIL members. In fact, she still sometimes collaborated with FMLN leadership informally, through her personal connections.[117]

Like Lilian, Felipe, also a FUNDABRIL board member, was skeptical that the veterans' organizing efforts would produce positive change for the FMLN. His own political career was truncated in 2001 because he had refused to align either with the CRS or with the renovadores in the internal dispute. As a result, both groups denied backing for the renewal of his contract as a senior municipal employee, and he lost his job. According to Felipe, the FMLN's internal conflicts led to a situation in which especially former cadres unwilling to align themselves with any internal faction were at risk of being purged.

In order to destroy someone's political career here it is enough to begin saying that "so-and-so has gone over to the Right," and start to circulate that [rumor]. "So-and-so has gone over to the Right, he became a Rightist." No one wants to speak to him because everyone thinks he has gone over to the Right. This is how people are politically destroyed. You just have to say that someone works for the CIA, that they are paid by the Right, you see? This has happened to many of us.[118]

After losing his municipal appointment, Felipe found employment with an NGO rooted in the FPL. Something similar had occurred to Felipe's fellow FUNDABRIL regular José, who said that in 2004 a former FAL cadre had successfully conspired against him to take over his position at the state's electoral authority. He then was unemployed for two years before procuring freelance lecturing at different universities, picking up on the career he studied for at the UES before the war broke out. Although not a founding member of FUNDABRIL, José was one of the most committed activists of the group, both in FUNDABRIL and in ASALVEG. In José's vision, after the peace accords the FMLN "turned into an electoral party with . . . Leftist discourse but with Rightist practices." José believed that "the FMLN institutionalized itself in order to play by democratic rules . . . , but it also adapted to the corrupt nature of Salvadoran democracy." According to José, clientelism was key to the FMLN's postwar adaptation.[119]

> The party cannot exist in the abstract, nor can its militants live in the abstract; they have to eat. . . . What the party does is to take . . . a little bit of the pie that it can use to guarante [access to] . . . the pot of tamales [the state's resources], . . . which they [the leaders] have tucked between their legs. . . . Be careful not to get close to the pot because they won't let you. Only when they tell you: "Come, take it." Right? That is the typical route to [political] advancement. . . . "Ah," they say, "this guy isn't coming to challenge me; he is going to help me become stronger." And they begin to insert you within the party's leadership structures, at ever higher levels. Hence, it is no accident that you will see the same faces [in different jobs]. The same faces, damn it, everyone knows who they are, right? . . . Now I see another phenomenon: the son or daughter of the historic leader now also becomes part of the new elite, taking possession of the highest-paid positions, without having the ability . . . and without having really the [moral] authority to be able to say: "I struggled to get here!"[120]

José considered that the PCS had been more successful at electoral politics than other FMLN factions. In part, he thought that this resulted from the PCS cadres' electoral experience in the 1970s, when the other factions were instead preparing for armed struggle. Additionally, he attributed postwar success to the PCS's embracing of conspiracy methods. José considered that "the PC [PCS] [was] very skillful at conspiring, but then adapted to the framework of elections."[121]

I also interviewed Hernán, an ASALVEG adviser, a member of the FUNDABRIL directorate, and one of Henríquez's intimates. Hernán held a job in the San Salvador municipal government. Years before, he had obtained this position through his FPL contacts, after internal conflicts in another municipality had sidelined him there. Now, he anticipated losing his job very soon, because of the personnel changes implemented by the new ARENA administration. In his view, the PCS owed its postwar success to its ability to maintain esprit de corps. In 1995, while "the FPL naïvely dissolve themselves . . . , on the other hand, . . . the PCS . . . don't dissolve. They continue to function . . . around an economic project for their people, which is fundamentally . . . access to political positions and access as well to . . . business ventures. For example, [mentions a leading former PCS member] is stockholder in around ten different companies, . . . mainly companies that work with the municipal governments."

According to Hernán, the PCS "functions like a Masonic lodge. . . . This is why they are so cohesive." José and Hernán both believed that, because of how the PCS controlled the FMLN, the FPL veterans could only be successful by recurring to conspiracy methods. Hernán believed they needed to be secretive in order to avoid being targeted, not only politically, but even physically. He was convinced the PCS still "[had] their hit men."[122]

At the end of the evening, José and I sometimes continued conversation in the FUNDABRIL office after the rest had left.[123] José considered that the veterans, and in particular the FPL veterans, had so much accumulated experience that they would not be easily sidelined or manipulated, if only they managed to organize themselves in a cohesive movement. Once organized, José thought, the FPL veterans would be handled with care by politicians and officials, because they knew that "these guys [could] cause problems."[124] Paradoxically, the veterans' accumulated experience also made organizing difficult. Many old conflicts and resentments were present among the veterans. In the case of ASALVEG, the association did well among the FPL veterans in San Vicente and Usulután, but it was unable to get much support in other FPL strongholds like Chalatenango, where local leaders were strong and preferred to set up separate groups. ASALVEG, on the other hand, was wary of accepting certain FPL veterans' leaders who it thought might subvert the association's internal discipline.[125]

José explained that many veterans rejected hierarchical structures. According to José, the veterans themselves might often overrate the importance of their experience and contribution, as in, "I am right because I fought like hell."[126] Although these difficulties sometimes irritated José, he had no doubt that he would continue to be involved in this and other, future efforts with the veterans. "I can't stop doing this because it is part of my life," he told me over coffee one evening, with what I perceived as a peculiar mix of determination and resignation.[127]

MV-END

"Welcome to the club of the dissatisfied," Juan Carlos joked when I arrived at the ALGES office to participate in a meeting of the Movimiento de Veteranos del Ejército Nacional para la Democracia (MV-END), the last of the three veterans' groups I engaged with.[128] Because Juan Carlos was also a war-wounded activist at ALGES, this organization allowed MV-END to occasionally use their office. On warm afternoons, we would sit out on the back patio, under the almond tree and by the side of the cracked and empty pool that reminded us that this house had once been a fancy residence before being converted into office space.

Juan Carlos's joke was intended to mark the difference between their group and the other veterans' groups I was working with for my study. They considered that, even though SV-FMLN and ASALVEG to a certain extent opposed each other, both groups responded to what they called "leadership cliques" within the FMLN, and both embraced "mercantilist" methods: the organizing of a more or less exclusive group in order to hoard benefits obtained through political participation. On the other hand, their group, they said, had no ambition to access any personal benefits for veterans. Instead, they struggled to unmask what they saw as the capture of the FMLN by a "new bourgeoisie" that had negotiated its interests with the Salvadoran oligarchy. For the time being, they were aware that they could aspire to little more than being "a stone in the shoe" of the powerful; in the long run, however, they hoped for a grand recovery of revolutionary horizons.

Like ASALVEG, MV-END was composed, in part, of those who had been marginalized from the FMLN after the failure of the veterans' movement in 2003–4. Though they identified themselves as a political collective and regularly published a political bulletin, from what I saw of

MV-END activities, it functioned more like a salon. The MV-END weekly meetings provided a handful of participants with the opportunity to exchange information and gossip and to analyze recent political developments. Only occasionally would the meeting conclude with a concrete plan for further political action. Mostly MV-END members seemed content to simply participate in their ongoing conversations, while sipping afternoon coffee we extracted, with ALGES's generous permission, from the large percolator in the office's waiting room.

MV-END was not legally constituted, nor did it possess internal regulations. "Membership" was informal. In all, I met two dozen participants, most of them ERP veterans, but also a few former RN and PRTC militants. MV-END's most important action radius consisted of former ERP networks. Furthermore, several MV-END members expressed strong admiration for Cayetano Carpio and sustained political contacts with a group of former FPL members who identified themselves as Carpio loyalists.[129]

Together with Juan Carlos, Demetrio functioned as the group's informal chair. They had both belonged to what they called the ERP's Marxist wing, one of the ERP's internal currents during the 1970s. Unlike top leaders Villalobos and Ana Guadalupe Martínez, the militants from this wing did not come from Catholic youth-organizing circles, but from PCS youth networks. Toward the end of the war and in the first years of peace, Demetrio had withdrawn from the movement, mainly out of discontent with the way the ERP had evolved. In the late 1990s, he decided to resume political activism, motivated in part by the weight of the losses suffered during the revolution. In his words, "I have to continue in the name of all those whom I persuaded [to join the revolutionary struggle] and who are now dead."[130]

The ERP's postwar internal conflicts had caused great bewilderment and left deep wounds among the former ERP militants active in MV-END. For example, one participant, a former ERP physician, said he still could not get his head around what had gotten into Villalobos. Demetrio sought answers in the past: he recounted incidents that should have served as a premonition for the precipitate abandonment of the revolutionary project by Villalobos and his group. MV-END veterans considered that, though most ERP militants rejected the ERP's exit from the FMLN, Villalobos's prestige initially prevented stronger internal rebellion. They lamented that the leadership's choices had turned the ERP militants into the object of pity and mockery on the part of militants of other PMOs.[131]

"This Shitty Peace": MV-END Perspectives on Postinsurgency

If in the meetings with the other veterans' groups I functioned mostly an observer, only intervening in the meeting proceedings on rare occasions, with MV-END the dynamic was different. In fact, the meetings I attended consisted of little more than extended informal conversations. Meeting participants addressed me directly and encouraged me to ask questions and ventilate opinions. Thus, the MV-END meetings I participated in largely evolved as conversations on the nature of El Salvador's postinsurgent transition.

The first group meeting I attended took place three days before Funes's official inauguration. The MV-END veterans applauded my research timing, since they considered that "now [was] the real reinsertion."[132] They referred to how former top echelons of the guerrilla had been awarded government positions. This asseveration was also partially true for the rank and file: "After the [Funes] victory, 1316 [the FMLN national offices] filled up with ex-guerrilleros looking for work."[133]

Even though the MV-END veterans considered that the FMLN as a political party was something very different from the guerrilla movement, they also argued that the only way to understand the FMLN today was to scrutinize revolutionary history. They extensively enumerated differences between the PMOs, as well as between subgroups within these PMOs. Prewar and wartime events had determined the mind-sets of specific groups of militants, so they explained. Invariably, present-day FMLN developments would be analyzed by discussing the previous roles and positions of current protagonists. As befits Marxists, they cherished their historical perspective and tended to apply this in a somewhat deterministic manner.

The ERP and RN leaderships' postwar shift toward social-democratic political positions should be interpreted, MV-END argued, as the leaderships' return to their origin. During the 1970s, some Catholic youth sectors had radicalized and entered the emerging guerrilla forces. These sectors, they said, ended up dominating leadership in the ERP and the RN. Their vision was Christian, not Marxist. MV-END thought of the FPL as a special case, in which the internal conflict, culminating in the dramatic events of 1983, had caused deep trauma and confusion among the militancy that persisted until present days. They referred to this as a state of "ideological orphanhood," which, in their view, contributed to the former FPL militants being prone to accept negotiations and clientelist arrangements.[134]

By their own accounts MV-END participants were involved in an impressive range of left-wing initiatives. Their strategy was to extend and consolidate a network of contacts to be capitalized upon in the future, when more favorable scenarios for revolutionary action were bound to emerge. For this to occur, they first needed to unmask what they saw as the current FMLN leadership's betrayal of the revolutionary project. This is why some of the MV-END members had participated actively in the Funes campaign, whose triumph they saw as a necessary step. "So long as the population believes in this instrument [electoral politics], our role, within . . . the frame of conspiracy, is to accompany the population, to be always on the inside." Ultimately, MV-END aimed to expose the FMLN as a counterrevolutionary force in order to facilitate the emergence of a genuine revolutionary alternative.

MV-END veterans thought of postwar conflicts within the FMLN not in terms of ideological disputes, but of factional power struggles between groups that had already traded in revolutionary aspirations, if they ever had them, for personal interests. In contrast, the MV-END veterans claimed, "[When we entered the revolution,] we weren't even thinking about coming out alive, much less of snagging ourselves a job." MV-END considered that the FMLN leadership had been successful in keeping the veterans subjugated and divided mainly by use of a belligerent left-wing discourse and by manipulation of the veterans' feeling of belonging. The connectedness of the veterans to their former PMO identities—"their umbilical cord," in Demetrio's words—allowed the leadership to play on preexisting loyalties and divisions, and to use the veterans as "cattle with which to win [a favorable] correlation [of power]" in the political playing field.[135] Juan Carlos seconded this assessment: "Now-a-days being a Leftist is . . . only about seeing how many [supporters] I have, how many you have; beyond that, there is nothing. . . . What they want is a herd of people who will show up! Yes! . . . He who has more head of cattle is the best leader and the most Leftist in this country!"[136]

Similar to the activists at FUNDABRIL, MV-END considered that the PCS had been more astute at postwar electoral politics than the other PMOs. They joked that PCS's ideological problem was that it confused being a communist with being a member of the Communist Party. Historically and presently, the PCS was far from what MV-END considered to be consistent Marxist positions and practices. Borrowing Trotsky's indictment of Stalin, they believed that the PCS had denaturalized popular participation in the party, established a bureaucracy with totalitarian tendencies, and nurtured manipulative electoral practices.[137]

"This shitty peace: what has it been good for?" Juan Carlos dropped as a question in one of the meetings. In MV-END's opinion, peace had been more of an obstacle than a gain for the cause of the revolution, and "for Marxist sectors, [the revolution] is still an outstanding debt."[138] MV-END saw renewed armed struggle as a likely necessity in the future. However, as far as I was able to determine, they were not actively preparing for it. MV-END participants saw their present role as "to accumulate [support] and to conspire for the construction of popular power," helping the political initiatives they were involved in fail, succeed, or radicalize.[139]

The declared loyalty to the revolution did not stop several participants in the MV-END meetings from also pursuing and obtaining government jobs, facilitated by the fact that, under Funes, several senior ERP cadres had obtained government positions. Demetrio rejected the notion that this was selling out. Instead he framed it as an opportunity to broaden conspiracy networks.

> We are also interested in inserting ourselves within government structures [another participant interrupts: "Yes, that's it!"]. We are trying to have influence, to place the greatest number of people possible [within government], and we are making progress. I am now a bureaucrat [he laughs]. . . . This is how it is, . . . you slowly go about inserting oneself . . . and there one has to do organizing work because there are other conspirators, on both sides. . . . So the question is who wins hegemony and control? So this is a new challenge that we face as veterans.[140]

After the meeting, Demetrio smilingly confided to me that his new job had also been a highly welcome relief, given his financial situation.

"We Better Be Prepared"

"Evaristo" was one of the political contacts that MV-END worked with or, perhaps more precisely, coconspired with. Evaristo was a former FPL combatant from Chalatenango involved in several political initiatives in which MV-END veterans also participated, including that of organizing disgruntled FMLN veterans. Although Demetrio told me that he did not trust Evaristo entirely, he said they concurred in terms of revolutionary disposition. FUNDABRIL members had also mentioned Evaristo several times to me. The FPL veterans there considered him difficult to work with. Some had told me he was a "radical" or "*un macho sin dueño*."[141] Other veterans suspected him of being an infiltrator financed by the Right.[142]

My first meeting with Evaristo doubled as a cheerful reencounter. It turned out we knew each other from back when I lived in Chalatenango, when he identified himself by a different name. We had common friends and had met and conversed several times back then. Because of his wartime achievements, Evaristo was something of a legend among the FPL's rank and file in Chalatenango. Surpassing many of his elders in skill and valor, he had been selected for the FPL's Special Forces while only a pre-adolescent child. Evaristo's body was riddled with scars, souvenirs of countless combats. After the accords, Evaristo entered the PNC. Simultaneously, he had gone back to school and studied law. He now supplemented his income by offering legal services, in his words, as a way of helping comrades with any legal troubles they encountered.

Like the MV-END veterans, Evaristo participated in several different political arenas, and in a range of different capacities. He said that the fact that "the FMLN leadership had betrayed the revolution" was not an impediment for him to work with the party, at different times, in order to obtain influence for the veterans, so he explained in our conversations.[143] In Evaristo's view, the prominent postwar role of the comandantes trumped the political growth of the revolutionary middle cadres and rank and file.

> Some party functionaries have been so cruel as to say: . . . "The only thing you [ex-combatants] know how to do is to fire bullets!" . . . If you say this you are killing him . . . ideologically. . . . [A combatant] is not just someone who fires bullets. This was a particular form of struggle, valuable at the time. . . . In fact, without this form of struggle we would not be in this new moment [today]. . . . When you treat a combatant, who has analytic capability, this way, he says [to himself]: "These bastards used me . . . , and now I am no one in this revolutionary process."[144]

Evaristo, on the contrary, looked at the former combatants as the country's true revolutionary vanguard. While power and privilege had corrupted many comandantes, Evaristo considered that most former combatants still possessed revolutionary clarity, expressed in their loyalty to the doctrines they were educated with. Evaristo claimed to be working on the formation of new revolutionary leadership, attained by the return of ideological training and debate among the veterans in combination with increased access to party positions and public office for the previously marginalized, "ideologically pure" veterans. Evaristo and his supporters tried to achieve this by competing locally with the official party candidates, knowing that many of the local party affiliates were ex-combatants sympathetic to his cause.[145] From what I was able to gather, the Chalatenango FMLN leadership despised Evaristo, but his figure had significant appeal among the former FPL rank and file, who saw him as one of their own.

It seemed to me that Evaristo's activism was as much social as political. His friends, the people he was close to, the people he felt at home with, were his former FPL comrades, the family that had been formed during the war, at the front in Chalatenango. At the end of my fieldwork period, Evaristo invited me to join him on an outing to the Sumpul River before we said our goodbyes. As I had been working elsewhere in Chalatenango the previous day, we met at the river around noon. Evaristo had bought fried chicken in Chalatenango City and had picked up close to a dozen friends and relatives on the way to the river, who had brought baskets with tortillas and hard-boiled eggs. After we all ate together, the children went swimming, and I sat down with Evaristo and several other veterans in a shady spot by the river.

One of Evaristo's friends was visiting from Sweden, where he had lived in exile since he had deserted from the FPL, after one of the comandantes had threatened to kill him. Another one had been working for many years as a personal bodyguard for a top FPL leader, but had become fed up, and was now trying to set up a small business, apparently with little success. The main topic that afternoon was which FPL leaders had screwed them over and which ones had stood up for them. Then the conversation turned to radical politics. If the leadership continued to squander the gains of the armed struggle, Evaristo suggested, it was only a matter of time before war would return. "We better be prepared," he said, with what seemed to me a mix of bitterness and temerity. His friends smiled and said nothing.[146]

EPILOGUE: THE FMLN VETERANS OBTAIN A BENEFIT PROGRAM

On August 16, 2010, Alex Segovia, one of the president's closest personal advisers and head of the Secretaría Técnica de la Presidencia (STP),[147] inaugurated a round table with different FMLN veterans' groups.[148] The fourteen participating veterans' associations soon clustered in two blocks (CONAVERS and Concertación Nacional).[149] Former FPL middle cadres headed both clusters, and both also included veterans' groups from the other PMOs.[150] The STP granted all representatives a small budget to help cover part of the organizing and transportation costs.[151] According to a government document, the development of the round-table process then proceeded as follows.

> Both entities [CONAVERS and Concertación Nacional] agreed with the [STP] proposal to orient the round-table dialogue toward the creation of an integrated program for men and women veterans in order to attend to the sector's basic needs and to work for their dignified insertion within national life. It is within this context that an agreement was reached to carry out a nationwide registration process of [FMLN] veterans. This way they [government officials] could identify their [the veterans'] current conditions and needs as input for the definition of an integral program. (STP 2012, 4)

Segovia's team coordinated seventy-eight registration "events" across the country, in which STP personnel registered the veterans' personal data and filled out a brief socioeconomic questionnaire for each veteran.[152] The STP registered 25,401 veterans over a three-month period (February–May 2011). The collected socioeconomic data indicated that registered veterans mostly subsisted by means of agricultural activities (55.6 percent) and suffered widespread poverty: "As a group they have an overall poverty rate of 86.9%, significantly above the national average of 36.5%" (STP 2012, 15).[153]

Interestingly, 70 percent of those registered had not participated in the UN demobilization process (STP 2012, 23). Throughout the process, the different veterans' groups privately accused each other of trying to include people who were not truly veterans. At the round table, the veterans agreed to include a screening mechanism by which all those who registered had to "identify the historic organization in which they were active, identify the type of unit or structure to which they belonged, indicate their pseudonym and the name or pseudonym of their two last leaders, and provide the name or pseudonym of three living veterans who knew them [during the war]" (5). These provisions might still allow the veterans' groups to include some nonveterans, but only with coaching and not indiscriminately.[154]

The three veterans' organizations that I followed during my fieldwork period responded to the round-table initiative in different ways. While ASALVEG was at the forefront, MV-END did not participate directly, but made sure they had a foot in the door. On the other hand, Alemán doubted whether SV-FMLN should participate. He rejected the idea of joining the round table as yet another veterans' association, since he wanted to emphasize the different nature of his group, not to be understood as a separate association but as the party's "official" veterans. Initially, Alemán's orientation was for SV-FMLN members to not participate in the registration. At the last minute, apparently to avoid being left out of the benefit program, Alemán did urge the veterans in his group to register, and organized buses to bring them to San Salvador.[155] However, SV-FMLN continued to abstain from institutional participation in the round-table process.

The round-table initiative triggered the reorganization and mobilization of different FMLN veterans' networks. Many new groups were launched, and groups existing only informally declared themselves to be an association in order to guarantee representation, and sometimes, but not always, they also backed this up with a formal organizational structure and statutes.[156] The FMLN veterans' movement in 2011 could be divided in four segments, which, apart from Concertación and CONAVERS, included SV-FMLN and MV-END.[157] As evident in table 7.1, a significant number of organizations were set up in the course of the round-table process itself, as a way for networks of veterans to obtain a formal status.

In January 2012, while celebrating the twentieth anniversary of the peace accords, President Funes formally launched the new program.[158] He told the crowd that the new program served to mend "the great historic shortcoming of the Salvadoran government . . . that of not having recognized the rights of the veterans," and that he had reserved $23 million for

Table 7.1. FMLN veterans' movement overview (June 2011 situation)

SV-FMLN (2003)

Sector de Veteranos del FMLN

Strategy: gain political influence by participation inside the FMLN party apparatus. Not a round-table member.

Concertación Nacional (2010)

ASALVEG (2009)
Asociación Salvadoreña de Veteranos y Veteranas de Guerra "Farabundo Martí"

Strategy: gain political influence through the STP round-table platform.

ASALDIG (1992)
Asociación Salvadoreña de Lisiados y Discapacitados de Guerra

AVDIES (2006)
Asociación de Veteranos para el Desarrollo Integral

COMANDANTE GONZALO (2010)
Asociación Comandante Gonzalo

AVERSAL (?)
Asociación de Veteranos Revolucionarios Salvadoreños

AVERD (2008)
Asociación de Veteranos Roque Dalton

FUNDELIDDI (2000)
Fundación de Lisiados y Discapacitados para el Desarrollo Integral

CONAVERS (2010)
AVEELSALCOMAR (2010)
Asociación de Veteranos de Guerra Comandante Marcial

Strategy: gain political influence through the STP round-table platform.

AVRAZ (2005)
Asociación de Veteranos Rafael Arce Zablah

ASVERS (2010)
Asociación de Veteranos Revolucionarios Salvadoreños

AVERCH (2010)
Asociación de Veteranos Revolucionarios de Chalatenango

ADG EL SALVADOR (2005)
Asociación de Discapacitados de Guerra de El Salvador

AVEGUEFOFA (2010)
Asociación de Veteranos de Guerra Frente Occidental Feliciano Ama

ASOVET (2010)
Asociación de Veteranos y Veteranas del FMLN histórico 12 de Abril

MV-END (2005)
Movimiento de Veteranos del Ejército Nacional para la Democracia

Unaligned, while trying to build hidden network in different groups. Not a round-table member.

the first three years of the program (2012–14), with measures including health-care benefits and pensions.[159] On May 26, 2012, many of those who had been present at the launch of the veterans' program once again mobilized for a rally in support of Funes on the third anniversary of his government. The massive event took place in the largest convention center of the country, with an estimated attendance of sixty thousand people. The veterans of CONAVERS and Concertación figured prominently among the organizers of the event.[160] Funes called on the crowd to build a "national alliance to deepen the changes" and to "overcome the systematic, iron opposition of these groups which lost their privileges and want to recover them in 2014 [the year of the next presidential elections]."[161] During the event, the veterans present petitioned Funes to promote a new law that would benefit the veterans and their families permanently.[162] With the benefit program in place, the next big step for the veterans' associations was the passage of legislation that would guarantee future benefits and protection.[163]

The round-table efforts had demonstrated that the veterans were a force to be reckoned with. One ASALVEG leader told me that their main political wager involved using the veterans' movement as a stepping-stone in the construction of a so-called third path, a social-democratic force that might occupy the void in El Salvador's political middle. Some of the people around Funes attempted to build such a third-path movement to extend their political influence beyond the 2009–14 presidency. ASALVEG was interested in this emerging scenario, but wary of being forced to take a public stand against the FMLN. ASALVEG, I was told, was more interested in the possibility of the FMLN negotiating with sectors like themselves in order to be able to win the 2014 elections. Several prominent ASALVEG members opposed moving too far from the FMLN. The association was trying to build alliances, looking for leverage to get the FMLN to be interested in making concessions to the veterans.[164] "I can tell you that the veterans are now in effervescence," an ASALVEG activist emailed me in an August 2012 update of the movement's political situation.[165]

THE MAKING OF THE FMLN VETERANS' MOVEMENT

FMLN veterans emerged as a political category in the first years of this century and have since played an important role in and around the FMLN.

Their ascendency constitutes a powerful reminder of the wartime roots of present-day political relations in El Salvador. At the heart of veterans' politics lies the claim that the FMLN accumulated substantial interpersonal debts in the process of the revolutionary war, debts that require repayment. Different veterans' organizations struggle over the same central issue: the distribution of the resources the FMLN has been able to obtain as a result of its performance as a political party. My comparative fieldwork with three veterans' groups allowed me to get a better understanding of the movement's complex internal politics. At their core, the groups responded to remnants of PMO networks seeking to gain a foothold in the political field, using veterans' networks as a springboard.

In these efforts, the veterans made use of (and were sometimes burdened by) the revolution's accumulated political history. They explained their ideological stances in veterans' organizing with frequent references to historical PMO relations and the FMLN's postwar internal conflicts. The affiliations, conflicts, and ruptures that occurred during the first wave of veterans' organizing in 2003–4 also played an important role in shaping the organizing efforts in what could be seen as a "second wave," set in motion with the Funes presidency.

Of the groups I studied, SV-FMLN provided the most insights into the internal dynamics of the FMLN as a political party. Their organizing revolved around "veteranship" as an element of distinction within party militancy, which allowed the veterans, and their leadership, to claim status within the party and access to resources related to party politics, such as government jobs. SV-FMLN tried to augment the weight of the veterans' sector within the FMLN by emphasizing their historical contribution, by framing themselves as a "moral reserve," and by participating in a range of party activities. Reasoning that without the contribution of those who fought the war, the FMLN leaders would have never gotten as far as they had, the veterans repeatedly explained that party leadership demonstrated too little sympathy for their plight and too little appreciation for their political efforts, which sometimes led to outbursts of frustration.

FUNDABRIL, on the other hand, functioned as a sort of reservoir of former FPL relations. As the Funes presidency reshuffled the context for veteran organizing, the connections that converged at FUNDABRIL became important to help build a new FMLN veterans' association. The emergence of ASALVEG did not so much respond to the rise of a new political actor, but rather constituted a reconversion of historical FPL networks into an organizational form befitting the circumstances of the Funes presidency. It was not so much the political pressure of groups like ASALVEG that prompted the government to establish a benefit program, but rather the promise of such a program that prompted veterans' groups to (re)organize. Beyond the pursuit of sectorial benefits, the round-table efforts allowed FMLN veterans to gain some foothold within El Salvador's political arena, building and negotiating political alliances.

MV-END embraced the second meaning of veteran: that of "experienced" rather than that of "former." They qualified themselves as "veterans who are not yet ideologically reinserted."[166] Being a revolutionary was a lifelong commitment, and to renounce revolutionary ideals a form of treason, they believed. The group attempted to reenact the conspiracy methods of the 1970s, expanding clandestine networks inside different movements and institutions, in order to accumulate influence that might enable them to rekindle the revolutionary fire should the political and economic crisis deepen, as they were convinced it would. At the same time, the concrete results of MV-END's work remained unclear to me, which led me to suspect that their capacities were distant from their ambitions.

Clientelist practices permeated the FMLN veterans' movement. SV-FMLN was relatively successful at getting FMLN officials to earmark postings for veterans in government institutions. They also attempted to influence the territorial distribution of state benefits, for example through the Ministry of Agriculture, though apparently with limited success. Members from ASALVEG and MV-END also profited from access to government jobs, through new government officials with roots in PMO networks. ASALVEG's main pursuit was to get its people into the round-table process, which they hoped would translate into benefits for affiliates. ASALVEG leadership sought a mediating role between veteran constituencies, the government, and other political actors. MV-END justified their access to government jobs as the expansion of conspiracy networks. From the perspective of all three groups, the ability to obtain concrete benefits constituted proof of political leverage. Hence, veterans commonly criticized the clientelism of other groups, but rarely reflected on their own clientelist practices, whose successes they presented as a source of legitimacy. Veterans hoped and expected that activism would generate professional opportunities, more modest for the rank and file, more sizable for the leadership.

The political imaginaries of the veterans' movement were heavily imbued with conspiracy thinking. More than a phantom of the past, conspiracy practices were seen as necessary to protect group interests from political rivals and enemies. For some FPL veterans, it was the FPL's initial withdrawal from conspiracy practices that had made them lose influence vis-à-vis the PCS in postwar FMLN affairs. The lesson they had extracted was that their postwar naïveté had contributed to the loss of political ground in comparison to those who they thought had continued to conspire in an electoral context. For SV-FMLN, infiltrators and potential traitors constituted the FMLN's internal enemy. Their task, as they saw it, was to protect the party from such enemies.

Under Funes, new political territories opened up for the FMLN veterans, providing opportunities to cash in on the veterans' historical contribution. SV-FMLN pressured FMLN leaders-turned-government-officials to provide opportunities for them. Simultaneously, some non-FMLN government officials were stimulating the creation of the veterans' territorial structures to help implement government programs.[167] Allegedly, the underlying objective here was to build constituencies that were not (fully) controlled by the FMLN. Although this claim is unverifiable, I suspected the veterans were right, since such a move helped reduce Funes's dependency on the FMLN at the time. Its practical use was demonstrated in May 2012, when Funes filled the National Convention Center without the FMLN summoning its militants to attend.

More even than the other two case studies, my fieldwork with the FMLN veterans' movement provided deep immersion into the political practices of Salvadoran postinsurgency. It was through ethnographic observation that I became aware of the extent to which the FMLN veterans have developed their own distinct "style" of politics, a style that combines discourses and practices acquired during the era of armed struggle with those of political patronage.

CHAPTER 8

_____

Salvadoran Politics and the Enduring Legacies of Insurgency

> *It is well known that the most radical revolutionary will become a conservative on the day after the revolution.*
>
> —Hannah Arendt, *Crisis of the Republic*

Justo, the old friend I had worked with on the recovery of the FPL archives (see chap. 1), had some good news. After years of renting a ramshackle office space, FUNDABRIL had finally acquired a permanent domicile in San Salvador. The foundation had recently moved into the property where Radio Farabundo Martí (RFM) functioned during the first postwar years, before the internal troubles led to the project's collapse, as described in chapter 4. After the RFM debacle, two things of value remained: the premises and the frequency rights, the latter being the more valuable of the two. A select group of FPL cadres previously involved in the RFM project owned the shares of these assets. Several RFM shareholders were also FUNDABRIL members, and FUNDABRIL's board had persuaded part of this group to remit their shares. Thus, FUNDABRIL was able to set up an office in the RFM's abandoned radio studios and offices.

Justo gave me a tour through the labyrinthine building I had last visited some twenty years earlier, when RFM was still functioning. It had been constructed as a large middle-class residence after World War II and since had been subjected to numerous additions and modifications. An exposition space, which featured a recently inaugurated exhibit on the history of Radio Farabundo Martí, was set up in what long ago had been the patio. The archive Justo and I had helped rescue from mold, moths, and mice now rested in orderly stands, filling a good-size room with walls covered in noise-absorbing egg cartons, the reminder of its previous use. Justo explained that several shareholders had ceded their stocks to FUNDABRIL, but not all. He was particularly upset that the largest shareholder, "Edgardo Cornejo," a former comandante and the radio network's last director, had refused to surrender his part. FUNDABRIL had had to buy him out by trading claims on the premises in for those on the—more profitable—frequency rights. For Justo, people like Edgardo Cornejo symbolized the revolution's decline. However, he was content with FUNDABRIL's having managed to secure the building. As long as there were comrades who continued to invest in collective projects like FUNDABRIL, the cause was not completely lost.

Since our work on the archives, Justo had continued to be involved in a range of projects around the recovery of the revolutionary movement's "historical memory." During the last years of the Funes presidency, he had also started working directly with the party again, putting an end to almost a decade of relative distance. After Sánchez Cerén's successful bid in 2014, Justo continued to operate inside as well as outside the FMLN, though he said he had not recovered his appetite for party politics. In a sense, he remained as disillusioned as before, but contrary to before, he now viewed the party as an opportunity to strengthen the work he was really passionate about: to dive deep into the history of the revolution and tell the stories of the people whose lives were touched by it.[1]

For Justo, the revolution had left many marvelous anecdotes of creativity, valor, and sacrifice, passages often not remembered or even documented. But most of all, his effort was about the many people who had not survived the revolutionary war. "People much better than I in human quality, . . . who did extraordinary things, beautiful things, . . . and who today are not here." According to Justo, the reason that the revolution went astray was that the best of its children died during the war. If only some of these extraordinary leaders were still alive, "things would be different, . . . the party would be different."

Even now, when Justo had partially reconciled himself with the FMLN, he could not help but contrast the current reality of the party with that of the revolution, in which "so many people shone so bright." For

Justo, the key to the revolutionary movement had not been its military dexterity or its organizational capacity. What made the revolution grow and prosper was the moral force of its participants, Justo said. Peasants like Apolinario Serrano, who in only a few years developed from an illiterate day-laborer into a torchbearer for the FPL. Or people like "Jesús Rojas" or Benjamín Valiente, sons of wealthy families, who nonetheless chose the side of the poor; or Comandante "Dimas Rodriguez," always preoccupied with the well-being of his combatants. For Justo, the revolution resembled the biblical story of David against Goliath. The movement was only made possible thanks to countless hands and hearts committed to the revolution, belonging to men and women willing to go through the fire for their comrades and for their people. To lose his revolutionary brothers and sisters was terrible enough; to forget them, inexcusable.

In spite of his undiluted admiration for the revolution and its heroes, Justo was not propagandist. He rallied for a type of memory work mindful of the multiplicity of experiences of all five revolutionary organizations. He contrasted that with the way a large part of the FMLN engaged in "historical memory," which revolved mainly around elevating the stature of Schafik Handal as the key leader of the Salvadoran revolution. Since his death in 2006, numerous murals have been painted and books published in his honor. A Schafik Handal museum was opened in San Salvador, and his tomb was transformed into the country's largest mausoleum (López Bernal 2015; Sprenkels 2011).

As Erik Ching (2016) points out, the stories of the past pushed by the FMLN comandantes have been quite different from those favored by the rank-and-file combatants. What Ching calls "the narrative battle" on the Salvadoran war and its legacy has unfolded not only between the antagonistic blocks of ARENA and FMLN supporters, but also inside the FMLN. While many of the comandantes published self-congratulatory memoirs and the FMLN's officially sanctioned commemoration practices increasingly steered towards Schafik Handal, other memory activists operating inside and around the FMLN were principally concerned with emphasizing rank-and-file contributions to the revolutionary war, and included critique on the role of the party leadership during and after the war (Velásquez Estrada 2015).

Filling the center of a traffic circle on a main traffic artery, one of the most impressive monuments erected in Handal's honor was adorned by a phrase the leader himself had employed to explain his vision on historical memory. "If we have to look at the past, let this only be to extract from it more firmness, reaffirmation of our revolutionary character." Instead of the selective use of the past that Handal proposed, and that his followers embraced, Justo favored an inclusive approach, which implied telling all the stories of the revolution, even those that might compromise the revolutionary movement's reputation. He was convinced that the truth was the only durable route towards reclaiming the dignity of all the participants in the movement. And however painful some of the stories that needed to be told were—like, for example, those on the internal purges—this was part of the experience of the revolution, and hence also of the lessons it should leave for future generations.

So lately Justo's life was dedicated to searching for the forgotten stories of the movement and sharing these with whoever wanted to listen, particularly his former comrades. He sometimes took out his guitar to play the songs of his best friend, a musician who had died in the ranks of the FPL, in order to keep them alive for posterity. He was passionate about documenting the life of some fallen comandante, but more so even about the life stories of forgotten peasants of some isolated hamlet that had joined the revolution. He talked about "unremembered comrades." He celebrated their stories of heroism, he laughed about their incredible adventures, and he lamented their painful mistakes or betrayals.

In a sense, Justo mined for the stories of the revolutionary war much like I have been mining for the stories of the postinsurgency throughout this book. Rather than seeking to exalt the leadership, or to reproduce the "official" stories they forward, we shared a commitment to try and democratize the historiography of the revolutionary movement, so as to include as many voices and perspectives as possible. Like me, Justo applied a prosopographical approach to his work, focusing on a variety of participants in the movement and conceiving of history writing always as a work in progress, ever in need of including more voices, particularly of those who actually took part, in order to improve our understanding of the historical process under scrutiny.

Though he saw the work I was doing as useful, Justo told me he would not have the stomach for it. For him, there was too much sadness in the realities of postinsurgency, too little inspiration. He was content that he could now count on the party's support for his historical memory work, but he remained highly skeptical about the FMLN's performance and about the stature of its leadership. In Justo's eyes, the FMLN was still a long way from overcoming the "big crash" it had suffered at war's end. Moral decline remained the lens through which Justo perceived party life.

THE POLITICS OF POSTINSURGENT ACCOMMODATIONS

Stories like Justo's and many others offered throughout this book demonstrate how the experience of insurgency, and in particular, its accumulated interpersonal relations, still echo among El Salvador's former insurgents, two decades after the end of the war. In general terms, postinsurgent accommodations did not lead to the disbandment of the relations that the insurgents had built up over the years, but rather to contentious changes in how these were structured and stratified. In spite of a significant erosion of the revolutionary movement's internal solidarity, the political imaginaries that had accompanied insurgency persisted, albeit dented and contested. Indeed, the experiences of postinsurgency complemented and complicated the imaginaries inherited from the revolution with increasingly pronounced internal inequality and disillusionment. The entanglements of former insurgents' personal life trajectories with the postwar itineraries of the political-military organizations imprinted postinsurgent politics with a particular set of characteristics.

The Growing Differentiation of the Movement

During the war, the PMOs formed an internal environment in which underlying tensions between individuals and subgroups, while certainly not absent, were generally subsumed in and subordinate to the shared experience of militancy and dedication to the cause. Though leadership was generally better off than rank and file, with few exceptions, all PMO militants, including leadership, lived in austerity.[2] All made considerable personal sacrifices. In spite of internal strains, most participants perceived the PMO sphere as one of transcendent internal solidarity. The revolutionary movement granted participants status and prestige, as they were part of a vanguard organization, with the peasant constituency seen as a sort of "chosen people." In a more mundane sense, for the peasant families that participated in the insurgency, victory would translate into access to land and other material benefits, so they were promised. Revolutionary triumph, it was said, would mean justice for all. Afterward, everyone would be equal.

With the peace accords, former insurgents sought to position themselves as favorably as possible in the emerging context. They did so collectively, but also as subgroups and individuals. This led to the insurgent participants gaining assets that facilitated the movement's reconversion to postwar politics, such as land and reintegration programs for constituents and leadership. However, these benefits also generated numerous tensions within the movement, as many considered they were not doled out evenhandedly. In fact, various subgroups and individuals were unevenly equipped to take advantage of the opportunities of peace. In part, this was related to the diversity of prewar backgrounds, which included a range from university-educated urbanites to illiterate peasants. In part, this was also related to the established wartime hierarchies, which had allowed those who performed well to gain responsibilities, status, and prestige.

The land transfer program (PTT) installed after the peace accords was of crucial importance for the insurgents' rural reconversion, not only in material terms, but also in symbolic terms. Though not sufficient to fulfill the aspirations of most peasant insurgents, the PTT allowed the PMOs to claim partial fulfillment of a historical promise to their constituents. As discussed in chapters 4 and 5, the different PMOs were able to each service their historical peasant constituencies through the PTT. Other peace stipulations also helped translate insurgent participation into concrete benefits, such as the FMLN quota for the new police force, which allowed a segment of ex-combatants to obtain permanent employment, or the different reinsertion packages and housing programs.

Nonetheless, the fact that these benefits did not live up to expectations generated earlier on put significant stress on the movement. Leadership attempted to explain the limitations by pointing out that the circumstances of negotiated peace were not those of a revolutionary triumph, and that further benefits would be contingent on the success of the movement in the postwar period. As Villalobos pointed out in 1993, the gains of the peace accords, and specifically of the land transfers, would have to serve as a foundation for the future development of the movement, enabling the movement to forward further claims.[3] The FMLN-affiliated NGOs attempted to provide additional benefits for historical insurgent constituencies, while at the same time trying to push them toward continued community activism geared both at obtaining further reconstruction benefits and at establishing a left-wing grassroots movement that could operate in partnership with the FMLN as a political party (Silber 2011).

At the same time, however, many movement participants perceived that the benefits of the struggle had become subject to uneven distribution in the postwar period. On the one hand, they saw a large part of the leadership rapidly taking on (or resuming) an urban middle-class lifestyle, financed with income obtained through public office or senior positions in NGOs and the like. With programs like Plan 600, described in chapter 4, leadership furthermore claimed additional reinsertion benefits for itself. Though some privileges for leadership had always existed, large differences in income were new to the movement. On the other hand, grassroots participants also witnessed significant local differences in access to benefits and projects. Former cadres frequently profited the most on the local level, and the overarching party leadership either facilitated such privilege or did little to avoid it. The grassroots experience of postinsurgency entailed the rise of what could be seen as a sort of "double inequality": a growing socioeconomic breach between national leadership and the grassroots base of the movement, as well as a similar process of differentiation taking place at the local level.

Power and Internal Solidarity

Former revolutionary participants complained about internal differentiation so frequently that this critique should be seen as one of the defining features of postinsurgency. They interpreted inequality mainly as correlated with the leadership privileges. Think of the FMLN veterans in the group loyal to the party continually joking about asking the guys in the ties (los corbatudos) for money (chap. 7). Or recall the outburst of former FPL cadre Rogelio when denied financial compensation for his party work by an FMLN deputy receiving a generous salary for her services (chap. 6). Imagine the frustration and humiliation felt when former guerrilla fighters found themselves repeatedly asking former comrades for a job or other favors, as described in chapters 6 and 7.

Though certainly some participants argued that their revolutionary aspirations remained intact, I consider that, by and large, the dynamics of postwar accommodation contributed to the implosion of the PMOs' moral universe. The ideological tenets of revolutionary struggle proved ill equipped to deal with the emerging circumstances of neoliberal peace (van der Borgh 2010). To argue that ideological baggage should be put overboard, as some leaders did, was difficult to accept for many participants, given that in previous years so many had sacrificed their lives in explicit dedication to these ideals. Indeed, part of the FMLN leadership successfully proceeded to marginalize the most enthusiastic reformers by accusing them of opportunism. This move made sense to many rank-and-file insurgents since most of these reformist leaders had publically reneged on earlier pledges. Many participants were furthermore bewildered by the intensity of the postwar power struggles taking place among the leadership, and interpreted these as further indication of moral decay. Some chose sides in these struggles. A few did so with an ideological zeal reminiscent of the PMO experience. However, the dominant sentiment I encountered among former insurgents was that of disillusionment.

Though this study's protagonists often complained that solidarity disappeared from their movement, I think it is more accurate to say postinsurgent solidarity differed with respect to previous conceptions. As becomes clear in chapter 6 and especially chapter 7, former insurgents in fact still laid extensive claims on the internal solidarity of the movement. However, if previously revolutionary solidarity implied an egalitarian understanding of internal reciprocity in the service of a higher purpose, later on the understanding of solidarity shifted toward a perception of historical debt. This led to many former insurgents approaching FMLN politicians to demand help with practical problems concerning everyday survival. This type of solidarity principally entailed mobilizing (public) resources made available through the FMLN's electoral success and directing them toward former participants in the armed struggle.

Solidarity acquired a different political rationale and thereby largely lost its revolutionary luster. Its reciprocity had become embedded in manifest inequality, and now implied the struggle over the distribution of benefits obtained through stratified political participation among leadership, militants, and constituents. Veterans claimed that, during the insurgent past, they contributed significantly to the creation of the power now wielded by the FMLN. They also contended that they could still contribute much through their organizing capacity and political experience. As one ASALVEG organizer reported, this included their capacity to kick up a racket.[4]

Postinsurgent Clientelism

With the exception of an important article by anthropologist Ainhoa Montoya (2015) on the political dynamics in a small city after the Funes election, clientelism has received remarkably little attention in the study of modern Salvadoran politics.[5] Most scholars focused first on revolution and civil war, and later on democratic transition. In the only 1980s article I was able to find on clientelism in El Salvador, David Mason (1986) argues that the weakening of the oligarchy and the civil war both contributed to a breakdown of clientelist relationships, but he does not examine how the war itself might also be reconfiguring such relationships, for example through the rise of ARENA as a political and electoral force. Subsequently, only a handful of studies even mention the existence of clientelism in postwar Salvadoran politics, and when they do, they summarily refer to the phenomenon as either an undesirable practice that needs be eliminated[6] or an obstacle to local development.[7]

The scarce attention to clientelism in postwar El Salvador contrasts with the renewed scholarly attention for this phenomenon elsewhere. As it has become increasingly clear that the successive waves of decolonization, developmentalism, revolutions, and what Huntington (1991) called "third wave" democratizations were all unsuccessful in rooting out patron-client networks, the topic has started to regain scholarly prominence (Chabal and Daloz 1999; Helmke and Levitsky 2004; van de Walle 2001; Vu 2010). The United Nations Development Programme's influential report on democracy in Latin America acknowledges the multilevel impact of "clientelism—networks . . . [that] generate privileges and exclusions, and usually implicate discretionary use of public resources—" on the region's governments (UNDP 2004, 183–84). Mushtaq Khan goes so far as to assert that "political contestation in developing countries is organized through the mobilization of patron-client factions, rather than through mobilization of class or economic interest groups" (2005, 705).

As van de Walle points out, "Clientelism exists in all polities. The forms it takes, its extent, and its political functions vary enormously, however, across time and place" (2007, 50). In the case of Latin America, a fresh wave of ethnography has zoomed in on the resilience and adaptability of patron-client networks as a central feature in modern social and political life.[8] In this growing body of work, clientelism appears as particularly salient in modern-day relationships between the large poor sectors of society and different types of elites.[9] For Latin Americans facing precarious livelihoods, clientelist relationships provide them with potential access to resources needed to solve essential problems in life. Often oversimplified as the exchange of votes for favors, political clientelism encompasses what Javier Auyero calls "the world of problem solving through political mediation" (2001, 181).

If clientelism is indeed a pervasive historical feature of Latin American politics, it is quite plausible that a political collective freshly inserted into the system might become compelled to engage in such practices. Thus, one way of looking at clientelist practices within and around the FMLN is to frame it as a product of the adaptation of the former insurgent movement to Salvadoran electoral politics, "with its corrupt character," as one of the veterans put it.[10] In this view, clientelism appears as one of the adjustments that the former insurgents made in responding to democratic transition. Nonetheless, my research demonstrated how clientelist relations largely evolved from the connections inherited from the insurgency, while at the same time representing the continuation of a phenomenon with even deeper historical roots stretching into the colonial and postcolonial periods (Ching 2014). By those directly involved, clientelism was certainly not seen as a form of corruption, but rather as something morally justified and desirable: it was framed as a form of solidarity. And it was morally linked to the interpersonal relations that were forged during the war. In the eyes of many former insurgents, participation in the revolutionary movement should indeed translate into lasting bonds of reciprocity.

As Auyero points out, clientelism is best understood when one zooms in on "the everyday dealings of political brokers, the practices and perspectives of so-called clients and the problem-solving networks that link 'clients,' brokers, and political patrons" (2000, 58). In these interactions, "clientelism does not sustain itself by material exchange alone. A network of affective relations embeds clientelism in power relations of aid and loyalty that masks the bare exchange of goods for electoral support" (Shefner 2012, 42). Clientelist transactions take place within a symbolic universe of political imaginaries, what Andrés Guerrero calls the "semantic field of reciprocity," which generates "a certain moral code that frames the individual strategies of the patron and the [clients] concerning distribution" (1991, 179). To produce and sustain their relations, patrons and clients make use of a range of "often subtle, hidden" sanctioning mechanisms (Helmke and Levitsky 2004, 733). Clients, far from being passive subjects, continually negotiate the relationship that ties them to the patron, laying claim on the patrons' obligation for reciprocity. On the other hand, patrons typically complain about the lack of dedication of those they see as their clients. In fact, neither patrons nor clients fully fulfill the other's expectations. Hence, patron-client relations are often "tinged with resentment, disappointment, disillusionment and bitterness" (Scheper-Hughes 1992, 117), indeed a common feature of the postinsurgent clientelism documented in this study.

Another factor that is crucial for understanding the dynamics of postinsurgent clientelism in El Salvador is that the former insurgents saw political adversaries as actively working to sustain their own clientelist support structures in connection to state resources. FMLN supporters perceived that, throughout ARENA's twenty years in office (1989 until 2009), ARENA participants were able to benefit extensively from their party's access to government. Those constructing the FMLN party structures and local networks saw themselves as engaged in a competition over state resources first and foremost with ARENA. Therefore, when the FMLN won the presidency in 2009, a common expression among the FMLN veterans was that now it was "our turn" (Ainhoa Montoya 2011, 2013). What it meant was that if previously other political groups had profited most from their ties to power holders, now it was the turn of those affiliated with the FMLN to access the state resources. Thus, in this new context, when ARENA-affiliated peasants were benefited with agricultural supplies, local FMLN supporters went to the national FMLN office to "denounce" this, because such resources, they argued, should now be "theirs."[11]

The experience of postinsurgent clientelism went beyond electoral trade-offs, and should be understood in the context of a complex, historically shaped social field. The relations between PMO leadership, cadres, and constituents built up during the insurgent period became restratified and reconfigured in the process of vying for different resources through engagement in postwar politics, mainly through the FMLN as a political party, but also, to a smaller extent, through NGOs or other institutions. Postinsurgent clientelist relations entailed significant internal competition for scarce resources as well as ongoing electoral confrontations with "enemy" political forces, mostly ARENA. Furthermore, postinsurgent clientelism was shaped and partially evaluated in the mirror of the revolutionary movement and its grand promises. Unmet expectations imbued postinsurgent clientelism with a strong emotional undercurrent, sometimes manifesting itself in cynicism.

Faction Building inside Postinsurgency

Clientelism is a two-way street: aspiring leaders relied on former comrades to back their claims to power, and these comrades also relied on the leaders they supported to reward them if the leaders attained power. As became clear in chapter 7, postinsurgent clientelism was intimately tied to disputes among (aspiring) leaders over paid positions and other resources. Aspiring leaders needed to be able to either mobilize constituents or convince FMLN leadership that they could do so. They needed to also gather support from above (from other leaders) in order to launch a candidacy or other power claims.

When an aspiring candidate organized supporters to mobilize in his or her support, such support would be partially fueled by the expectations of future rewards. For example, a successful candidate would eventually be able to offer loyal collaborators a government job, might back the community leader for a local political position, and might be able to channel aid to communities that provided support. Exchanges of support took place on various interconnected levels, from the community up to the party's upper echelons. A local leader might function as a patron towards his or her constituents, while operating more like a client in relation to more senior leadership on a regional or national level. In this sense, postinsurgent clientelism to a degree provided subtle and flexible hierarchies. It might in fact be difficult to find a client or a patron in an absolute sense, as participants took on different roles and positions at different times in order to produce the desired trade-offs. Clientelism provided space to accommodate and reward different participants in various ways.

However, the ability to dispense rewards should not be exaggerated. I found El Salvador's postinsurgent clientelism to be, in general terms, rather precarious, and largely unsatisfying in terms of its redistributive capacities. Factional conflicts were, furthermore, recurrent. Plausibly, the precariousness fed such conflict, since the resources up for distribution compared unfavorably to the needs of those involved. Hence factions might be useful for hoarding scarce resources in such a way as to obstruct contenders and to privilege in-group interests (Tilly 2006). In my view, postinsurgent factionalism should be understood both as a legacy of the revolutionary movement and as a product of clientelism. Revolutionary history helped fuel clientelism through the existence of close ties and strong expectations between former PMO members. At the same time—as the case studies show—this revolutionary history served as a device for exclusion, supporting divisionary claims regarding which former insurgents were worthy of power and benefits, and which were not.

Factional clientelism appears with particular clarity in the FMLN veterans' movement. Although ideological debates also sometimes took place, most participants seemed particularly interested in the practical political trade-offs involved. A common metaphor the veterans used was that of the "ladder," in which those who were not leaders were used for others to climb. Thus, according to one research participant, the organizers of the veterans' movement "build a ladder in order to say, whether it be to the political commission [of the FMLN] or to the Friends of Mauricio [Funes]:[12] 'Look, we are strong.'"[13]

In a similar vein, another veteran reached the following conclusion about the leaders' agenda: "You see, when the FMLN veterans' movement is formed it is because the leadership of the movement wants . . . to show up with ten thousand affiliates and ask for positions within the party and within the municipal and legislative governments. Not to defend the needs of the ex-combatants and their families for health, work, housing. . . . No! This is secondary."[14]

Regardless of individual perceptions as to which agenda carries priority (the "public" agenda of benefits for constituents or the "hidden" agenda of the leaders), the fact is that veteran politics hinges on the interconnection between the two. The better positioned the leaders, the better they may facilitate future benefits for constituents. Various leaders wooed possible constituents, often people they had been connected with since the war. As I noticed during fieldwork, some veterans participated with several, potentially competing, political factions simultaneously. And then sometimes the conflict between different leaders and factions escalated to the extent that participation in rival groups became untenable, forcing constituents to make a choice between groups or to tone down political participation, as occurred, for example, within the veterans' movement in 2004.

Understanding the Saliency of Conspiracy

Initially, I viewed with skepticism the perception, widespread among former insurgents, that postwar Salvadoran politics was pervaded by conspiracy.[15] I inferred that the phenomenon mainly pointed at the existence of deep political distrust. But gradually I came to understand that a number of former insurgents also conceived of conspiracy as a (legitimate) method of building political power. I eventually asked dozens of informers whether they saw conspiracy as a relevant part of the experience of postinsurgency. Invariably, the response was affirmative. "Conspiracy is part of the ABC of Salvadoran politics," I was told.[16]

As dealt with in chapter 2, conspiracy played a crucial role before and during the war, as a characteristic feature of the insurgents' political-military efforts as well as those of their enemies.[17] Tom Gibb, who covered the war in El Salvador for the BBC, wrote that "conspiracies . . . were the stuff of war in El Salvador" (2000, 223). Indeed, during the 1970s and 1980s, both Salvadoran revolutionaries and anticommunists received extensive training in conspiratorial methods for clandestine warfare.[18] But if war and conspiracy are a familiar mix, democratic transition and conspiracy are certainly not. Why then would (the imaginary of) conspiracy have endured after the peace accords?

A former FAL cadre I interviewed extensively witnessed that PMO cadres with conspiratorial experience subsequently applied it to their advantage in the postwar context.

> The work method they [the leaders] used was a conspiratorial one, founded upon personal intrigues; it gave the best results. . . . [What] they sought to control was, in the first place, the internal power apparatus of the FMLN . . . within the municipality or the department. . . . Following the elections [of 1994] . . . an internal struggle ensued for political offices. It was already apparent that being in office made it easy to get to where the money was. . . . The huge majority in this period was in it for this reason. . . . They were fighting over the bones . . . biting, kicking and using below-the-belt methods. . . . They began to manipulate groups, in the communities. . . . There was another structure, another step above, which controlled these [local]

control groups. . . . They carried out their intrigues, . . . and above them there were four or five people who pulled everyone else's strings, you see.[19]

In this narrative of postinsurgent politics, conspiracy is seen as a tool that militants use to forward personal and factional interests in (local) electoral politics. When asked what type of manipulation was used, the FAL veteran whom I cited above mainly referred to seeking strategic advantage through the manipulation of the personal flaws or weaknesses of local leaders, provoking attitudes or behavior that would make them prone to blackmail or public humiliation. He also claimed that, if this was not successful, some used intimidation, threats, and violence.[20] A strategy former insurgents commonly referred to was that of "*la camita*,"[21] which implied seeking the confidence of someone in order to have them do or say something that then could be used to marginalize them.[22] Several informers also emphasized the importance of slander in the microdynamics of postinsurgent politics.

> If they want to marginalize someone from the party structures, the first thing they do is to call the person an infiltrator. This is the first rumor [spread], the classic one; . . . or that the person is an enemy agent, you see? Or an ARENA member. Another type of rumor is that of a sexual nature. . . . For example, this is how they can shake someone off: "Have you heard? So-and-so is harassing so-and-so." You see? But first they get the woman's okay to do so, see? And maybe the gal is provoking him and he just goes along with it, you see? "He is harassing me." You see? They now made it true that he is harassing her. But the underlying intent is to marginalize him. . . . The other: economic corruption. The rumor: "He has stolen so much [money]." . . . Since the norm is business beneath fine tablecloths and behind the curtains. . . . And when they can't accuse someone of anything else, . . . "He is gay." This is a rumor that has a lot of weight here. . . . And people, well, what they do is, everyone begins to spread the rumor around.[23]

In the passage above, slander is conceived as a form of conspiracy that participants in postinsurgency recur to with the purpose of undermining the competitor's position and strengthening their own. Several examples of conspiratorial thinking also appear in the case studies presented in the previous chapters. Consider the underground campaigning in Ellacuría to vote for a non-FMLN candidate (chap. 5) or the veterans' frequent references to infiltrators (chap. 7). Save a few exceptions, these are not "spectacular" forms of conspiracy. Instead, most examples point to the use of conspiratorial methods to advance the aims of factionalist interests within the framework of electoral politics.

However, postinsurgency in El Salvador has also witnessed more elaborated cases of conspiracy, leaving darker threads to unwind. For example, in 1997, the FMLN's PCS faction was implicated in a scandal around the abduction of several wealthy Salvadorans. These kidnappings for ransom began to take place at the end of the war, and continued well after the peace accords.[24] The PCS tie was eventually deemed proven by a Salvadoran court, but the extent to which top leadership was involved remained unclear. It was rumored, but never substantiated, that the PCS used money obtained through the kidnappings to finance its postwar ascendency within the FMLN. Nonetheless, the most resounding case of postwar political conspiracy was the July 5, 2006, killings involving FMLN militant Mario Belloso, referred to in chapter 7. The Belloso case, including the manipulation various politicians engaged in during its aftermath, tragically and painfully demonstrated that conspiracy continued to be a valuable currency in postwar Salvadoran politics, for both Left and Right.[25]

Postinsurgent participants, indeed, widely believed in the relevance of conspiracy, though its actual reach was difficult to qualify. Several postwar political scandals strongly suggested the use of conspiracy, both among former insurgents and among right-wing adversaries. Some of my informers recalled the wartime training many cadres received in conspiratorial techniques. However, the fact that the insurgents brought a reservoir of conspiratorial skills with them into postwar democratic transition does not automatically mean they also put them to work. In the revolutionary mind-set, the use of such tools was justified as legitimate and necessary when fighting a war against a formidable enemy. One might suppose that with the peace accords the moral justification for conspiracy disappeared or became much less evident.

Nonetheless, my findings suggest that some (aspiring) leaders may have sought and found ways to adjust their experience with conspiracy to

matic trade-offs and negotiations that helped to tie together different actors within the field of postinsurgency, harnessing identities such as "friends, factions and followers,"[28] but also appealing to in-groups' solidarity with roots in insurgent identities. Appealing to deeply entrenched distrust, postinsurgent participants also frequently mobilize wartime categories like enemies, traitors, or death squads to make sense of postwar politics. Finally, the imaginary of conspiracy placed us squarely in a mode of politics in which political identities and events are material for deceit and manipulation.

I hold that these different understandings of postinsurgent politics are not separate universes, but instead interact in myriad ways to produce the lived experience of postinsurgent politics. Several activists, for example, framed electoral politics as a continuation of the war with other means, playing on von Clausewitz's famous definition of war as politics by other means. Or, in another example, even an extremely loyal FMLN militant like Rafael (chap. 7), who spoke extensively with me regarding his revolutionary convictions, complained on numerous occasions about the political maneuvering taking place inside his party, which he called "Machiavellian."[29]

Many former insurgents borrowed from all five imaginaries in their daily participation in postinsurgent politics. Like Mische's activists, they switched from one to the other according to the setting, the audience, and the objectives associated with the occasion or the specific point they sought to make. Some dominant tendencies could be identified. For one, in public discourse directed at large audiences susceptible to media coverage, emphasis tended to be on the imaginaries and identities associated with democracy and revolution, with the communicators often seeking to connect the two imaginaries, playing down contradictions between them. With elections upcoming, imaginaries from the war would be widely used to galvanize historical loyalties, as well as to counteract anticommunist fearmongering by ARENA (Ainhoa Montoya 2013). On the other hand, in private meetings and gatherings, former insurgents tended to emphasize political trade-offs and negotiations taking place, and to comment or speculate on the strategies different political actors employ.[30] Political opponents and competitors were analyzed and, no less frequently, disqualified, often by means of "authentic 'inside information,' indiscreetly revealed" (Ashfort 2005, 66). On such occasions, conspiracy was given significant and explicit attention.

Participants in postinsurgent Salvadoran politics seemed keenly aware of the possible advantages of conducting different types of politics strategically and in a parallel manner (Jasper 2006, 9). Hence, for example, the ASALVEG organizers in chapter 7 were, according to FPL veteran José, "engaged in conspiracy" in order to strengthen their faction, while simultaneously also appealing to the democratic frame of citizen inclusion when publicly engaging with the round table of the Funes presidency. Behind the scenes, however, the negotiations with the government mostly involved clientelist trade-offs.

AT THE START OF THE FMLN'S SECOND TERM IN GOVERNMENT

The 2014 presidential ballot for the FMLN was an FPL affair. Salvador Sánchez Cerén, Funes's vice-president and the FPL's former top comandante, was joined by Oscar Ortíz, another former FPL comandante, as his second. As described in chapter 7, Ortíz was one of the few reformist leaders that had managed to survive the postwar purges and stay inside the FMLN. His inclusion on the ballot was seen by most militants as an attempt to appeal to disaffected former insurgents and moderate sectors outside of the party.

Funes had ended his presidency with relatively high popular approval ratings, though opinions on the quality of his administration varied. A large part of the FMLN militancy complained about his alleged authoritarian stance, his lack of commitment to the party, and his attempts to create his own political platform (Allison and Martín Alvarez 2012, 112). Several observers wondered how it was possible that Funes had protected retired officers involved in human rights violations while allowing the military to increment its political influence.[31] Some reputable journalists questioned the Funes administration's transparency.[32] He had also lost the confidence of certain civil society activists who had rallied behind him before, after his presidential support for the 743 decree, an attempt to rein in the independence of the country's Supreme Court, whose rulings had started to contain the power of the executive and the political parties, generating annoyance within the leaderships of both ARENA and FMLN (Freedman 2011; Moodie 2013b; Zulueta-Fülscher 2013).

Nonetheless, the FMLN and ARENA stood neck and neck in the polls, and the FMLN gaining another term was a distinct possibility.

Funes became the star campaigner, using every opportunity at hand during his last months as president to launch verbal attacks on ARENA. The FMLN won the elections by the tiny margin of just of 6,364 votes, or 0.22 percent of the total tally (TSE 2014). Similar to what happened in the elections of 2006, when the FMLN retained the capital city by just forty-four votes, FMLN militants quickly mobilized to "defend the triumph." ARENA militants took to the streets elsewhere in the capital to voice accusations of fraud and to demand recounts.[33] After a tense week, the Electoral Tribunal declared Sánchez Cerén the winner, and eligible to take office on June 1, 2014. Becoming the president by such a small margin of votes was not a comfortable point of departure. And in subsequent months his government regularly received criticism for meager performance, particularly from the country's leading newspapers, mostly right-wing bulwarks, but also occasionally from more prestigious outlets such as *El Faro*.

When Justo and I met for coffee in July 2015, the topic of the day was the "golpe blando," the "soft coup."[34] The FMLN leadership had recently denounced an alleged ARENA plot to bring down Sánchez Cerén, echoing similar accusations against the opposition by Nicolás Maduro in Venezuela and Rafael Correa in Ecuador.[35] According to FMLN secretary general Medardo González, the soft coup consisted of a secret plan to discredit the FMLN and destabilize the government by use of sabotage and other manipulative tactics. One of González's strongest accusations was that, conniving with the MS13 and 18 gangs, ARENA was manipulating a surge in homicide rates and assaults in order to deepen the country's ongoing security crisis.[36] The FMLN had started organized efforts to neutralize this threat, which consisted of a media campaign and a protest rally in the center of San Salvador.

For Justo, the idea of the soft coup was far-fetched. Rather than always accusing ARENA, he thought the FMLN should stop seeking scapegoats and focus on improving government performance. Justo speculated that the FMLN leadership probably didn't even believe in the existence of a coordinated right-wing plan. The campaign against the soft coup, so he considered, was meant for FMLN militants, to provide them with additional motivation to stand strong against criticism and to stay united against a common enemy. According to Justo, those who attended the rally were mostly "their employees," people whose jobs depended on the FMLN, and who therefore had to embrace the party line rather uncritically, although some "true believers" had also made an appearance.[37]

Nonetheless, in spite of the precarious political reality of Sánchez Cerén's first year in office, the FMLN still qualified as a hugely successful party. To understand the strengths and limitations of the FMLN's performance, we should note several factors. For one, it is necessary to look at ARENA, which, after emerging strong from the war, governed the country until 2009. Well connected to historical elites, deeply rooted in the country's conservative networks, and building on a significant rural constituency with previous paramilitary ties, ARENA profiled itself after the war as a modern, good-for-business party (Wade 2016). ARENA's economic reform, however, mostly benefited the upper classes, and in contrast proved quite disastrous for the country's peasantry, and many scholars consider that ARENA's neoliberal stance helped push Salvadoran families toward illegal labor migration (Andrade-Eekhoff and Silva-Avalos 2003; Arias Peñate 2010; Bull 2013a; Gammage 2006; Segovia 2002; Velásquez Carrillo 2012).

Furthermore, over the years, corruption scandals and internal strife increasingly wore out ARENA (Wade 2016; Wolf 2009). ARENA's wartime history, closely linked to the death squads, continued to dent ARENA's reputation. As we saw in chapter 2, Robert d'Aubuisson, ARENA founder and historical leader, was also a key figure behind the terror of the late 1970s and early 1980s. The UN Truth Commission found him directly responsible for ordering the assassination of Monseñor Oscar Arnulfo Romero. And while in 2014 the Vatican declared Romero to be "blessed," leaving the archbishop well on route to becoming a saint, ARENA became increasingly divided between those wanting to distance themselves from D'Aubuisson and those who continued to defend him. Still, ARENA won the largest faction in parliament in the 2015 elections, and its fierce competition with the FMLN continued.

The successes of the Left in other countries in the region constitute another factor affecting FMLN's success, since these have arguably created a favorable public climate for left-wing ascendency across the continent (Chodor 2014; Queirolo 2013). Most important, however, as described in chapter 7, is Venezuela. In 2005 the FMLN used Venezuelan capital to set up a significant commercial venture called Alba Petroleo. It started with diesel and gasoline, and later also moved into other products such as food supplies. The financial means of Alba enterprises—estimated by the reputable digital newspaper *El Faro* at close to a billion dollars since 2006[38]—helped provide stability to the party apparatus and allowed the FMLN to compete more effectively with ARENA in electoral campaigning. The FMLN leadership, furthermore, learned to negotiate pacts with influential figures external to the party, for example to strengthen electoral bids, as occurred with Mauricio Funes in 2009, and in 2015 with Nayib Bukele, the mayor of San Salvador for the period 2015–18.

A final factor is that—in spite of revolutionary rhetoric—the FMLN gradually embraced a less ideological and a more patrimonial approach to politics. This connected with the strong reciprocal ties that were built in the movement over the years and that have been amply documented in this study. The remnants of the cadre system served as a foundation for this process. Access to state resources further fueled this dynamic. Public employment, in turn, helped to strengthen the party, as those that obtained their positions through party contacts were then strongly urged to participate in party activities as well as to contribute part of their salary; "la cuota partidaria."

This certainly does not mean that the contemporary FMLN militancy was only motivated by personal economic interests. Historical affiliation, loyalty to the movement and (part of) its leadership, and ideological factors were also important. I found, however, that such factors coexisted with clientelist arrangements, and to a certain extent had become mutually dependent for most participants. As documented in chapter 7, ideology was used to justify clientelist arrangements, for example when offering low-ranking government jobs to FMLN militants became framed as a way to counteract the institutional control of right-wing forces seeking to sabotage the FMLN project.

All these factors together also help explain why the FMLN administration has received mixed reviews from international scholars. While in 2009 Forrest Colburn, writing for the *Journal of Democracy*, considered the FMLN triumph as crucial step to much-needed constructive reform (2009, 152), in his more recent article in this same journal he described the FMLN administration as generally lacking ideas, increasing external debts, and producing only meager benefits for the country (Colburn and Cruz 2014). On the other hand, Cannon and Hume, in *Democratization*, considered that the FMLN government's "increased inclusion of previously excluded civil society groups in policy-making structures has opened up possibilities for progressive, inclusive measures" (2012, 1050). Perla and Cruz-Feliciano, in *Latin American Perspectives*, considered that "given the international correlation of forces arrayed against them, [the

FMLN is] making significant improvements in the daily lives of [Salvadoran] citizens" (2013, 101), a position also defended by Clark (2015) in relation to advances in the Ministry of Health. Nonetheless, analysts further to the left like James Petras conceive the FMLN as sell-outs "shifting to the right" (2015), while the International Communist League speaks of "the bourgeois FMLN" (2015). As we have seen throughout this book, all of these positions can also be found among the former participants in the insurgent movement in El Salvador.

According to the opinion polls performed by the UCA's Instituto Universitario de Opinión Pública (IUDOP), the broader Salvadoran citizenry evaluated the government's performance over 2015 at 5.18 on a scale of 10, manifesting significant "disenchantment regarding the expectations of change generated by the government when taking power" (IUDOP 2016, 6).[39] In August 2016, the reputation of left-wing Salvadoran politics received a significant blow when former president Funes was charged with corruption. Rather than facing justice in El Salvador, Funes requested and received political exile in Daniel Ortega's Nicaragua, where he has lived since then.[40] With El Salvador facing a deep and protracted crisis in matters of security and overall state performance, the challenges for the FMLN administration would be daunting enough without such scandals.[41] The FMLN government record thus far indeed reflects the depth of these challenges and the various ups and downs with which government officials and party leadership have navigated them.

A key argument of this book is that, on a deeper level, the performance of the FMLN relies strongly on the adjustment of the insurgency's internal relations to the context of electoral politics, producing strengths as well as limitations. The FMLN's historical militancy has been partially reconverted to form the core of an electoral machine able to field tens of thousands of people for campaigning and on election day (Almeida 2010). PMO factionalism allowed the FMLN to reshape its leadership networks, and eventually helped to reconvert its wartime trust networks into a relatively stable leadership with historical stature and rather firm control of the party apparatus (Allison and Martín Alvarez 2012). Though competing left-wing factions have emerged, most recently around the figure of Mauricio Funes, they have thus far been unable to gain ascendency over the FMLN's top governing bodies.

The reconversion of the former insurgency into a political machine feeds into a particular kind of clientelism. With the FMLN's electoral success, the internal inequality of the movement became big enough for solidarity to become gradually replaced by clientelist relations. Embracing more patrimonial forms of politics helped the FMLN to reshape its ties with historical constituencies as well as to connect to new constituencies, and thus effectively compete with ARENA, a party which itself strongly relied on clientelism to maintain allegiance among rural constituencies and to strengthen buy-in among urban entrepreneurs.

Hence, as pointed out by José in chapter 7, the FMLN's success depended in part on its capacity to adapt to El Salvador's lackluster political realities. In line with the developments of other countries in the region, these realities have dampened enthusiasm for postwar democratization in El Salvador. Torres-Rivas (2010) speaks of Central America's "bad democracies," while Lehoucq (2012) refers to "low-quality democracies," embattled by inequality, violence, and immigration, where "perverse state institutions" have helped to "reproduce criminal violence after peace" (J. Cruz 2015, 170). Though forces like the FMLN manifestly aim to reverse such negative developments, the question remains to what extent they might be successful in this enormous task, taking into account both the deep challenges of the region's present context and the party's weaknesses and contradictions.

TOWARD A THEORY OF POSTINSURGENCY

The specific ways in which an insurgent movement's accumulated history may help shape postwar adjustment processes is still very much underappreciated and understudied. As the Salvadoran case clearly demonstrates, participation in insurgency generates strong in-group expectations, putting very significant political strains on the ensuing transition process. This has been documented beyond the case of El Salvador, most rigorously by Southall, in *Liberation Movements in Power: Party and State in Southern Africa* (2013), and by Kriger in her work on guerrilla veterans in Zimbabwe (2003). The most eloquent account comes from the late Nadine Gordimer, in her novel *No Time like the Present*, about former ANC militants in postinsurgent South Africa (2012).[42]

In spite of the PMOs' dissolution, PMO itineraries were omnipresent in the field of postinsurgency. They became crucial components of leadership and faction building. It is telling that throughout the postwar decades the FMLN's political commission continued to consist almost exclusively of former PMO cadres, dominated by PCS and FPL. As we saw in the case studies, when former PMO cadres obtained senior postings, they frequently relied on their previous comrades to fill out the positions under their command. Old PMO power relations were thus sometimes reproduced in government institutions. A friend who, through her PMO connections, had obtained a midlevel job in the Funes administration complained that "the same ones as always end up with the jobs." She was referring to older cadres who occupied the best positions, leaving little space for younger, better-educated candidates. This was exacerbated by the fact that, according to her, the party leaders internally "still maintain quotas, there always have to be people from the PC [PCS] and from the 'Fs' [FPL]."[43]

During the war, PMO cadres functioned as mobilizing agents as well as gatekeepers to different sectors and communities. In the framework of the insurgency, the PMO cadres were subject to supervision and evaluation by superiors, but after the peace accords this control slacked, and with it, the cadres were known to partially privatize their individual position of power within the community, NGO, or union. Cadres also frequently attempted to convert their "revolutionary credit" into a position of political leadership in the new context. This phenomenon was especially salient among the comandantes—the majority of whom attempted a career in public office—but also quite noticeable among midlevel cadres. Eventually, as we saw in the case study chapters, the cadre legacy played an important role in the structuring of internal inequality and in the emergence of factional clientelism within the field of postinsurgency.

Especially during the 1990s, the experience of postinsurgency was dominated by the phenomenon of disillusionment, something that mainly made sense in the light of the expectations that participants in the revolutionary movement had previously held. Nonetheless, contrary to what some social movement literature suggests, in the Salvadoran case disillusionment did not always translate into demobilization.[44] I met many highly disillusioned ex-combatants who nonetheless were still active in the FMLN or social movement work. Furthermore, with postinsurgency being a lengthy and drawn-out process, many of those who opted for exit early on ended up reconnecting in subsequent years. What disillusionment did do was to contribute to the experience of postinsurgency as a less idealistic or anti-idealistic form of politics, sometimes leading to cynicism. Much more than simply a catalyst for demobilization, disillusionment became part of the shared experience of postinsurgency.

Social movement literature pays little attention to internal differentiations between (groups of) participants in the movement, differentiations that I found played an important role in postinsurgent transition. This lack of attention is correlated with the literature's limited concern for the political intricacies of internal hierarchies as well as for the matter of leadership in general (Campell 2005, 63). However, as we saw, the experience of postinsurgency is impossible to understand without the matter of internal inequality, and the tension between this factor and that of proclaimed solidarity. To accommodate this finding, it might be useful to infuse social movement scholarship with a dose of elite theory. For this purpose, I do not propose to look at left-wing leaders as skilled manipulators of egalitarian discourses in search of personal power, as Michels (1962) and Pareto (1991) did, but rather to consider internal power differences as a highly dynamic and contentious component of the experience of postinsurgency.

As we have seen, such power differentials do not only set apart different participants, but also help to connect them, through various forms of exchange and redistribution of power and privilege. The lack of consideration of internal power arrangements has made social movement theory largely oblivious to the phenomenon of clientelism. Elite theory, on the other hand, contributes little understanding to the ongoing dynamics of bottom-up claim making within the field of postinsurgency. It overestimates leadership's strategic advantage and underestimates that of constituents. It oversimplifies the relationships that hold them together. If social movement theory could benefit from integrating certain notions of elite theory, the same might well be true the other way around.

A final implication of my research findings is that what we have learned about postinsurgency might also constitute an invitation to revisit the experience of insurgency itself. For example, to what extent should we interpret postinsurgent factional clientelism as a distinctly new way of organizing internal relations? Indeed, the revolutionary movement explicitly rejected clientelist politics as practiced by the regime and the oligarchy. But does this also mean that there were no clientelist trade-offs in the movement before and during the war? To address such matters it is necessary to reexamine the nature of the movement's internal relationships even more closely than I have done in this study. It might be useful to consider, for example, how, in the 1970s, the insurgent movement might have drawn on existing clientelist relationships, like compadrazgo, in order to help build the movement, something already insinuated by the data that Cabarrús presented on Aguilares (1983). In this vein, another issue is how PMO capacity to mobilize different resources through NGOs and other entities, for example in the refugee camps, helped to shape the relationships between rural insurgent constituents and the rest of the movement. To what extent, for example, might the revolutionary organizations have played a role in the emergence of the alleged "*asistencialismo*" (aid dependency) among Salvadoran peasant refugees in Honduras?[45] In all, I think it is not unlikely that clientelist practices and imaginaries already played a role in the development of the revolutionary movement from the 1970s onward. But I believe this was of minor importance in comparison to the imaginary of revolutionary militancy and that of the peasant insurgents as the "chosen people."[46]

These observations also connect to more theoretical discussions regarding the type of (local) governance arrangements an insurgent movement might bring into existence (Mampilly 2011; Tilly 1978, 1985; Wickham-Crowley 1987, 1992, 2015). By and large, our understanding of insurgent governance is still very much limited by the fact that such arrangements include important clandestine facets difficult to document or research. The advantage of the Salvadoran case is that it is now possible to perform in-depth research efforts on wartime internal affairs. As the former insurgent peasants from Ellacuría indicated, they now share stories that were previously off-limits for outsiders. What we can learn from those stories is that Salvadoran guerrilla government as such was made effective on the local level through the intricate personal and organizational ties that, often covertly, intertwined segments of the local population with the guerrilla. The fact that the PMO cadre system was very hierarchical does not mean that it did not help to incorporate and represent different subgroups within the insurgent polity on different levels. The PMOs' internal governance system was permeable for local participants. Thus, unlike Weinstein (2007), who conceives of rebel government as fundamentally driven by strategic decision-making at the top of the organization, we must acknowledge that the dynamic of guerrilla government also pertains to the regulation of different constituents. In other words, insurgent governance also constitutes a set of arrangements in which power is produced, disputed, and distributed internally. I believe that the ongoing negotiation of internal power was an important feature of the Salvadoran insurgent movement. The contention between different insurgent subgroups that we have seen emerge so clearly and publicly in the postwar period must already have taken place—in a more subdued manner—before and during the war.

THE ENDURING LEGACIES OF INSURGENCY IN EL SALVADOR

The end of the war implied drastic changes for El Salvador's insurgent movement, but it did not mean a fresh start. The former insurgents took with them into this new phase the accumulated relationships and imaginaries of insurgency, and sought different ways of collectively accommodating to the emerging circumstances. In comparison to the apparently clear-cut categories of war, the aftermath gave way to confusing times, with actors repositioning and realigning, and political meanings and identities often wandering in flux (Strazzari 2008). Because of long-standing—but temporarily repressed—socioeconomic and political differences, insurgent participants held different cards that facilitated, or hindered, social, political, and economic ascendency in the postwar context.

The insurgent accommodations that took place after the peace accords did not end the phenomenon of left-wing revolutionary militancy in El Salvador. Leadership emphasized that "the struggle continued" and, in that sense, political demobilization was not warranted. Former insurgents nonetheless debated the extent to which postwar political militancy could still be considered "revolutionary." While some saw the electoral ascendency of the FMLN, and the political trade-offs that came with it, as important steps on the road toward deeper socialist-oriented societal transformations, others interpreted it as opportunism or even as betrayal. Certain activists saw the breach between FMLN discourse and FMLN political practice as the main obstacle to the advancement of a left-wing agenda. Others mainly looked at right-wing sabotage as the culprit.

Indeed, the continued electoral rivalry between ARENA and FMLN, combined with the rooting of this rivalry in wartime divides, stimulated a type of politics heavily informed by the existence of an enemy that required defeating. As we saw in chapter 7, the stakes involved in the contest with ARENA served to legitimate the use of a range of nondemocratic means, including the abolition of most of the internal democratic mechanisms that the FMLN experimented with during its first decade as a political party. The ongoing antagonism with ARENA not only produced an "external enemy" for the FMLN to defeat, but also contributed to the discernment of an internal enemy within the party itself. It fed a conspiracy mind-set, in which the party was seen as an infiltrated entity, with certain activists accused of secretly serving the enemy and acting as a fifth column within the party.[47] Internal suspicion, in turn, strengthened the leadership's hold on the party, by providing scapegoats and justifying purges and the stepping up of control mechanisms for party activists. As described in chapter 7, factions of party activists also drew on the conspiracy mind-set in order to discredit internal competitors.

My fieldwork findings suggest that clientelism's success lay in the fact that former insurgents, on different levels, saw it as an effective tool for electoral competition. On the one hand, clientelism offered a powerful instrument to achieve effective aggregate structuring of political relationships from top to bottom, and vice versa. On the other hand, clientelism helped to sustain collective political identities over time because it offered resources to sustain in-group solidarity. The identities and imaginaries of the war provided emotionally powerful devices to help structure the groups that entered in competition. For some party activists, the semantic prominence of the war and the enemy might have helped to conceal the fact that, in the postinsurgent decades, left-wing Salvadoran politics evolved from revolutionary vanguardism toward a version of electoral clientelism, and that, as a political party, the former revolutionaries adopted, albeit in a new jacket, some of the political practices that they originally had taken up arms against.[48]

As with clientelism, the saliency of conspiracy in postinsurgent politics can also be seen both as a legacy of insurgency and as part of an older tradition within Salvadoran politics. Secret plotting by dissident factions, for example around coups, was an essential part of how Salvadoran politicians operated throughout the twentieth century.[49] My fieldwork indicates that some former insurgents used behind-the-scenes plotting in addition to public debate and formal electoral procedures. Participants also saw elements on the Right as commonly engaging secretive political practices. Indeed, conspiracy thinking is not exclusive to FMLN circles, but is also common among Salvadoran right-wing activists.[50] How significant and effective this secretive plotting might be vis-à-vis other aspects of Salvadoran politics remains a matter of speculation. In the eyes of many of the veterans I worked with, conspiracy continued to be a factor of utmost importance.

Throughout this study we have seen how insurgent networks, relationships, and political imaginaries played crucial roles in shaping the postinsurgent political arena. The sectarianism for which the Salvadoran revolutionaries were well known in the 1970s resurfaced forcefully in the 1990s. Former insurgent subgroups laid divergent claims on what they saw as the heritage of revolution. Underneath the disputes, the insistence that earlier participation and sacrifice have earned them the right to political ascendency constituted a common thread. This helps explain what, in my eyes, emerged as this study's main paradox. Even if many former insurgents criticized the prevalence of clientelism and factionalism in Salvadoran democracy, they also, by and large, internalized these organizational methods. One of Ellacuría's community leaders reflected on the bittersweet irony of this phenomenon: "As Schafik [Handal] said . . . : 'We are going to immerse ourselves within the system in order to change the system and not so that the system changes us.' . . . This was Schafik's vision, to be able, over time, to change the system. But it ended up the other way around: the system changed us, right? It's that simple! . . . The system has absorbed us."[51]

In this sense, my study concurs with Edelberto Torres-Rivas's retrospective analysis of Central America's political turmoil as revolutions that did not generate revolutionary transformations (2011). Nonetheless, more than two decades after the end of war, the experience of insurgency continued to deeply mark the Salvadoran political landscape. The enduring character of insurgent legacies becomes particularly evident when one considers the life trajectories of those involved in the revolutionary movement on different levels. On the local level, insurgent legacies included tangible changes in settlement patterns and property relations. In urban environments, significant sectors and institutions were also still very much permeated by their insurgent antecedents.

El Salvador's former insurgency developed into a power bloc able to compete effectively with political contenders for access to and control of the state, thereby mostly enlarging the inclusiveness of El Salvador's political arena and boosting postwar electoral democracy. However, at the same time the practical dimensions of these transformations became permeated with traditional and conservative notions of politics, which in turn generates the question to what extent the former insurgents actually achieved political innovation, or whether, instead, they helped outfit "old-style" politics in a new ideological jacket. In my view, the results are mixed. Insurgency and its aftermath did modify Salvadoran power relations profoundly, only not necessarily always in manners that enhanced equality or egalitarianism. As the former insurgents amassed postwar power, they also frequently relied on mundane or traditional political practices rather than transformative ones.

Notes

CHAPTER 1. ECHOES OF REVOLUTION

1. Farabundo Martí National Liberation Front.

2. Tim Golden, "The Salvadorans Make Peace in a 'Negotiated Revolution,'" *New York Times*, January 5, 1992, http://www.nytimes.com/1992/01/05/weekin review/the-world-the-salvadorans-make-peace-in-a-negotiated-revolution .html?pagewanted=all&src=pm.

3. Relevant titles include Arnson (1999), Baranyi and North (1996), Bird and Williams (2000), Boyce (1995, 1999), Burgerman (2000), Call (2002), Cañas and Dada (1999), Córdova Macías, Ramos, and Loya Marín (2007), de Soto and del Castillo (1994), del Castillo (1997, 2001), Doyle, Johnstone, and Orr (1997), Grenier and Daudelin (1995), Johnstone (1995), Juhn (1998), MacLeod (2006), Montgomery (1995b), Orr (2001), Pearce (1999), Spence (2004), and Tulchin and Bland (1992).

4. This positive reputation of the Salvadoran peace process has endured for several decades. For example, one of Colombian president Santos's principal advisers for the 2012–16 peace negotiations in La Habana was Joaquín Villalobos, a former FMLN comandante. Simultaneously, also the Colombian guerrilla of the Fuerzas Armadas Revolucionarias de Colombia (Revolutionary Armed Forces of Colombia; FARC) has taken the Salvadoran experience as a key reference. Colombian newspapers, such as *El Tiempo* and *El Espectador*, have reported extensively on the role of El Salvador in the peace process.

5. Translated by the author from the original in Spanish. In the remainder of this study, all quotes from originals in Spanish have been translated by the author, unless otherwise indicated.

6. On the transfer of power to the FMLN as a test for El Salvador's democracy, see Almeida (2009, 2010), Becker (2009), and Colburn (2009).

7. Observers also point to other factors relevant to Latin America's "left turn," such as left-wing varieties of political pragmatism (or opportunism, depending on observers' positions) and shifts in left-wing political repertoires. For contrasting political views on Latin America's left turn, see Castañeda and Morales (2007) and Petras and Veltmeyer (2009). Regarding contemporary adjustments within the Latin American left, Benjamin Arditi asks, "How can we speak of a turn to the left if we are unsure about what counts as the left?" (2008, 59).

8. On the "pink tide," see, for example, Bull (2013b), Cameron and Hershberg (2010), Isbester (2011), and Levitsky and Roberts (2011).

9. In calling attention to the breach between the international observers' enthusiasm and local rank-and-file anxieties, I aim not to argue which perspective on El Salvador's political transition is more truthful or genuine. The obvious inference here is that appreciation of a large and complex political transition process is highly contingent on the range of particular positions and interests involved. For a political scientist, what requires explanation is likely to be of a different order than what requires explanation from the perspective of a former insurgent. Within each group, further subgroup differences in preferred interpretations and explanations are also bound to exist. Rather than seeking to evaluate which perspective is most truthful, I believe it may be much more beneficial to analyze how these various perspectives offer different and possibly complementary insights on the political dynamics of the transition process.

10. For the analysis of postwar transition in El Salvador as neoliberal peace, see Moodie (2010), Silber (2011), Smith-Nonini (2010), and van der Borgh (2010).

11. The interviewees are included in the List of Protagonists, a list which also contains a handful of research protagonists that I did not interview. The gender division of my interviewees (29 percent women, 71 percent men) roughly corresponds to the estimate of women making up 30 percent of the total FMLN participants during the war (Pampell Conaway and Martínez 2004, 3; Viterna 2013, 267–68).

12. Popular Liberation Forces.

13. More details about my time with the FPL can be found in chap. 3.

14. Armed Forces of Liberation.

15. Salvadoran Communist Party.

16. I use pseudonyms for all people featuring in this study, with the exception of well-known public figures.

17. Justo's story is based on interviews (August 11, 2009; August 20, 2009; July 24, 2015) and field notes (May 8, 2009; May 23, 2009; June 4, 2009; August 3, 2009; August 11, 2009; August 20, 2009; May 26, 2011; May 28, 2011; February 19, 2012; May 10, 2014; September 28, 2014; February 14, 2015; July 24, 2015).

18. Interview with Justo (August 20, 2009).

19. Beatriz Cortéz introduced the concept "the esthetics of cynicism" to analyze Castellanos Moya's work and that of several of his contemporaries (2010). In *La diáspora* (1989), his debut novel, Castellanos Moya reviews some of the experiences of an FPL collective functioning in Mexico City during the 1980s. While *La diáspora* speaks to early revolutionary disenchantment, his novel *El Asco: Thomas Bernhard en San Salvador* (1997) presents a ferocious satire of postinsurgency and of the country's political affairs in general. The book caused uproar in El Salvador. Castellanos Moya received death threats shortly after publishing *El Asco* and left the country. Other Castellanos Moya novels that deal with

postwar affairs and sentiments are *Baile con serpientes* (1996), *La diabla en el espejo* (2000), *El arma en el hombre* (2001), *Donde no estén ustedes* (2003), *Indolencia* (2004), *Insensatez* (2005), and, most recently, *El sueño del retorno* (2013).

20. The most authoritative source on D'Aubuisson's role in political violence is the United Nations' Truth Commission for El Salvador (United Nations 1993). Other sources include Escobar Galindo (2002), Galeas (2004), Lauria-Santiago (2005), Melara Minero (2012), Pyes et al. (2004), and Sprenkels (2011).

21. On partisanship and memory politics in postwar El Salvador, see Ching (2016), Juárez (2011), and Sprenkels (2011, 2012).

22. Incidents of intra-activist violence have been documented during all postwar electoral campaigns, but have become much more common after 1999. The Procuraduría para la Defensa de los Derechos Humanos (PDDH; National Counsel for the Defense of Human Rights) produces an observation report on each election which includes electoral violence. One particularly noteworthy case took place in November 2003, when Antonio Saca was campaigning for the presidency and visiting the northern province of Chalatenango. In one community, the activists were forced to take off their ARENA shirts (which were demonstratively burnt) before they were allowed to continue on their way (field notes, January 3, 2009). This episode was part of a wider scolding of ARENA campaigners in the repopulated communities of Northeastern Chalatenango, who were angry that the ARENA authorities had failed to coordinate their activities with local leaders, and also failed to respect petitions made by locals to abstain from certain types of activities. The ensuing interactivist violence resulted in twenty-three people being wounded. See "Enfrentamiento 23 heridos reportan ARENA y FMLN," *La Prensa Grafica*, November 28, 2003. For a left-wing perspective on these events, see "ARENA and the electoral violence in the northeast of Chalatenango," in UCA's *Proceso*, http://www.uca.edu.sv/publica/proceso /proci1076.html#Politics.

23. See, for example, "Censor vs. trol," *La Prensa Gráfica*, November 15, 2015.

24. There has been some scholarly attention to the development of ARENA during the war (Gordon 1989; Stanley 1996) and to the postwar adjustments of ARENA networks at the elite level (Wade 2016; Wood 2000). However, the issue of how broader ARENA party networks, including those embedded in the armed forces and the paramilitary structures, readjusted to peace remains a lacuna to be addressed in future research.

25. Though approaching social field theory from different academic traditions, both scholars contributed greatly to thinking about the centrality of relations in social life, and about the patterning of such relations in particular groups or fields (Emirbayer 2010).

26. A social field might partially overlap with formal institutions, such as a political party, but one should be cautious about equating such a formal structure

with a social field, since the latter tends to connect different social actors with different roles and positions that do not necessarily or exclusively come together in a formal institution. Therefore Bourdieu argues against "the tendency to privilege substances—here, the real groups, whose numbers, limits, members, etc., one claims to define—at the expense of *relationships*" (1985, 723; emphasis original).

27. Besides El Salvador, well-known cases include South Africa, Angola, Guatemala, Cambodia, Burundi, Nepal, East Timor, and Mozambique, among many others.

28. Examples of such studies include Allison (2006); Burnell (2006); Deonandan, Close, and Prevost (2007); de Zeeuw (2008); Dudouet (2009); Holland (2016); Jarstad and Sisk (2008); Lee (1992); Manning (2004, 2007, 2008); Martí i Puig, Garcé, and Martín (2013); Söderberg-Kovacs (2007); and Southall (2013).

29. Cited in Linz (2006, 24).

30. The "law" reads as follows: "It is organization which gives birth to the domination of the elected over the electors, of the mandataries over the mandators, of the delegates over the delegators. Who says organization, says oligarchy" (Michels 1962, 401).

31. Elite theory is commonly associated with Italian sociology. Gaetano Mosca, for example, forwarded the idea that the principle of government consisted of the rule of the minority over the majority. For Mosca, "class struggle . . . does not take place primarily between the ruling class and the masses but between a ruling elite and a subaltern elite claiming to represent the interests of the masses" (Finocchiaro 1999, 26). Vilfredo Pareto famously stated that "the history of man is the history of continuous replacement of certain elites: as one ascends, another declines" (1991, 36) and that "the rise of the new elite appears as the vindication of the humble and weak against the powerful and strong" (41). Robert Michels also lived and worked extensively in Italy, and is often considered an exponent of Italian elitism. Antonio Gramsci introduced Italian elite theory into Marxist thought. For critical overviews of Italian sociological elitism, see Adamson (1980), Bellamy (1987), and Finocchiaro (1999).

32. See Trotsky (1969, 1972, 1994).

33. Gramsci's conceptualization of hegemony does not refer solely to the dominance of traditional powers, but also to the construction of alternative power, as in revolutionary hegemony among the subaltern (Gramsci 1971, 53–55, 146).

34. On Gramsci and Mariátegui, see Biegel (2005) and Löwy (2008). On Gramsci and Freire, see McLaren and Leonard (1993). Gramsci's work was also important in relation to liberation theology, responsible for mobilizing many Latin American Christians into revolutionary activism. For different considerations of Gramsci's influence amongst Latin American revolutionaries, see Aricó (1988), Becker (1993), and García Canclini (1986).

35. The Spanish terms used by Guevara are *ángel tutelar* and *sacerdote verdadero* (1961b, 51–52).

4. Scholarly work on the relational and organizational aspects associated with armed struggle has gained momentum over the last few years, for instance (1) by acknowledging that, in armed conflicts, "violence . . . forms part of claim making's central rationale" (Tilly and Tarrow 2008, 136), (2) by paying attention to the conscious efforts of the people involved (Selbin 2010, 191), or (3) by trying to redeem the "puzzling absence" of organizational aspects of the groups and movements involved (Weinstein 2007, 34; see also Staniland [2014] and Wood [2008]).

5. The overall chronology is as follows: (1) years of active clandestinity (pre-1980), (2) active resistance (1980–82), (3) military initiative (mid-1982 to 1983), and (4) heightened guerrilla control (1984–92), as cited in Binford (1999, 11). A former PCS cadre proposes a similar, though slightly modified, chronology of insurgent development (Araujo 2011).

6. Well-known accounts of this event, which came to be known as "La Matanza del 32," can be found in T. Anderson (2001) and Dalton (1972 [1993]). Recent revived academic interest in the 1932 events centers upon the question of the relative importance of the Communist Party in the rebellion and the relationship between the communists and the indigenous villagers who participated in the revolt (Gould and Lauria-Santiago 2008; Lindo-Fuentes, Ching, and Lara Martínez 2010). For an analysis of the long-term impact of 1932 on El Salvador's revolutionary Left, see Lindo-Fuentes, Ching, and Lara Martínez (2010, 213–48).

7. For an anecdotal account of the PCS in the decades after 1932, see Dalton (1972 [1993]).

8. United Front of Revolutionary Action.

9. Christian Democratic Party.

10. Renovative Action Party.

11. Revolutionary People's Army.

12. Armed Forces of National Resistance.

13. Revolutionary Party of the Central American Workers.

14. Emphasis original.

15. For a retrospect on Lenin's theoretical and strategic contributions, see Lih (2006) and Shandro (2007).

16. Interview with "Demetrio," May 19, 2009.

17. Hannah Arendt points out that during much of the twentieth century the revolutionary Left resisted embracing violence as a core strategy, in spite of the success of the Russian revolution. Instead, it was right-wing fascism that went for carnage. She identifies Mao Tse-tung's "Power grows out of the barrel of a gun" and especially Frantz Fanon's book *The Wretched of the Earth* as turning points (Arendt 1969, 8–21). Fanon's view of violence as an essential maturation element of the revolutionary process resonated well with supporters of different types of liberation movements emerging at the time, who endured severe

persecution by repressive and militarized regimes or colonial forces. Jean-Paul Sartre, in his 1963 foreword to Fanon's book, acclaims the liberating power of revolutionary violence, stating that "this irrepressible violence . . . is man recreating himself" (2007, lv), and that, in taking up arms and fighting, the oppressed, "by this mad rage . . ., have become men" (lii).

18. His influential idea concerning the need to establish an active nucleus of guerrilla activity (the *foco*) as the revolutionary vanguard was based on the conviction that the practice of revolutionary violence would provoke increasing repression and persecution by the (military) establishment, and thus help push revolutionaries toward clandestine and violent means, while simultaneously unleashing "the wave of hate that repression creates" and catalyzing popular "awareness of the possibility of victory through violent struggle" (Guevara 1961a, 63).

19. Revolutionary mystique.

20. Militancy can be characterized as a type of political engagement based on an "ideology of conflicting interests" that combines an inclination toward concrete and confrontational actions, high levels of personal commitment, and strong reliance on collective membership mobilization (Kelly 1996).

21. Marta Harnecker's omnipresent *Basic Concepts of Historical Materialism* (2005) provided ideological guidance for many aspiring guerrillas. It is hard to overestimate the influence of this text. Jorge Castañeda writes that Harnecker became Latin America's second-best-selling author of all time, after Gabriel García Márquez (1993, 70). See also Kruijt (2008, 55–56).

22. Interviews with Demetrio (May 19, 2009), "José" (December 3, 2009), and Justo (August 20, 2009). See also some of the memoirs produced by participants in the insurgency of the 1970s, like M. Hernández (2009), Peña Mendoza (2009), Rico Mira (2003), and Sánchez Cerén (2008).

23. Aware of the possible consequences of this strategy, the document quotes a fragment of Che Guevara's 1967 speech called "Message to the Tricontinental":

> And these battles shall not be mere street fights with stones against tear-gas bombs, nor shall they be pacific general strikes; neither shall it be the battle of a furious people destroying in two or three days the repressive scaffolds of the ruling oligarchies; the struggle shall be long, harsh, and its front shall be in the guerrillas' refuge, in the cities, in the homes of the fighters—where the repressive forces shall go seeking easy victims among their families—in the massacred rural population, in the villages or cities destroyed by the bombardments of the enemy. They are pushing us into this struggle; there is no alternative apart from preparing it and deciding to undertake it. (FPL 1974, 7)

24. Interview with "Rafael" (December 1, 2009).

25. June 21 National Association of Salvadoran Educators.

26. Hence many Latin American revolutionaries became attentive to what scholars like Barrington Moore had pointed out: the key importance of peasant involvement in rebellions as part of the process of social transformation of societies (1966). Gerrit Huizer, a Dutch social scientist whose extensive fieldwork in Latin America included sojourns in rural communities in El Salvador, pointed out that the commonly held stereotype of "passive peasants" reluctant to change was misleading, and that Latin American peasants had a long history of struggle and resistance, though not always manifest and often small scale (1973). The argument would be reworked and refined in James Scott's well-known *Weapons of the Weak* (1987). Huizer thought the climate for (revolutionary) peasant movements was increasingly favorable. But he added: "Whether [this] . . . will be utilized depends to a large extent on the willingness of urban allies to support and guide the peasant organization" (1973, 159). His ideas resonated well with left-wing intellectuals eager to pull the peasants into Latin America's revolutionary buildup.

27. For a comprehensive overview of the liberation theology and its impact in Latin America, see Burdick and Hewitt (2000) and Rowland (2007).

28. Cabarrús, a Guatemalan Jesuit, was at the time a doctoral candidate in anthropology. He combined his participation in the Jesuits' pastoral work in Aguilares with ethnographic fieldwork for his thesis, which was eventually published in the form of the book referred to in this text.

29. Christian base communities were "working groups of lay people who applied progressive interpretations of Church teachings to the political and social issues of the time" (Kruijt 2008, 49).

30. Various references to such incentives can be found in Cabarrús's 1983 study (200, 236, 249–50, 280).

31. Christian Federation of Salvadoran Peasants.

32. Nationalist Democratic Organization.

33. See Gordon (1989, 185). The two most important government institutions offering rural development projects at the time were Fomento y Cooperación Comunal (FOCCO; Community Development and Cooperation) and the Banco de Fomento Agropecuario (BFA; Agricultural Development Bank). Both used ORDEN networks as channels into rural communities.

34. Available documentation on ORDEN and Salvadoran paramilitaries in general is scarce, and, beyond Cabarrús, scholarship so far holds few empirical data on the local rural dynamics of paramilitary organization and its development in relation to the emerging conflict. Mazzei provides the best historical overview study of Salvadoran paramilitary organizations (2009). More-general accounts that also ponder the role of the paramilitary structures include Ching, López Bernal, and Tilley (2007), Menjívar Ochoa (2006), Pyes et al. (2004), Stanley (1996), and United Nations (1993).

35. Salvadoran Communal Union.

36. National Conciliation Party.

37. *Compadrazgo* can be translated as "godparenthood," an important traditional institution based on bonds of reciprocity between godparents on the one hand and their godchildren and the children's families on the other. For descriptions of the institution of compadrazgo in El Salvador, see Martín-Baró (1973) and Montes (1978).

38. For example, while in the community of El Jicarón, the organizers built the local group in explicit opposition to the wealthiest man in town and those families allied with him (260–61), and in the community of El Rodeo the organizers built the local group around the support of the wealthiest family in town (Cabarrús 1983, 225–26).

39. Confirming this view, Anaya Montes argues that in the early 1970s "there are a great many institutions or organizations that in one way or the other control the peasant" (1972, 75), and lists several pages of specific examples of organizations, programs, and projects existing in the Salvadoran countryside in the late 1960s and early 1970s. Referring particularly to the case of Chalatenango, Bataillon argues that the changes of the 1950s and 1960s lead to a situation in which "subsistence farmers modulate their relationships with local elites through the clergy, the State and the military" (2008, 115).

40. Chris van der Borgh points out that the cooperative peasant movement in Chalatenango in the 1970s already received funding from Dutch and German NGOs (2003, 80). More details on different projects related to the cooperative movement and the churches are available in Chávez (2010).

41. Interviews with Carmen (December 14, 2009) and "Reyes" (March 31, 2010). An example of the PDC nationwide expansion in the 1960s is the fact that this party won over a third of El Salvador municipal governments in the 1966 elections, including San Salvador (Bataillon 2008, 103).

42. The links between the PMOs and the Catholic Church networks were facilitated through the existence of previous relations of a good part of the militant students with Catholic youth organizations, particularly Acción Católica Universitaria Salvadoreña (ACUS; Salvadoran Catholic University Action) and Juventud Estudiantil Católica (JEC; Catholic Student Youth). I thank Alberto Martín Alvarez for pointing this out to me.

43. Interview with Reyes (March 31, 2010).

44. Union of Rural Workers.

45. Alas refers here to the different PMOs that eventually integrated into the FMLN. However, in 1975 the panorama of the revolutionary organizations was still slightly different: the RN was in the process of splitting off from the ERP. The PRTC did not yet exist, and the PCS had not set up its military arm yet, but was nevertheless also politically active in the countryside. By the late 1970s, political control of the peasant communities in and around the Guazapa area was mostly in the hands of the RN, the FPL, and a small contingent supportive of the PCS.

46. The participation of different PMOs in the dispute over the bases around Suchitoto was related to the fact that the Alas brothers did promote liberation theology, but were not recruited at the time by a specific PMO. Therefore, they allowed different groups to enter their area of influence. In several cases, priests who had already been recruited or were collaborating closely with a specific PMO functioned as gatekeepers, keeping other PMOs out of their area of influence (Alas 2003, 237; Cabarrús 1983, 146). This factor helps explain the territorial distribution of the areas of influence of the different PMOs that later integrated into the FMLN. Clergy influenced by liberation theology represented a significant sector in El Salvador's Catholic Church in the early to mid-1970s, but did not dominate the entire church. "Outside the Archdiocese of San Salvador, . . . most of the other dioceses had conservative bishops who prevented individual pastoral agents from forming Christian base communities or other parish-based projects" (A. Peterson 1997, 56). Documented examples of pastoral work overflowing into revolutionary peasant organizing include David Rodriguez's work in San Vicente and La Paz (Gibb 2000; Sánchez 2015), Miguel Ventura's work in Morazán (Binford 1999; M. López Vigil 1987), the brothers Alas in Suchitoto (Alas 2003) and Rutilio Grande in Aguilares (Cabarrús 1983; Cardenal 1986), and Benito Tovar in Chalatenango (Ascoli 2001; Chávez 2010). These areas also became the most important guerrilla battlefronts during the 1980s.

47. Almeida and Urbizagástegui identified fifty popular musical groups that worked with the insurgents between 1975 and 1992 (1999, 13).

48. Several urban parishes set up Christian base communities and promoted radical political organizing in ways similar to the one described by Cabarrús. Examples include Father Ernesto Barrera in Ciudad Delgado, Father Alfonso Navarro en San Salvador, Father Rafael Palacios en Santa Tecla, and Father Octavio Ortíz in San Antonio Abad. The book *La semilla que cayó en tierra fértil* (Consejo de Mujeres Misioneras por la Paz 1996) provides testimonies from participants in urban Christian base communities. A few Protestant churches also developed similar communities, for example the Emmanuel Baptist Church. Its pastor, Augusto Cotto, became one of the leaders of the RN. Anna Lisa Peterson offers a comprehensive overview of the experience of Christian base communities in El Salvador (1997). On the part of the high school students, the largest organization was Movimiento Estudiantil Revolucionario de Secundaria (Revolutionary Movement of High School Students; MERS), affiliated with the FPL (Harnecker 1993, 124).

49. Democratic Nationalist Union.

50. Dagoberto Gutiérrez, one of the leaders of the Salvadoran Communist Party in the 1970s, wrote a well-known essay reflecting on these debates called "Nuestra polémica con la ultraizquierda" (M. Hernández 2009). See also PCS (2011, 103).

51. Interviews with Demetrio (June 29, 2009) and Rafael (December 1, 2009). See also Chávez (2010) and M. Hernández (2009).

52. Disputes focused mainly, though not exclusively, on the matter of how military and organizational efforts should be linked for maximum revolutionary leverage. The ERP, for example, argued in favor of preparing a popular insurrection, while the FPL organized for lengthy and sustained confrontation (Dunkerley 1985; Harnecker 1983; M. McClintock 1985).

53. For a discussion of the different ideological currents among the Salvadoran PMOs in the 1970s, see Byrne (1996, 33–43).

54. The Revolutionary Popular Bloc.

55. The Unified Popular Action Front.

56. February 28 Popular League.

57. Former RN comandante Macías Mayora claims the RN war chest at some point amassed $50 million (1997, 285) (unless otherwise noted, all references to dollars are to US dollars). This seems a bit steep. But several authors agree that successful kidnapping operations in the late 1970s and early 1980 did provide the RN with very substantial resources (M. Hernández 2009; Rico Mira 2003). On the other hand, according to some sources, the ERP might have lost a substantial part of the money accumulated through kidnappings when Alejandro Rivas Mira, the organization's top leader, deserted and reportedly took a significant amount of money with him, leaving most of the responsibility for leadership of the ERP in the hands of Joaquín Villalobos (M. Hernández 2009, 122). Interview with Demetrio (May 19, 2009).

58. For an interesting debate on the historical value of Dalton's rendering of Mármol's story, see the works by Lindo Fuentes, Ching, and Lara Martínez (2010) and Gould and Lauria-Santiago (2008).

59. Similarly, FPL's Cayetano Carpio wrote an account of his detention and torture by the Salvadoran authorities during the 1960s, called *Secuestro y Capucha* (1979), while PRTC's Nidia Díaz published a testimonio of her captivity during the civil war (1988). See also Stephen (1994).

60. For an edited volume on the role of writers in the Salvadoran revolution, see Yánez et al. (1985).

61. The best-known Salvadoran revolutionary bands were Yolocamba I-ta (FPL), Cutumay Camones (ERP), and Banda Tepehuani (PCS) (Judson 2002).

62. Eastern Region Agriculturalist Front; Female Front.

63. The most comprehensive account of D'Aubuisson's efforts to organize a clandestine militant right-wing movement in the period 1979–81 can be found in Galeas (2004), especially in the extensive interview featured there with Fernando Sagrera. Escobar Galindo coined the idea of D'Aubuisson as the artifice of El Salvador's "militant right" (2002, 87). See also Melara Minero (2012) and Sprenkels (2011).

64. Scholars Paul Almeida (2008) and Charles Brockett (2005) recently dedicated book-length studies theorizing on this phenomenon in their respective analyses of the Salvadoran "protest cycle" that preceded the civil war. Brockett calls this the "protest-repression paradox," something he encountered in his research on both El Salvador and Guatemala. It reads as follows: "Repression generally succeeds in smothering contention if the prior level of mobilization was low. However, if state violence is increased after a protest cycle/cycle of contention is well underway, this repression is more likely to provoke even higher levels of challenge, both nonviolent and violent, rather than deter contention" (2005, 327). For Almeida, the 1960s in El Salvador constituted a period of relative political liberalization, laying the groundwork for civil society groups to organize to defend their interest. Subsequently, "if regimes close down this political opening they risk much more disruptive and violent forms of political action by the newly disenfranchised but organized groups" (2008, 217).

65. Interviews with Carmen (December 14, 2009) and "Herminia" (December 4, 2009).

66. I refer to the rural areas with active popular church parishes during the 1970s. References can be found in Ascoli (2001, 44–51), Sprenkels (2001, 51–57; 2009, 19) and van der Borgh (2003, 103–6).

67. This estimate is based on the annex of the UN Truth Commission report (United Nations 1993) and confirmed by the more comprehensive list of victims presented by Comité Pro-Monumento for the Monument for Civilian Victims of El Salvador's Civil War, located in the Cuscatlán park of San Salvador (Comité Pro-Monumento 2001). The UN Truth Commission, by mandate, did not take into account any acts of violence that occurred before 1980, omitting 1970s cases from its report.

68. An example of such an improvised camp was in the Chalatenango hamlet of Las Aradas. The refugees chose the place because it was far from military outposts and on the other side of the Sumpul River from Honduras. They would thus be able to move into Honduras should the army get too close. On May 14, 1980, heavy rains had swollen Sumpul's current. The Honduran army closed off the Honduran side of the river, collaborating with the massacre perpetrated by the Salvadoran forces. The refugees at Las Aradas had only a few pistols at their disposal for defense. Between three hundred and six hundred people were assassinated, the second-worst massacre of the war (Morales and Navas 2006; Sprenkels 2015; United Nations 1993).

69. See Sprenkels (2001, chap. 3).

70. Little has been written on the urban clandestine guerrilla organizing in El Salvador. Manlio Argueta's novel *Caperucita en la Zona Roja* (1977) describes some of the early clandestine urban dynamics in the 1970s. Rico Mira (2003) offers a personal account of his experience within the RN. García Dueñas and

Espinoza (2010) and M. Hernández (2009) focus on the details around the assassination of Roque Dalton, thus offering a glimpse into the urban dynamics of the ERP in the mid-1970s. Sprenkels (2001) includes a chapter dedicated to FPL safe houses during the 1980s. For an excellent insiders account of the urban guerrilla in Guatemala in 1981 (with many parallels to the Salvadoran experience) see Payeras (1987). A recent book by Galeas (2013) offers an partially novelized account of the internal dynamics of the first years of the ERP.

71. Gilberto told me this as we were traveling together from Mexico to El Salvador. He had left the FPL in 1983, after Carpio's suicide, and was returning to El Salvador for the first time after years of exile. His brother, a member of the FPL leadership, had arranged for him to travel together with us.

72. Democratic Revolutionary Front.

73. In spite of support from Cuba and Nicaragua, the insurgents lacked weaponry. One RN comandante from Guazapa stated that during the offensive he had led three hundred to four hundred combatants and only sixty had rifles (cited in Montgomery 1995a, 117). The situation was similar on other fronts. The other organizations accused the ERP of hoarding the weapons that came in via Nicaragua. Because of how the different PMOs were positioned in the military fronts throughout the country, the ERP controlled the main routes to and from Nicaragua. Interview with José (November 15, 2009).

74. Brian Bosch, former US military adviser and scholar of El Salvador's civil war, estimates that by late 1980 the FMLN had four thousand full-time combatants (1999, 61). Estimates of the total number of effective guerrillas vary according to sources and were also manipulated in relation to the objectives of the war. In a 1981 interview, one FMLN commander placed the insurgency's strength at four thousand armed guerrillas and more than five thousand militia members (cited in Montgomery 1995a, 116).

75. Interviews with Beatriz (February 12, 2010), "Dolores" (December 2, 2009), "Fidel" (December 2, 2009), José (November 15, 2009), "Moisés" (August 27, 2009), Rafael (December 1, 2009), "Rogelio" (December 10, 2009), "Sebastián" (September 12, 2009), and "Umberto" (May 15, 2009).

76. Starting in 1980, Salvadoran insurgents set up various press agencies, such as SALPRESS (Agencia Salvadoreña de Prensa/Salvadoran Press Agency; FPL affiliated), COMIN (Comando International de Información/International Information Commando; ERP affiliated), NOTISAL (Agencia de Información y Análisis de El Salvador/El Salvador Information and Analysis Agency; PCS affiliated), and AIP (Agencia Independiente de Prensa/Independent Press Agency; RN affiliated), all operating in Managua and/or Mexico City (Leonhard 1999, 16).

77. Masses.

78. Interviews with Carmen (December 14, 2009) and Justo (August 20, 2009).

79. Different accounts of these large-scale military operations and the en-suing guindas can be found in Ascoli (2001), Binford (1997), Bourgois (1982), Danner (1994), de Witte (1989), Metzi (1988), Pearce (1986), Serrano Serrano and León Castillo (2017), Sprenkels (2001, 2002), Todd (2010), and Wright (1994).

80. Interview with "David" (December 20, 2009).

81. Todd (2010) provides the most extensive account of the refugee camps in Honduras.

82. Interview with Carmen (January 7, 2010). *Compañera* roughly translates as "comrade" or "partner." *Caramba* is a common expression meaning roughly "wow" or "dammit."

83. A few scholars have pointed out that the Salvadoran guerrilla frequently recruited children (Courtney 2010; Verhey 2001). From what I learned, among the peasant guerrilla supporters it was considered normal that boys could become fighters in the guerrilla forces at around fourteen or fifteen years of age. Some-times, younger boys would perform various tasks for the guerrilla, like that of a messenger or auxiliary. The participation of underage girls in various tasks was not uncommon either. Courtney estimates that around 20 percent of the Salva-doran guerrilla forces were made up of child soldiers (2010, 524). Verhey indicates that in the Salvadoran Armed Forces fresh recruits would frequently be under eighteen years of age—estimates run up to 80 percent (2001, 7).

84. The PCS-FAL had difficulty recruiting because they did not have a sig-nificant peasant constituency. As part of an internal FMLN agreement, the PCS-FAL was allowed to start working and recruiting in Mesa Grande in the mid-1980s. However, the refugees were already organized into two blocks: the RN and the FPL, the latter being the largest force. The PCS-FAL was able to overcome this obstacle in part by offering potential combatants better conditions for incor-poration, like boots, clothes, and stipends. Thus, the PCS-FAL was also able to in-corporate some members from Mesa Grande. Interviews with "Arturo" (June 29, 2011) and "Pablo" (June 29, 2011).

85. For an extensive description of the use of militia forces by the Salva-doran PMOs, see Moroni Bracamonte and Spencer (1995, 67–71).

86. For description and analysis of the role of women in the FMLN, see Kampwirth (2004); Luciak (2001); Rivera et al. (1995); Vázquez, Ibáñez, and Mur-guialday (1996); and Viterna (2013).

87. Metzi (1988) describes FPL health work during the 1980s in Chalat-enango. Espinoza (2007) provides a retrospect on the work of a physician at the service of the FPL. FUNDABRIL (2012) offers a structured and detailed account on the organization and evolution of the health system within the FPL for two war fronts (Chalatenango and Cuscatlán-Cabañas).

88. Interview with Carmen (December 14, 2009). Carmen coordinated ex-pansion work for the FPL in one area of Chalatenango between 1983 and 1985.

89. In this operation, FPL Special Forces had the lead, supported by regular FPL guerrilla forces as well as RN and FAL troops. See David Spencer (1996) and Salazar (2016) for detailed accounts.

90. The case described by Macías Mayora is an example of an infiltrator who reached a high position in the organization and worked for several years in coordination with the enemy while participating in the PMO. Macías Mayora ventures that "maybe in the 'successful' work of [the infiltrator]—and his successors—an explanation can be found for the successes of the Armed Forces in the western part of El Salvador, and to the very weak or non-existent presence of the FMLN in Santa Ana, for the duration of the war" (1997, 280). Investigative journalist Tom Gibb offers an extensive account of this case of infiltration in the RN and the destruction it caused (2000).

91. Recall the earlier reference in this chapter to the RN war chest obtained through kidnappings and bank robberies in the 1970s (under "Mass Organizations and PMO Expansion").

92. Interview with José (December 3, 2009). José, a former FPL midlevel cadre, was present in Managua at the time of the events and later participated in the FPL's international work.

93. The FPL split-off organization would become known as "la Fracción" and operate militarily under the name of Frente Clara Elizabeth Ramírez or simply Frente Clara, which had been the name of the FPL's urban front in and around San Salvador. Another group of FPL dissidents formed an organization called Movimiento Obrero Revolucionario (MOR) (Alvarenga 1993; Morales Carbonell 1999). According to José, the latter gained some international support halfway into the 1980s. The former continued to operate militarily and politically for several years, but in the margins, mainly in San Salvador and around the university. They were harassed by the PMOs integrated into the FMLN, especially by the FPL. Interviews with "Antonio" (July 29, 2009), José (December 3, 2009), and Umberto (May 15, 2009).

94. Interview with José (December 3, 2009). See also Morales Carbonell (1999).

95. Interviews with David (December 20, 2009), "Félix" (March 6, 2010), and "Tino" (July 16, 2009). For more details, see chap. 6 on the life trajectories of guerrilla fighters.

96. Benítez Manaut claims the volume of insurgent troops initially fell from some twelve thousand in 1983 to roughly six thousand in 1986 (1988, 11). See also Bosch (1999).

97. Local Popular Power.

98. Field notes (November 22, 2009).

99. Francisco Metzi, a Swiss internationalist who worked for the FPL in Chalatenango from 1982 to 1985, comments on the basic organizational structure of the Chalatenango Front in this period, situating the PPL under the FPL's

military and political command (1988, 219). On the issue of adaptation, he wrote: "The people's war is a school for the emerging society that wages it. Mobility and change are permanent, not just in terms of spaces and places, but the forms and the structures as well" (1988, 12).

100. Field notes (November 22, 2009).

101. An important contributor to international pressure on human rights performance was the Central American peace process, initiated with Contadora sessions (1983–85) and continued in Esquipulas I and II (1986–87).

102. Two-faced power.

103. Interview with José (December 3, 2009).

104. Ibid.

105. Interview with "Napoleón" (February 23, 2011).

106. On the repopulation movement see Cagan and Cagan (1991), Compher and Morgan (1991), Edwards and Tovar Siebentritt (1991), Lungo, Umaña, and Rivero (1996), Macdonald and Gatehouse (1995), A. Peterson (2005), Sollis (1992), and Todd (2010).

107. Among other sources, based on interviews with "Anastasio" (December 15, 2009), "Angela" (May 11, 2009), Dolores (December 2, 2009), "Felipe" (January 30, 2010), Félix (March 6, 2010), José (December 15, 2009), and "Marcelo" (March 31, 2010).

108. Even though the government and the guerrilla soon resumed negotiations, and this time with very serious intent to reach an agreement, intense and sustained military confrontation continued in the years 1990 and 1991. These military actions were seen mainly as operations designed to send (symbolic) messages to the negotiation table. Interview with "Evaristo" (December 15, 2009).

109. The quick postoffensive regrouping of the urban networks was demonstrated by the 1990 May Day parade, dominated by the revolutionary groups and with a reported eighty thousand people marching (Fitzsimmons and Anner 1999, 106). See also Wood (2003, 172, 184) and Sprenkels (2005, 66–67).

110. In table 2.1, the category "mixed" refers to organizations combining grassroots work with tasks typical for NGOs, such as fund-raising and project implementation. Table 2.2 excludes organizations affiliated to Salvadoran PMOs operating outside El Salvador. Several social organizations were themselves composed of smaller organizations at the grassroots level. For example, FENASTRAS, controlled by the RN, consisted of a federation of twenty-one smaller labor unions which all held close ties to the RN. Similarly, FEASIES federated three of such unions within the sphere of the FPL, while the FUSS united five small PCS-aligned unions (Stewart and Jiménez 1993). These three labor federations appear as three single organizations in tables 2.1 and 2.2. Similarly, the ERP-linked NGOs CIAZO (education) and ASPS (health care) started out as programs embedded in the larger NGO FASTRAS and evolved into separate NGOs toward the end of the war. Organizations with historical roots from before the emergence

of the PMOs, such as the teachers' union ANDES and several of the trade unions, were known to suffer from internal disputes between members linked to different PMOs.

111. Interview with "Martín" (February 20, 2012).

112. The parties participating in the Democratic Convergence alliance were the MNR (Movimiento Nacional Revolucionario/Revolutionary National Movement), the MPSC (Movimiento Popular Social Cristiano/Popular Social Christian Movement), and the PSD (Partido Social Demócrata/Social Democratic Party) (Montgomery 1995a, 208). Later, the UDN, a party set up by the PCS in 1970, would also join the CD (see chap. 4).

113. National Union of Salvadoran Workers.

114. Human Rights Commission of El Salvador.

115. To illustrate the extent of the PMOs' political control, one of the cadres in charge of political work within the UES explained to me that, after 1984, the decision of who was to become the new rector of the UES would be made by the General Command of the FMLN. Interview with Umberto (May 15, 2009). On the influence of the FMLN in the UES, also see Grenier (1999).

116. General Association of Salvadoran University Students.

117. Quezada and Martínez (1995) present several cases of smaller organized student organizations linked to specific PMOs during the late 1980s and early 1990s, but these groups were not very stable, and I have not been able to establish which ones were actually active in 1991.

118. As explained earlier in this chapter (see under "Involving the Peasants in the Revolution"), the relationship between the FPL and the Jesuits goes back to the Aguilares experience, one of the FPL founding pillars. Several Jesuit priests and seminarians became part of the FPL in the 1970s and early 1980s. In 1992, one member of the FPL's top leadership (the fifteen-member political commission) was an active Jesuit priest, and another former Jesuit and top FPL leader had recently been killed. (Antonio Cardenal, Comandante "Jesús Rojas," was killed, together with several staff members, on April 11, 1991, in an army ambush in Chalatenango.) Several other FPL leaders and cadres had close historical ties with the Jesuits.

119. Interview with José (December 15, 2009). Abundant material on international solidarity work around El Salvador can be found in the archives of the International Institute of Social History (IISH) in Amsterdam. Documentation reaches into the mid-1990s and includes internal documents of some of these committees.

120. Interviews with "Emanuel" (August 28, 2007), José (December 15, 2009), and "Mauricio" (December 12, 2007).

121. As it turned out, in the 1992–95 period, ensuring adequate international financing proved to be more difficult than anticipated. The lack of funding became one of the most serious threats to the peace process. Chief ne-

gotiators and high-ranking UN personnel had to work many extra hours and exert severe political pressure in order to procure acceptable levels of financial support for implementation of established agreements. Interview with Martín (August 26, 2009).

122. Extensive accounts of the negotiations can be found in Juhn (1998), McCormick (1997), and Samayoa (2002).

123. For a description of life and community in urban guerrilla safe houses, the most thorough account comes from Payeras (1987) on the guerrilla in Guatemala. Sprenkels (2001, 177–243) and Ward (2011) offer accounts on urban safe houses sustained by the FPL guerrilla, including Salvadoran operations in Honduras. For extensive descriptions of daily life at the front line in El Salvador, see (among others), for the FPL, Metzi (1988), Perales (1986), and Shaull (1990); for the ERP, Ibarra Chávez (2009) and Vásquez and Escalón Fontan (2012).

124. Interview with "Miriam" (March 6, 2009).

125. Interview with Beatriz (January 23, 2010).

126. Interview with Máximo (August 27, 2009).

127. The definition Lalich offers of a transcendent belief system is the following: "The overarching ideology that binds adherents to the group and keeps them behaving according to the group's rules and norms. It is transcendent because it offers a total explanation of past, present, and future, including a path to salvation. Most important, the group also specifies the exact methodology, or recipe, for the personal transformation necessary to qualify one to travel on that path" (2004, 17). Lalich's work is inspired, among other sources, by her personal experience as a militant of a Marxist-Leninist political party in the United States.

128. For a former militant's testimony concerning the level of dedication to the revolutionary cause, see Sprenkels (2001, 180–81).

129. Consider the declarations by former FAL comandante Dagoberto Gutiérrez in a 2010 interview. "Did the FMLN exist? No. What existed then? Five organizations. The political understanding between five organizations was called FMLN. But, besides the five organizations nothing else existed. There never was anything else! We decided everything in the political commissions of the five organizations, which was what really existed." "Plática con Dagoberto Gutiérrez: Me hice comunista a partir de mi experiencia con Dios," *El Faro*, August 29, 2010, http://www.elfaro.net/es/201008/el_agora/2340/?st-cuerpo=3.

130. For the 1970s, the best sources indicating distrust and strife among different insurgent groups are these organizations' own clandestine publications (see, e.g., FLACSO and Fundación Gallardo 2011). Recent investigative work into the assassination of revolutionary militant and poet Roque Dalton at the hands of fellow ERP members is also illustrative (García Dueñas and Espinoza 2010). Furthermore, M. Hernández documented several instances of interinsurgent violence in the 1970s, including the assassination of members of rival left-wing groups (2009). For the 1980s, exemplary cases include the internal crisis and

split-off in the FPL (Morales Carbonell 1999; Rojas 1986) and divisive struggles over internal hegemony within the insurgency (Grenier 1999; Zaid 1981). Distrust among former insurgents continued in the 1990s. Joaquín Villalobos, for example, accused rival FMLN leaders of manipulating the implementation of the peace accords (1999).

131. For diverse reflections on the personal costs of Salvadoran insurgent participation, see Rivera et al. (1995) and Sprenkels (2001, 2002).

132. In the case of Roque Dalton, for example, political differences with the ERP leadership at the time emerged, as well as an accusation that he was an infiltrated CIA agent (Didion 1983, 33; García Dueñas and Espinoza 2010).

133. Based on Byrne (1996, 104), Macías Mayora (1997, 279–88), Perales (1986, 107–12), and interviews with David (December 2, 2009), Ever (December 15, 2009), and "Luis" (January 12, 2010; January 22, 2012).

134. More on this episode in chap. 5.

135. Well-known defections of insurgent leaders include those of Comandante "Alejandro Montenegro" (ERP) in 1983, "Miguel Castellanos" (FPL) in 1985, and Pablo Salvador Cárcamo (FPL) in 1989. See Hudson (1988), Menzel (1994), and Rojas (1986). Accused of collaborating with the enemy, Miguel Castellanos (real name: Napoleón Romero) was assassinated by an FPL commando in 1989 (United Nations 1993, 252–53).

136. The PCS-FAL constituted a partial exception to this development. Unlike the other PMOs, it only inherited a very limited peasant constituency from the 1970s. Even though the FAL tried to amend this in the course of the war, they had to rely on combatants of urban origin to a significantly larger extent than the other PMOs.

CHAPTER 3. INTERLUDE

1. A pupusería is a place where a typical Salvadoran dish is served: *pupusas*, a kind of tortilla filled with cheese, beans, pork, etc.

2. Short for *compañeros* (comrades).

3. One of the slogans the FMLN used after the signing of the peace accords.

4. Central American University "José Simeón Cañas."

5. FECCAS stands for Federación Cristiana de Campesinos Salvadoreños (Christian Federation of Salvadoran Peasants), and UTC for Unión de Trabajadores del Campo (Union of Rural Workers). The most comprehensive account of these organizations' origins, growth, and dissolution into the guerrilla can be found in Cabarrús (1983).

6. In 2000 I conducted an extensive biographical interview with Jon Cortina which offers a detailed personal account of his accompaniment of the peasant movement and the repopulated communities (Sprenkels 2009).

7. Accounts of the work I was involved in during the 1990s in Chalatenango can be found in Sprenkels (2001, 2015) and Ward (2011).

8. Association for the Search for Disappeared Children.

9. I worked for Pro-Búsqueda from 1994 until 2002, fulfilling, in turn, the roles of head of research, general coordinator, and adviser. For more information on this organization and its activities, see Sprenkels (2001, 2003b, 2015) and Ward (2011) or visit the institutional website (www.probusqueda.org.sv).

10. Juan Serrano's testimony can be found in Serrano Serrano and León Castillo (2017).

11. Central American term for someone that traffics human beings to the North in exchange for payment.

12. I do not know whether the issue of Galán's pickup truck was discussed in the FPL's political commission and what measures, if any, were taken. At the time, I heard contradictory declarations on this topic from different leaders. What I do know is that the matter was not satisfactorily clarified to the broader Chalatenango FPL constituency and that the irritation this incident had caused continued to be felt long afterwards. After Galán's death, the pickup truck was taken over by his replacement. When his responsibilities in the capital increased, he left Chalatenango and took the vehicle with him to San Salvador.

13. Guerrilla combatants.

14. I offer a detailed analysis of this topic in *The Price of Peace: The Human Rights Movement in Postwar El Salvador* (2005).

CHAPTER 4. POSTINSURGENT RECONVERSION

1. Several consultants have produced "lessons learned" reports on the reintegration of the Salvadoran guerrilla (Barillas Villalta 1999; Cassafranco et al. 1997; Chávez 2008; Oliver 2000; Pampell Conaway and Martínez 2004; Segovia 2008; Denise Spencer 1997), but serious academic interest has been quite limited thus far, and it has focused almost exclusively on gender aspects.

2. See chap. 1, e.g., under "Postinsurgency as a Historically Constructed Social Field."

3. As troops assembled, an emergency program was set up to support the FMLN camps with temporary housing, food, personal items, and health care. The program cost $8.2 million and was paid for mostly by the Norwegian government (Guáqueta 2005, 15).

4. Fundación 16 de Enero (cited in Barillas Villalta 1999, 7).

5. Barillas Villalta (1999) and Fundación 16 de Enero (1993). This latter study concerns a large survey among demobilized women in 1993. Eighty-eight percent of the women that participated in the sample indicated they resided in predominantly rural municipalities in the former conflict areas, while only

12 percent resided in the cities. In fact, most of the respondents listed as their place of residence one of the repopulated communities in the former conflict zones. For original data, see Fundación 16 de Enero (1993, 23–28).

6. See, for example, FMLN (1992a and 1992b) and USAID (1994a).

7. In Spanish: De Comandantes Guerrilleros a Empresarios.

8. In the end, 598 FMLN officials participated in the program, receiving benefits amounting to US$12,000 on average. The exact extent of the benefits depended on the leadership categories assigned by the FMLN ("A" for the PMO leadership, "B" for senior cadre, and "C" for midlevel cadre), with the highest category receiving the higher personal amounts (FMLN 1992b, 1992c; Luciak 2001, 131–32; USAID 1994a, 36).

9. Based on USAID (1994a, 35–38). The complete list of NRP reinsertion programs with corresponding numbers of FMLN beneficiaries by the end of 1994 reads as follows: 1. scholarships for ex-combatants (690); 2. agricultural and vocational training (7,870); 3. livestock and agricultural technical assistance for ex-combatants (6,000); 4. agricultural credit and technical assistance for farmers (5,473); 5. microenterprise development for ex-combatants (1,156); 6. land transfer for ex-combatants (2,712 ex-combatants and 6,157 FMLN squatters) (note: these are the 1994 figures; the final figures were much higher); 7. emergency shelter for ex-combatants (571); 8. agricultural starter kits (8,800); 9. household furnishings (10,747); 10. academic refresher course (415); 11. Plan 600 (598); 12. assistance for war-wounded (2,500).

10. By January 1995, 6,311 ex-combatants (of a total of 7,500 planned beneficiaries) had benefited from housing projects in any of three different categories: provisional, progressive, and permanent (Sención Villalona 1995, 85–86). Some additional housing program projects were implemented at a later stage, granting some kind of housing assistance to most rural ex-combatants.

11. See USAID 1994a, 35–38. Plan 600 is not contemplated in these figures. In practice, Plan 600 was mostly granted as an additional benefit "on top of" of participation in other tracks. The extent to which the FMLN officers took advantage of the reintegration possibilities available varied.

12. In Spanish: Fondo de Protección de Lisiados y Discapacitados a Consecuencia del Conflicto Armado.

13. Based on the bulletin *Al Tope*, no. 11–12 (2002): 5–12, published by Asociación de Lisiados de Guerra de El Salvador "Héroes de Noviembre del 89" (ALGES; Association of War-Wounded of El Salvador, Heroes of November '89). See also "Lisiados de Guerra: Saldando Viejas cuentas," *Voces Semanario*, February 5–11, 2010.

14. The evaluations nonetheless contribute limited insight on the quality and sustainability of the reintegration achieved. One assessed that "practitioners [wrongly] defined reinsertion as a move back into pre-conflict communities, [while] ex-combatants tended to have expectations of social mobility" (CREA

1996, 38). A Central American overview study on reintegration also echoes that "[rural] ex-combatants in many cases had no real agricultural vocation" (Bendaña 1999, 112).

15. Interview with Umberto (May 20, 2009). COPAZ was the National Commission for Peace Consolidation.

16. See SIEP (2009). This veteran PCS leader describes the separation as follows:

> In practice it is perceived that the UDN uses a different discourse than that within the FMLN. It was urgent to resolve [the situation]. And so we did. A political agreement was reached by which those who wished to continue within the UDN were free to do so, but no longer as PCS militants. The Fundación Cuscatlán was left to the UDN along with furniture, equipment, and three months' salary for the leadership. It was an amicable and democratic separation agreement. Later the UDN, together with the MPSC and the MNR, created the Democratic Convergence. And thus ended the relationship between the UDN and the PCS, weeks after the signing of the peace accords.

17. Interview with Umberto (May 20, 2009). Umberto was a senior staff member of the Fundación Cuscatlán at the time. In 1993, he publically denounced death threats and attacks from PCS militants directed at the Fundación Cuscatlán office and at him personally. He also affirms that "the Communist Party killed the Foundation; they cut off all contacts" that allowed for the external funding of projects.

18. Editorial of *El Diario de Hoy*, March 19, 1993.

19. *Diario Latino*, March 18, 1993.

20. The Truth Commission included detailed descriptions of ten exemplary cases in the chapter dedicated to FMLN violence: nine cases of individual or multiple assassinations and one case regarding kidnapping. Of these, responsibilities were attributed and confirmed in eight cases: PRTC, 1; FAL, 1; FPL, 1; ERP, 2; and FMLN, 2, these last two without a faction being specified. In two of the described cases, one with alleged links to the FPL and another to the ERP, the Truth Commission was unable to establish responsibilities because it had been unable to resolve doubts and contradictions in the investigative process (United Nations 1993). See also Ladutke (2004, 111–13) and Sprenkels (2005, 70).

21. Top ERP leaders named in the report were Joaquín Villalobos ("Atilio"), Jorge Meléndez ("Jonas"), Ana Sonia Medina ("Mariana"), Mercedes del Carmen Letona ("Luisa"), Ana Guadalupe Martínez ("María"), and Marisol Galindo (United Nations 1993, 139).

22. Declarations in *Diario Latino*, March 18, 1993.

23. Ibid.

24. Interviews with Demetrio (May 26, 2009; May 29, 2009).

25. Interviews with Demetrio (June 29, 2009), Jorge (January 19, 2010), and Tino (May 29, 2009; July 16, 2009).

26. For an in-depth analysis of the political impact of the UN Truth Commission report, see Sprenkels (2012).

27. Villalobos had already advanced several elements of this position in a well-known article for *Foreign Policy* (1989).

28. For an overview of the ERP's political position in 1993, see PRS-ERP (1993b).

29. From Revolutionary Army of the People to Renovated Expression of the People.

30. Other documentation on this case includes PRS-ERP (1993a, 1993b).

31. Several ERP representatives from Usulután sent a letter to the FMLN's political commission requesting support. Interview with Jorge (January 19, 2010). Jorge also provided me with a copy of this letter.

32. Interviews with Fabio (August 28, 2009), Felipe (January 30, 2010), and Moisés (August 27, 2009).

33. Nejapa is located in the department of San Salvador, close to the capital city. Other municipalities where the FMLN won the 1994 elections were Arcatao, Las Vueltas, San José Las Flores, and San Antonio Los Ranchos (Chalatenango); Jocoaitique, Meanguera, Arambala, El Rosario, and Perquín (Morazán); Tecoluca and San Esteban Catarina (San Vicente); Suchitoto (Cuscatlán); El Paisnal (San Salvador); and Cinquera (Cabañas). Based on TSE (1994, 51). Nayelly Loya Marín (2008, 66) writes that the FMLN won sixteen municipalities in 1994, but she does not provide a list.

34. The twenty-one parliamentary seats won by the FMLN in 1994 were divided as follows: FPL, 6; PCS, 5; ERP, 5; RN, 3; PRTC, 2. See Luciak (2001, 424).

35. *Diario Latino*, May 2, 1994; *La Noticia*, May 4, 1994; *La Prensa Gráfica*, May 5, 1994.

36. "Comunicado de Prensa de la Comisión Política y Diputados del ERP y RN," *La Prensa Gráfica*, May 6, 1994.

37. Declarations in *El Diario de Hoy*, May 5, 1994.

38. Salvadoran Revolutionary Front.

39. *La Noticia*, May 6, 1994; *La Prensa Gráfica*, May 7, 1994; *El Diario de Hoy*, May 7, 1994.

40. Reprinted in *La Noticia*, May 4, 1994.

41. *La Prensa Gráfica*, May 8, 1994; *El Diario de Hoy*, May 9, 1994.

42. *La Noticia*, May 10, 1994; *El Diario de Hoy*, May 10, 1994; *Diario Latino*, May 10, 1994.

43. *El Diario de Hoy*, May 10, 1994.

44. "Expresión Renovadora del Pueblo," *Boletín Informativo*, no. 4, December 1994. The excerpt is from page 2 of the bulletin.

45. Felipe refers here to the internal conflict within the FPL that resulted in the assassination of the organization's second in command, Mélida Anaya Montes, and the suicide of its secretary general, Cayetano Carpio. See chap. 2.

46. Interview with Felipe (January 30, 2010).

47. "Resolución Final de la II Convención Nacional del FMLN," cited in Hernández Pico (1995). See also Luciak (2001, 229).

48. The PRTC formally dissolved on July 30, 1995; the PCS on August 5, 1995; and the FPL on December 9, 1995. Allison and Martín Alvarez (2012, 103) and Luciak (2001, 231).

49. Revolutionary Tendency.

50. Interviews with Angela (May 11, 2009), Emanuel (August 28, 2007), and "Ronaldo" (August 20, 2009). Field notes (March 13, 2013).

51. Democratic Party.

52. See "College Row over Guerilla [sic] Student," *Oxford Mail*, March 16, 1999, http://www.oxfordmail.co.uk/archive/1999/03/16/Oxfordshire+Archive /6636795.College_row_over_guerilla_student/.

53. Based on field notes (May 7, 2009; May 28, 2009; July 16, 2009) and interviews with "Fabio" (August 28, 2009), "Ignacio" (September 6, 2009), "Jorge" (January 19, 2010), Moisés (August 27, 2009), and Tino (May 29, 2009).

54. This document is entitled *Análisis de la situación interna del FMLN*, dated October 1995. Available in the archives of Fundación 1 de Abril (FUNDABRIL).

55. Interviews with Fabio (August 28, 2009), Ignacio (September 6, 2009), Jorge (January 19, 2010), Moisés (August 27, 2009), and Tino (May 29, 2009). See also Luciak (2001, 191).

56. FMLN, Documentos de la III Convención Nacional, available at the FMLN headquarters in San Salvador.

57. Revolutionary Socialist Current.

58. "Sobre el debate interno en el FMLN," *Proceso* 811, June 17, 1998.

59. Interviews with Emanuel (August 28, 2007), Hernán (March 11, 2010), and José (December 15, 2009).

60. Interview with Emanuel (August 28, 2007).

61. See the CRS bulletin *¡Farabundo! Corriente revolucionaria y socialista del FMLN*, no. 12, 1999, p. 2, available in the archives of FUNDABRIL.

62. After the 1999 convention, the seats in the 50-member national council were divided as follows: CRS, 25; renovadores, 19; terceristas, 6. Fabio Castillo, considered a moderate CRS follower, was elected party leader. See "Empate en el FMLN obligó a negociar," *El Diario de Hoy*, May 27, 1999.

63. During the war, Humberto Centeno participated in the PCS-FAL. The quote is from "F.M.L.N. Expels Former Presidential Candidate Facundo Guardado from Party," *NotiCen: Central American and Caribbean Affairs*, October 11,

2001, https://www.thefreelibrary.com/EL+SALVADOR%3A+F.M.L.N.+EXPELS
+FORMER+PRESIDENTIAL+CANDIDATE+FACUNDO...-a079085226.

64. Renovation Movement.

65. Social Democratic Party.

66. See "Ruptura renovadores no tiene regreso," *La Prensa Gráfica*, April 4, 2002; "Soy del FMLN," *El Diario de Hoy*, April 4, 2002.

67. United Democratic Center.

68. "Denuncias efemelenistas por asalto a la Asamblea," *La Prensa Gráfica*, December 5, 2002.

69. CORDES: Asociación para la Cooperación y el Desarrollo Comunal de El Salvador (Salvadoran Association for Communal Development and Cooperation).

70. CRIPDES: Christian Committee for the Displaced of El Salvador.

71. FUNDE: Fundación Nacional para el Desarrollo (National Development Foundation); MAM: Movimiento de Mujeres "Mélida Anaya Montes" (Mélida Anaya Montes Women's Movement); ISD: Iniciativa Social para la Democracia (Social Initiative for Democracy).

72. PROESA: Fundación Promotora de Productores y Empresarios Salvadoreños (Foundation for the Promotion of Salvadoran Producers and Entrepreneurs).

73. CODECOSTA: Coordinadora para el Desarrollo de la Costa (Coordinator for the Development of the Coast).

74. Note that the NGO affiliation to different PMOs described in this section was not really public information, even in the postwar period. Since the peace accords diminished government repression toward insurgent activists, security provisions within the different organizations linked to the insurgency were relaxed, and the affiliation of the organizations to particular factions of the FMLN ceased to be the carefully guarded secret information it had previously been. However, most NGOs did not disclose their affiliation and did not discuss the matter in public. One of the reasons for this was that few practical gains were to be obtained from showcasing historical ties to a particular faction of the insurgency. Such confessions, if no longer a security problem, could still make these organizations susceptible to criticism or scrutiny. Instead, these organizations preferred to position themselves simply as "civil society organizations," since this capacity equipped them better to court a broad array of national actors and, especially, international agencies to obtain support for different projects. These affirmations are based on my own experience in NGO work in El Salvador.

75. REDES: Fundación Salvadoreña para la Reconstrucción y el Desarrollo (Salvadoran Foundation for Reconstruction and Development).

76. CRD: Coordinadora para la Reconstrucción y el Desarrollo (Coordinator of Reconstruction and Development). Interview with Emanuel (August 28, 2007).

107. One relevant exception is that of the women's group Las Dignas, which I return to later in this chapter.

108. The description of the events around COMAFAC is based on Sprenkels (2005, 86–89). The quotations I use have previously been published in this source. COMAFAC stands for Comité de Madres y Familiares Cristianos de Presos, Desaparecidos y Asesinados (Christian Committee of Mothers and Relatives of Prisoners, the Disappeared and the Assassinated).

109. Group interview at COMAFAC (July 28, 2003). From Sprenkels (2005, 88).

110. Ibid.

111. "Pronunciamiento público COMAFAC ante el FMLN," manuscript dated April 18, 1994.

112. Group interview at COMAFAC (July 28, 2003). From Sprenkels (2005, 88). Note that the events took place in between the first and the second rounds of the 1994 presidential elections.

113. Interview with a COMAFAC member (July 17, 2003). From Sprenkels (2005, 89).

114. Ibid.

115. The remaining activists at COMAFAC blame Villalobos for using his international contacts to stop the funding. Interview with a COMAFAC member (July 14, 2003). From Sprenkels (2005, 89).

116. For an account of the internal disputes within CDH-ES during the 1990s, see Sprenkels (2005, chap. 6).

117. Interviews with Hernán (March 11, 2010), Lilian (January 23, 2010), and Sebastián (September 12, 2009).

118. More on this subject in chaps. 6 and 7. Interviews with Hernán (March 11, 2010) and Sebastián (September 12, 2009).

119. Furthermore, during the transition process the PMOs had moved a lot of senior cadres into the capital city, a relatively expensive setting, which translated into higher stipends and increased operational costs.

120. Field notes (September 15, 2011).

121. Many urban insurgents had aborted studies because of their participation in the revolution. Other beneficiaries included insurgents who had grown to adulthood during the war. They often had significant political experience, but little formal training.

122. Interview with "Ana" (November 9, 2007).

123. This combination of negotiated reforms and imposed neoliberal adjustment has prompted several scholars to characterize El Salvador's transition as "neoliberal peace" (Smith-Nonini 2010; van der Borgh 2004).

124. Interview with Lilian (January 23, 2010).

125. Quoted in Sprenkels (2005, 79).

CHAPTER 5. INSIDE CHALATENANGO'S FORMER "PEOPLE'S REPUBLIC"

1. The quote is from the back cover of Cagan and Cagan (1991).

2. For a detailed overview of this large body of literature, see Martín Alvarez and Sprenkels (2014).

3. The term *repobladores* is used locally to identify the inhabitants of the repopulations.

4. The two partial exceptions are Elisabeth Wood's well-documented account of the ERP's work with peasant supporters in Usulután during the period 1988–93 (2003) and Leigh Binford's analysis of ERP-civilian relations in northern Morazán during the war (1999).

5. As a matter of security as well as strategy, PMO ties were always denied or left unconfirmed to outsiders. For more on clandestinity, see Sprenkels (2005, chap. 4).

6. Thompson writes of twenty-five church-sponsored camps in the early 1980s (1995, 116). These camps were often located in church facilities like convents or retreats, such as Domus María, San José de la Montaña, and Planes de Renderos. Later, the Catholic Church closed several smaller camps and attempted to concentrate the displaced in larger facilities, like Calle Real, in Ciudad Delgado, and the Zaragoza camp (Americas Watch 1991, 114). Other churches, e.g., the Baptists and the Lutherans, managed smaller camps.

7. Apart from the Honduran camps, there were much smaller groups of Salvadoran peasant refugees exiled in Nicaragua, Costa Rica, and Panama (a few hundred in each country). For partial accounts of the Salvadoran refugee communities in Costa Rica, see Quizar (1998); for Panama, see Berríos Chicas (2008); for Nicaragua, see Morel (1991) and Nueva Esperanza Support Group (1999).

8. See Binford (1997, 38) and Todd (2010, 106). Interviews with Pablo (May 29, 2011), Gerardo (January 24, 2010), and Napoleón (February 23, 2012).

9. These were distributed as follows: some 12,000 in Mesa Grande, 8,400 in Colomoncagua, and 1,500 in San Antonio. Estimates based on Cagan and Cagan (1991), Compher and Morgan (1991, 4), Hammond (1993, 109), Montes (1989, 39), and Todd (2010, 90).

10. For a review of these negotiations and their political implications see CARECEN (1988), Edwards and Tovar Siebentritt (1991, chaps. 8 and 9), Schrading (1991), Todd (2010, chap. 7), and Wood (2003, chap. 5).

11. Key elements of this process were the Contadora sessions (1983–85) and Esquipulas I and II (1986–87).

12. While the Salvadoran government promoted repatriation schemes for individual families, refugee leadership pushed for collective return to areas under

FMLN influence, a proposal the government in turn rejected (van der Borgh 2003, 108).

13. The Salvadoran Catholic Church paved the way for the repopulation process by taking the lead in negotiating the 1985 repopulation of Tenancingo. Both the FMLN and the Salvadoran military agreed to respect civilians and to not establish permanent presence within the repopulated areas of Tenancingo. The repobladores in this case included nonaffiliated families, as well as FMLN supporters and government supporters. They were all original prewar inhabitants of the town. Though a few violent incidents did take place, the Tenancingo experiment confirmed that, in the political and military context of the moment, repopulation initiatives were viable (Wood 2003, 136–47). Thus, it prepared the way for the establishment of the first insurgent repopulations. Different from the case of Tenancingo, the repopulations of 1986 were directly linked to the PMOs and did not allow for noninsurgency supporters to participate (137).

14. In 1982, the Salvadoran government had set up an agency called CONADES (Comisión Nacional para los Desplazados/National Commission for the Displaced), which in subsequent years attempted to organize and care for groups of internally displaced. CONADES was connected to CONARA (Comisión Nacional para la Restauración de Areas/National Commission for Reconstruction), a multimillion-dollar US-funded rural development program fundamentally aimed at consolidating support for the government among the rural population (Sollis 1992, 51). This program included the promotion of resettlement of peasant families in areas affected by the war, in a scheme that also aimed at strengthening government control over such areas (Edwards and Tovar Siebentritt 1991, 47; Sollis 1992, 59–60). CONADES resettlement efforts were only able to enlist small numbers of people, most of whom already held political ties with the governing party or with the military (Sollis 1992, 51). CONADES furthermore assisted small numbers of displaced families that had decided to break away from the insurgency. The Salvadoran government by and large accepted the idea in itself of establishing new settlements for the displaced and the refugees. The political issues at stake were where they would be located and who would control the resettlement project.

15. Close to a hundred people participated in the occupation of the church (interview with Carmen, December 14, 2009).

16. Based on Keune (1995) and interviews with Carmen (December 11, 2008; December 14, 2009). See also Edwards and Tovar Siebentritt (1991) for a version that does not implicate the FPL.

17. I base this figure on an interview with Carmen (December 14, 2009), an FPL cadre who acted as one of the organizers of the repopulation effort. In existing written sources, the figure reported varies. Todd (2010, 197) writes that 120 *families* participated in repopulating San José Las Flores, subsequently joined by

an additional 500 local refugees previously roaming the area. Of the repobladores from Las Flores interviewed by Lou Keune, a woman identified as Juana Alberto indicated that 18 families participated in the initial repopulation effort, while Elías Menjívar mentions 26 as the number of families (Keune 1995, 241–42). A recent report on Las Flores mentions 36 families that participated in the original repopulation effort, totaling 126 individuals. See "Las Flores de la Guerra," *El Faro*, January 15, 2007, http://archivo.elfaro.net/secciones/noticias/20070115 /noticias7_20070115.asp.

18. Pastoral support would continue to be important in subsequent years. For example, the Jesuits provided accompaniment for the repopulations of northeastern Chalatenango. Some priests who had helped organize the peasant movement in the 1970s reunited with their former flock in the repopulations. Priests played important roles because they were capable of intermediating with the military. They also served as channels for relief projects. See, for example, Nueva Esperanza Support Group (1999), Sprenkels (2009, 26–33), and Wright (1994).

19. The repopulation of El Barrillo, near Suchitoto, was set up in July 1986, mostly with repobladores captured a few months earlier as masas of the RN in Guazapa during a military operation called *Operación Fénix*. Later that year, the Lutheran Church organized a repopulation to the village of Panchimilama, located south of the capital in the department of La Paz (Edwards and Tovar Siebentritt 1991, 52–59). Here, the repobladores were connected to the PCS-FAL, mostly families from San Vicente (personal correspondence with a former employee of the Lutheran Church, March 23, 2012). The FPL masas in San Vicente also attempted to create more permanent settlements, for example in San Carlos Lempa in June 1986. The military captured and evacuated eighty families only a few days after they established themselves in this abandoned community, and after a sojourn in the military garrison of Zacatecoluca, they were sent to Calle Real. From there, the next year, several families involved in the San Carlos Lempa repopulation attempt tried again, this time in the location of Santa Cruz, Berlin, in Usulután. Alvarenga and Baumgärtner 2008. See also McElhinny 2006, 349.

20. The refugees negotiated the repatriation with the Salvadoran and Honduran governments, under auspices of the Office of the United Nations High Commissioner for Refugees (UNHCR). On October 17, 1987, the first group of 4,313 refugees from Mesa Grande entered El Salvador in a massive caravan with strong international accompaniment. After the border crossing, the 110 buses and trucks split in three groups. The largest group went to repopulate Las Vueltas, Guarjila, and Arcatao, all in northeastern Chalatenango; a second traveled to Copapayo, Cuscatlán, on the edge of Cerrón Grande Reservoir; and a third to Santa Marta, Cabañas (Edwards and Tovar Siebentritt 1991, 85). In August of 1988 San Antonio Los Ranchos would be repopulated as well (Compher and Morgan 1991, 8; Todd 2010, 204).

21. Interviews with Carmen (December 11, 2008; December 14, 2009) and Pablo (May 29, 2011; February 21, 2012).

22. For a listing of different collective repatriations from Honduras, see Edwards and Tovar Siebentritt (1991, 137–38).

23. The largest RN repopulations in the area of Suchitoto were Aguacayo and El Barrillo.

24. Binford (1997), Cagan and Cagan (1991), and Macdonald and Gatehouse (1995) offer the most extensive accounts of the repopulation of northern Morazán. See also Todd (2010, 216).

25. McElhinny (2006) and Wood (2003) both document the repopulation process of the coastal plains in detail. Wood focuses on the ERP in Usulután, and McElhinny focuses on the FPL in San Vicente.

26. The repopulations affiliated with the PRTC were Nuevo Gualcho, in the Usulután department, and Nacaspilo, on the border between the departments of San Vicente and Cabañas. Besides the demobilization camp in Guazapa (Ciudadela Guillermo Ungo), the PCS-FAL founded the repopulation of Panchimilama in La Paz as well as two repopulations in Chalatenango (Las Minas and Los Alas) and a community in Jucuarán, Usulután. Interviews with Napoleón (February 23, 2012) and "Wilber" (May 17, 2009; May 19, 2009).

27. Examples can be found in Americas Watch (1991, 115), Lindsay-Poland (1989), Smith-Nonini (2010, 111–12), Sprenkels (2009, 27–34), Todd (2010, 213), and Wood (2003, 149), among others.

28. See, for example, Sprenkels (2009) for a description of several incidents in the repopulations of northeastern Chalatenango.

29. See, for example, Keune (1995, 250) and Sprenkels (2009, 27–34).

30. For examples of civilian mobilization in the repopulations, see Cagan and Cagan (1991), Keune (1995), and Sprenkels (2009). For an analysis of the role that different human rights groups and their international contacts played in defending the rights of people captured by the military in this period, see Sprenkels (2005) and Sprenkels and van der Borgh (2011).

31. Coordinator of the Repopulated Communities of Chalatenango. Shortly after the peace accords, the CCR changed its name to Coordinadora de Comunidades y Repoblaciones de Chalatenango (Coordinator of Communities and Repopulations of Chalatenango). Several years after the war it again changed its name to Coordinadora de Comunidades en Desarrollo de Chalatenango (Coordinator of Communities in Development of Chalatenango). The organization kept using the original acronym.

32. Christian Committee for the Displaced of El Salvador.

33. Interview with Carmen (December 11, 2008). For more on CRIPDES, see chap. 4, under "The NGO Boom."

34. See Binford (1999) for an analysis of PMO hegemony in Morazán. Also, interviews with Carmen (December 11, 2008; December 14, 2009), Napoleón (February 23, 2012), and Pablo (May 29, 2011; February 21, 2012).

35. Elisabeth Wood's work on the ERP in Usulután documents these land occupations extensively. From 1986 onward, the ERP was supporting local farmers in the occupation of abandoned properties to found cooperatives (2003, 166). Invading such properties helped solve the farmers' needs for land while at the same time refueling historical demands for agrarian reform (chap. 6). Wood reports on a 1992 meeting between ERP leader Villalobos and ERP supporters in Usulután, where Villalobos emphasized the need to multiply land claims to enhance the possible transfer of land to FMLN sympathizers. Villalobos furthermore indicated that this land would "form the economic base of the FMLN's future political party" (2003, 176).

36. Interview with Ignacio (July 6, 2009). Additionally, several of the guerrilla's demobilization camps also turned into permanent settlements.

37. When one includes smaller settlements, the number becomes higher. See, e.g., McElhinny (2006) and Merlos and Moreno (2004) for exhaustive listings of the repopulations in southern San Vicente.

38. Hamlet or small village.

39. Small rural district, containing one or several small villages.

40. According to "Renato," a Guancora native currently living in the city of Aguilares, the families in Guancora were uncertain who was behind this and other crimes. Renato considered that the imminence of the war fed common crime. Interview (January 22, 2012).

41. Interview with Dorotea (November 28, 2009).

42. "Everyone went off to different places, staying with family members, renting a house, boarding with friends. Aguilares, Sonsonate, Santa Ana, La Nueva [Concepción], Suchitoto. The poorest (families) went to Misata. That area was thickly overgrown, all mountainsides, and that's where people went to build their little shack." Interview with Renato (January 22, 2012).

43. According to Renato, it is unclear which group was responsible for their assassination. Interview (January 22, 2012).

44. Ibid.

45. The description of prewar Guancora and the hamlets' abandonment is based on interviews with Dorotea (November 28, 2009), Gerardo (January 24, 2010), and Renato (January 22, 2012).

46. Interview with Gerardo (January 24, 2010).

47. Interview with Marta (November 25, 2009).

48. Interview with Pablo (May 29, 2011). Also interview with Marta (November 25, 2009).

49. Interview with Pablo (May 29, 2011). In effect, Pablo led the repopulation of Guancora, but left his own family in Mesa Grande at the time. His family later also returned from Honduras and settled in Guancora.

50. Based on the life trajectories of Pablo's family and interviews with Pablo (May 29, 2011; February 21, 2012).

51. Interview with Pablo (May 29, 2011).

52. Interview with Arturo (May 29, 2011).

53. Interviews with Marta (November 25, 2009) and Pablo (May 29, 2011; June 3, 2012).

54. It was not the last repatriation; close to a thousand refugees still stayed behind. Interviews with Marta (November 25, 2009) and Pablo (January 25, 2010). Also, Edwards and Tovar Siebentritt (1991, 137).

55. Interviews with Gerardo (January 24, 2010), Marta (November 25, 2009), and Pablo (May 29, 2011).

56. Interview with Pablo (May 29, 2011).

57. Interview with Gerardo (January 24, 2010).

58. Interview with Pablo (June 3, 2012).

59. Interview with Arturo (May 29, 2011).

60. Ibid.

61. Interview with Gerardo (January 24, 2010).

62. Interview with Arturo (May 29, 2011); field notes (May 29, 2011).

63. Interview with Pablo (June 3, 2012).

64. Conversation with Pablo; field notes (February 21, 2012).

65. Interview with Gerardo (January 24, 2010).

66. Interview with Marta (November 25, 2009).

67. Interview with Arturo (May 29, 2011).

68. Field notes (May 29, 2011). Also, interviews with Medardo (January 25, 2010) and Arturo (May 29, 2011).

69. Americas Watch (1991, 158) and CODEHUCA (1992, 40); interview with Marta (November 25, 2009).

70. From the words of a song composed to commemorate the massacre. It is sung each year on February 11, at the commemoration of the massacre in Ellacuría. Field notes (February 11, 2010).

71. *La Prensa Gráfica*, February 15, 1990.

72. Based on conversation with María, mother of two of the children killed during the massacre. Field notes (February 11, 2010).

73. Ciudad Segundo Montes adopted this name on March 25, 1990, in honor of one of the Jesuits martyred by the Salvadoran army in the November 1989 massacre at the UCA (Cagan and Cagan 1991, 152). Ignacio Ellacuría, a Jesuit priest and one of El Salvador's foremost left-wing intellectuals, was also assassinated in this massacre. The Salvadoran military committed this crime in the early

morning of November 16, 1989, during the FMLN's military offensive in the capital. For more about this event and the 1989 offensive, see chap. 2.

74. Some people in the community claim that Ignacio Ellacuría himself, before he was murdered, had visited the community in the company of Jon Cortina (field notes, February 11, 2010). If true, this event could only have taken place between October 28, the day the repobladores arrived, and November 10. With the start of the offensive, on November 11, travel would have been impossible. It is now impossible to confirm this information with Jon Cortina (he died in 2005). However, in extensive interviews and personal conversations I held with Jon Cortina concerning the events of November 1989, he never mentioned this visit. Also, in the description of the inauguration of Comunidad Ignacio Ellacuría in a book dedicated to the Jesuit Martyrs of the UCA, no reference is made to Ellacuría's possible previous presence in this particular community (Carranza 1990, 324–26).

75. Tojeira's speech at this occasion is reproduced in Carranza (1990, 321–23).

76. In 1990, the FPL command in Chalatenango appointed Pablo to the FPL expansion team in the western part of Chalatenango. He returned to live in Ellacuría in 1992. Interview with Pablo (February 21, 2012).

77. I think Arturo here refers to the need to recruit in communities not yet contributing to the guerrilla army.

78. Interview with Arturo (February 3, 2010).

79. Ten out of a total of eighteen.

80. In this larger nearby repopulation, the popular education school was much larger and the popular health system was quite developed, in part due to the presence of foreign health workers and strong international support for the community.

81. Pablo points out that enemy informers were also active inside Mesa Grande, and that the different PMOs resorted to clandestine organizational techniques as well as repressive ones in order to prevent informers from damaging PMO interests.

82. Interview with Gerardo (January 24, 2010).

83. It involved a different organizational structure that operated separately from the community organization, though partially embedded within it.

84. Interview with Gerardo (January 24, 2010).

85. Guerrilla fighters frequently used elastic bands to close off the trousers above the boots. These bands left marks on the skin.

86. Interview with Gerardo (January 24, 2010).

87. Ibid.

88. Ibid.

89. Based on interviews with several former FPL combatants in Chalatenango: David (December 20, 2009), Hernán (March 11, 2010), and Justo (Au-

gust 20, 2009). With regard to the repopulation of Santa Marta, Philippe Bourgois documents a case of a female *repobladora* accused of being an informer and executed by the guerrilla (2001, 25).

90. The reconstruction of postwar events in Ellacuría is based on interviews with Ellacuría inhabitants "Medardo" (January 25, 2010), Arturo (February 3, 2010; May 29, 2011), Marta (November 25, 2009), "Nicolás" (February 22, 2012), Pablo (May 29, 2011; February 21, 2012), Rigoberto (January 25, 2010), Santos (February 21, 2012), Severina and Santos (March 1, 2010), and Yancy (February 22, 2012), as well as notes taken during fieldwork in Ellacuría.

91. Pablo points out that many FPL-affiliated families from Cabañas left Santa Marta. Most settled in communities close to Suchitoto: "A lot of people that live around Suchitoto, many people from those communities, fled from Santa Marta. They now live in Milingo [a repopulation near Suchitoto]. They now live in all those communities, those that left, fleeing from the RN." Interview (May 29, 2011).

92. According to Arturo, "The PC [PCS] projects came with a lot of resources" (interview, May 29, 2011). As was the case in other PCS-FAL-affiliated repopulations (see, for example, the case of Panchimilama, mentioned earlier in this chapter), the Lutheran Church established a local chapter in Las Minas and coordinated a range of different support projects for this repopulation.

93. Interviews with Arturo (February 3, 2010; May 29, 2011) and Nicolás (February 22, 2011).

94. Interview with Arturo (February 3, 2010).

95. The term *tenedor* refers to an occupant of land in a repopulated settlement at the end of the war.

96. See "Las Flores de la Guerra," *El Faro*, January 15, 2007, http://archivo .elfaro.net/secciones/noticias/20070115/noticias7_20070115.asp._

97. Reconstruction of the story of the repopulation of El Roble is based on an interview with Pablo (February 21, 2012); on conversations with Santos, Severina, and Yancy from Ellacuría (February 21, 2012) and with "Mariana" from El Roble (February 22, 2012), registered in field notes; and on personal communication with Yancy (February 28, 2012).

98. Interview with Renato (February 21, 2012).

99. Interview with Arturo (February 3, 2010).

100. Chris van der Borgh, reviewing postwar reconstruction in Chalatenango, describes how this "labyrinth of good intentions" increasingly entangled itself as different actors, different projects, and different development logics stumbled into each other at the community level (2003, 205).

101. A meeting house for women.

102. "The Planes de Guancora Cooperative, established in 1994, had 60 members at its height. It administered collective plots of land and distributed

credit for fertilizers and pesticides, which were paid for with the earnings from the collectively harvested grains. From 1999 onwards, the cooperative lost strength and now [2002] it is practically inactive" (Calderón Vandenberg 2002, 36–37).

103. For a description of the different NGOs active in postwar Ellacuría and their activities, see Calderón Vandenberg (2002).

104. Interview with Arturo (February 3, 2010).

105. Interviews with Medardo (January 25, 2010) and Rigoberto (January 25, 2010).

106. At the time of this research, five young people from Ellacuría were attending university: four in the capital of San Salvador, and one in a local branch of the university in Chalatenango city.

107. Conversation with Yancy; field notes (January 7, 2010).

108. Susan Bibler Coutin offers the most detailed examination thus far of the phenomenon of postwar migration from El Salvador to the United States, which includes an extensive analysis of the family dynamics associated with migrations and remittances (2007, chap. 5). For a comprehensive overview study of the phenomenon, see Andrade-Eekhoff and Silva-Avalos (2003). For a specific account of migration in relation to a repopulated community in Chalatenango, see Silber (2011).

109. Interview with Arturo (February 3, 2010).

110. Ibid.

111. Ibid.

112. Conversation with Pablo; field notes (May 29, 2011).

113. Interview with Arturo (February 3, 2010).

114. Ibid.

115. Derived from comments expressed in the Ellacuría's community survey as well as from fieldwork notes.

116. The term "contrario" was commonly used in the war to indicate someone who sympathized or participated with the enemy.

117. Field notes (February 21, 2012).

118. Interviews with Pablo (May 29, 2011; February 21, 2012), Santos (February 21, 2012), Severina and Santos (March 1, 2010), and Yancy (February 22, 2012).

119. Interview with Pablo (February 21, 2012).

120. Calderón Vandenberg found that of a total of 119 homes, 64 depended partially or completely on land assigned by the community directive for agriculture (2002, 39–40).

121. Interview with Arturo (February 3, 2010).

122. Field notes (May 29, 2011). The PTT operated with a bond system that most beneficiaries in the community found confusing and not transparent. If the beneficiary rejected a plot of land offered to them or otherwise waited too long to use their bond, they ran the risk of not being able to use it at all. Properties were

often bought by putting together several bonds to add up to the value of one property for sale, to be subdivided among individual beneficiaries later. To divide properties amongst different beneficiaries, sometimes lotteries were used to avoid accusations of favoritism. Nonetheless, as intermediaries between the bank, the owners, and the beneficiaries, the community directorate played a key role in the process of assigning who got what. Interviews with Arturo (February 3, 2010) and Santos (February 21, 2012). Calderón Vandenberg shows that seventy-three homes in Ellacuría farmed land they owned privately (2002, 40).

123. On the other hand, those favored with better lands claimed they had acted promptly when opportunities arose, while those who had waited too long often ended up having to settle for less. As a consequence, the families less favored by the PTT relied mostly on being assigned communal lands.

124. These community associations are known as Asociación de Desarrollo Comunal (ADESCO) or Communal Development Association.

125. For an extensive analysis of the role of community associations in postwar development in Chalatenango, see van der Borgh (2003).

126. Apart from the farmlands, Ellacuría's directorate and its namesakes also held most "urban" properties (properties inside the village itself), as the terrains to be used for construction had mostly been acquired with donated funds. A part of this had been transferred to the beneficiaries of housing projects in the 1990s. Other tracts had been assigned for community infrastructure, like the school, or as a location for community projects. The directorate would, furthermore, distribute small plots among community members, for example to young couples looking to establish an independent home. Some of these transactions had been met with approval; others had generated rumors and accusations regarding favoritism and misappropriation.

127. Interview with Yancy (February 22, 2012).

128. Interviews with Pablo (February 21, 2012) and Yancy (February 22, 2012). One practical factor that allegedly impeded property transfer is the fact that such a transaction implies fees for legal services and registration. Even though these costs were relatively low in relation to the value of the land, the community directorate had generally been reluctant to incur in such expenses. Since the issue of namesakes constituted a long-standing problem in several of the repopulated communities, CORDES and CCR managed a joint project a few years ago in order to address this issue. However, the results for Ellacuría were very meager. According to detractors, the reason for this was that the prestanombres conditioned their signature on receiving benefits in return, such as the cession of other community properties to their name.

129. Field notes (February 22, 2012).

130. Interview with Santos and Severina (March 1, 2010).

131. Interview with Santos (February 21, 2012).

132. Member of the National Guard.

133. The review of this family's position in the community is based on interviews with Santos (February 21, 2012) and Yancy (February 22, 2012), as well as field notes (February 21, 2012; February 22, 2012).

134. Conversation with Santos and Severina; field notes (February 21, 2012).

135. One of the issues that further colored the interpretation of this "public service" discourse in the eyes of some Ellacuría residents was that some tasks performed by community leaders could be interpreted both as service and as privilege, and separating the two could be very difficult. For example, the community directorate had a vehicle at their disposal, which was used for a range of purposes in the community. Only a few people were allowed to drive the vehicle, Arturo among them. The vehicle was used to transport Ellacuría inhabitants to the hospital in case of emergency or to take the local soccer team to matches outside the community. At the same time, the margin of control the designated drivers held over the vehicle gave them the opportunity to attend meetings outside the community, to run errands, and to provide an occasional personal favor. Interview with Yancy (February 22, 2012).

136. Paragraph based on field notes (March 2, 2010; May 31, 2011) and interviews with Arturo (February 3, 2010), Marta (November 25, 2009), and Nicolás (February 22, 2012).

137. Admittedly, the fact that he left his own family behind in Mesa Grande in 1989 and only had them repatriated when the security situation improved had dented his local reputation (see earlier in this chapter).

138. Field notes (February 21, 2012); interviews with Pablo (May 29, 2011; February 21, 2012; March 6, 2012). For more details on the postwar dispute between renovadores and ortodoxos, see chaps. 4 and 7.

139. Interview with "Sergio" (March 12, 2010).

140. Interview with Pablo (May 29, 2011). Former FPL central committee member Felipe confirmed Pablo's account regarding the arrangements and conflicts between FPL and RN in Santa Marta (interview, February 25, 2012).

141. Interview with Pablo (May 29, 2011).

142. Interview with Pablo (February 21, 2012); field notes (February 21, 2012).

143. Interview with Juan (December 12, 2009).

144. Ibid.

145. Ibid. The term "cacique" refers to the traditional strong man.

146. Ibid. As in other parts of Latin America, compadrazgo is an important social and religious institution in El Salvador, especially in the rural areas. Montes (1978) points to the importance of compadrazgo in regulating Salvadoran patron-client relations.

147. The three previous paragraphs are based on field notes (February 13, 2012).

148. The quotations below are from an interview with Alex (March 18, 2010). The other sections regarding the situation in Guarjila are based on this same interview as well as field notes (March 18, 2010).

149. Conversations with "Balbina" and Oscar; field notes (February 14, 2012).

150. The description of the initiative to legalize the name of Comunidad Ignacio Ellacuría is based on field notes (February 22, 2012) and interviews with Medardo (January 25, 2010), Arturo (February 3, 2010), and Marta (November 25, 2009).

151. Field notes (February 22, 2012).

152. Based on interviews with Pablo (January 25, 2010; May 29, 2011; February 21, 2012; June 3, 2012).

CHAPTER 6. POSTWAR LIFE TRAJECTORIES OF FORMER GUERRILLA FIGHTERS

1. "Snowballing" refers to building a sample making use of the informers' personal connections with other potential informers. See King and Horrocks (2010, 34) for a discussion of snowballing in social research.

2. Foundation for Development.

3. Field notes (July 8, 2009; January 15, 2010); interview with "María Ester" (January 15, 2010).

4. Latin American School of Medicine.

5. Field notes (July 28, 2009).

6. Field notes (December 28, 2009; January 8, 2010; January 11, 2010; July 28, 2012).

7. Museum of the Word and Image.

8. Institute for Historical, Anthropological, and Archaeological Studies.

9. I accessed potential photographs for life-trajectory reconstruction by asking former combatants I knew and by looking in the different archives I had access to. I then made a first selection of several dozen photographs based on the criteria of group size and the visibility of individual characteristics that might facilitate identification. I also tried to obtain photographs of combat units that had operated in different areas of the country and/or belonged to different factions of the FMLN. However, once I had obtained a promising photograph, it was often difficult to determine where to start with the reconstruction. Where and when was the picture taken? What political-military organization did the fighters belong to? These questions could often only be answered when someone appearing in the picture had been located. And sometimes this proved to be a difficult task. Once I had identified and located the first survivor, speaking with him or her would then provide several leads that would help speed up the process of

tracing the rest of the photograph. But finding the first one was sometimes difficult. Thus, for the largest part of my fieldwork, I carried around maps of photographs everywhere I went, in the hope of gathering bits of information that would eventually allow me to build a sizable sample. Having a better idea of whom to approach for specific bits of information regarding guerrilla units, I was able to make more headway with pictures portraying FPL units than with those of other organizations, in spite of my attempts to spread the sample.

10. One example is the delegation of Dutch journalists headed by Koos Koster, who had already visited the front on several occasions. The four journalists were murdered in 1982 by the Salvadoran army while on their way to a liberated zone in Chalatenango (Broere 2007; United Nations 1993).

11. Field notes (March 9, 2010).

12. Field notes (February 12, 2010). For example, a Salvadoran NGO called Equipo Maíz publishes a yearly calendar with hundreds of photographs of revolutionaries who fell in the struggle.

13. Interviews with Angela (May 11, 2009), "Josefina" (December 28, 2009), and "Ruth" (May 27, 2009).

14. This paragraph is based on my own recollections of this episode.

15. Interview with Wilber (May 19, 2009).

16. Insurgent leaders sometimes labeled this fear as the "M-19 scenario," in reference to how repressive forces had decimated former Colombian guerrilla organization M-19 after it publicly destroyed its weapons to participate in the 1990 elections (Dudouet 2009, 41; Sánchez-Blake 2002). Unión Patriótica, an earlier initiative by the Colombian FARC to partially demobilize and participate in an electoral process, was also met by rampant paramilitary violence, leaving thousands dead in the mid-1980s (Theidon 2007, 72). During 1993 and early 1994, the fear that Wilber and other former insurgents had felt about the possibility of renewed persecution was rekindled by a series of assassinations, attacks, and death threats on former insurgents that, the UN confirmed, were politically motivated (Morales, Pohl, and Racicot 1995, 339–407). The incidents were not enough to sabotage the FMLN participation in the 1994 election and other key aspects of the implementation of the peace accords, but they did increase apprehensions and uncertainties among former insurgents about the process as a whole. A description of the paramilitary structures behind some of the cases can be found in the report of the special UN commission that was set up to investigate remaining paramilitary structures (Grupo Conjunto 1994). See also Samayoa (2002, 620), who mentions a few additional cases that affected the FPL specifically.

17. Based on interviews with Wilber (May 17, 2009; May 19, 2009) and informal conversation with Sandro and Wilber; field notes (February 17, 2010; February 18, 2010).

18. Interview with Wilber (May 19, 2009).

19. Field notes (February 17, 2010; February 18, 2010).

20. Field notes (February 18, 2012).

21. Reconstruction of the life trajectories derived from this photograph was possible with the support of a former PRTC collaborator as well as the former platoon leader for this unit and several ex-combatants featured in the photograph.

22. As explained in chap. 2, most guerrilla fighters were of rural descent. In the period around the 1989 offensive the PMOs temporarily incorporated larger numbers of fighters of urban descent.

23. My rendering of David's story relies on a lengthy interview (December 20, 2009) as well as several informal conversations sustained in the course of the reconstruction of the photographs (field notes, June 2, 2009, and March 8, 2010). The appreciation of who David was during the war additionally relies on comments other FPL members made about him in my presence.

24. Interview with David (December 20, 2009).

25. Ibid.

26. Ibid.

27. One harboring resentments.

28. Interview with David (December 20, 2009).

29. Field notes (April 8, 2010).

30. Blood sausage.

31. He refers to her income as a deputy, a sizable salary for Salvadoran standards at the time. Rogelio's story is based on interviews (December 10, 2009; December 18, 2009) and field notes (April 8, 2010).

32. Field notes (January 12, 2010).

33. Informal conversation with Gabino in Chalatenango; field notes (March 12, 2010).

34. Field notes (January 14, 2010).

35. The reconstruction of the life trajectories was done through the cooperation of David, of one of the surviving combatants appearing in the photograph, and of several people in their respective networks.

36. Carmen described to me the case of defection of two FPL guerrilla fighters in Chalatenango. Interview (December 14, 2009).

37. Field notes (December 15, 2009).

38. Interview with David (December 20, 2009).

39. The story of Mariano is based on field notes (March 11, 2010), as well as on a long-standing personal relationship with the author.

40. Although a few earlier references to the Mayo Sibrián killings exist elsewhere (Castro 1999, 18; Gibb 2000, 321–37; McElhinny 2006, 354–58), a book called *Grandeza y miseria en una guerrilla* offers the first extensive account of the events based on testimonies of family members and some of the FPL cadres involved (Galeas and Ayalá 2008). The book caused considerable controversy, among other reasons because it was published in the midst of the campaign for the 2009 presidential election. The authors directly accused Salvador Sánchez

Cerén (Comandante "Leonel González"), at the time Mauricio Funes's running mate, of being responsible for the abuses. While Comandante "Mayo Sibrián" was in charge at the San Vicente front, Sánchez Cerén, as the organization's general secretary, was responsible for all FPL operations. The book furthermore zooms in on those elements that might help to build a case against Sánchez Cerén. In short, the authors and their informants claim that Sánchez Cerén, responsible for Sibrián within the FPL's chain of command, knew about the killings and did nothing or too little, too late to stop them. In an attempt to move beyond politicized or propagandistic views on the purges, UES historian Jorge Juárez has recently initiated an academic project on Mayo Sibrián and the San Vicente front.

41. The FPL's top leader after Carpio's death in 1983 (see chap. 2). Vice-president of El Salvador for the period 2009–14. Elected president of El Salvador for the period 2014–19. Known in the war as Comandante "Leonel González."

42. This section is based on interviews with Luis (May 29, 2009; June 4, 2009; August 14, 2009; January 21, 2010; January 22, 2010; February 9, 2010) and field notes (June 2, 2009; June 4, 2009; July 2, 2009; August 8, 2009; August 18, 2009).

43. Interview (February 9, 2010).

44. Number 10 in the photograph stayed in touch with many of his former comrades and provided most of the information for the reconstruction of the life trajectories on this picture. Two other FPL veterans, not included in the picture, contributed additional information (field notes, January 24, 2010; February 1, 2010; February 9, 2010).

45. Interview with Dolores (December 2, 2009).

46. Ibid.

47. Ibid.

48. Ibid.

49. Interview with Tino (May 29, 2009).

50. Ibid.; field notes (May 28, 2009).

51. Interview with Ignacio (July 6, 2009).

52. Based on interviews and conversations with Tino (May 29, 2009; July 16, 2009); field notes (May 28, 2009).

53. Based on interview with Segundo (May 22, 2009) and field notes (May 22, 2009; January 11, 2010; February 12, 2010).

54. Photograph 6.11 was reconstructed with the help of Moisés, Rubén, and a handful of other RN veterans. Yuri Escamilla helped facilitate the reconstruction process.

55. Field notes (January 22, 2010).

56. Interview with Moisés (August 27, 2009).

57. Interview with Beatriz (February 12, 2010).

58. Ibid.

59. The sample I present here comes with certain limitations inherent in its size and other methodological particularities. A larger sample might have shown more variation in livelihood scenarios, as well as greater precision in the relative weight of different options. Also, it is necessary to take into account that the sample represents a snapshot of the situation at the time of the reconstruction of the different life trajectories, and that, naturally, the individuals in the sample do not have "frozen" lives. Furthermore, it was impossible to verify all the life trajectory information directly with each individual portrayed. Although I spoke with many of those depicted in the photographs, for a significant number of the individuals in the sample I had to rely on information provided by their former comrades. I then double-checked available life trajectory data with at least two veterans familiar with the individual in question. A final caveat is needed on the possible effects of the distribution of the photographs in relation to the different PMOs. As I have pointed out earlier, I was more successful in my efforts with former FPL combatants than with members of the other groups. When considering the differences in size between the five PMOs, we see that the RN and the ERP are especially underrepresented in the sample (which contains only one photograph of each, showing relatively small units). This warrants some caution in our weighing of the sample findings regarding "between-PMO" distinctions. Ideally, future research efforts would look to extend the sample presented here in terms of size and in terms of enhanced representation of the different PMOs in the sample.

60. Interviews with Felipe (January 30, 2010) and Lilian (January 23, 2010).

61. Interviews with Hernán (March 11, 2010), Lilian (January 23, 2010), and Sebastián (September 12, 2009).

62. Interviews with Hernán (March 11, 2010) and Sebastián (September 9, 2009).

63. Municipal Police Force.

64. Interviews with Carlos (December 17, 2009), Hernán (March 11, 2010), and Pedro (December 11, 2008).

65. This was as true for the FMLN supporters as it was for ARENA supporters. The militancies of both parties were partially inserted into the state, with the FMLN holding a significant number of legislative seats and municipalities, whereas ARENA relied upon its control of the central government.

66. Interview with Carlos (December 17, 2009).

67. Central American Parliament.

68. Interview with Juan (December 12, 2009).

69. Division for the Protection of Important Persons.

70. Interview with Ignacio (July 6, 2009).

71. Interview with Pedro (December 11, 2008).

72. Reliable figures on the number of Salvadorans living outside the country do not exist. The lowest existing figure suggests that at least 10 percent of the

Salvadoran population was residing in the United States in 2000. The highest available estimates establish the total migration rate at close to 20 percent of the population, with 90 percent residing in the United States (Andrade-Eekhoff 2003; Kandel 2002).

73. Field notes (May 29, 2009).

74. One exception was the case of El Zapotal (in photo 6.7). Fighters recruited from this town just before the 1989 offensive mostly returned to their hometown after the demobilization process, even though El Zapotal was not an FMLN-affiliated community.

75. Field notes (June 2, 2009).

76. Based on an interview with David (December 20, 2009) as well as several informal conversations and on field notes (June 2, 2009; March 8, 2010; March 19, 2010).

77. The literal meaning is "plugs."

78. Interview with David (December 20, 2009).

79. Ibid.

80. Ibid.

81. Field notes (June 2, 2009; December 17, 2009; November 30, 2009).

82. Field notes (August 11, 2009).

CHAPTER 7. FMLN VETERANS' POLITICS

1. Veterans' Sector of the FMLN.

2. I attended the weekly Monday-night meetings of this group between August 2009 and February 2010. During this period I also separately interviewed several of SV-FMLN's regular participants.

3. Fundación 1 de Abril (First of April Foundation).

4. Between June 2009 and April 2010, I participated in various meetings; helped organize FUNDABRIL's archive, which contained remnants of the FPL's historical archive; and interviewed several FUNDABRIL members.

5. Movement of War Veterans from the National Army for Democracy.

6. I attended seven group meetings as well as several informal gatherings, interviewed two participants separately, and sustained regular conversations with "Demetrio" and "Juan Carlos," the group's principal animators, between August 2009 and April 2010.

7. Based on an interview with Luis, one of the organizers of the first national meeting (June 4, 2009). A copy of the invitation flyer containing basic information of the event is available in the FUNDABRIL archives.

8. Interview with "Memo" (January 26, 2010).

9. The FMLN war-wounded started out with a single unitarian association (ASALDIG), which lobbied for the creation of a protection fund for the war-

wounded, with benefits that included health-care provisions and disability pensions (Denise Spencer 1997, 48–50). When the government installed such a fund in 1993, ASALDIG was granted a seat on the board. ASALDIG members often disagreed on how to confront the ARENA government's limited cooperation with the fund. The FMLN's internal conflicts during 1993–95 also had strong repercussions inside ASALDIG, which suffered from bickering between the two largest blocks, the FPL and the ERP. As a result, ASALDIG leadership rarely agreed on a common strategy with regard to how to pressure the fund and the government into enhanced compliance. In 1996, ASALDIG's internal crisis deepened, leading to an abscission and to the formation of a new group called ALGES, spearheaded by former FPL members. FMLN leadership recognized ALGES as the official representation of the FMLN's war-wounded, to the detriment of ASALDIG. ALGES obtained formal association status in 1997. However, the new group was unable either to invalidate ASALDIG's seat on the board of the fund or to take ASALDIG's place in that seat. Discredited and without FMLN support, ASALDIG continued to be divided and weak in subsequent years, which later led to new split-offs resulting in the creation of a group called Fundación de Lisiados y Discapacitados para el Desarrollo Integral (FUNDELIDDI; Foundation of War-Wounded and Disabled for Integral Development) in 2000 and a group called Asociación de Discapacitados de Guerra (ADG; Association of Those Disabled in War) in 2005. From the date of its founding, ALGES grew quickly to become by far the largest group. Apart from drawing members away from ASALDIG, ALGES actively pursued the incorporation of new members who had not been registered in the 1993 census of the fund's beneficiaries. ALGES also allowed non-FMLN war-wounded, including former military and civilians, to join the group. In 2001, ALGES and the Salvadoran government negotiated reforms that allowed them to take a seat on the council of the fund and to register new beneficiaries. ALGES proved successful on other levels as well. It quickly expanded its organizational structures, and its membership grew from 423 (1997) to 4,823 (2002), 6,201 (2006), and 7,109 (2010). Besides access to government benefits, ALGES actively sought "reinsertion" opportunities for their members, either through internationally funded projects or by lobbying municipal councils. For example, ALGES persuaded several large municipalities governed by the FMLN to grant them the contract for the public restrooms. During 2004 alone, ALGES was able to negotiate contractual employment for 115 of its members. ALGES also established an emergency fund to support the member families in the case of accidents, illness, or death. This fund was financed in part through an agreement with the FMLN legislative faction, which donated 1 percent of the monthly salary of the entire staff. Based on interviews with "Chabelo" (August 1, 2009), Luis (June 4, 2009; August 14, 2009), and Memo (January 26, 2010), as well as descriptions from ALGES's own bulletin, called *Al Tope*.

    10. Salvadoran Association of War-Wounded and Disabled Veterans.

11. See *Al Tope*, no. 17 (2004): 2.

12. Interviews with Luis (June 4, 2009) and Memo (January 26, 2010).

13. On these expulsions and the internal development of the FMLN as a political party until 2001, see chap. 4.

14. Interviews with Demetrio (May 26, 2009) and Félix (March 6, 2010).

15. Interviews with Demetrio (May 26, 2009), Félix (March 6, 2010), and Luis (June 4, 2009; August 14, 2009).

16. Force for Change.

17. "FMLN eligió a su formula presidencial," *Diario Co Latino*, July 28, 2003; "FMLN se decidió por Schafik," *El Diario de Hoy*, July 28, 2003.

18. Interviews with Cándido (July 23, 2009), Demetrio (May 26, 2009), Luis (June 4, 2009; August 14, 2009), and Tino (May 29, 2009).

19. According to my sources, the CRS leadership blocked the meeting when it became clear that Schafik Handal would not be able to attend because of other, previous commitments. Interviews with Demetrio (May 26, 2009) and Luis (June 4, 2009; August 14, 2009).

20. Field notes (June 20, 2009).

21. Ibid. Apart from interviews with several veterans involved in these efforts, the description of the events around the Nejapa assembly and the FMLN veteran movement that year is based on documents and newspaper clippings provided to me by veterans. The Acta de Constitution del Sector Veteranos de Guerra del FMLN, adopted on this day, holds 1,432 individual signatures. Document available in the FUNDABRIL archives.

22. "Veteranos del FMLN piden participación," *El Diario de Hoy*, October 6, 2003; "Veteranos divididos en la campaña," *El Diario de Hoy*, November 17, 2003.

23. Interviews with Luis (February 9, 2010) and Rubén (December 7, 2009), and meeting with MV-END (March 16, 2010).

24. "Veteranos divididos en la campaña."

25. "Se adhieren a la propuesta del gobierno del FMLN," *Diario Co Latino*, November 17, 2003.

26. See declarations by Salvador Sánchez Cerén in "Veteranos divididos en la campaña."

27. On February 28, 2004, the veterans organized a "victory caravan" in the capital in support of Schafik. According to the veterans, the caravan included more than 150 motor vehicles. See *Veteranos en Marcha*, no. 4 (2004): 2. *Veteranos en Marcha* was presented as the informative bulletin of the "Veteranos de Guerra del Frente Farabundo Martí para la Liberación Nacional."

28. Note the parallel with Facundo Guardado's downfall after his loss at the 1999 presidential election. See chap. 4.

29. Based on interviews with several participants in the veterans' movement at the time: Cándido (July 23, 2009), Demetrio (May 19, 2009; May 26, 2009),

Félix (March 6, 2010), Luis (May 29, 2009; June 4, 2009; February 9, 2010), and Tino (May 29, 2009; July 16, 2009).

30. See IDHUCA (2004). For an account of the 2004 campaign from the perspective of the CRS, see Bichkova de Handal (2009) and Regalado (2011).

31. According to reports, local FMLN leaders and residents were angry that ARENA authorities had failed to properly coordinate the tour with the municipal councils and community leaders in the area. Allegedly, when locals asked the ARENA campaigners to abstain from behavior such as chanting their party hymn, which dates from the war and calls for the physical elimination of the "Reds," they sang the hymn anyway. Mutual insults accompanied the campaign tour during that day across several communities. Local youth hurled stones at the ARENA campaigners. Toward the end of the day, when returning to Guarjila from San José Las Flores, the caravan encountered a roadblock. The car with the candidate in it quickly turned around in search of another route out of the area. Local FMLN activists trapped several buses full of ARENA campaigners. They threw bee hives at the buses and forced them to take off their ARENA shirts, which they subsequently burnt, before the ARENA partisans were allowed to continue on their way. ARENA reported that twenty-three activists were wounded that day. Based on field notes (January 3, 2009); interview with Alex (March 18, 2010); "Enfrentamiento 23 heridos reportan ARENA y FMLN," *La Prensa Gráfica*, October 28, 2003; "ARENA y la violencia electoral en el nororiente de Chalatenango," *Proceso*, no. 1076 (December 3, 2003).

32. See Garibay (2004, 33) and Handal (2007, 10–12). Also, "Handal aceptó la derrota, pero no felicitó a Saca," *El Diario de Hoy*, March 22, 2004; and "Ya vine de donde andaba," *La Prensa Gráfica*, March 27, 2004.

33. Examples include an ongoing scholarship program, established in 1999, for Salvadorans selected by the FMLN to study at Cuba's Escuela Latinoamericana de Medicina (ELAM) and the agreement between FMLN municipalities and the Venezuelan government that paved the way for the establishment of Alba Petroleo in El Salvador in 2005.

34. Veterans on the march.

35. *Veteranos en Marcha*, no. 7 (2004): 1.

36. Ibid., no. 9 (2004): 1.

37. Ibid., no. 7 (2004): 1.

38. Ibid., no. 16 (2004): 4.

39. Ibid., 1.

40. "Fuerza del Cambio insiste en el empate técnico," *Diario Co Latino*, November 9, 2004; "Ortíz no acepta los resultados," *El Diario de Hoy*, November 9, 2004.

41. Deputies who abandoned the FMLN legislative faction in this period included Ileana Rogel, Hector Córdova, Nicolás García, and Miguel Navarrete.

42. See the FMLN bulletin *Correo Semanal de la CP*, no. 106 (2005): 4.

43. Based on coverage of the events in Salvadoran newspapers. See, e.g., "Nuevas deserciones farabundistas," *El Diario de Hoy*, June 8, 2005; "Los antihandalistas no acudirán a las urnas," Ibid., July 17, 2005; "Nepotismo en los cargos del FMLN," Ibid., July 15, 2005; "Partido de izquierda satisfecho con resultados de elecciones internas," *Diario Co Latino*, July 18, 2005; "FDR . . . nueva izquierda . . . una luz al final del túnel," Ibid., July 4, 2005; "FDR cuenta con 25 mil firmas," Ibid., September 1, 2005; "Los efemelenistas retan al gobierno," *El Diario de Hoy*, April 13, 2004; "Ortíz no acepta resultados," Ibid., November 9, 2004.

44. First, the FDR was unable to get timely approval from the Tribunal Supremo Electoral (TSE) to participate in the upcoming 2006 legislative and municipal elections. FDR leadership resolved to temporarily integrate within Cambio Democrático (CD), the new name of the previously suspended CDU. With only two deputies and fewer than a handful of municipal victories, the CD performed poorly in the election, and FDR access to public office was extremely limited. However, since the FDR hadn't participated formally as a party, it was able to avoid cancelation and was thus allowed a new electoral bid in 2009, again without success. In fact, in 2009 FDR won the municipal election only in the city of Acajutla, which they won in coalition with the CD. Specific data on electoral results of the CD and the FDR in 2006 and 2009 can be found in TSE (2006, 2009).

45. Interviews with Demetrio (May 26, 2009), Félix (March 6, 2010), and Luis (June 4, 2009; August 14, 2009).

46. *Veteranos en Marcha*, no. 18 (2005): 1–8.

47. Interviews with Félix (March 6, 2010), Hernán (March 11, 2010), and José (December 15, 2009).

48. State Intelligence Office.

49. Based on interviews with participants within these diverse currents: Demetrio (May 19, 2009; June 26, 2009), Evaristo (December 15, 2009), "Jerónimo" (December 27, 2009), Luis (August 14, 2009; February 9, 2010), Rafael (February 14, 2010), and Tino (May 29, 2009).

50. Interviews with Demetrio (May 26, 2009), Jerónimo (December 27, 2009), and Magdalena (August 12, 2009).

51. For the electoral results, see TSE (2006). For reports on the tension during and after the elections, and particularly with regard to the municipal government of San Salvador, see Salvadoran newspaper coverage, e.g., "FMLN y ARENA se declaran ganadores de la alcaldía capitalina," *Diario Co Latino*, March 13, 2006; "Indagan al FMLN," *El Diario de Hoy*, March 16, 2006.

52. Interviews with Demetrio (May 26, 2009; June 29, 2009), Luis (August 14, 2009), and Tino (May 29, 2009).

53. Interviews with Demetrio (May 26, 2009; June 29, 2009) and Luis (August 14, 2009).

54. "Concentración 'pacífica' se torna violenta en Suchitoto," *Diario Co Latino*, July 3, 2007; "Protestas terminan en disturbios en Suchitoto," *La Prensa Gráfica*, July 3, 2007; "Trece detenidos por desordenes," Ibid.

55. Based on the author's personal participation in an international campaign to free those accused of terrorism in Suchitoto. For newspaper coverage, see "Concentración 'pacífica' se torna violenta en Suchitoto"; "Organizaciones sociales piden liberar a capturados," *Diario Co Latino*, July 3, 2007; "Trece detenidos por desordenes"; "Colombianizan a El Salvador . . . persecución a simpatizantes del FMLN" and "FMLN califica detenidos como presos políticos," *Diario Co Latino*, July 7, 2007.

56. "Funes–Sánchez Cerén formula FMLN 2009," *La Prensa Gráfica*, September 28, 2007.

57. For academic accounts of the Funes election and the subsequent transition of power, see Almeida (2010), Azpuru (2010), Cannon and Hume (2012), Luis González (2011), Motta and Gutiérrez (2011), Torres-Rivas (2009), and Viterna (2012).

58. I performed fieldwork with various veteran groups from May 2009 until April 2010, and during subsequent follow-up visits (May–June 2011 and February 2012). Also, interview with Patricia (July 13, 2009).

59. "Gobierno se reivindica con lisiados de guerra," *Diario Co Latino*, February 3, 2010.

60. Field notes (July 13, 2009).

61. The following paragraphs are based my attendance at dozens of meetings of the FMLN Veterans' Sector and related field notes.

62. Additionally, I was allowed to ask SV-FMLN participants for personal interviews. Alemán himself agreed to one interview, but did not want it recorded.

63. Some of the meetings I attended in late 2009 and early 2010 were held in 1316, since the 229 office was under renovation at the time.

64. In and around San Salvador, public transportation becomes scarce, irregular, and frequently also more expensive after 8:30 p.m.

65. Confidential employee designation.

66. Field notes (August 24, 2009).

67. My rendering of the August 24, 2009, meeting of the FMLN Veterans' Sector is based on field notes.

68. Field notes (August 31, 2009).

69. Ibid.

70. My rendering of the August 31, 2009, meeting of the FMLN Veterans' Sector is based on field notes.

71. National Administration of Aqueducts and Sewerage.

72. Based on field notes (September 7, 2009).

73. Field notes (November 30, 2009; January 25, 2010).

74. The project was cosponsored by a reputable FMLN militant and senior state official, who had arranged the artistic design of the monument and also helped fund-raising by selling bonds.

75. Field notes (August 26, 2009).

76. Field notes (September 7, 2009). Norman Quijano was elected mayor of San Salvador on January 18, 2009, for the ARENA party.

77. Field notes on veteran meetings (September 21, 2009; October 5, 2009; October 12, 2009).

78. Field notes (November 11, 2009). See also "FMLN conmemora 20 aniversario," *Diario Co Latino*, November 11, 2009.

79. This extract is from the manuscript.

80. I requested and obtained a copy of the text from him after the meeting had ended.

81. Field notes (November 23, 2009).

82. Field notes (November 30, 2009).

83. Field notes (January 4, 2010).

84. My rendering above of the January 4, 2010, meeting is based on field notes.

85. Based on field notes (January 10, 2010).

86. Because I was in the Netherlands at the time, I was unable to attend the inauguration ceremony. A report of the event can be found in "'En los 14 departamentos debería haber un monumento a los caídos': Sigfrido Reyes," *Diario Co Latino*, November 15, 2010.

87. Field notes (August 18, 2009).

88. Field notes (July 13, 2009; August 18, 2009).

89. When I started my fieldwork, the effort of building a veteran "census" had already kicked off some months before, with the help of some FMLN militants working at the UES School of Medicine. Alemán provided me with a copy of the census form that had been used, which was quite rudimentary. Based on this form, I prepared a few comments regarding the possibilities that the information-recollection tool would offer in terms of socioeconomic indicators for the veterans' sector. This was discussed in my presence at the meeting of the veterans' national directorate. It was agreed that I coordinate my technical assistance with the compañero from the UES in charge of the project, who was also present at this meeting. We agreed on a midweek work meeting at his office, but he stood me up. I made some new attempts at coordinating a meeting with him via telephone and email, also without results. Field notes (August 26, 2009; August 31, 2009).

90. Field notes (August 31, 2009).

91. Ibid.

92. Field notes (November 30, 2009).

93. Field notes (January 25, 2012).

94. Field notes (August 26, 2009).

95. Ibid.

96. Field notes (August 24, 2009; August 26, 2009; August 31, 2009; November 23, 2009; January 28, 2010).

97. Field notes (January 28, 2010). With regard to my own role: I told Alemán once again that I would be happy to provide technical assistance, but that I was unable to process the forms myself. I did provide him with a contact with students at the UES who might be willing and able to help, and I arranged a face-to-face meeting of these students with Alemán.

98. Interviews with Rafael (January 6, 2010; January 14, 2010).

99. Field notes (April 5, 2010).

100. Field notes (February 27, 2010); interview with José (December 15, 2009).

101. Some FPL militants continued to be incarcerated abroad after the war in El Salvador ended. As far as I know, there were prisoners in Nicaragua (connected to the 1993 explosion of an FPL secret arms-storage chamber in the Santa Rosa neigborhood of Managua) and in Brazil (connected to an attempted kidnapping of a businessman).

102. Field notes (June 20, 2009).

103. Interview with Lilian (January 23, 2010).

104. Field notes (June 24, 2009).

105. See "Acta de Constitución de FUNDABRIL," *Diario Oficial de la República de El Salvador*, February 17 (vol. 370, no. 34), 2006.

106. Based on a meeting with several FUNDABRIL members. Field notes (June 20, 2009).

107. Field notes (June 20, 2009).

108. Field notes (August 17, 2009).

109. Interview with Dora (August 17, 2009).

110. Salvadoran Association of FMLN War Veterans "Farabundo Martí."

111. Field notes (August 9, 2009).

112. Field notes (September 30, 2009).

113. Interview with Cándido (July 23, 2009); field notes (September 30, 2009).

114. Based on an interview with Cándido (July 23, 2009) and field notes (July 23, 2009).

115. Interview with Lilian (January 23, 2010).

116. Ibid.

117. Ibid.

118. Interview with Felipe (January 30, 2010).

119. Interview with José (December 15, 2009); fieldnotes (June 20, 2009; August 13, 2009; September 30, 2009).

120. Interview with José (December 15, 2009).

121. Ibid.

122. Field notes (March 17, 2010).

123. Interview with José (December 15, 2009); field notes (June 20, 2009).

124. Field notes (April 7, 2010).

125. Based on interviews with Félix (March 6, 2010), Hernán (March 11, 2010), and José (December 15, 2009; May 26, 2011), and field notes (February 20, 2012).

126. Field notes (August 20, 2009).

127. Interview with José (December 15, 2009); field notes (June 20, 2009).

128. Field notes (March 2, 2010).

129. For more on Cayetano Carpio, the founder of the FPL, see chap. 2.

130. Field notes (May 19, 2009).

131. This description of MV-END is based on field notes (May 18, 2009; May 28, 2009; June 2, 2009; June 4, 2009; June 23, 2009; June 29, 2009; July 2, 2009; July 16, 2009; August 18, 2009; August 28, 2009; March 2, 2010; May 24, 2011; February 20, 2012); interviews with Demetrio (May 19, 2009; May 26, 2009; August 18, 2009; June 29, 2009), Fabio (August 28, 2009), Luis (May 29, 2009; June 4, 2009; August 14, 2009; January 12, 2010; January 22, 2010; February 9, 2010), and Tino (May 29, 2009; July 16, 2009); transcriptions of MV-END meetings (March 9, 2010; March 16, 2010); MV-END newsletters (July 5, 2007; November 29, 2007; February 4, 2008; February 11, 2009; April 13, 2009; April 16, 2011); and the participation of an MV-END representative in a public event (May 27, 2011).

132. Field notes (May 28, 2009).

133. Field notes (June 23, 2009).

134. Based on transcriptions of MV-END meetings (March 9, 2010; March 16, 2010) and interviews with Demetrio (May 19, 2009; May 26, 2009; June 29, 2009; August 18, 2009).

135. MV-END meeting (March 9, 2010).

136. Juan Carlos's words in an MV-END meeting (March 16, 2010).

137. MV-END meeting (March 9, 2010). See also *MV-END boletín*, November 29, 2007.

138. MV-END representative's statement at a public conference (May 27, 2011). Also MV-END meeting (March 9, 2010).

139. MV-END meeting (March 9, 2010).

140. Ibid.

141. "A mule without an owner," i.e., someone who does not submit to authority.

142. The description of Evaristo's political activities is based on field notes (December 15, 2009; March 28, 2010; February 20, 2012) and interviews with Demetrio (June 29, 2009), Evaristo (December 15, 2009), Félix (March 6, 2010), José (December 15, 2009), Juan (December 12, 2009), and Luis (August 14, 2009; February 9, 2010), as well as an interview with a government official (June 1, 2011).

143. Field notes (February 20, 2012).

144. Interview with Evaristo (December 15, 2009).

145. Based on interview with Evaristo (December 15, 2009) and field notes (December 15, 2009; March 28, 2010; February 20, 2012).

146. Field notes (March 28, 2010).

147. Technical Secretariat of the Presidency.

148. When I returned to the Netherlands in April 2010, after a three-year stay in El Salvador, the FMLN veterans were only beginning to become the subject of new government policies directed at them. In subsequent months, veterans' organizing intensified further as the opportunities to become involved in a government benefit program became more concrete. I documented this process in two follow-up visits (May–June 2011 and February 2012), complemented by newspaper coverage and electronic communication with several veterans. These findings offer additional and complementary insights into FMLN veterans' politics in its broader context.

149. CONAVERS stands for Coordinadora Nacional de Asociaciones de Veteranos y Veteranas Revolucionarios Salvadoreños del FMLN (National Coordinator of Associations of Salvadoran Revolutionary FMLN Veterans). Concertación Nacional loosely translates as National Coalition. Of the groups that I had included in my fieldwork, ASALVEG was particularly active in this initiative. Like ASALVEG, several other veterans' groups had been set up, reorganized, or reenergized in anticipation of the round table. Some groups were organized territorially, others by PMO affiliation, others in a combination of these ways. They all claimed to represent significant numbers, but in most cases, government officials had no idea of how many veterans belonged to each group. Interview with a STP government official (June 1, 2011); see also STP (2012, 3–4).

150. While ASALVEG was the leading organization for the Concertación, CONAVERS was headed by the FPL veterans' associations from El Paisnal and Chalatenango.

151. Interview with José (May 26, 2011); field notes (June 1, 2011; February 20, 2012).

152. The government's registration process was directed at "those who formed part of one of the historic organizations which constituted the FMLN during the armed conflict and who were called [to register] by one of the different organizations participating in the veterans' round-table dialogue" (STP 2012, 5).

153. The difference between the census and the sample I presented in the previous chapter with regard to the number of veterans who depend on agricultural activities for survival is quite remarkable: 55.6 percent in the government survey and 20 percent in my own survey. I suspect this is mainly due to the survey method employed. In the STP survey, the data were based on voluntary inscription into a census and with the perceived purpose of serving as the vehicle for a government support program for the (proclaimed) veterans inscribed. By design,

the government sample also disregarded the veterans not present in El Salvador at the time of the survey.

154. Interview with José (May 26, 2011).

155. Personal correspondence (April 27, 2011); interview with José (May 26, 2011).

156. I thank Liliana Trejo for her assistance in consulting with the different veterans' movement participants on the full names and dates of establishment of the different organizations involved in Concertación Nacional and CONAVERS. Additional information was collected in an interview with Memo (January 26, 2010) and with an STP government official (June 1, 2011). After June 2011, a few additional veterans' groups emerged and applied to be accepted at the round table. These are not included in the present overview.

157. This summary shows that, apart from ALGES, the other organizations of war-wounded that were established over the years now also participated in the coordination efforts of the veterans' movements. During the remainder of 2011 and in 2012, several other organizations appeared that also attempted to gain a seat at the round table. Furthermore, different veterans' groups would sometimes change their political allegiances at the round table in the course of time. Since the veterans' movement was a volatile one, even the coordinators of the Concertación and CONAVERS had difficulties keeping track of exactly which groups were on board.

158. Curiously, two days before Funes announced the new benefit program, a small group of FMLN veterans and war-wounded occupied the San Salvador cathedral to launch several new demands. Two Concertación members, FUNDELIDDI and Asociación de Veteranos Revolucionarios Salvadoreños (AVERSAL; Association of Salvadoran Revolutionary Veterans), were involved in this protest. The MV-END veterans said they supported the occupation, since in their mind it helped reveal the limited commitment the Funes government actually had to the cause of the veterans and war-wounded. ASALVEG veterans, on the other hand, considered the occupation an act of desperation by a few veteran leaders with tiny constituencies who had little influence with other members of the round table, and had little to show for their presence there. The Catholic Church hierarchy complained repeatedly and bitterly about the occupation, which interfered with religious activities at the cathedral. They considered that the veterans were disrespecting the church and needed to find other ways to express their demands. The PDDH tried to negotiate with the veterans to persuade them to abandon the cathedral. The veterans finally left the building on April 16, 2012, after ninety-six days of occupation. It was announced to the press that they had negotiated, with the mediation of prominent church members and human rights defenders, a personal meeting with the head of the STP to discuss their demands. Field notes (February 20, 2012). See also coverage in local newspapers: "Sindicatos piden solución a demandas de ex combatientes," *Diario*

Co Latino, February 23, 2012; "Arzobispo exige le devuelvan catedral," *El Diario de Hoy*, March 19, 2012; "Conflicto por toma de catedral sigue sin resolverse," *Diario Co Latino*, March 19, 2012; "Tras 96 días, abren puertas de Catedral," *El Mundo*, April 16, 2012; "Arzobispo dice que ocupación de catedral es sacrilegio," *El Mundo*, April 8, 2012.

159. "Presentan Programa de Atención a Veteranos del FMLN," *El Diario de Hoy*, January 13, 2012. See also "Presidente Funes anuncia programa de beneficios para veteranos y veteranas del FMLN," *Diario Co Latino*, January 14, 2012; "Funes anuncia beneficios para los veteranos de guerra FMLN," *La Prensa Gráfica*, January 14, 2012. Digital newspaper *El Faro* pointed out that Funes "argued that the preceding governments prioritized the care for ex-combatants from the armed forces, and that now, as an act of justice, he would develop this program to aid the ex-guerrillas." See "Funes anuncia plan de atención a miles de exguerrilleros," *El Faro*, January 16, 2012, http://www.elfaro.net/es/201201/noticias/7169/.

160. "Presidente Funes recibe apoyo de organizaciones sociales," *Diario Co Latino*, May 28, 2012; "Presidente Funes se compromete a dejar un país con cambios irreversibles," *Diario Co Latino*, May 28, 2012.

161. "Funes le hace guiño al pueblo antes de 1 junio," *El Diario de Hoy*, May 27, 2012.

162. "Funes llama a formación de la unidad por el cambio," *La Prensa Gráfica*, May 27, 2012.

163. Field notes (February 20, 2012). See also *Boletín Informativo FUNDA-BRIL* 1, no. 5 (August 2012).

164. Based on conversations and personal correspondence with members of ASALVEG and MV-END. Field notes (February 20, 2012).

165. Personal correspondence (August 17, 2012).

166. MV-END representative's statement at a public event (May 27, 2011).

167. Indeed, the figures the government presented in 2012 on the supposed universe of FMLN veterans in the country said more about the particular logic with which they pursued registration of potential beneficiaries for the program than it said about the actual numbers or status of FMLN veterans in the country.

CHAPTER 8. SALVADORAN POLITICS AND THE ENDURING LEGACIES OF INSURGENCY

1. Justo's story is based on interviews (August 11, 2009; August 20, 2009; July 24, 2015) and field notes (May 8, 2009; May 23, 2009; June 4, 2009; August 3, 2009; August 11, 2009; August 20, 2009; May 26, 2011; May 28, 2011; February 19, 2012; May 10, 2014; September 28, 2014; February 14, 2015; July 24, 2015).

2. Interview with Martín, a senior FPL cadre during the war (February 20, 2012).

3. Report of a speech by Joaquín Villalobos during an ERP meeting, rendered by Wood (2003, 175–76).

4. Compare with Javier Auyero's account of the connections between clientelism and political riots in Argentina (2007, 151; 2010, 130).

5. Montes (1978) authored the only substantial study I know of that is concerned specifically with the phenomenon of compadrazgo in El Salvador. Some recent publications on Salvadoran history pay some attention to clientelism and patronage as historical phenomena: see Ching (2004, 2014), Gould and Lauria-Santiago (2008), and Lindo-Fuentes, Ching, and Lara Martínez (2010).

6. See Artiga-González (2007, 34), J. Cruz (2001, 24), and Dodson, Jackson, and O'Shaughnessy (2001, 55).

7. See Bland (2011), Cosgrove (2002), and McElhinny (2004).

8. Examples of in-depth consideration of contemporary patron-clients relations in different Latin American settings include Arias (2006), Auyero (1997, 2000, 2001, 2007, 2012), Eaton (2006), Escobar (2000), Gay (1994, 2006), Gootenberg and Reygadas (2010), Hilgers (2008), Pansters (2012), Perlman (2009), and Scheper-Hughes (1992).

9. Nancy Scheper-Hughes, for example, uses the concept to disentangle the uneasy interaction between the well-off and the poor in a small city in northern Brazil. She describes a strongly stratified but wholly interdependent society in which "each class behaves, in its own realm, as a group to whom things are entitled: service, homage, loyalty, on the one hand, and the basic necessities of life, on the other" (1992, 117).

10. Interview with José (December 15, 2009).

11. Field notes (August 31, 2009). For further description of this episode, see chap. 7.

12. This organization was formed to support Mauricio Funes's candidacy for president.

13. Interview with Luis (August 14, 2009).

14. Interview with Tino (July 16, 2009).

15. In academic terms, the discussion of political conspiracy is delicate terrain. Scholarly attempts to uncover the "true" nature of events manipulated by conspirators may easily sink into the murky waters of speculation. Deniability and manipulation of meaning or perception are elements integrated within its design. This makes it understandable that, as Jeffrey Bale has pointed out, "very few notions nowadays generate as much intellectual resistance, hostility and derision within academic circles as a belief in the historical importance or efficacy of political conspiracies" (2007, 47). Political conspiracy refers to "secret but often mundane political planning" (53) for the covert manipulation of political relationships. And while "dirty tricks" (Marx 1974, 438) may be effective political tools used in many different settings, political scientists often ignore the existence of a conspiratorial dimension of politics altogether, reducing accounts of it to

anecdote or paranoia (Bradley 2005; Keeley 1999). True, academic consideration of political conspiracies is a complicated task, not in the least because the manipulation and secrecy endemic to conspiracies thoroughly complicate empirical-data gathering. In effect, conspiracies are designed to be untraceable. Furthermore, speculation regarding false or nonexistent conspiracies can also be used for political manipulation. For the researcher taking on the challenge of studying conspiracy, there is also the risk of being drawn in, something most academics rightfully see as a threat to their work.

16. Group interview with veterans of MV-END (May 24, 2011).

17. In the context of the Cold War, clandestine plotting became a common political practice in the continent, both on the Left and the Right side of the political spectrum. Think of the clandestine networks of the political-military organizations active in most countries of the continent, whose raison d'être was to be involved in secret plotting for the violent overthrow of the military and right-wing governments (Castañeda 1993). Or the right-wing terrorists who cooked up numerous anticommunist counterinsurgency plots, executed by paramilitary groups, right-wing politicians, and army officers, often supported by the CIA, and exemplified by such infamous names as Plan Condor and the Iran-Contra scandal. The United States allocated enormous resources to secret operations fighting communism in Latin America and all over the world (Jackson 1990). In the 1980s, CIA director William Casey would be quoted as saying that "covert action [was] the 'keystone' of U.S. policy in the Third World" (Agee 1992, 2).

18. The former received senior training mostly in Cuba, while the latter attended courses in places like the School of the Americas and Taiwan.

19. Interview with Rafael (December 11, 2009).

20. Ibid.

21. Literally "the small bed," a popular expression that refers to a plot to frame someone.

22. Interviews with Chabelo (August 1, 2009), Justo (August 20, 2009), and Tino (May 26, 2009).

23. Interview with Fabio (August 28, 2009).

24. The best-known victim of these kidnappings was adolescent Andrés Suster, member of an affluent family, in September 1995. During the adolescent's 354 days of captivity, the case aroused massive media attention and nurtured all kinds of speculation. In 1997, when it became clear that clandestine structures of the PCS had been involved, the right-wing press focused its attacks on PCS leader Schafik Handal. In the courts, the case dragged on for several years, and Handal managed to stay clear of penal prosecution. Comandante "Marcelo," one of Handal's close collaborators and the former second in command of PCS-FAL, was condemned together with other former PCS cadres. "Marcelo" disappeared and remains a fugitive to this day. Sprenkels (2011, 20).

25. See PDDH (2006), Moodie (2010, 212), and Sprenkels (2014a).

26. This view echoes an interpretation of Latin American politics based on the mobilization of "power capacities," as proposed by Charles Anderson. This scholar conceives of Latin American politics as a "process consist[ing] of manipulation and negotiation among power contenders" (1967, 97). Power contenders substantiate their claims through the presumption or mobilization of different power capacities—including (the threat of) violence (91). For a recent application of this analytical framework, see Bataillon (2008).

27. Drawing on the work of Cornelius Castoriadis and Claude Lefort, Adams, Smit, and Straume (2012) conceive of such imaginaries as connected to cultural projects of power.

28. The phrase "friends, factions and followers" refers to the title of a classic volume on political clientelism edited by Schmidt et al. (1977).

29. Interview with Rafael (December 16, 2009).

30. This observation partially echoes Timur Kuran's analysis of the differences between public and private speech on politics (1997). However, it should be noted that the division I observed within postinsurgent politics between public and private speech is far from absolute, and that, contrary to what Kuran suggests in his work, both dimensions conflate elements of truth and falsity. References to the political imaginaries of clientelism and conspiracy may also be detectable in public speech, especially by insiders, and those of democracy and revolution also invade private conversation. But the division is certainly significant enough to create a semantic breach between the experience of postinsurgent politics as documented in fieldwork and the image of postinsurgent politics that may emerge from reviewing the FMLN party program or listening to the leadership's public discourse.

31. See Sprenkels (2012) for a review of Funes's human rights politics. See van der Borgh and Savenije (2015) and Wolf (2015, 284) for the new role of the military in security under Funes.

32. For example, digital news platform *El Faro* (http://www.elfaro.net/) published several research articles on Funes's unwarranted use of public funds or involvement in nepotism.

33. See, for example, "La derecha de El Salvador pide conteo voto por voto," *El País*, March 11, 2014; "ARENA continúa con sus acusaciones de fraude," *Diario Co Latino*, March 14, 2014.

34. "FMLN asegura 'la derecha' está planificando un 'golpe blando' contra el GOES," *La Prensa Gráfica*, July 27, 2015. See also "Las amenazas de golpe y acciones desestabilizadoras se repiten: Roberto Viera," *Diario Co Latino*, July 25, 2015; "De los tipos de Golpes de Estado," *Diario Co Latino*, July 24, 2015.

35. See, for example, "El 'golpe suave' in Venezuela en cinco pasos," Telesur, February 20, 2014, http://www.telesurtv.net/news/El-golpe-suave-en-Venezuela -en-cinco-pasos-20140220-0054.html.

36. In an interesting parallel, ARENA has also frequently accused the FMLN of conspiring with the gangs. See, for example, Zilberg (2007).

37. Interview with Justo (July 24, 2015).

38. "La millonaria revolución de Alba," *El Faro*, January 19, 2014, https://www.elfaro.net/es/201401/noticias/14423/.

39. Further conclusions of the report include that "the discontent of the population with regard to the present government and its capacity to respond to the most pressing needs of the population is translating into . . . a clear erosion of the image of the party in power. To the country's difficult national situation we add the perception that we have a government with low capacity to formulate effective responses to the country's main problems, making it understandable that a large part of the population is pessimistic and fearful regarding the country's future" (IUDOP 2016, 6).

40. "Nicaragua da asilo político al expresidente Funes, investigado por cinco delitos de corrupción," *El Faro*, September 6, 2016, http://elfaro.net/es /201609/el _salvador/19214/Nicaragua-da-asilo-pol%C3%ADtico-al-expresidente -Funes-investigado-por-cinco-delitos-de-corrupci%C3%B3n.htm.

41. See J. Cruz (2015), van der Borgh and Savenije (2015), and Wolf (2017) for recent discussions of El Salvador's security crisis and its impacts on state governance.

42. The proliferation of veterans' organizations participating in politics is most common following successful "national liberation" wars, as studies on Namibia (Metsola 2006, 2010), South Africa (Adonis 2008; Hart 2007; Southall 2007), Mozambique (Wiegink 2014, 2015), and Kosovo (Ströhle 2010) indicate.

43. Field notes (August 3, 2009).

44. Tilly and Tarrow, for example, use the concept of disillusionment as a mechanism for demobilization of social movements (2008, 98).

45. For different positions regarding the alleged aid dependency of the insurgency's peasant supporters, contrast Binford (2010, 542), Silber (2011, 97), and Todd (2010, 162).

46. For a reflection on changes in the political imaginary of participants in the Salvadoran insurgent movement after the peace accords, see Peterson and Peterson (2008).

47. On the political functionality of the idea of the internal enemy, see Galli (2009).

48. To those who have read Leon Trotsky the pattern will sound familiar.

49. See, for example, Cáceres Prendes (2012), Castro Morán (1987), Ching (2014), and Williams and Walter (1997).

50. Erik Ching's work on how political actors tell different stories regarding the Salvadoran civil war offers insight into this (2016).

51. Interview with Arturo (February 3, 2010).

References

Adams, Jacqueline. 2003. "The Bitter End: Emotions at a Movement's Conclusion." *Sociological Inquiry* 73:84–113.

Adams, Suzy, Jeremy Smit, and Ingerid Straume. 2012. "Political Imaginaries in Question." *Critical Horizons* 13 (1): 5–11.

Adamson, Walter. 1980. *Hegemony and Revolution: A Study of Antonio Gramsci's Political and Cultural Theory.* Berkeley: University of California Press.

Adonis, Cyril. 2008. *"We Need to Do It for Ourselves": An Evaluation of the CSVR Ex-combatant Policy Dialogue Project.* Johannesburg: Centre for the Study of Violence and Reconciliation.

Agee, Phillip. 1992. "Tracking Covert Actions into the Future." *Covert Action Quarterly* 42 (1): 1–21.

Agosta, Diana. 2007. "Constructing Civil Society, Supporting Local Development: A Case Study of Community Radio in Postwar El Salvador." *Democratic Communiqué* 2 (1): 4–26.

Alarcón Medina, Rafael. 2015. "Digitalización, clase social y formación social electrónica en El Salvador rural." In *Conflictos y sujetos emergentes: Episodios en la transformación rural neoliberal,* edited by Antonio Fuentes Díaz, 19–56. Puebla: Benemérita Universidad Autónoma de Puebla, Instituto de Ciencias Sociales y Humanidades.

Alas, José Inocencio. 2003. *Iglesia, Tierra y Lucha Campesina: Suchitoto, El Salvador, 1968–1977.* San Salvador: Asociación de Frailes Franciscanos.

Alegría, Claribel, with D. J. Flakoll. 1983. *No me agarran viva: La mujer salvadoreña en lucha.* Mexico City: Serie Popular Era.

Allison, Michael. 2006. "The Transition from Armed Opposition to Electoral Opposition in Central America." *Latin American Politics and Society* 48 (4): 137–62.

Allison, Michael, and Alberto Martín Alvarez. 2012. "Unity and Disunity within the FMLN." *Latin American Politics and Society* 54 (4): 89–118.

Almeida, Paul. 2008. *Waves of Protest: Popular Struggle in El Salvador, 1925–2005.* Minneapolis: University of Minnesota Press.

———. 2009. "Social Movements, Political Parties, and Electoral Triumph in El Salvador." *NACLA Report on the Americas* 42 (6): 16–21.

———. 2010. "El Salvador: Elecciones y movimientos sociales." *Revista de Ciencias Políticas* 30 (2): 319–34.

Almeida, Paul, and Rubén Urbizagástegui. 1999. "Cutumay Camones: Popular Music in El Salvador's National Liberation Movement." *Latin American Perspectives* 26 (2): 13–42.

Alvarenga, Chepe. 1993. "Las otras historias prohibidas de Pulgarcito." Manuscript. Published by Centro de Documentación de los Movimientos Armados July 25, 2006, http://www.cedema.org/ver.php?id=1453.

Alvarenga, Ester, and Ulf Baumgärtner. 2008. "Entrevista con Alejandro Valladares, líder campesino de las FPL." Manuscript.

Alvarez, Antonio. 2003. *La Tierra, Seguridad, Desarrollo*. Washington, DC: Chemonics International.

Alvarez, Antonio, and Joaquín Chávez. 2001. *Tierra, Conflicto y Paz*. San Salvador: Ediciones CEPAZ.

Americas Watch. 1991. *El Salvador's Decade of Terror: Human Rights since the Assassination of Archbishop Romero*. New Haven: Yale University Press.

Anaya Montes, Mélida. 1972. *La segunda gran batalla de ANDES 21 DE JUNIO*. San Salvador: Editorial Universitaria.

Anderson, Charles. 1967. *Politics and Economic Change in Latin America: The Governing of Restless Nations*. Princeton: Van Nostrand.

Anderson, Jon Lee. 1993. *Guerrillas*. London: HarpersCollins.

———. 1997. *Che Guevara: A Revolutionary Life*. New York: Grove Press.

Anderson, Thomas. 1981. *The War of the Dispossessed: Honduras and El Salvador, 1969*. Lincoln: University of Nebraska Press.

———. 2001. *El Salvador, 1932: Los sucesos politicos*. San Salvador: Concultura.

Andrade-Eekhoff, Katharine. 2003. *Remesas, migración y vínculos con la micro y pequeña empresa en El Salvador*. San Salvador: FLACSO.

Andrade-Eekhoff, Katharine, and Claudia Marina Silva-Avalos. 2003. *Globalization of the Periphery: The Challenges of Transnational Migration for Local Development in Central America*. San Salvador: FLACSO.

Ankersmit, Frank. 2002. *Political Representation*. Stanford: Stanford University Press.

Arana, Ana. 1994. "The Smiling Chameleon." *Bulletin of the Atomic Scientists* 50 (6): 36–39.

Araujo, Américo Mauro. 2011. "Un tiempecito después de terminada la guerra: Períodos y fases de la guerra Salvadoreña." Manuscript.

Arditi, Benjamin. 2008. "Arguments about the Left Turns in Latin America: A Post-Liberal Politics?" *Latin American Research Review* 43 (3): 59–81.

Arendt, Hannah. 1969. *On Violence*. New York: Harvest Books.

———. 1972. *Crises of the Republic*. San Diego: Harcourt Brace & Company.

Aretxaga, Begoña. 2000. "'A Fictional Reality': Paramilitary Death Squads and the Construction of State Terror in Spain." In *Death Squad: The Anthropology of State Terror*, edited by Jeffrey A. Sluka, 46–69. Philadelphia: University of Pennsylvania Press.

Argueta, Manlio. 1977 (1981). *Caperucita en la Zona Roja.* San Salvador: UCA Editores.

———. 1980 (1985): *Un día en la vida.* San José: EDUCA.

Arias, Enrique Desmond. 2006. *Drugs and Democracy in Rio de Janeiro: Trafficking, Social Networks, and Public Security.* Chapel Hill: University of North Carolina Press.

———. 2009. "Ethnography and the Study of Latin American Politics: An Agenda for Research." In *Political Ethnography: What Immersion Contributes to the Study of Power,* edited by Edward Schatz, 239–54. Chicago: University of Chicago Press.

Arias Peñate, Salvador. 2010. *Atlas de la pobreza y la opulencia en El Salvador.* San Salvador: UCA Editores.

Aricó, José. 1988. *La cola del diablo: Itinerario de Gramsci en América Latina.* Caracas: Nueva Sociedad.

Armstrong, Robert, and Janet Rubin. 1983. *El Salvador, el rostro de la revolución.* San Salvador: UCA Editores.

Arnson, Cynthia. 1982. *El Salvador: A Revolution Confronts the United States.* Washington: Institute for Policy Studies.

———. 1999. *Comparative Peace Processes in Latin America.* Stanford: Stanford University Press.

Artiga-González, Alvaro. 2006. "Entre la oposición y el gobierno tras doce años de elecciones." *Revista Centroamericana de Ciencias Sociales* 3 (2): 49–83.

———. 2007. *Gobernabilidad y democracia en El Salvador: Bases teóricas y metodológicas para su medición.* San Salvador: UCA Editores.

———. 2015. *El Sistema Político Salvadoreño.* San Salvador: Programa de las Naciones Unidas para el Desarrollo.

Ascoli, Juan Fernando. 2001. "Memoria de la historia: Organización y lucha de las comunidades del nororiente del departamento de Chalatenango (1974–1994)." Unpublished book manuscript.

Ashfort, Adam. 2005. *Witchcraft, Violence and Democracy in South Africa.* Chicago: University of Chicago Press.

Auyero, Javier, comp. 1997. *¿Favores por Votos? Estudios sobre clientelismo político contemporáneo.* Buenos Aires: Editorial Losada.

Auyero, Javier. 2000. "The Logic of Clientelism in Argentina: An Ethnographic Account." *Latin American Research Review* 35 (3): 55–81.

———. 2001. *Poor People's Politics: Peronist Survival Networks and the Legacy of Evita.* Durham, NC: Duke University Press.

———. 2003. *Contentious Lives: Two Argentine Women, Two Protests, and the Quest for Recognition.* Durham, NC: Duke University Press.

———. 2007. *Routine Politics and Violence in Argentina: The Gray Zone of State Power.* Cambridge: Cambridge University Press.

———. 2010. "Clandestine Connections: The Political and Relational Makings of Collective Violence." In *Violent Democracies in Latin America*, edited by Enrique Desmond Arias and Daniel Goldstein, 108–32. Durham, NC: Duke University Press.

———. 2012. *Patients of the State: The Politics of Waiting in Argentina*. Durham, NC: Duke University Press.

Azpuru, Dinorah. 2010. "The Salience of Ideology: Fifteen Years of Presidential Elections in El Salvador." *Latin American Politics and Society* 52 (2): 103–38.

Azucena, Miguel Angel, et al. 2005. *El Cipitío en El Salvador Sheraton: Un round de 11 días en 10 años de guerra*. San Salvador: Grupo Amate.

Bale, Jeffrey. 2007. "Political Paranoia v. Political Realism: On Distinguishing between Bogus Conspiracy Theories and Genuine Conspiratorial Politics." *Patterns of Prejudice* 41 (1): 45–60.

Baloyra, Enrique. 1982. *El Salvador in Transition*. Chapel Hill: University of North Carolina Press.

Baranyi, Stephen, and Liisa North. 1996. *The United Nations in El Salvador: The Promise and Dilemmas of an Integrated Approach of Peace*. Toronto: Centre for Research on Latin America and the Caribbean, York University.

Barillas Villalta, Alberto. 1999. *Proyecto educativo y la conversión social de excombatientes*. San Salvador: Fundación Empresarial para el Desarrollo Educativo.

Bataillon, Gilles. 2008. *Génesis de las guerras intestinas en América Central (1960–1983)*. Mexico City: Fondo de Cultura Económica.

Baumgärtner, Ulf. 1998. *La cuestión agraria en El Salvador*. San Salvador: Ediciones Heinrich Böll.

Becker, Marc. 1993. *Mariátegui and Latin American Marxist Theory*. Athens: Ohio University Press.

———. 2009. "Winds of Political Change in El Salvador: The FMLN's Historic Victory." *Against the Current* 24 (2): 7–8.

Bellamy, Richard. 1987. *Modern Italian Social Theory: Ideology and Politics from Pareto to the Present*. Stanford: Stanford University Press.

Bendaña, Alejandro. 1999. *Demobilization and Reintegration in Central America: Peace-building Challenges and Responses*. Managua: Centro de Estudios Internacionales.

Benford, Robert, and David Snow. 2000. "Framing Processes and Social Movements: An Overview and Assessment." *Annual Review of Sociology* 26:611–39.

Benítez Manaut, Raúl. 1988. "La Guerra Total en El Salvador." In *El Salvador: Guerra, Política y Paz (1979–1988)*, edited by Edgar Jiménez et al., 1–22. San Salvador: CINAS.

———. 1989. *La teoría militar y la guerra civil en El Salvador*. San Salvador: UCA Editores.

Berger, John. 1992. *Keeping a Rendezvous*. New York: Vintage Books.

Berríos Chicas, José Gilberto. 2008. "La Experiencia Colectiva de la Repoblación: El Papel de la Memoria Histórica en la Construcción Identitaria en las Comunidades del Bajo Lempa (Nueva Esperanza y Ciudad Romero)." Tesis de licenciatura, Universidad Tecnológica de El Salvador.

Berryman, Phillip. 2004. *Religious Roots of Rebellion: Christians in Central American Revolutions*. Eugene, OR: Wipf & Stock.

Bertaux, Daniel. 1995. "Social Genealogies Commented on and Compared: An Instrument for Observing Social Mobility Processes in the 'Longue Durée.'" *Current Sociology* 43:69–88.

Bertaux, Daniel, and Catherine Delcroix. 2000. "Case Histories of Families and Social Processes: Enriching Sociology." In *The Turn to Biographical Methods in Social Sciences*, edited by Prue Chamberlayne, Joanna Bornat, and Tom Wengraf. Abingdon: Routledge.

Bertaux, Daniel, and Paul Thompson. 2007. Introduction to *Pathways to Social Class: A Qualitative Approach to Social Mobility*, edited by Daniel Bertaux and Paul Thompson, 1–31. New Brunswick, NJ: Transaction Publishers.

Bibler Coutin, Susan. 2007. *Nations of Emigrants: Shifting Boundaries of Citizenship in El Salvador and the United States*. Ithaca, NY: Cornell University Press.

Bichkova de Handal, Tatiana. 2009. *Recuerdos sin peinar: Mi vida con Schafik*. San Salvador: Ediciones El Independiente.

Biegel, Fernanda. 2005. "Una mirada sobre otra: El Gramsci que conoció Mariátegui." *Estudos de Sociologia* 10 (18 and 19): 23–49.

Biekart, Kees. 1999. *The Politics of Civil Society Building: European Private Aid Agencies and Democratic Transitions in Central America*. Utrecht: International Books.

Binford, Leigh. 1996. *The El Mozote Massacre: Anthropology and Human Rights*. Tucson: University of Arizona Press.

———. 1997. "Grassroots Development in the Conflict Zones of Northeastern El Salvador." *Latin American Perspectives* 24 (2): 56–79.

———. 1999. "Hegemony in the Interior of the Salvadoran Revolution: The ERP in Northern Morazán." *Journal of Latin American Anthropology* 4 (1): 2–45.

———. 2002. "Violence in El Salvador: A Rejoinder to Philippe Bourgois's 'The Power of Violence in War and Peace: Post-Cold War Lessons from El Salvador.'" *Ethnography* 3 (2): 177–95.

———. 2004. "Peasants, Catechists, Revolutionaries: Organic Intellectuals in the Salvadoran Revolution, 1980–1992." In Lauria-Santiago and Binford, *Landscapes of Struggle*, 105–25.

———. 2010. "A Perfect Storm of Neglect and Failure: Postwar Capitalist Restoration in Northern Morazán, El Salvador." *Journal of Peasant Studies* 37 (3): 531–57.

Bird, Shawn, and Philip Williams. 2000. "El Salvador: Revolt and Negotiated Transition." In *Repression, Resistance, and Democratic Transition in Central*

America, edited by Thomas Walker and Ariel Armony, 25–46. Wilmington, DE: Scholarly Resources.

Blair, Harry, et al. 1995. *Civil Society and Democratic Development in El Salvador: A CDIE Assessment*. Washington, DC: USAID.

Bland, Gary. 2011. "Supporting Post-conflict Democratic Development? External Promotion of Participatory Budgeting in El Salvador." *World Development* 39 (5): 863–73.

Blumberg, Rea Lesser. 2001. "Risky Business: What Happens to Gender Equality and Women's Rights in Post-conflict Societies? Insights from NGO's in El Salvador." *International Journal of Politics, Culture and Society* 15 (1): 161–73.

Bonasso, Miguel, and Ciro Gómez Leyba. 1992. *Cuatro minutos para las doce: Conversaciones con el comandante Schafik Handal*. Puebla: Periodistas Asociados Latinoamericanos.

Bonner, Raymond. 1984. *Weakness and Deceit: U.S. Policy and El Salvador*. New York: Times Books.

Bosch, Brian. 1999. *The Salvadoran Officer Corps and the Final Offensive of 1981*. Jefferson, NC: McFarland.

Bourdieu, Pierre. 1984. *Distinction: A Social Critique of the Judgement of Taste*. London: Routledge.

———. 1985. "The Social Space and the Genesis of Groups." *Theory and Society* 14 (6): 723–44.

———. 1990. *The Logic of Practice*. Stanford: Stanford University Press.

Bourgois, Philippe. 1982. "What US Foreign Policy Faces in Rural El Salvador: An Eyewitness Account." *Monthly Review* 37 (1): 14–30.

———. 2001. "The Power of Violence in War and Peace: Post–Cold War Lessons from El Salvador." *Ethnography* 2 (1): 5–34.

———. 2002. "The Violence of Moral Binaries: Response to Leigh Binford." *Ethnography* 3 (2): 221–31.

Boyce, James. 1995. "External Assistance and the Peace Process in El Salvador." *World Development* 23 (12): 2101–16.

Boyce, James, ed. 1999. *Ajuste hacia la Paz: La política económica y la reconstrucción de posguerra en El Salvador*. Mexico City: PNUD and Plaza y Valdés Editores.

Bradley, Richard. 2005. "Paranoia, Conspiracy Theories and the Presidential Election of 2004." *Cultural Studies/Critical Methodologies* 5 (3): 338–45.

Brands, Hal. 2010. *Latin America's Cold War*. Cambridge, MA: Harvard University Press.

Brockett, Charles. 1990. *Land, Power, and Poverty: Agrarian Transformation and Political Conflict in Central America*. Winchester, MA: Unwin Hyman.

———. 2005. *Political Movements and Violence in Central America*. Cambridge: Cambridge University Press.

Broderick, Joe. 2000. *El guerrillero invisible*. Bogotá: Intermedio Editores.

Broere, Marc, ed. 2007. *Overleven Verplicht: 25 jaar na de moord op de Nederlandse Journalisten in El Salvador.* Amsterdam: Onze Wereld Media.

Brysk, Alison. 2000. *From Tribal Village to Global Village: Indian Rights and International Relations in Latin America.* Stanford: Stanford University Press.

Bull, Benedicte. 2013a. "Diversified Business Groups and the Transnationalisation of the Salvadorean Economy." *Journal of Latin American Studies* 45 (2): 265–95.

———. 2013b. "Social Movements and the 'Pink Tide' Governments in Latin America: Transformation, Inclusion and Rejection." In *Democratization in the Global South: The Importance of Transformative Politics*, edited by Kristian Stokke and Olle Törnquist, 75–99. Basingstoke: Palgrave.

Burdick, John, and W. E. Hewitt. 2000. *The Church at the Grassroots in Latin America: Perspectives on Thirty Years of Activism.* Westport, CT: Praeger.

Burgerman, Susan. 2000. "Building the Peace by Mandating Reform: United Nations–Mediated Human Rights Agreements in El Salvador and Guatemala." *Latin American Perspectives* 27 (3): 63–87.

Burnell, Peter, ed. 2006. *Globalising Democracy: Party Politics in Emerging Democracies.* London: Routledge.

Byrne, Hugh. 1996. *El Salvador's Civil War: A Study of a Revolution.* Boulder, CO: Lynne Rienner Publishers.

Cabarrús, Carlos Rafael. 1983. *Génesis de una Revolución: Análisis del Surgimiento y Desarrollo de la Organización Campesina en El Salvador.* Mexico City: Ediciones de la Casa Chata.

Cáceres Prendes, Jorge. 2012. "El juicio a los alzados del 2 de abril de 1944: Memoria histórica, mito y drama." *Identidades* 4 (2): 11–42.

Cagan, Beth, and María Juliá. 1998. "Maintaining Wartime Gains for Women: Lessons from El Salvador." *International Social Work* 41 (4): 405–15.

Cagan, Beth, and Steve Cagan. 1991. *This Promised Land, El Salvador: The Refugee Community of Colomoncagua and Their Return to Morazán.* New Brunswick, NJ: Rutgers University Press.

Calderón Vandenberg, Mauricio. 2002. "Perfil de Salud en la Comunidad Ignacio Ellacuría de Mayo 2001 a Mayo 2002." Tesis para optar al título de Doctor en Medicina, Universidad de El Salvador.

Call, Charles. 2002. "Democratisation, War and State-Building: Constructing the Rule of Law in El Salvador." *Journal of Latin American Studies* 35 (4): 827–62.

Cameron, Maxwell, and Eric Hershberg, eds. 2010. *Latin America's Left Turns: Politics, Policy and Trajectories of Change.* Boulder, CO: Lynne Rienner Publishers.

Campbell, John L. 2005. "Where Do We Stand? Common Mechanisms in Organizations and Social Movements Research." In *Social Movements and Organization Theory*, edited by Gerald Davis, Doug McAdam, W. Richard Scott, and Mayer N. Zald, 41–48. Cambridge: Cambridge University Press.

Cañas, Antonio, and Héctor Dada. 1999. "Political Transition and Institutionalization in El Salvador." In *Comparative Peace Processes in Latin America*, ed. Cynthia Arnson, 69–96. Washington, DC: Woodrow Wilson Center Press.

Cañas, Roberto. 2002. "Elecciones a la vista y diplomacia activada." *Revista Envío Digital*, no. 242. http://www.envio.org.ni/articulo/1147.

Cannon, Barry, and Mo Hume. 2012. "Central America, Civil Society and the 'Pink Tide': Democratization or Dedemocratization?" *Democratization* 19 (6): 1039–64.

Cardenal, Rodolfo. 1986. *Historia de una esperanza: Vida de Rutilio Grande*. San Salvador: UCA Editores.

CARECEN (Central American Refugee Center). 1988. *After 7 Years in Honduras . . . Salvadoran Refugees Turn Home*. Washington, DC: Central American Refugee Center.

Carpio, Salvador Cayetano. 1979. *Secuestro y capucha en un país del "mundo libre."* San José: Editorial Universitaria Centroamericana.

———. 1999. *Nuestras montañas son las masas: Documentos y escritos de la revolución salvadoreña*. Vienna: Der Keil.

———. 2011. *Nuestras montañas son las masas*. Segunda edición. Con una nota de Tulita Alvarenga. San Salvador: Carpio-Alvarenga Editores.

Carranza, Salvador, ed. 1990. *Mártires de la UCA*. San Salvador: UCA Editores.

Carter, Brenda, and David Loeb, eds. 1989. *A Dream Compels Us: Voices of Salvadoran Women*. San Francisco: New Americas Press.

Cassafranco, Roldán, Maria Virginia, Margarita Mooney Suárez, and Carlos Lecaros Zavala. 1997. *Demobilization, Reintegration and Pacification in El Salvador*. San José: Arias Foundation for Peace and Human Progress.

Castañeda, Jorge. 1993. *La utopía desarmada*. Mexico City: Joaquín Mortiz.

———. 1997. *Compañero: The Life and Death of Che Guevara*. London: Bloomsbury.

Castañeda, Jorge, and Marco Morales. 2007. "The Left Turn Continues." *Brown Journal of World Affairs* 13 (2): 201–10.

Castellanos Moya, Horacio. 1989. *La diáspora*. San Salvador: UCA Editores.

———. 1996. *Baile con serpientes*. San Salvador: Dirección Nacional de Publicaciones.

———. 1997. *El Asco: Thomas Berhard en San Salvador*. San Salvador: Editorial Arcoiris.

———. 2000. *La diabla en el espejo*. Ourense: Linteo Ediciones.

———. 2001. *El arma en el hombre*. Barcelona: Tusquets.

———. 2003. *Donde no estén ustedes.* Barcelona: Tusquets.

———. 2004. *Indolencia.* Barcelona: Tusquets.

———. 2005. *Insensatez.* Barcelona: Tusquets.

———. 2013. *El sueño del retorno.* Barcelona: Tusquets.

Castro, Iván. 1999. "Niños perdidos en la guerra: La historia de Emiliano." *Tendencias* 75:11–18.

Castro Morán, Mariano. 1987. *Función política del ejército salvadoreño en el presente siglo.* San Salvador: UCA Editores.

Cea, José Roberto. 1981. *Los herederos de Farabundo.* San Salvador: Editorial Universitaria.

———. 1984. *Ninel se fue a la guerra.* San Salvador: Canoa Editores.

———. 1989. *Díme con quién andas, y . . .* San Salvador: Canoa Editores.

Center for the Study of the Americas. 1983. *Listen, Companero: Conversations with Central American Revolutionary Leaders.* Berkeley, CA: Solidarity Publications.

Chabal, Patrick, and Jean Pascal Daloz. 1999. *Africa Works: Disorder as Political Instrument.* Oxford: James Curry.

———. 2006. *Culture Troubles: Politics and the Interpretation of Meaning.* Chicago: University of Chicago Press.

Chávez, Joaquín Mauricio. 2010. "The Pedagogy of Revolution: Popular Intellectuals and the Origins of the Salvadoran Insurgency, 1960–1980." PhD thesis, New York University.

———. 2014. "Catholic Action, the Second Vatican Council, and the Emergence of the New Left in El Salvador (1950–1975)." *The Americas* 70 (3): 459–87.

Ching, Erik. 2004. "Patronage and Politics under General Maximiliano Martínez, 1931–1939: The Local Roots of Military Authoritarianism in El Salvador." In Lauria-Santiago and Binford, *Landscapes of Struggle*, 50–70.

———. 2014. *Authoritarian El Salvador: Politics and the Origin of the Military Regimes, 1880–1940.* Notre Dame, IN: University of Notre Dame Press.

———. 2016. *Stories of Civil War in El Salvador: A Battle over Memory.* Durham, NC: University of North Carolina Press.

Ching, Erik, Carlos Gregorio López Bernal, and Virginia Tilley. 2007. *Las masas, la matanza y el martinato en El Salvador.* San Salvador: UCA Editores.

Chodor, Tom. 2014. *Neoliberal Hegemony and the Pink Tide in Latin America.* Basingstoke: Palgrave.

Christia, Fotini. 2014. *Alliance Formation in Civil Wars.* Cambridge: Cambridge University Press.

Churchill, Lindsey. 2014. *Becoming the Tupamaros: Solidarity and Transnational Revolutionaries in Uruguay and the United States.* Nashville: Vanderbilt University Press.

CIREFCA (Conferencia Regional sobre Refugiados Centroamericanos). 1989. "Declaration and Concerted Plan of Action in Favour of Central American

Refugees, Returnees and Displaced Persons." *International Journal of Refugee Law* 1 (4): 582–96.

Clark, Mary. 2015. "The New Left and Health Care Reform in El Salvador." *Latin American Politics and Society* 57:97–118.

Clements, Charles. 1984. *Witness to War: An American Doctor in El Salvador.* New York: Bantam Books.

CODEHUCA (Comisión Centroamericana de Derechos Humanos). 1992. *Perdonando el Asesinato: Diez años de masacre en El Salvador.* San José: Secretaria de Comunicación y Prensa de CODEHUCA.

Colburn, Forrest. 2009. "The Turnover in El Salvador." *Journal of Democracy* 20 (3): 143–52.

Colburn, Forrest, and Arturo Cruz. 2014. "El Salvador's Beleaguered Democracy." *Journal of Democracy* 25 (3): 149–58.

Comité Pro-Monumento. 2001. *Suplemento nombres para no olvidar: Listado de víctimas civiles de violaciones a los derechos humanos, 1970–1992.* San Salvador: Co-Latino.

Compher, Vic, and Betsy Morgan. 1991. *Going Home: Building Peace in El Salvador; The Story of Repatriation.* New York and London: Apex Press.

Consejo de Mujeres Misioneras por la Paz. 1996. *La semilla que cayó en tierra fértil.* San Salvador: Consejo de Mujeres Misioneras por la Paz.

Córdova Macías, Ricardo, Carlos Ramos, and Nayelly Loya Marín. 2007. "La contribución del Proceso de Paz en la Construcción de la Democracia en El Salvador." In *Construyendo la democracia en sociedades posconflicto: Guatemala y El Salvador, un enfoque comparado,* edited by Dinorah Azpuru et al., 53–287. Guatemala City: F&G Editores.

Cortéz, Beatriz. 2010. *La estética del cinismo: Pasión y el desencanto en la literatura centroamericana de posguerra.* Guatemala City: F&G Editores.

Cortina Orero, Eudald. 2015. "Comunicación insurgente y proceso revolucionario en El Salvador (1970–1992)." Tesis de doctorado, Universidad de Santiago de Compostela.

Cosgrove, Serena. 2002. "Levels of Empowerment: Marketers and Microenterprise-Lending NGOs in Apopa and Nejapa, El Salvador." *Latin American Perspectives* 29 (5): 48–65.

Costa, Gino. 1999. *La Policía Nacional Civil de El Salvador (1990–1997).* San Salvador: UCA Editores.

Courtney, Jocelyn. 2010. "The Civil War That Was Fought by Children: Understanding the Role of Child Combatants in El Salvador's Civil War, 1980–1992." *The Journal of Military History* 74 (2): 523–56.

Crandall, Russell. 2016. *The Salvador Option: The United States in El Salvador, 1977–1992.* Cambridge: Cambridge University Press.

CREA (Creative Associates International). 1996. "Impact Evaluation: Reinsertion of Ex-Combatants in El Salvador; Final Report for USAID." Manuscript.

Cruz, José Miguel. 2001. ¿Elecciones para qué? *El impacto del ciclo electoral 1999–2000 en la cultura política salvadoreña.* San Salvador: FLACSO.

———. 2015. "The State and the Reproduction of Violence in Post-transition El Salvador and Guatemala." In *Non-state Challenges in a Re-ordered World: The Jackals of Westphalia,* edited by Stefano Ruzza, Anja Jakobi, and Charles Geisler, 157–74. London: Routledge.

Cruz, María del Carmen. 2004a. "Orígenes de la educación popular en Chalatenango: Una innovación educativa." *Estudios Centroamericanos* 671:897–925.

———. 2004b. "La educación popular en las comunidades para el desarrollo de Chalatenango." *Estudios Centroamericanos* 672:1045–71.

Cummings, Andrew. 2007. *Against All Odds: Building Innovative Capabilities in Rural Economic Initiatives in El Salvador.* San Salvador: FUNDE.

Dada Hirezi, Héctor, ed. 2002. *Más allá de las elecciones: Diez años después de los acuerdos de paz.* San Salvador: FLACSO.

Dalton, Roque. 1962. *El turno del ofendido.* La Habana: Casa de las Américas.

———. 1972 (1993). *Miguel Mármol: Los sucesos de 1932 en El Salvador.* San Salvador: UCA Editores.

———. 1974 (1999). *Las historias prohibidas del Pulgarcito.* Mexico City: Siglo XXI.

———. 1975 (1984). *Poemas clandestinos.* Puebla: Universidad Autónoma de Puebla.

———. 1975 (1993). *Pobrecito poeta que era yo . . .* San Salvador: UCA Editores.

Danner, Mark. 1994. *The Massacre at El Mozote: A Parable of the Cold War.* New York: Vintage Books.

Darling, Juanita. 2007. "Radio and Revolution in El Salvador: Building a Community of Listeners in the Midst of Civil War, 1981–1992." *American Journalism* 24 (4): 67–93.

———. 2008. The 3R's of El Salvador's Civil War: Revolution, Religion and Radio. *Journal of Media and Religion* 7 (3): 132–49.

Das, Veena, ed. 1990. *Mirrors of Violence: Communities, Riots and Survivors in South Asia.* Oxford: Oxford University Press.

Debray, Régis. 1967. *Révolution dans la révolution? Lutte armée et lutte politique en Amérique latine.* Paris: Maspero.

De Bremond, Ariane. 2007. "The Politics of Peace and Resettlement through El Salvador's Land Transfer Programme: Caught between the State and the Market." *Third World Quarterly* 28 (8): 1537–56.

Degregori, Carlos Iván. 2012. *How Difficult It Is to Be God: Shining Path's Politics of War in Peru, 1980–1999.* Madison: University of Wisconsin Press.

de Herrera, Norma. 2011. *La mujer en la revolución salvadoreña.* San Salvador: Instituto de Investigación, Capacitación y Desarrollo de la Mujer.

del Castillo, Graciana. 1997. "The Arms-for-Land Deal in El Salvador." In Doyle, Johnstone, and Orr, *Keeping the Peace,* 342–65.

———. 2001. "Post-conflict Reconstruction and the Challenge to International Organizations: The Case of El Salvador." *World Development* 29 (12): 1967–85.

Delugan, Robin Maria. 2012. *Reimagining National Belonging: Post-Civil War El Salvador in a Global Context.* Tucson: University of Arizona Press.

Deonandan, Kalowatie. 2007. "Revolutionaries to Politicians: Can the Transition Succeed?" In Deonandan, Close, and Prevost, *From Revolutionary Movements to Political Parties,* 227–45. New York: Palgrave Macmillan.

Deonandan, Kalowatie, David Close, and Gary Prevost, eds. 2007. *From Revolutionary Movements to Political Parties: Cases from Latin America and Africa.* New York: Palgrave Macmillan.

de Soto, Alvaro, and Graciana del Castillo. 1994. "Obstacles to Peacebuilding." *Foreign Policy* 94:69–83.

de Witte, Michael. 1989. *Dagboek uit El Salvador.* Berchem: Uitgeverij EPO.

de Zeeuw, Jeroen, ed. 2008. *From Soldiers to Politicians: Transforming Rebel Movements after Civil War.* Boulder, CO: Lynne Rienner Publishers.

———. 2010. "'Sons of War': Parties and Party Systems in Post-war El Salvador and Cambodia." *Democratization* 17 (6): 1176–1201.

Díaz, Nidia. 1988. *Nunca estuve sola.* San Salvador: UCA Editores.

Dickson-Gómez, Julia. 2002. "The Sound of Barking Dogs: Violence and Terror among Salvadoran Families in the Postwar." *Medical Anthropology Quarterly* 16 (4): 415–38.

———. 2004. "'One Who Doesn't Know War, Doesn't Know Anything': The Problem of Comprehending Suffering in Postwar El Salvador." *Anthropology and Humanism* 29 (2): 145–58.

Didion, Joan. 1983. *Salvador.* New York: Vintage Books.

Dodson, Michael, Donald Jackson, and Laura O'Shaughnessy. 2001. "Political Will and Public Trust: El Salvador's Procurator for the Defense of Human Rights and the Dilemmas of Institution-Building." *Human Rights Review* 2 (3): 51–75.

Doggett, Martha. 1993. *Death Foretold: The Jesuit Murders in El Salvador.* Washington, DC: Georgetown University Press.

Domínguez, Jorge, and Marc Lindenberg, eds. 1997. *Democratic Transitions in Central America.* Gainesville: University Press of Florida.

Doyle, Michael, Ian Johnstone, and Robert Orr, eds. 1997. *Keeping the Peace: Multidimensional UN Operations in Cambodia and El Salvador.* Cambridge: Cambridge University Press.

Duarte, José Napoleón, with Diana Page. 1986. *Duarte: My Story.* New York: G. P. Putnam's Sons.

Dudouet, Veronique. 2009. *From War to Politics: Resistance/Liberation Movements in Transition.* Berlin: Berghof.

Dunkerley, James. 1985. *The Long War: Dictatorship and Revolution in El Salvador.* New ed. London: Verso.

Eaton, Kent. 2006. "The Downside of Decentralization: Armed Clientelism in Colombia." *Security Studies* 15 (4): 533–62.

Edwards, Beatrice, and Gretta Tovar Siebentritt. 1991. *Places of Origin: The Repopulation of Rural El Salvador.* Boulder, CO: Lynne Rienner Publishers.

Eisenbrandt, Matt. 2017. *Assassination of a Saint: The Plot to Murder Óscar Romero and the Quest to Bring His Killers to Justice.* Berkeley: University of California Press.

Emirbayer, Mustafa. 2010. "Tilly and Bourdieu." *The American Sociologist* 41:400–422.

Escalona, María Teresa. 2003. "La radio como instrumento de lucha política: Radio Farabundo Martí (1982–1992)." In *Memoria del Primer Encuentro de Historia de El Salvador,* edited by Carlos Gregorio López Bernal, 257–80. San Salvador: Dirección de Publicaciones e Impresos.

Escobar, Arturo, and Sonia Alvarez, eds. 1992. *The Making of Social Movements in Latin America: Identity, Strategy and Democracy.* Boulder, CO: Westview Press.

Escobar, Cristina. 2000. "Bullfighting Fiestas, Clientelism and Political Identities in Northern Colombia." In *The Collective and the Public in Latin America: Cultural Identities and Political Order,* edited by Luis Roniger and Tamar Herzog, 174–91. Brighton: Sussex Academic Press.

Escobar Galindo, David. 2002. *Tiempos de reconstruir, tiempos de recordar . . .* San Salvador: Ricaldone.

Espinoza, Eduardo. 2007. *Relatos de una guerra.* San Salvador: Imprenta y Editorial Universitaria.

Estudios Centroamericanos. 1993. "Crónica del mes: Junio." *Estudios Centroamericanos* 536:607–17.

Falquet, Jules-France. 1997. "Les salvadoriennes et la guerre civile révolutionnaire." *CLIO: Histoire, femmes et sociétés* 5:117–31.

———. 2001. "División sexuelle du travail révolutionnaire: Réflexions à partir de l'expérience salvadorienne." *Cahiers d'Amérique latine* 40:109–28.

———. 2002. "Le mouvement des femmes dans la 'démocratisation' d'après-guerre au Salvador." *Cahiers du Genre* 33:179–200.

Falzon, Mark-Anthony. 2009. Introduction to *Multi-sited Ethnography: Theory, Praxis and Locality in Contemporary Research,* edited by Mark-Anthony Falzon, 1–24. Farnham: Ashgate.

Finocchiaro, Maurice. 1999. *Beyond Left and Right: Democratic Elitism in Mosca and Gramsci.* New Haven: Yale University Press.

Fitzsimmons, Tracy, and Mark Anner. 1999. "Civil Society in a Postwar Period: Labor in the Salvadoran Democratic Transition." *Latin American Research Review* 34 (3): 103–28.

FLACSO (Facultad Latinoamericana de Ciencias Sociales). 1995. *El Proceso Electoral 1994*. San Salvador: FLACSO.

FLACSO and Fundación Gallardo, eds. 2011. *Prensa Clandestina: El Salvador, 1970–1975*. Edición facsimilar numerada. San Salvador: FLACSO.

Fligstein, Neil, and Doug McAdam. 2012. *A Theory of Fields*. Oxford: Oxford University Press.

Flores Macal, Mario. 1980. "El Movimiento Sindical Salvadoreño: Características Principales." *Anuario de Estudios Centroamericanos* 6:17–24.

FMLN (Frente Farabundo Martí para la Liberación Nacional). 1992a. *Acuerdos hacia una nueva Nación: Recopilación de los acuerdos de paz suscritos con el gobierno de El Salvador*. San Salvador: FMLN.

———. 1992b. "De Comandantes Guerrilleros a Empresarios: Un Proyecto para la Reinserción Económica de los Oficiales del Ejército Nacional para la Democracia del FMLN." San Salvador, 18 de noviembre de 1992. Manuscript.

———. 1992c. "Programa de Reinserción Económica de Oficiales del FMLN." Manuscript.

Foley, Michael. 1996. "Laying the Groundwork: The Struggle for Civil Society in El Salvador." *Journal of Interamerican Studies and World Affairs* 38 (1): 76–104.

———, with George Vickers and Geoff Thale. 1997. *Tierra, paz y participación: El desarrollo de una política agraria de posguerra en El Salvador y el papel del Banco Mundial*. Washington, DC: WOLA.

———. 2010. "Cautionary Tales: Soft Intervention and Civil Society." In *Strengthening Peace in Post–Civil War States: Transforming Spoilers into Stakeholders*, edited by Matthew Hoddie and Caroline Hartzell, 163–88. Chicago: University of Chicago Press.

Foran, John. 1997. "Discourses and Social Forces: The Role of Culture and Cultural Studies in Understanding Revolutions." In *Theorizing Revolutions*, edited by John Foran, 197–220. London: Routledge.

———. 2005. *Taking Power: On the Origins of Third World Revolutions*. Cambridge: Cambridge University Press.

FPL (Fuerzas Populares de Liberación Farabundo Martí). 1973. "Estrella Roja (Número 1)." Manuscript.

———. 1974. "Elementos Estratégicos Revolucionarios." Manuscript.

———. 1992. "Reunión ampliada del Comité Central: Estrategia Parcial para el período de Post-Guerra, 1992–1994." Manuscript.

———. 1994. "Readecuaciones partidarias en 1994: Comisión de Construcción del Partido; Informe elaborado para el Comité Central." Dated February 1994. Manuscript.

Frankland, Gene, and Benoît Rihoux. 2008. "Conclusion: The Metamorphosis of Amateur-Activist Newborns into Professional-Activist Centaurs." In *Green Parties in Transition: The End of Grass-Roots Democracy?*, edited by Gene Frankland, Paul Lucardie, and Benoît Rihoux, 259–88. Farnham: Ashgate.

Freedman, Elaine. 2011. "Decreto 743: ¿Qué hay tras todo esto?" *Revista Envío Digital*, no. 352. http://www.envio.org.ni/articulo/4360.

Frundt, Henry. 2002. "Central American Unions in the Era of Globalization." *Latin American Research Review* 37 (3): 7–53.

Fuentes Díaz, Antonio, ed. 2015. *Conflictos y sujetos emergentes: Episodios en la transformación rural neoliberal*. Mexico City: Benemérita Universidad Autónoma de Puebla.

FUNDABRIL. 2009. "Diagnóstico: Situación socioeconómica de los/las veteranos de guerra del FMLN en dos zonas del país." Manuscript.

FUNDABRIL (Fundación 1 de Abril), ed. 2012. *La otra cara de la guerra: Salvador vidas; Experiencia de la sanidad guerrillera en Chalatenango y Cinquera, El Salvador*. San Salvador: FUNDABRIL.

Fundación 16 de Enero. 1993. "Diagnóstico sobre la situación de las mujeres excombatientes del FMLN." San Salvador. Manuscript.

Galeas, Geovani. 2004. *Mayor Roberto D'Aubuisson: El rostro más allá del mito*. San Salvador: La Prensa Gráfica.

———. 2013. *Héroes bajo sospecha: El lado oscuro de la guerra salvadoreña*. San Salvador: Editorial Athena.

Galeas, Geovani, and Berne Ayalá. 2008. *Grandeza y miseria en una guerrilla: Informe de una matanza*. San Salvador: Centroamérica 21.

Galli, Carlo. 2009. "On War and on the Enemy." *The New Centennial Review* 9 (2): 195–219.

Gammage, Sarah. 2006. "Exporting People and Recruiting Remittances: A Development Strategy for El Salvador?" *Latin American Perspectives* 33 (6): 75–100.

García Canclini, Néstor. 1986. "Gramsci y las culturas populares en América Latina." *Dialéctica* 40 (18): 13–33.

García Dueñas, Lauri, and Javier Espinoza. 2010. *¿Quién asesinó a Roque Dalton? Mapa de un largo silencio*. San Salvador: Indole Editores.

Garibay, David. 2004. "Salvador, les défis du renouvellement: Le FMLN et les élections de 2003 et 2004." *Problèmes d'Amérique latine* 54 (3): 33–52.

———. 2006. "Un partido de izquierda radical frente a las reivindicaciones de género: Entre el estancamiento de los números y la afirmación de la radicalidad; El caso del FMLN en El Salvador." *Política* 46:141–71.

Gay, Robert. 1994. *Popular Organization and Democracy in Rio de Janeiro: A Tale of Two Favelas*. Philadelphia: Temple University Press.

———. 2006. "The Even More Difficult Transition from Clientelism to Citizenship: Lessons from Brasil." In *Out of the Shadows: Political Action and the Informal Economy in Latin America*, edited by Patricia Fernández-Kelly and Jon Shefner, 195–217. University Park: Pennsylvania State University Press.

Gibb, Tom. 2000. "Under the Shadow of Dreams: El Salvador's Revolutionaries." Unpublished book manuscript.

Gill, Lesley. 2004. *The School of the Americas: Military Training and Political Violence in the Americas.* Durham, NC: Duke University Press.

Goffman, Erving. 1961. *Asylums: Essays on the Social Situation of Mental Patients and Other Inmates.* Chicago: Aldine.

———. 1974. *Frame Analysis: An Essay on the Organization of the Experience.* New York: Harper Colophon.

Gómez, Ileana. 2001. "Rebuilding Community in the Wake of War: Churches and Civil Society in Morazán." In *Christianity, Social Change, and Globalization in the Americas,* edited by Anna Lisa Peterson, Manuel Vásquez, and Philip Williams, 123–42. New Brunswick, NJ: Rutgers University Press.

González, Leonel. 1992. Prólogo [foreword] to *Acuerdos hacia una nueva nación: Recopilación de los acuerdos de paz suscritos con el gobierno de El Salvador,* by FMLN. San Salvador: FMLN.

González, Luis Armando. 2003. "De la ideología al pragmatismo: Ensayo sobre las trayectorias ideológicas de ARENA y el FMLN." *Estudios Centroamericanos,* no. 661–62:1173–1202.

———. 2006. "La muerte de Schafik Handal y su significado para la izquierda." *Estudios Centroamericanos* 687:96–100.

———. 2011. "El FMLN salvadoreño: De la guerrilla al gobierno." *Nueva Sociedad* 234:143–59.

González, Medardo. 2010. *Memorias del Camino para compartir: Entrevista con Medardo González, comandante Milton, coordinador general del FMLN.* San Salvador: Editorial Morazán.

González, Olga. 2011. *Unveiling Secrets of War in the Peruvian Andes.* Chicago: University of Chicago Press.

Goodale, Mark, and Nancy Postero, eds. 2013. *Neoliberalism, Interrupted: Social Change and Contested Governance in Contemporary Latin America.* Stanford: Stanford University Press.

Gootenberg, Paul, and Luis Reygadas. 2010. *Indelible Inequalities in Latin America: Insights from History, Politics, and Culture.* Durham, NC: Duke University Press.

Gordimer, Nadine. 2012. *No Time like the Present.* London: Bloomsbury.

Gordon, Sara. 1989. *Crisis Política y Guerra en El Salvador.* Mexico City: Siglo Veintiuno Editores.

Gott, Richard. 1970. *Guerrilla Movements in Latin America.* London: Nelson and Sons.

Gould, Jeffrey. 2015. "Ignacio Ellacuría and the Salvadorean Revolution." *Journal of Latin American Studies* 47 (2): 285–315.

Gould, Jeffrey, and Aldo Lauria-Santiago. 2008. *To Rise in Darkness: Revolution, Repression, and Memory in El Salvador, 1920–1932.* Durham, NC: Duke University Press.

Gramsci, Antonio. 1971. *Selections from the Prison Notebooks*. New York: International Publishers.

Grandin, Greg. 2004. *The Last Colonial Massacre: Latin America in the Cold War*. Chicago: University of Chicago Press.

———. 2007. *Empire's Workshop: Latin America, the United States, and the Rise of the New Imperialism*. New York: Holt & Company.

Graziano, Frank. 1999. *The Millennial New World*. New York: Oxford University Press.

Greene, Samuel, and Stacy Keogh. 2009. "The Parliamentary and Presidential Elections in El Salvador, March 2009." *Electoral Studies* 28 (4): 666–69.

Grenier, Yvon. 1996. "From Causes to Causers: The Etiology of Salvadoran Internal War Revisited." *Journal of Conflict Studies* 16 (2). http://journals.hil .unb.ca/index.php/JCS/article/view/11812/12630.

———. 1999. *The Emergency of Insurgency in El Salvador: Ideology and Political Will*. Pittsburgh: University of Pittsburgh Press.

Grenier, Yvon, and Jean Daudelin. 1995. "Foreign Assistance and the Market-Place of Peacemaking: Lessons from El Salvador." *International Peacekeeping* 1 (3): 350–64.

Grupo Conjunto. 1994. *Informe del grupo conjunto para la investigación de grupos armados ilegales con motivación política en El Salvador*. San Salvador.

Guáqueta, Alejandro. 2005. *Desmovilización y reinserción en El Salvador: Lecciones para Colombia*. Bogotá: Fundación Ideas para la Paz.

Guerrero, Andrés. 1991. *La semántica de la dominación: El concertaje de indios*. Quito: Ediciones Libri Mundi.

Guevara, Ernesto Che. 1961a. "Cuba: An Exceptional Case?" *Monthly Review* 13 (3–4): 56–71.

———. 1961b (2006). *La Guerra de Guerrillas: Edición autorizada con corecciones*. La Habana: Ocean Sur.

———. 1970. *Obras, 1957–1967*. Vol. 2. La Habana: Casa de las Américas.

———. 1994. *The Bolivian Diary of Ernesto Che Guevara*. New York: Pathfinder.

Hammes, Thomas. 2005. "Insurgency: Modern Warfare Evolves into a Fourth Generation." *Strategic Forum* 214:1–7.

Hammond, John. 1993. "War-Uprooting and the Political Mobilization of Central American Refugees." *Journal of Refugee Studies* 6 (2): 105–22.

———. 1998. *Fighting to Learn: Popular Education and Guerrilla War in El Salvador*. New Brunswick, NJ: Rutgers University Press.

Handal, Schafik. 2004. *El FMLN y la vigencia del pensamiento revolucionario en El Salvador*. San Salvador: Instituto Schafik Handal.

———. 2007. *Atentados contra el estado de derecho y la voluntad del pueblo*. San Salvador: Instituto Schafik Handal.

Harnecker, Marta. 1969 (2005). *Los conceptos elementales del materialismo histórico*. Mexico City: Siglo Veintiuno.

———. 1983. *Pueblos en Armas: Entrevistas a los principales comandantes guerrilleros de Nicaragua, El Salvador, Guatemala.* Mexico City: Universidad Autónoma de Guerrero.

———. 1993. *Con la mirada en alto: Historia de las Fuerzas Populares de Liberación a través de entrevistas con sus dirigentes.* San Salvador: UCA Editores.

Harper, Douglas. 2002. "Talking about Pictures: A Case for Photo Elicitation." *Visual Studies* 17 (1): 13–26.

———. 2003. "Reimagining Visual Methods: Galileo to Neuromancer." In *Collecting and Interpreting Qualitative Materials*, edited by Norman Denzin and Yvonna Lincoln, 717–32. 2nd ed. London: Sage.

Hart, Gillian. 2007. "Changing Concepts of Articulation: Political Stakes in South Africa Today." *Review of African Political Economy* 34 (111): 85–101.

Helmke, Gretchen, and Steven Levitsky. 2004. "Informal Institutions and Comparative Politics: A Research Agenda." *Perspectives on Politics* 2 (4): 725–40.

Henríquez Consalvi, Carlos. 2010. *Broadcasting the Civil War in El Salvador: A Memoir of Guerrilla Radio.* Austin: University of Texas Press.

Hernández, Alfonso. 1981. *León de Piedra: Testimonios de la lucha de clases en El Salvador.* No publication information.

Hernández, Marco. 2009. "El Salvador: La revolución inconclusa." Unpublished book manuscript.

Hernández Pico, Juan. 1995. "El pacto: ¿Autoritarismo o democratización?" *Revista Envío Digital*, no. 161. http://www.envio.org.ni/articulo/143.

Hernández Rivas, Georgina. 2011. "Conservación y gestión de la memoria del conflicto armado salvadoreño." In *Conflicto, memoria y pasados traumáticos: El Salvador contemporáneo*, edited by Eduardo Rey Tristán and Pilar Cagiao Vila, 241–54. Santiago: Universidad de Santiago de Compostela.

———. 2015. "Cartografía de la memoria: Actores, lugares y prácticas en El Salvador de posguerra (1992–2015)." Tesis doctoral, Universidad Autónoma de Madrid.

Herrera, Morena, et al. 2008. *Movimiento de Mujeres en El Salvador, 1995–2006: Estrategías y miradas desde el feminismo.* San Salvador: FUNDE.

Hilgers, Tina. 2008. "Causes and Consequences of Political Clientelism: México's PRD in Comparative Perspective." *Latin American Politics and Society* 50 (4): 123–53.

Hipsher, Patricia. 2001. "Right- and Left-Wing Women in Post-Revolutionary El Salvador: Feminist Autonomy and Cross-Political Alliance Building for Gender Equality." In *Radical Women in Latin America: Left and Right*, edited by Victoria González and Karen Kampwirth, 133–64. University Park: Pennsylvania State University Press.

Hirschman, Albert. 1970. *Exit, Voice, and Loyalty: Responses to Decline in Firms, Organizations, and States.* Cambridge, MA: Harvard University Press.

Holland, Alisha. 2016. "Insurgent Successor Parties: Scaling Down to a Party after War." In *Challenges of Party-Building in Latin America*, edited by Steven Levitsky et al., 273–304. New York: Cambridge University Press.

Hudson, Rex. 1988. *Castro's America Department: Coordinating Cuba's Support for Marxist-Leninist Violence in the Americas.* Washington, DC: Cuban American National Foundation.

Huizer, Gerrit. 1973. *Peasant Rebellion in Latin America.* London: Penguin Books.

Humphreys, Macartan, and Jeremy Weinstein. 2007. "Demobilization and Reintegration." *Journal of Conflict Resolution* 51 (4): 531–67.

Huntington, Samuel. 1991. *Democratization in the Late Twentieth Century.* Norman: University of Oklahoma Press.

Ibarra Chávez, Héctor. 2009. *La Brigada Rafael Arce Zablah: Una historia contada por sus protagonistas.* Mexico City: Ediciones Expediente Abierto.

IDHUCA (Instituto de Derechos Humanos de la UCA). 2004. *Informe electoral 2004: Observatorio Ciudadano de las Elecciones Presidenciales El Salvador 2004.* San Salvador: UCA.

International Communist League. 2014. "El Salvador: Ex-Guerrillas Remain at Helm of Capitalist State." *Workers Vanguard*, no. 1046. http://www.icl-fi.org/english/wv/1046/elsalvador.html.

Isbester, Katharine, ed. 2011. *The Paradox of Democracy in Latin America: Ten Country Studies of Division and Resilience.* Toronto: University of Toronto Press.

IUDOP (Instituto Universitario de Opinión Pública). 2016. "Los salvadoreños y las salvadoreñas evalúan la situación del país a finales de 2015." *IUDOP Boletín de Prensa* 30 (1): 1–16.

Jackson, William. 1990. "Congressional Oversight of Intelligence: Search for a Framework." *Intelligence and National Security* 5 (3): 113–47.

Jarstad, Anna, and Timothy Sisk. 2008. *From War to Democracy: Dilemmas of Peacebuilding.* Cambridge: Cambridge University Press.

Jasper, James. 2006. *Getting Your Way: Strategic Dilemmas in the Real World.* Chicago: University of Chicago Press.

———. 2011. "Emotions and Social Movements: Twenty Years of Theory and Research." *Annual Review of Sociology* 37:285–303.

Jennings, Kathleen. 2008. "Unclear Ends, Unclear Means: Reintegration in Postwar Societies—The Case of Liberia." *Global Governance* 14 (3): 327–45.

Jiménez, Edgar, et al., eds. 1988. *El Salvador: Guerra, política y paz (1979–1988).* San Salvador: CINAS.

Joes, Anthony James. 2006. *Resisting Rebellion: The History and Politics of Counterinsurgency.* Lexington: University Press of Kentucky.

Johnstone, Ian. 1995. *Rights and Reconciliation: UN Strategies in El Salvador.* Boulder, CO: Lynne Rienner Publishers.

Juárez, Jorge. 2011. "Memoria e historia reciente en El Salvador: La necesidad de nuevos mitos en el presente salvadoreño." In *Conflicto, memoria y pasados traumáticos: El Salvador contemporáneo*, edited by Eduardo Rey Tristán and Pilar Cagiao Vila, 275–84. Santiago: Universidad de Santiago de Compostela.

———. 2015. "Mayo Sibrián en el frente paracentral." Paper presented at 55th International Congress of Americanists, San Salvador, July.

Judson, Fred. 2002. "Central American Revolutionary Music." In *Music and Marx: Ideas, Practice, Politics*, edited by Regula Burckhardt Qureshi, 204–35. London: Routledge.

Juhn, Tricia. 1998. *Negotiating Peace in El Salvador: Civil-Military Relations and the Conspiracy to End the War.* New York: St. Martin's Press.

Kalyvas, Stathis. 2006. *The Logic of Violence in Civil War.* Cambridge: Cambridge University Press.

Kamenitsa, Lisa. 1998. "The Complexity of Decline: Explaining the Marginalization of the East German Women's Movement." *Mobilization* 3 (20): 245–63.

Kampwirth, Karen. 2004. *Feminism and the Legacy of Revolution: Nicaragua, El Salvador, Chiapas.* Athens: Ohio University Press.

Kandel, Susan. 2002. *Migraciones, medio ambiente y pobreza rural en El Salvador.* San Salvador: PRISMA.

Kapmeyer, Rolando. 2004. "Agrarian Reform and Development in El Salvador: A Case Study from the Lower Lempa River Region." PhD diss., Philipps University, Marburg.

Katayanagi, Mari. 2002. *Human Rights Functions of United Nations Peacekeeping Operations.* Dordrecht: Martinus Nijhoff.

Kay, Cristóbal. 2015. "The Agrarian Question and the Neoliberal Rural Transformation in Latin America." *European Review of Latin American and Caribbean Studies* 100:73–83.

Keeley, Brian L. 1999. "Of Conspiracy Theories." *Journal of Philosophy* 96 (3): 109–26.

Kelly, John. 1996. "Union Militancy and Social Partnership." In *The New Workplace and Trade Unionism*, edited by Peter Ackers, Chris Smith, and Paul Smith, 77–109. London: Routledge.

Keune, Lou. 1995. *Sobrevivimos la guerra: La historia de los pobladores de Arcatao y San José Las Flores.* El Salvador: Adelina Editores.

Khan, Mushtaq. 2005. "Markets, States and Democracy: Patron-Client Networks and the Case for Democracy in Developing Countries." *Democratization* 12 (5): 704–24.

King, Nigel, and Christine Horrocks. 2010. *Interviews in Qualitative Research.* London: Sage.

Kirkpatrick, Jeane. 1987. "Dictatorship and Double Standards." In *El Salvador: Central America in the New Cold War*, edited by Marvin Gettleman et al., 14–34. 2nd ed. New York: Grove Press.

———. 1988. *Legitimacy and Force.* Vol. 2. New Brunswick, NJ: Transaction Publishers.

Köpcke, Bettina. 1999. "Partizipation in Krieg und Frieden: Erfahrungen im Basisgesundheitswesen von drei Wiederbesiedlungen Chalatenangos, El Salvador, Mittelamerika, 1986–1996." PhD diss., Universität Heidelberg.

Kowalchuk, Lisa. 2003a. "Peasant Struggle, Political Opportunities, and the Unfinished Agrarian Reform in El Salvador." *Canadian Journal of Sociology* 28 (3): 309–40.

———. 2003b. "From Competition to Cooperation: Threats, Opportunities, and Organizational Survival in the Salvadorean Peasant Movement." *European Review of Latin American and Caribbean Studies* 74:43–63.

———. 2004. "The Salvadoran Land Struggle in the 1990s: Cohesion, Commitment, and Corruption." In Lauria-Santiago and Binford, *Landscapes of Struggle,* 187–206.

———. 2005. "The Discourse of Demobilization: Shifts in Activist Priorities and the Framing of Political Opportunities in a Peasant Land Struggle." *The Sociological Quarterly* 46:237–61.

Krämer, Michael. 1998. *El Salvador, unicornio de la memoria.* San Salvador: Ediciones MUPI.

Krauss, Clifford. 1991. *Inside Central America: Its People, Politics, and History.* New York: Simon & Schuster.

Krauze, Enrique. 2011. *Redeemers: Ideas and Power in Latin America.* New York: HarperCollins.

Kriesi, Hanspeter. 1996. "The Organizational Structure of New Social Movements in a Political Context." In *Comparative Perspectives on Social Movements,* edited by Doug McAdam, John McCarthy, and Mayer N. Zald, 152–84. Cambridge: Cambridge University Press.

Kriesi, Hanspeter, et al. 1995. *New Social Movements in Western Europe: A Comparative Analysis.* Minneapolis: University of Minnesota Press.

Kriger, Norma. 2003. *Guerrilla Veterans in Post-War Zimbabwe: Symbolic and Violent Politics, 1980–1987.* Cambridge: Cambridge University Press.

Kruijt, Dirk. 2008. *Guerrillas: War and Peace in Central America.* London: Zed Books.

———. 2017. *Cuba and Revolutionary Latin America: An Oral History.* London: Zed Books.

Kuran, Timur. 1997. *Private Truths, Public Lies: The Social Consequences of Preference Falsification.* Cambridge, MA: Harvard University Press.

Ladutke, Lawrence. 2004. *Freedom of Expression in El Salvador: The Struggle for Human Rights and Democracy.* Jefferson, NC: McFarland.

———. 2008. "Understanding Terrorism Charges against Protesters in the Context of Salvadoran History." *Latin American Perspectives* 35 (6): 137–50.

Lalich, Janja. 2004. *Bounded Choice: True Believers and Charismatic Cults.* Berkeley: University of California Press.

Lauria-Santiago, Aldo. 2005. "The Culture and Politics of State Terror and Repression in El Salvador." In *When States Kill: Latin America, the U.S., and Technologies of Terror,* edited by Cecilia Menjívar and Néstor Rodriguez, 85–114. Austin: University of Texas Press.

Lauria-Santiago, Aldo, and Leigh Binford, eds. 2004. *Landscapes of Struggle: Politics, Society, and Community in El Salvador.* Pittsburgh: University of Pittsburgh Press.

Lazo, José Francisco. 1995. "Elecciones y lecciones . . . ¿Qué pasó en marzo de 1994?" *Realidad: Revista de Ciencias Sociales y Humanidades* 43:109–90.

Lee, Hong Yung. 1992. *From Revolutionary Cadres to Party Technocrats in Revolutionary China.* Berkeley: University of California Press.

Lehoucq, Fabrice. 2012. *The Politics of Modern Central America: Civil War, Democratization, and Underdevelopment.* Cambridge: Cambridge University Press.

Lenin, Vladimir. 1969 (1902). *What Is to Be Done? Burning Questions of Our Movement.* New York: International Publishers.

Leonhard, Ralf. 1999. *Ondas rebeldes, ondas conformes.* San Salvador: Ediciones Heinrich Böll.

Levitsky, Steven, and Kenneth Roberts, eds. 2011. *The Resurgence of the Latin American Left.* Baltimore: Johns Hopkins University Press.

Levitsky, Steven, et al., eds. 2016. *Challenges of Party-Building in Latin America.* New York: Cambridge University Press.

Lichbach, Mark. 1987. "Deterrence or Escalation? The Puzzle of Aggregate Studies of Repression and Dissent." *Journal of Conflict Resolution* 31 (2): 266–97.

Lih, Lars. 2006. *Lenin Rediscovered: 'What Is to Be Done?' in Context.* Leiden: Brill.

Lindo-Fuentes, Héctor, and Erik Ching. 2012. *Modernizing Minds in El Salvador: Education Reform and the Cold War, 1960–1980.* Albuquerque: University of New Mexico Press.

Lindo-Fuentes, Héctor, Erik Ching, and Rafael Lara Martínez. 2010. *Recordando 1932: La Matanza, Roque Dalton y la Política de la Memoria Histórica.* San Salvador: FLACSO.

Lindsay-Poland, John. 1989. "Unwelcome in El Salvador: For Those Who Come to Help; Threats, Deportation, Even Death." *The Progressive* 53 (5): 32–35.

Linz, Juan. 1978. *Crisis, Breakdown and Reequilibration.* Baltimore: Johns Hopkins University Press.

———. 2006. *Robert Michels, Political Sociology, and the Future of Democracy.* New Brunswick, NJ: Transaction Publishers.

López Bernal, Carlos Gregorio. 2015. "Schafik Jorge Handal y la 'unidad' del FMLN de postguerra: Entre la memoria y la historia; El Salvador, 1992–

2015." Paper presented at the 55th International Congress of Americanists, San Salvador, July.

López Vigil, José Ignacio. 1991. *Las Mil y Una Historias de Radio Venceremos*. San Salvador: UCA Editores.

López Vigil, María. 1987. *Muerte y Vida en Morazán: Testimonio de un sacerdote*. San Salvador: UCA Editores.

Löwy, Michael. 2008. "Communism and Religion: José Carlos Mariátegui's Revolutionary Mysticism." *Latin American Perspectives* 35 (2): 71–79.

Loya Marín, Nayelly. 2008. *El comportamiento electoral en las elecciones municipales: El Salvador, 1994–2006*. San Salvador: FundaUngo.

Luciak, Ilja. 1999. "Gender Equality in the Salvadoran Transition." *Latin American Perspectives* 26 (2): 43–67.

———. 2001. *Después de la revolución: Igualdad de género y democracia en El Salvador, Nicaragua y Guatemala*. San Salvador: UCA Editores.

Lungo, Mario. 1987. *La lucha de masas en El Salvador*. San Salvador: UCA Editores.

Lungo, Mario, Nidia Umaña, and Alicia Rivero. 1996. *Desarraigo y reasentamiento: La construcción de comunidades en los asentamientos humanos de las zonas ex-conflictivas de El Salvador*. San Salvador: FUNDASAL.

Macdonald, Mandy, and Mike Gatehouse. 1995. *In the Mountains of Morazán: Portrait of a Returned Refugee Community in El Salvador*. London: Latin America Bureau.

Macías Mayora, Julio César. 1997. *La guerrilla fue mi camino: Epitafio para César Montes*. Guatemala City: Editorial Piedra Santa.

MacLeod, Lisa Hall. 2006. *Constructing Peace: Lessons from UN Peacebuilding Operations in El Salvador and Cambodia*. Lanham, MD: Lexington Books.

Maddison, Sarah, and Sean Scalmer. 2006. *Activist Wisdom: Practical Knowledge and Creative Tension in Social Movements*. Sydney: University of New South Wales Press.

Majano, Adolfo. 2009. *Una oportunidad perdida: 15 de octubre 1979*. San Salvador: Indole Editores.

Mampilly, Zachariah. 2011. *Rebel Rulers: Insurgent Governance and Civilian Life during War*. Ithaca, NY: Cornell University Press.

Manning, Carrie. 2004. "Armed Opposition Groups into Political Parties: Comparing Bosnia, Kosovo, and Mozambique." *Studies in Comparative International Development* 39 (1): 54–77.

———. 2007. "Party-Building on the Heels of War: El Salvador, Bosnia, Kosovo and Mozambique." *Democratization* 14 (2): 253–72.

———. 2008. *The Making of Democrats: Elections and Party Development in Postwar Bosnia, El Salvador, and Mozambique*. New York: Palgrave Macmillan.

Manning, Carrie, and Ian Smith. 2016. "Political Party Formation by Former Armed Opposition Groups after Civil War." *Democratization* 23 (6): 972–89.

Manwaring, Max, and Court Prisk. 1988. *El Salvador at War: An Oral History of Conflict from the 1979 Insurrection to the Present.* Washington, DC: National Defense University Press.

Manzano Merino, Ana Carolina. 1994. *Mapa de la comunidad de ONGs: Sombrillas y Consorcios.* San Salvador: USAID.

Mao Tse-tung. 1971. *Selected Readings from the Works of Mao Tse-tung.* Peking: Foreign Language Press.

Marcus, George. 1995. "Ethnography in/of the World System: The Emergence of Multi-Sited Ethnography." *Annual Review of Anthropology* 24:95–117.

Marighella, Carlos. 1969 (2008). *Minimanual of the Urban Guerrilla.* St. Petersburg, FL: Red and Black Publishers.

Martí i Puig, Salvador, and Carlos Figueroa Ibarra, eds. 2006. *La izquierda revolucionaria en Centroamérica: De la lucha armada a la participación electoral.* Madrid: Catarata.

Martí i Puig, Salvador, Adolfo Garcé, and Alberto Martín. 2013. "¿Liderazgo, organización o ideología? Las diferentes vías de adaptación partidaria de los movimientos guerrilleros. Los casos de Nicaragua, El Salvador y Uruguay." *Revista Española de Ciencia Política* 33:57–79.

Martín Alvarez, Alberto. 2004. "De movimiento de liberación a partido político: Articulación de los fines organizativos en el FMLN salvadoreño (1980–1992)." PhD diss., Universidad Complutense de Madrid.

———. 2006. "El Frente Farabundo Martí para la Liberación Nacional: De movimiento de liberación a partido político." In *La izquierda revolucionaria en Centroamérica: De la lucha armada a la participación electoral,* edited by Salvador Martí y Puig and Carlos Figueroa Ibarra, 91–128. Madrid: Catarata.

———. 2010. "Ideología y Redes Sociales en el Surgimiento de Violencia Política: El Frente Farabundo Martí para la Liberación Nacional." Article presented at the 14th Encuentro de Latinoamericanistas Españoles, Santiago de Compostela, Spain, September 16–18.

———. 2011. "De guerrilla a partido político: El Frente Farababundo Martí para la Liberación Nacional (FMLN)." *Historia y Política* 25 (1): 207–33.

———. 2014. "Del partido a la guerrilla: Los orígenes de las Fuerzas Populares de Liberación Farabundo Martí." In *Historia y debates sobre el conflicto armado salvadoreño y sus secuelas,* edited by Jorge Juárez, 55–62. San Salvador: Editorial Universitaria.

Martín Alvarez, Alberto, and Eudald Cortina Orero. 2014. "The Genesis and Internal Dynamics of El Salvador's People's Revolutionary Army." *Journal of Latin American Studies* 46 (4): 663–89.

Martín Alvarez, Alberto, and Ralph Sprenkels. 2014. "La izquierda revolucionaria salvadoreña: Balance historiográfico y perspectivas de investigación."

In *El estudio de las luchas revolucionarias en América Latina (1959–1996): Estado de la cuestión*, edited by Martín López Ávalos, Verónica Oikión Solano, and Eduardo Rey Tristán, 212–40. Zamora, Michoacán: El Colegio de Michoacán.

Martín-Baró, Ignacio. 1973. "Psicología del campesino salvadoreño." *Estudios Centroamericanos* 297:476–95.

———. 1989. "La institucionalización de la guerra." *Revista de Psicología de El Salvador* 8 (33): 223–45.

Martínez, Ana Guadalupe. 1978. *Las cárceles clandestinas de El Salvador.* San Salvador: UCA Editores.

Martínez Peñate, Oscar. 1995. *El Salvador: Del conflicto armado a la negociación, 1979–1989.* Ontario, CA: Bandek Enterprises.

Marx, Gary. 1974. "Thoughts on a Neglected Category of Social Movement Participant: The Agent Provocateur and the Informant." *The American Journal of Sociology* 80 (2): 402–42.

Mason, David. 1986. "Land Reform and the Breakdown of Clientelist Politics in El Salvador." *Comparative Political Studies* 18 (4): 487–516.

Mata, Mario, and Julio Martínez. 2009. *Movimientos sociales de campesinos e indígenas en El Salvador.* San Salvador.

Mazzei, Julie. 2009. *Death Squads or Self-Defense Forces? How Paramilitary Groups Emerge and Challenge Democracy in Latin America.* Chapel Hill: University of North Carolina Press.

McAdam, Doug, John McCarthy, and Meyer N. Zald. 1988. "Social Movements." In *Handbook of Sociology*, edited by Neil Smelser, 695–738. Beverley Hills, CA: Sage.

McAdam, Doug, Sidney Tarrow, and Charles Tilly. 2001. *Dynamics of Contention.* Cambridge: Cambridge University Press.

McClintock, Cynthia. 1998. *Revolutionary Movements in Latin America: El Salvador's FMLN and Peru's Shining Path.* Washington, DC: United States Institute of Peace.

McClintock, Michael. 1985. *The American Connection: State Terror and Popular Resistance in El Salvador.* London: Zed Books.

McCormick, David. 1997. "From Peacekeeping to Peacebuilding." In *Keeping the Peace: Multidimensional UN Operations in Cambodia and El Salvador*, edited by Michael Doyle, Ian Johnstone, and Robert Orr, 282–311. Cambridge: Cambridge University Press.

McElhinny, Vincent. 2004. "Between Clientelism and Radical Democracy: The Case of Ciudad Segundo Montes." In Lauria-Santiago and Binford, *Landscapes of Struggle*, 147–65.

———. 2006. "Inequality and Empowerment: The Political Foundations of Post-War Decentralization and Development in El Salvador, 1992–2000." PhD diss., University of Pittsburgh.

McLaren, Peter. 2000. *Che Guevara, Paulo Freire, and the Pedagogy of Revolution.* Lanham, MD: Rowman & Littlefield.

McLaren, Peter, and Peter Leonard, eds. 1993. *Paulo Freire: A Critical Encounter.* London: Routledge.

McMullin, Jaremey. 2013. "Integration or Separation? The Stigmatisation of Ex-combatants after War." *Review of International Studies* 39 (2): 385–414.

McReynolds, Samuel. 2002. "Land Reform in El Salvador and the Chapultepec Peace Accord." *Journal of Peasant Studies* 30 (1): 135–69.

Medrano, Juan Ramón. 1992. "Revolución Democrática." Tesis para estrategia del FMLN. Manuscript.

Medrano, Juan Ramón, and Walter Raudales. 1994. *Ni militar ni sacerdote: De suedónimo Balta.* San Salvador: Ediciones Arcoiris.

Melara Minero, Lidice Michelle. 2012. "El asesinato de los dirigentes del FDR en la construcción discursiva de Roberto d'Aubuisson." *Identidades* 2 (4): 108–26.

Mena Sandoval, Francisco Emilio. 1990. *Del ejército nacional al ejército guerrillero.* San Salvador: Ediciones Arcoiris.

Menéndez Rodríguez, Mario. 1984. *El Salvador: Una auténtica guerra civil.* San José: Editorial Universitaria Centroamericana.

Menjívar Larín, Rafael. 2006. "Apéndice 4: Reflexiones sobre la insurección urbana." In *Tiempos de Locura: El Salvador, 1979–1981,* by Rafael Menjívar Ochoa, 272–96. Segunda edición ampliada. San Salvador: FLACSO.

Menjívar Ochoa, Rafael. 2006. *Tiempos de locura: El Salvador, 1979–1981.* Segunda edición ampliada. San Salvador: FLACSO.

Menzel, Sewall. 1994. *Bullets versus Ballots: Political Violence and Revolutionary War in El Salvador, 1979–1991.* Coral Gables, FL: North-South Center.

Merino, José Luis. 2011. *Comandante Ramiro: Revelaciones de un guerrillero y líder revolucionario salvadoreño.* Mexico City: Ocean Sur.

Merlos, Enrique, and María Elena Moreno. 2004. "Una mirada desde la experiencia del SES en el sur de Tecoluca." In *Desarrollo económico local en Centroamérica: Estudios de comunidades globalizadas,* edited by Guillermo Lathrop and Juan Pablo Pérez Saínz. 99–138. San José: FLACSO.

Metsola, Lalli. 2006. "'Reintegration' of Ex-combatants and Former Fighters: A Lens into State Formation and Citizenship in Namibia." *Third World Quarterly* 27 (6): 1119–35.

———. 2010. "The Struggle Continues? The Spectre of Liberation, Memory Politics and 'War Veterans' in Namibia." *Development and Change* 41 (4): 589–613.

Metzi, Francisco. 1988. *Por los caminos de Chalatenango con la salud en la mochila.* San Salvador: UCA Editores.

Michels, Robert. 1962. *Political Parties: A Sociological Study of the Oligarchical Tendencies of Modern Democracy.* Glencoe, IL: The Free Press.

Mijango, Raúl. 2007. *Mi Guerra: Testimonio de toda una vida.* San Salvador.

Mische, Ann. 2008. *Partisan Publics: Communication and Contention amongst Brazilian Youth Activist Networks.* Princeton: Princeton University Press.

Moallic, Benjamin. 2010. "Victoire des anciens révolutionnaires ou ascension d'un nouveau personnel politique? Les réaménagements de l'espace politique salvadorien après les élections de 2009." *Problèmes d'Amérique latine* 78 (4): 111–29.

———. 2014. "De la guerra a sus memorias: Surgimiento de una profesión militante y recomposición de los revolucionarios (Nicaragua–El Salvador, 1992–2009)." *Trace* 66: 82–98.

Molinari, Lucrecia. 2013. "Contrainsurgencia y represión al movimiento sindical en El Salvador (1963–1972)." Paper presented at 10th Jornadas de Sociología Facultad de Ciencias Sociales, University of Buenos Aires, June 1–6, 2013.

Montes, Segundo. 1978. *El Compadrazgo: Una estructura de poder en El Salvador.* San Salvador: UCA Editores.

———. 1989. *Refugiados y repatriados: El Salvador y Honduras.* San Salvador: Instituto de Derechos Humanos, UCA.

Montgomery, Tommie Sue. 1982. *Revolution in El Salvador: Origins and Evolution.* Boulder, CO: Westview Press.

———. 1995a. *Revolution in El Salvador: From Civil Strife to Civil Peace.* 2nd ed. Boulder, CO: Westview Press.

———. 1995b. "Getting to Peace in El Salvador: The Roles of the United Nations Secretariat and ONUSAL." *Journal of Interamerican Studies and World Affairs* 37 (4): 139–72.

Montobbio, Manuel. 1999. *La metamorfosis del pulgarcito: Transición Política y Proceso de Paz en El Salvador.* Barcelona: Icaria Editorial.

Montoya, Ainhoa. 2011. "'Neither War nor Peace': Violence and Democracy in Post-War El Salvador." PhD diss., University of Manchester.

———. 2013. "The Violence of Cold War Polarities and the Fostering of Hope: The 2009 Elections in Postwar El Salvador." In *Central America in the New Millennium: Living Transition and Reimagining Democracy,* edited by Jennifer Burrell and Ellen Moodie, 49–63. New York: Berghahn Books.

———. 2015. "The Turn of the Offended: Clientelism in the Wake of El Salvador's 2009 Elections." *Social Analysis* 59 (4): 101–18.

Montoya, Aquiles. 1993. *La nueva economía popular: Una aproximación teórica.* San Salvador: UCA Editores.

———. 2001. "Community Economic Development in El Salvador." In *Transcending Neoliberalism: Community-Based Development in Latin America,* edited by Henry Veltmeyer and Anthony O'Malley, 154–83. Sterling, VA: Kumarian Press.

Moodie, Ellen. 2010. *El Salvador in the Aftermath of Peace: Crime, Uncertainty and Transition to Democracy.* Philadelphia: University of Pennsylvania Press.

———. 2013a. "Inequality and Intimacy between Sister Communities in El Salvador and the United States." *Missiology: An International Review* 41 (2): 146–62.

———. 2013b. "Democracy, Disenchantment , and the Future in El Salvador." In *Central America in the New Millennium: Living Transition and Reimagining Democracy*, edited by Jennifer Burrell and Ellen Moodie, 96–114. New York: Berghahn Books.

Moore, Barrington. 1966. *Social Origins of Dictatorship and Democracy: Lord and Peasant in the Making of the Modern World*. Boston: Beacon Press.

Morales, David, and Zaira Navas, eds. 2006. *Masacres: Trazos de la historia salvadoreña narrados por las víctimas*. Mejicanos: Centro para la Promoción de los Derechos Humanos "Madeleine Lagadec."

Morales, Evelyn, Lina Pohl, and Denis Racicot. 1995. "Situación de Derechos Humanos en el Marco Electoral." In *El Proceso Electoral 1994*, by FLACSO, 339–408. San Salvador: FLACSO.

Morales Carbonell, José Antonio. 1999. "El suicidio de Marcial ¿Un asunto concluido? Salvador Cayetano Carpio." In *Nuestras montañas son las masas: Documentos y escritos de la revolución salvadoreña*, by Salvador Cayetano Carpio, 26–75. Vienna: Der Keil.

Morel, Augusto. 1991. *Refugiados salvadoreños en Nicaragua*. Managua: ACRES.

Moreno, Elsa. 1997. *Mujeres y Política en El Salvador*. San José: FLACSO.

Moroni Bracamonte, José Angel, and David Spencer. 1995. *Strategy and Tactics of the Salvadoran FMLN Guerrillas: Last Battle of the Cold War, Blueprint for Future Conflicts*. Westport, CT: Praeger.

Motta, Stefano, and Dagoberto Gutiérrez. 2011. "Ideología y poder popular en El Salvador: La metamorfosis del FMLN y las posibilidades de construcción de un nuevo sujeto." *Revista Brasileira de Estudos Latino-Americanos* 1 (1): 81–112.

Navas, María Candelaria. 2007. "De guerrilleras a feministas: Origen de las organizaciones de mujeres post-conflicto en El Salvador (1992–1995)." Paper presented at the Segundo Encuentro Nacional de Historia, San Salvador, July 16–20.

Nepstad, Sharon Erica. 2001. "Creating Transnational Solidarity: The Use of Narrative in the U.S.–Central America Peace Movement." *Mobilization* 6 (1): 21–36.

———. 2004. *Convictions of the Soul: Religion, Culture, and Agency in the Central America Solidarity Movement*. Oxford: Oxford University Press.

Nilsson, Anders. 2005. *Reintegrating Ex-Combatants in Post-War Societies*. Stockholm: Swedish International Development Cooperation Agency.

North, Liisa. 1985. *Bitter Grounds: Roots of Revolt in El Salvador*. Toronto: Between the Lines.

Nueva Esperanza Support Group. 1999. *Like Gold in the Fire: Voices of Hope from El Salvador; War, Exile and Return, 1974–1999.* Nottingham: Russell Press.

Nugent, Daniel. 1993. *Spent Cartridges of Revolution: An Anthropological History of Namiquipa, Chihuahua.* Chicago: University of Chicago Press.

Oliver, Johanna. 2000. "Seeking a Return to Normalcy for Central America's Ex-combatants." In *War Force to Work Force: Global Perspectives on Demobilization and Reintegration,* edited by Natalie Pauwels, 260–94. Baden-Baden: Nomos.

Oñate, Andrea. 2011. "The Red Affair: FMLN-Cuban Relations during the Salvadoran Civil War, 1981–92." *Cold War History* 11 (2): 133–54.

Orr, Robert. 2001. "Building Peace in El Salvador: From Exception to Rule." In *Peacebuilding as Politics: Cultivating Peace in Fragile Societies,* edited by Elizabeth Cousens and Chetan Kumar, 165–67. Boulder, CO: Lynne Rienner Publishers.

Orrellana, Luis, Nicola Foroni, and Marden Nochez. 1998. "REFLECT and institutional Change: The Experience of CIAZO in El Salvador." *PLA Notes* 32:77–81.

Owens, Lynn. 2009. *Cracking under Pressure: Narrating the Decline of the Amsterdam Squatters.* Amsterdam: Amsterdam University Press.

Pampell Conaway, Camille, and Salomé Martínez. 2004. *Adding Value: Women's Contributions to Reintegration and Reconstruction in El Salvador.* Cambridge: Hunts Alternatives Fund.

Pansters, Wil, ed. 2012. *Violence, Coercion, and State-Making in Twentieth-Century Mexico: The Other Half of the Centaur.* Stanford: Stanford University Press.

Pareto, Vilfredo. 1991. *The Rise and Fall of Elites: An Application of Theoretical Sociology.* New Brunswick, NJ: Transaction Publishers.

Payeras, Mario. 1987. *El trueno en la Ciudad: Episodios de la lucha armada urbana del 1981 en Guatemala.* Mexico City: Juan Pablos Editor.

PCS (Partido Comunista de El Salvador). 2011. "45 años de sacrificada lucha revolucionaria, 1930–1975." In *Prensa Clandestina, El Salvador, 1970–1975,* edited by FLACSO and Fundación Gallardo, 79–106. Edición facsimilar numerada. San Salvador: FLACSO.

PD (Partido Demócrata). 1995. "Discurso pronunciado por Joaquín Villalobos en el Acto de constitución del Partido Demócrata (en organización)." Dated March 28, 1995. Manuscript.

PDDH (Procuraduría para la Defensa de los Derechos Humanos). 2006. "Informe preliminar sobre los sucesos del 5 de julio de 2006." Manuscript.

Pearce, Jenny. 1986. *Promised Land: Peasant Rebellion in Chalatenango, El Salvador.* London: Latin American Bureau.

———. 1999. "Peace-Building in the Periphery: Lessons from Central America." *Third World Quarterly* 20 (1): 51–68.

Peceny, Mark, and William Stanley. 2010. "Counterinsurgency in El Salvador." *Politics & Society* 38 (1): 67–94.

Peña Mendoza, Lorena. 2009. *Retazos de mi vida: Testimonio de una revolucionaria salvadoreña.* Mexico City: Ocean Sur.

Perales, Iosu. 1986. *Chalatenango, viaje por la guerrilla salvadoreña.* Madrid: Editorial Revolución.

Perla, Héctor. 2008. "Si Nicaragua venció, El Salvador vencerá: Central American Agency in the Creation of the U.S.–Central American Peace and Solidarity Movement." *Latin American Research Review* 43 (2): 136–58.

Perla, Héctor, and Héctor Cruz-Feliciano. 2013. "The Twenty-First-Century Left in El Salvador and Nicaragua: Understanding Apparent Contradictions and Criticisms." *Latin American Perspectives* 40 (3): 83–106.

Perlman, Janice. 2009. *Favela: Four Decades of Living on the Edge in Rio de Janeiro.* Oxford: Oxford University Press.

Peterson, Anna L. 1997. *Martyrdom and the Politics of Religion: Progressive Catholicism in El Salvador's Civil War.* Albany: State University of New York Press.

———. 2005. *Seeds of the Kingdom: Utopian Communities in the Americas.* Oxford: Oxford University Press.

Peterson, Anna L., and Brandt Peterson. 2008. "Martyrdom, Sacrifice, and Political Memory in El Salvador." *Social Research* 75 (2): 511–42.

Peterson, Brandt. 2006. "Consuming Histories: The Return of the Indian in Neoliberal El Salvador." *Cultural Dynamics* 18 (2): 163–88.

Petras, James. 2015. "The Demise of Incumbents: Resurgence of the Far Right and the Absence of the Consequential Left." The James Petras Website, November 6. http://petras.lahaine.org/?p=2061.

Petras, James, and Henry Veltmeyer. 2009. *What's Left in Latin America? Regime Change in New Times.* Farnham: Ashgate.

Piñeiro, Manuel. 2006. *Che Guevara and the Latin American Revolution.* 2nd ed. New York: Ocean Press.

Pink, Sarah. 2004. "Visual Methods." In *Qualitative Research Practice*, edited by Clive Seale, Giampietro Gobo, Jaber Gubrium, and David Silverman, 361–76. London: Sage.

Pirker, Kristina. 2007. "La redefinición de lo posible: Guerra civil y proceso de paz en las biografías de militantes de la izquierda salvadoreña." *Revista Centroamericana de Ciencias Sociales* 4 (2): 3–29.

———. 2008. "La redefinición de lo posible: Militancia y movilización social en El Salvador (1970–2004)." PhD diss., Universidad Nacional Autónoma de México.

Pirker, Kristina, and Omar Nuñéz. 2011. "Puente, retaguardia y voz: La Ciudad de México en el trabajo político-militar del FMLN." *Revista Izquierdas* 10:85–96.

Polletta, Francesca. 2006. *It Was Like a Fever: Storytelling in Protest and Politics.* Chicago: University of Chicago Press.

Popkin, Margaret. 2000. *Peace without Justice: Obstacles to Building the Rule of Law in El Salvador.* University Park: Pennsylvania State University Press.

PRS-ERP (Partido de la Revolución Salvadoreña—Ejército Revolucionario del Pueblo). 1992. "Discusión sobre estrategia: Minutas de la reunión de Jocoaitique." Dated March 22, 1992. Manuscript.

———. 1993a. "Carta a la dirección nacional y militantes del PRS-ERP: Asamblea de militantes reunidos en San Miguel." Dated November 8, 1993. Manuscript.

———. 1993b. "Informe posición de la dirección nacional del ERP sobre problemas internos en el partido." Dated November 10, 1993. Manuscript.

———. 1993c. "Resolución de la asamblea de congreso sobre problemas internos." Dated November 10, 1993. Manuscript.

Pyes, Craig, et al. 2004. *Los escuadrones de la muerte en El Salvador.* Segunda edición. San Salvador: Editorial Jaraguá.

Queirolo, Rosario. 2013. *The Success of the Left in Latin America: Untainted Parties, Market Reforms, and Voting Behavior.* Notre Dame, IN: University of Notre Dame Press.

Quezada, Rufino Antonio, and Hugo Roger Martínez. 1995. *25 años de estudio y lucha: Una cronología del movimiento estudiantil.* San Salvador.

Quintanilla Gómez, Nelson. 2010. "Elecciones 2009 y Campaña Política: Desafíos para la democracia salvadoreña." *Cuadernos de Ciencias Sociales* 1 (3): 27–44.

Quizar, Robin Ormes. 1998. *My Turn to Weep: Salvadoran Refugee Women in Costa Rica.* Westport, CT: Bergin & Garvey.

Rabe, Stephen. 2011. *The Killing Zone: The United States Wages Cold War in Latin America.* Oxford: Oxford University Press.

Radu, Michael. 1998. "Practitioners of Revolution." In *Violence and the Latin American Revolutionaries,* edited by Michael Radu, 82–105. New Brunswick, NJ: Transaction Publishers.

Ramírez, Sergio. 1999. *Adiós Muchachos: Una memoria de la revolución Sandinista.* Bogotá: Aguilar.

Ramos, Carlos. 1998. "El Salvador: Transición y procesos electorales a fines de los 90." *Nueva Sociedad* 158:28–39.

———. 1999. "El año pre-electoral: Dinamismos y escenarios de los actores políticos." In *Actores, Agendas y Escenarios en El Salvador 1998,* edited by Carlos Ramos, Carlos Acevedo, and Guillermo Padilla, 1–53. San Salvador: FLACSO.

Ramos, Carlos, and Carlos Briones. 1999. *Las elites: Percepciones y actitudes sobre los procesos de cambio político y de transformación institucional en El Salvador.* San Salvador: FLACSO.

Regalado, Roberto. 2011. *FMLN: Un gran tsunami de votos rojos.* Mexico City: Ocean Sur.

Richmond, Oliver, and Jason Franks. 2009. *Liberal Peace Transitions: Between Statebuilding and Peacebuilding.* Edinburgh: Edinburgh University Press.

Rico, José María. 1997. *Justicia penal y transición democrática en América Latina.* Mexico City: Siglo XXI Editores.

Rico Mira, Carlos Eduardo. 2003. *En silencio tenía que ser: Testimonio del conflicto armado en El Salvador, 1967–2000.* San Salvador: Editorial Universidad Francisco Gavidia.

Rivera, Ana Kelly, et al., eds. 1995. ¡¿Valió la pena?! Testimonios de salvadoreñas que vivieron la guerra. San Salvador: Editorial Sombrero Azul.

Rojas, Javier. 1986. *Conversaciones con el comandante Miguel Castellanos.* Santiago de Chile: Editorial Andante.

Roque Baldovinos, Ricardo. 2016. "Estética y política: Contracultura y revolución en El Salvador (1960–1980)." *Cultura de Guatemala* 37 (2): 33–52.

Rowland, Christopher, ed. 2007. *The Cambridge Companion to Liberation Theology.* 2nd ed. Cambridge: Cambridge University Press.

Rubin, Jeffrey. 1998. "Ambiguity and Contradiction in a Radical Popular Movement." In *Cultures of Politics, Politics of Culture: Re-visioning Latin American Social Movements*, edited by Sonia Alvarez, Evelina Dagnino, and Arturo Escobar, 141–64. Boulder, CO: Westview Press.

Russell, Philip. 1984. *El Salvador in Crisis.* Austin: Colorado River Press.

Salazar, Armando. 2016. *Los secretos de El Paraíso.* San Salvador: UCA Editores.

Salazar, Armando, and María del Carmen Cruz. 2012. *CCR: Organización y Lucha Popular en Chalatenango.* Chalatenango: Asociación de Comunidades para el Desarrollo de Chalatenango, CCR.

Samayoa, Salvador. 2002. *El Salvador: La reforma pactada.* San Salvador: UCA Editores.

Samayoa, Salvador, and Guillermo Galván. 1979. "El movimiento obrero en El Salvador: ¿Resurgimiento o agitación?" *Estudios Centroamericanos* 369–70:793–800.

Sánchez, Peter. 2015. *Priest under Fire: Padre David Rodríguez, the Catholic Church, and El Salvador's Revolutionary Movement.* Gainesville: University Press of Florida.

Sánchez-Blake, Elvira. 2002. "El legado del desarme: Voces y reflexiones de las excombatientes del M-19." *The Journal of Latin American Anthropology* 7 (1): 254–75.

Sánchez Cerén, Salvador. 2008. *Con sueños se escribe la vida: Autobiografía de un revolucionario salvadoreño.* Mexico City: Ocean Sur.

Santacruz Giralt, María. 2003. *Una aproximación al estudio sobre las clases medias y su comportamiento político.* San Salvador: Friedrich Ebert Stiftung and UCA Editores.

Sollis, Peter. 1992. "Displaced Persons and Human Rights in El Salvador." *Bulletin of Latin American Research* 11 (1): 49–67.

Sontag, Susan. 1977. *On Photography*. London: Penguin Books.

Southall, Roger. 2007. "Ten Propositions about Black Economic Empowerment in South Africa." *Review of African Political Economy* 111:67–84.

———. 2013. *Liberation Movements in Power: Party and State in Southern Africa*. Woodbridge: James Curry.

Spence, Jack. 2004. *War and Peace in Central America: Comparing Transitions toward Democracy and Social Equality in Guatemala, El Salvador, and Nicaragua*. Cambridge: Hemisphere Initiatives.

Spencer, David. 1996. *From Vietnam to El Salvador: The Saga of the FMLN Sappers and other Guerrilla Special Forces in Latin America*. Westport, CT: Praeger.

Spencer, Denise. 1997. *Demobilisation and Reintegration in Central America*. Bonn: International Center for Conversion.

Sprenkels, Ralph, ed. 2001. *El día más esperado: Buscando a los niños desaparecidos de El Salvador*. San Salvador: Asociación Pro-Búsqueda de Niñas y Niños Desaparecidos y UCA Editores.

———. 2002. "Erst verdrängt und dann vergessen." *Lateinamerika Nachrichten* 331:34–39.

———. 2003a. *La Paz en Construcción: Un estudio sobre la problemática de la niñez desaparecida por el conflicto armado en El Salvador*. San Salvador: Asociación Pro-Búsqueda.

———. 2003b. *Lives Apart: Family Separation and Alternative Care Arrangements during El Salvador's Civil War*. Stockholm: Save the Children.

———. 2004. "Heridas Pasadas, heridas presentes: Actualidad de la experiencia de la guerra en El Salvador, analizada desde la búsqueda de niñas y niños desaparecidos." In *Educar desde la memoria: Experiencias pedagógicas para la paz, la democracia y la equidad de género*, edited by Gloria Guzmán, Ena Peña, Begoña Ballesteros, and Mujeres por la Dignidad y la Vida [Las Dignas]. San Salvador: Las Dignas.

———. 2005. *The Price of Peace: The Human Rights Movement in Postwar El Salvador*. Amsterdam: Cuadernos del CEDLA.

———. 2009. *Caminar con el Pueblo: Entrevista con Jon Cortina*. San Salvador: Ediciones Populares.

———. 2011. "Roberto d'Aubuisson versus Schafik Handal: Militancy, Memory Work and Human Rights." *European Review of Latin American and Caribbean Studies* 91:15–30.

———. 2012. "La guerra como controversia: Una reflexión sobre las secuelas políticas del informe de la Comisión de la Verdad para El Salvador." *Identidades* 2 (4): 68–89.

———. 2014a. "Arena, FMLN y los sucesos del 5 de Julio de 2006 en El Salvador: Violencia e imaginarios políticos." *Trace* 66:62–81.

———. 2014b. "Las relaciones urbano-rurales en la insurgencia salvadoreña." In *Historia y debates sobre el conflicto armado salvadoreño y sus secuelas*, edited by Jorge Juárez, 25–44. San Salvador: Editorial Universitaria.

———. 2014c. "Reintegration or Reconversion? Probing the Nature of Disarmament, Demobilisation and Reintegration (DDR) Processes in Fragile Settings." IS Academy Research Brief. Wageningen: Wageningen University.

———, ed. 2015. *Stories Never to Be Forgotten: Eyewitness Accounts from the Salvadoran Civil War*. Tempe: Arizona State University Press.

———. Forthcoming. "Among Comrades: (Dis)trust in Ethnographic Fieldwork with Former Salvadoran Revolutionaries." In *Risky Anthropology*, edited by Kees Koonings, Dennis Rodgers, and Dirk Kruijt. London: Zed Books.

Sprenkels, Ralph, and Chris van der Borgh. 2011. "De politiek van civiele diplomatie: Burgeroorlog en mensenrechten in El Salvador." In *Civic Diplomacy: Diplomatie tussen macht en mensenrechten*, edited by Beatrice de Graaf and Duco Hellema, 81–98. Utrecht: SIM Publicaties.

———. 2017. "Precarious Itineraries: The 'Longue Durée' of Recovery and Livelihoods in a Post-war Salvadoran Village." In *Facing Fragilities: People, Aid and Institutions in Socio-Economic Recovery*, edited by Thea Hillhorst, Bart Weijs, and Gemma van der Haar, 63–81. London: Routledge.

Staniland, Paul. 2014. *Networks of Rebellion: Explaining Insurgent Cohesion and Collapse*. Ithaca, NY: Cornell University Press.

Stanley, William. 1996. *The Protection Racket State: Elite Politics, Military Extortion, and Civil War in El Salvador*. Philadelphia: Temple University Press.

Stephen, Lynn. 1994. *Hear My Testimony: María Teresa Tula, Human Rights Activist of El Salvador*. Boston: South End Press.

Stewart, Stephen, and Daniel Jiménez. 1993. *AIFLD-AID Cooperative Agreement in El Salvador: Final Report Mid-Term Evaluation*. San Salvador: USAID.

STP (Secretaría Técnica de la Presidencia de la República de El Salvador). 2012. "Resultados del registro de veteranos y veteranas del FMLN." Official government document.

Strazzari, Francesco. 2008. "Between 'Messy Aftermath' and 'Frozen Conflicts': Chimeras and Realities of Sustainable Peace." *Human Security Journal* 2:45–66.

Ströhle, Isabel. 2010. "The Politics of Reintegration and War Commemoration: The Case of the Kosovo Liberation Army." *Südosteuropa* 58 (4): 478–519.

Suárez Salazar, Luis, and Dirk Kruijt. 2015. *La revolución cubana en nuestra América: El internacionalismo anónimo*. La Habana: Ruth Casa Editorial. E-book.

Tarrow, Sidney. 1998. *Power in Movement: Social Movements and Contentious Politics.* Cambridge: Cambridge University Press.

———. 2005. *The New Transnational Activism.* Cambridge: Cambridge University Press.

Theidon, Kimberly. 2007. "Transitional Subjects: The Disarmament, Demobilization and Reintegration of Former Combatants in Colombia." *The International Journal of Transitional Justice* 1 (1): 66–90.

Thompson, Martha. 1995. "Repopulated Communities in El Salvador." In *The New Politics of Survival: Grassroots Movements in Central America,* edited by Minor Sinclair, 109–52. New York: Monthly Review Press.

Tilly, Charles. 1978. *From Mobilization to Revolution.* New York: Random House.

———. 1985. "War Making and State Making as Organized Crime." In *Bringing the State Back In,* edited by Peter Evans, Dietrich Rueschemeyer, and Theda Skocpol, 35–60. Cambridge: Cambridge University Press.

———. 1997. *Roads from Past to Future.* Lanham, MD: Rowman and Littlefield.

———. 2002. *Stories, Identities, and Political Change.* Lanham, MD: Rowman and Littlefield.

———. 2003. *The Politics of Collective Violence.* Cambridge: Cambridge University Press.

———. 2004. *Social Movements, 1786–2004.* Boulder, CO: Paradigm.

———. 2005a. *Identities, Boundaries and Social Ties.* Boulder, CO: Paradigm.

———. 2005b. *Trust and Rule.* Cambridge: Cambridge University Press.

———. 2006. "Poverty and the Politics of Exclusion." Background paper for the World Bank.

———. 2008a. *Contentious Performances.* Cambridge: Cambridge University Press.

———. 2008b. *Explaining Social Processes.* Boulder, CO: Paradigm.

Tilly, Charles, and Sidney Tarrow. 2008. *Contentious Politics.* Boulder, CO: Paradigm.

Todd, Molly. 2010. *Beyond Displacement: Campesinos, Refugees, and Collective Action in the Salvadoran Civil War.* Madison: University of Wisconsin Press.

Torres-Rivas, Edelberto. 2009. "La difícil existencia de las izquierdas centroamericanas." *A Contracorriente* 6 (2): 1–20.

———. 2010. "Las democracias malas en Centroamérica." *Nueva Sociedad* 226 (3–4): 52–66.

———. 2011. *Revoluciones sin cambios revolucionarios: Ensayos sobre la crisis en Centroamérica.* Guatemala: F&G Editores.

Trotsky, Leon. 1969. *"The Permanent Revolution" and "Results and Prospects."* New York: Pathfinder Press.

———. 1972. *The Revolution Betrayed: What Is the Soviet Union and Where Is It Going?* New York: Pathfinder Press.

————. 1994. *In Defense of Marxism: The Social and Political Contradictions of the Soviet Union.* New York: Pathfinder Press.

TSE (Tribunal Supremo Electoral). 1994. *Escrutinio final para concejos municipales elecciones 20 de marzo de 1994.* San Salvador: Imprenta Nacional.

————. 1997. *Memoria Especial Elecciones, 1997.* San Salvador: Imprenta Nacional.

————. 2000. *Memoria Especial Elecciones, 2000.* San Salvador: Imprenta Nacional.

————. 2003. *Memoria Especial Elecciones, 2003.* San Salvador: Imprenta Nacional.

————. 2006. *Memoria Especial Elecciones, 2006.* San Salvador: Imprenta Nacional.

————. 2009. *Memoria Especial Elecciones, 2009.* San Salvador: Imprenta Nacional.

————. 2014. *Memoria Especial Elecciones, 2014.* San Salvador: Imprenta Nacional.

Tulchin, Joseph, and Gary Bland. 1992. *Is There a Transiton to Democracy in El Salvador?* Boulder, CO: Lynne Rienner Publishers.

Ueltzen, Stefan. 1993. *Die Radios der FMLN.* Bonn: Infostelle El Salvador.

UNDP (United Nations Development Programme). 2004. *La Democracia en América Latina: Hacia una democracia de ciudadanas y ciudadanos.* Buenos Aires: Alfaguara.

United Nations. 1993. *From Madness to Hope: The 12-Year War in El Salvador; Report of the Commission on the Truth for El Salvador.* New York: United Nations.

————. 1995. *The United Nations and El Salvador, 1990–1995.* New York: The United Nations Blue Book.

Urbina González, Yanci. 2006. "Análisis del ámbito interno del FMLN: 1980–2004." MA thesis in political science, Universidad Centroamericana "José Simeón Cañas."

USAID (United States Agency for International Development). 1994a. "El Salvador: The First Three Years of the Peace and National Recovery Project (519-0394); Lessons Learned." Manuscript.

————. 1994b. "El Salvador: Evaluation of the Peace and National Recovery Project; AID Evaluation Summary." Manuscript.

Valle, Victor Manuel. 1993. *Siembra de vientos: El Salvador, 1960–69.* San Salvador: CINAS.

van der Borgh, Chris. 2003. *Cooperación externa, gobierno local y reconstrucción posguerra: La experiencia de Chalatenango, El Salvador.* Amsterdam: Rozenberg Publishers.

————. 2004. "Triple Transition and Governance in El Salvador." In *Good Governance in the Era of Global Neoliberalism: Conflict and Depolitisation in Latin*

America, Eastern Europe, Asia and Africa, edited by Jolle Demmers, Alex E. Fernández Jilberto, and Barbara Hogenboom, 101–16. London: Routledge.

———. 2010. "The Practice of International Interventions in El Salvador: Problems of Building a Liberal Peace." Paper presented at the Max-Planck-Institut, Freiburg.

van der Borgh, Chris, and Wim Savenije. 2015. "De-securitising and Re-securitising Gang Policies: The Funes Government and Gangs in El Salvador." *Journal of Latin American Studies* 47 (1): 149–76.

van de Walle, Nicolas. 2001. "The Impact of Multi-Party Politics in Sub-Saharan Africa." *Forum for Development Studies* 28 (1): 6–42.

———. 2007. "Meet the New Boss, Same as the Old Boss? The Evolution of Political Clientelism in Africa." *Patrons, Clients, and Policies: Patterns of Democratic Accountability and Political Competition*, edited by Herbert Kitschelt and Steven Wilkinson, 50–67. Cambridge: Cambridge University Press.

van Leeuwen, Mathijs. 2010. "To Conform or to Confront? CSOs and Agrarian Conflict in Post-Conflict Guatemala." *Journal of Latin American Studies* 42 (1): 91–119.

Vásquez, Lucio, and Sebastián Escalón Fontan. 2012. *Siete Gorriones*. San Salvador: Ediciones MUPI.

Vázquez, Norma, Cristina Ibáñez, and Clara Murguialday. 1996. Mujeres—montaña: Vivencias de guerrilleras y colaboradoras del FMLN. Madrid: Horas y HORAS.

Velásquez Carrillo, Carlos. 2012. "The Persistence of Oligarchic Rule in El Salvador: Neoliberal Transformation, and the Retrenchment of Privilege and Inequality in the Post–Civil War Period." PhD diss., York University.

Velásquez Estrada, Ruth Elizabeth. 2015. "Grassroots Peacemaking: The Paradox of Reconciliation in El Salvador." *Social Justice* 41 (3): 69–86.

Verboven, Koenraad, Myriam Carlier, and Jan Dumolyn. 2007. "A Short Manual to the Art of Prosopography." In *Prosopography Approaches and Applications: A Handbook*, edited by Katharine Keats-Rohan, 35–70. Oxford: University of Oxford, Linacre College Unit for Prosopographical Research.

Verhey, Beth. 2001. *Prevention, Demobilization and Reintegration of Child Soldiers: Lessons Learned from El Salvador*. Washington, DC: World Bank.

Vilas, Carlos. 1986. *The Sandinista Revolution: National Liberation and Social Transformation in Central America*. New York: Monthly Review Press.

Villalobos, Joaquín. 1989. "A Democratic Revolution for El Salvador." *Foreign Policy* 74: 103–22.

———. 1999. *Sin vencedores ni vencidos: Pacificación y reconciliación en El Salvador*. San Salvador: Instituto para un Nuevo El Salvador INELSA.

———. 2001. *La Policía Nacional Civil de El Salvador como instrumento de la pacificación y democratización*. San Salvador: Instituto para un Nuevo El Salvador.

Viterna, Jocelyn. 2003. *When Women Wage War: Explaining the Personal and Political Outcomes of Women's Guerrilla Participation in the Emerging Democracy of El Salvador.* PhD diss., Indiana University.

———. 2012. "The Left and 'Life' in El Salvador." *Gender & Politics* 8 (2): 248–54.

———. 2013. *Women in War: The Micro-Processes of Mobilization in El Salvador.* Oxford: Oxford University Press.

Voss, Kim. 1996. "The Collapse of a Social Movement: The Interplay of Mobilizing Structures, Framing and Political Opportunities in the Knights of Labor." In *Comparative Perspectives of Social Movements,* edited by Doug McAdam, John McCarthy, and Meyer N. Zald, 227–58. Cambridge: Cambridge University Press.

Vu, Thuong. 2010. *Paths to Development in Asia: South Korea, Vietnam, China, and Indonesia.* Cambridge: Cambridge University Press.

Wacquant, Loïc. 1990. "Exiting Roles or Exiting Role Theory? Critical Notes on Ebaugh's *Becoming an Ex*." *Acta Sociologica* 33 (4): 397–404.

Wade, Christine. 2008. "El Salvador: The Success of the FMLN." In *From Soldiers to Politicians: Transforming Rebel Movements after Civil War,* edited by Jeroen de Zeeuw, 33–54. Boulder, CO: Lynne Rienner Publishers.

———. 2016. *Captured Peace: Elites and Peacebuilding in El Salvador.* Athens: Ohio University Press.

Waller, Michael. 1991. *The Third Current of Revolution: Inside the "North American Front"of El Salvador's Guerrilla War.* Lanham, MD: University Press of America.

Ward, Margaret. 2011. *Missing Mila, Finding Family: An International Adoption in the Shadow of the Salvadoran Civil War.* Austin: University of Texas Press.

Wedeen, Lisa. 2010. "Reflections on Ethnographic Work in Political Science." *Annual Review of Political Science* 13:255–72.

Weinstein, Jeremy. 2007. *Inside Rebellion: The Politics of Insurgent Violence.* Cambridge: Cambridge University Press.

Whitfield, Teresa. 1995. *Paying the Price: Ignacio Ellacuría and the Murdered Jesuits of El Salvador.* Philadelphia: Temple University Press.

Wickham-Crowley, Timothy. 1987. "The Rise (and Sometimes Fall) of Guerrilla Governments." *Sociological Forum* 2 (3): 473–99.

———. 1992. *Guerrillas and Revolution in Latin America: A Comparative Study of Insurgents and Regimes since 1956.* Princeton: Princeton University Press.

———. 2015. "Del Gobierno de Arriba al Gobierno de Abajo . . . and Back: Transitions to and from Rebel Governance in Latin America, 1956–1990." In *Rebel Governance in Civil War,* edited by Ana Arjona, Nelson Kasfir, and Zachariah Mampilly, 47–73. Cambridge: Cambridge University Press.

Wiegink, Nikkie. 2014. "Beyond Fighting and Returning: Social Navigations of Former Combatants in Central Mozambique." PhD diss., Utrecht University.

———. 2015. "Former Military Networks a Threat to Peace? The Demobilisation and Remobilisation of Renamo in Central Mozambique." *Stability: International Journal of Security and Development* 4 (1): 1–16.

Williams, Philip, and Knut Walter. 1997. *Militarization and Demilitarization in El Salvador's Transition to Democracy.* Pittsburgh: University of Pittsburgh Press.

Wittig, Katrin. 2016. "Politics in the Shadow of the Gun: Revisiting the Literature on 'Rebel-to-Party Transformations' through the Case of Burundi." *Civil Wars* 18 (2): 137–59.

Wolf, Sonja. 2009. "Subverting Democracy: Elite Rule and the Limits to Political Participation in Post-war El Salvador." *Journal of Latin American Studies* 41 (3): 429–65.

———. 2015. "Formal and Informal Security Governance in the Americas." *Latin American Research Review* 50 (3): 275–85.

———. 2017. *Mano Dura: The Politics of Gang Control in El Salvador.* Austin: University of Texas Press.

Wood, Elisabeth. 1999. "Los acuerdos de paz y la reconstrucción de posguerra." In *Ajuste hacia la paz: La política económica y la reconstrucción de posguerra en El Salvador,* edited by James Boyce, 103–40. Mexico City: PNUD and Plaza y Valdés Editores.

———. 2000. *Forging Democracy from Below: Insurgent Transitions in South Africa and El Salvador.* Cambridge: Cambridge University Press.

———. 2003. *Insurgent Collective Action and Civil War in El Salvador.* Cambridge: Cambridge University Press.

———. 2008. "The Social Processes of Civil War: The Wartime Transformation of Social Networks." *Annual Review of Political Science* 11:539–61.

Wright, Scott. 1994. *Promised Land: Death and Life in El Salvador.* Maryknoll, NY: Orbis Books.

Yánez, Gabriela, et al., eds. 1985. *Mirrors of War Literature and Revolution in El Salvador.* New York: Monthly Review Press.

Zaid, Gabriel. 1981. "Colegas enemigos: Una lectura de la tragedia salvadoreña." *Vuelta* 56:9–27.

Zamora, Rubén. 1998. *El Salvador: Heridas que no cierran; Los partidos políticos en la post-guerra.* San Salvador: FLACSO.

———. 2003. *La izquierda partidaria salvadoreña: Entre la identidad y el poder.* San Salvador: FLACSO.

Zilberg, Elana. 2007. "Gangster in Guerrilla Face: A Transnational Mirror of Production between the USA and El Salvador." *Anthropological Theory* 7 (1): 37–57.

Zulueta-Fülscher, Kimana. 2013. "Contributing to Democratic Consolidation and Sustainable Peace in El Salvador and the Philippines." Discussion Paper. German Development Insititute.

Index

www.ingramcontent.com/pod-product-compliance
Lightning Source LLC
Chambersburg PA
CBHW060321100426
42812CB00003B/844